LIVING ISLAM

Pakistan's North-West Frontier has long been associated with Islamic fundamentalism and tribal politics. Magnus Marsden has spent several years living here amongst the people of Chitral. His experiences show that, in fact, most Muslims in the region are committed to leading their lives as good Muslims, and do not support the teachings of fundamentalist Islamist movements. This book explores their philosophy, which rests on the interaction between mind and spirit, enhanced through the creative force of poetry, music and dance. These celebrations form a central part of life in Chitral. Challenging assumptions powerful in both popular and scholarly work on Islam, the book makes a significant contribution to our understanding of the place of religion in Pakistani society, and in the Muslim world more generally. It will be of interest to scholars of Pakistan and students and anthropologists researching the nature of Islam and religion in the contemporary world.

MAGNUS MARSDEN is a fellow of Trinity College and the Graduate Officer in Research at the Centre of South Asian Studies, the University of Cambridge. He lectures on the anthropology of Islam, as well as on religion and politics in Pakistan.

D1500753

LIVING ISLAM

Muslim Religious Experience in Pakistan's
North-West Frontier

MAGNUS MARSDEN

University of Cambridge

CAMBRIDGE
UNIVERSITY PRESS

CAMBRIDGE UNIVERSITY PRESS

Cambridge, New York, Melbourne, Madrid, Cape Town, Singapore, São Paulo, Delhi

Cambridge University Press
The Edinburgh Building, Cambridge CB2 8RU, UK

Published in the United States of America by Cambridge University Press, New York

www.cambridge.org
Information on this title: www.cambridge.org/9780521617659

First published 2005
Reprinted 2008

Printed in the United Kingdom at the University Press, Cambridge

A catalogue record for this publication is available from the British Library

ISBN 978-0-521-85223-4 hardback
ISBN 978-0-521-61765-9 paperback

Contents

List of maps   *page* vi
Acknowledgements   vii
Note on transliteration   x
Glossary of Khowar words used in text   xi

1. Introduction   1
2. Rowshan: Chitral village life   37
3. Emotions upside down: affection and Islam in present
    day Rowshan   51
4. The play of the mind: debating village Muslims   85
5. *Mahfils* and musicians: new Muslims in Markaz   122
6. Scholars and scoundrels: Rowshan's amulet-making *ulama*   157
7. To eat or not to eat? Ismai'lis and Sunnis in Rowshan   193
8. Conclusion   239

Bibliography   264
Index   290

Maps

1. Pakistan   *page* xv
2. Chitral district   xvi

Acknowledgements

It is ten years since I first visited Chitral, and it would have been impossible to live there and complete the research on which this book is based without the friendship, hospitality and warmth many of the region's people showed me. Unfortunately, I cannot name them all here. In Rowshan I have benefited from long lasting friendship with Muzafar and Jamila Hussein, Qamar-ul Haq and Habiba, Aziz Ahmed, and Shamsudin and Parvakichi Kai. Aftab Hussein, his mother, father and sisters were a constant source of affection during my stay in Rowshan, as were Charunaich Kai, Qazi Mehboob and their children. Tikadar Ghloam Qadir, Mawlana Sahib, Sultan Nigah and Amin Shah were all sources of valued advice and hospitality during my stay in Rowshan. Babu Lal, Fauji Lal, Collegie Lal, Jan Lal, Amin Lal and their families have for long welcomed me into their homes both in Rowshan and in Markaz. Subadar, his brother, Havildar, and their families showered me with unremitting hospitality, happiness and encouragement during my stay in Rowshan. Hazar Baig was and is a real friend, and he also gave me especially deep insights into the nature of Chitral life and the Islamic tradition.

In particular, it was Mir Hussein and his family, especially his brother, Sardar Hussein, mother, wife and sister, Hamida Kai, who have given me a house and a family in Chitral, and have done most to make my many stays in Rowshan both enjoyable and academically rewarding. In Markaz, Nizar Wali Shah was a source of boundless entertainment, friendship and amusement, as were other Markaz folk, especially Mansoor Ali Shabab, Aftab Alam Aftab, Manuwar Ghamgin, Jabar, Sa'dat Hussein Makhfi, Shahid, and many more. Abdul Wali Khan and his family also showed me great hospitality on my visits to Markaz, as did Abdur Rauf, his brother, Subadar, and their sisters.

The research upon which this book was based was not, however, confined to the villages of Chitral. In Peshawar, after arriving late at night and exhausted from the daylong journey from Chitral, I was always given gracious and unending hospitality by Zarak Saleem Jan and his wife, Palwasha. In Lahore, Alia Hamid and her husband Shehreyar Hamid helped introduce me to the Punjab. Whilst in Karachi, Sadiq-ur-Rehman, among many other Chitral friends, provided me insights into yet another dimension of Chitral life.

Two of my closest friends died during the writing of this book. In Markaz I benefited from great hospitality and conversation with Wali Ur Rehman. His death shortly after I left Chitral in October 2002, as my friend told me on the telephone when he relayed the sad news to me, means that the shade of Chitral will never be as cool again. He is sorely missed. Shireen Lal was also a man deeply loved by many in the region, and his death in February 2003 makes Rowshan seem an empty place. My thoughts remain with his wife and children.

On returning to Great Britain in the aftermath of 11 September 2001, I have been able to talk about Chitral and have been shown Chitrali hospitality by Sher Gul, his wife and children in London. Ali Sher has been a constant companion in debate and discussion, and Shah Hussein has offered great support with my work and helped refine my transliteration of Khowar words into English. Israr has always been ready to answer my questions and share his fascinating insights into Chitral life with me.

Financial support for this research was provided in the form of a research studentship by the Economic and Social Research Council. I should like also to thank Trinity College, Cambridge for making a number of further research visits to Chitral possible. Emma Rothschild and the Centre for History and Economics at King's College have also generously supported the research on which this book is based. At the Centre, Inga Huld Markan, Sunil Amrith, Rosie Vaughan, Rosanne Flynn and Jo Maybin have offered great support. I have also received generous support from Peter and Azra Meadows at the University of Glasgow. And I am particularly grateful to Akbar Ahmed, who gave me my research visa while he was High Commissioner in London. At Cambridge University Press, Marigold Acland, Isabelle Dambricourt and Valina Rainer all helped greatly guiding the book into production.

Cambridge friends and colleagues, Vera Skirvskaja, Fiona Scorgie, Bene Rousseau, Mark Elliot, Nico Martin and Soumhya Venkatesan have all offered invaluable companionship. Perveez Mody-Spencer has given ceaseless encouragement and advice. Tom Burston and Alex MacDonald have offered an unflagging source of friendship, as has William Fletcher who also helped produce the maps presented within.

The Centre for South Asian Studies at the University of Cambridge has provided an excellent setting in which to refine the arguments of the PhD thesis upon which this book is based, and I am grateful to Rajnarayan Chandarvarkar, Chris Bayly, Kevin Greenbank, William Gould, Rachel Rowe, Barbara Roe and Jan Thulborn for providing such a welcoming atmosphere there. Since joining the Centre, Kaveri Gill has witnessed the fraught final months of the preparation of this book, and given great boosts to my energy and perseverance.

The examiners of my PhD thesis, James Laidlaw and Michael Gilsenan, provided me with encouragement and greatly needed criticism, as have two anonymous Cambridge University Press reviewers. Above all, the supervisor of the thesis, Susan Bayly, has been an academic guide without comparison, and has constantly reminded me that there is something other than the anthropology of Islam: to her my sincerest and unending thanks.

Finally, there is a Khowar proverb, 'parents' hearts are on their children, children's hearts on stones' (*nan-taatan hardi azhelian suri, azhelian hardi darbokhtan suri*). This suitably reflects the support, during sometimes difficult times, my mother, father and brother have given to me during the course of my long interaction with Chitral and the region's people, and it is to them that this book is dedicated. I, of course, take sole responsibility for the shortcomings and any errors that remain. Following anthropological convention, pseudonyms are used for all people and small places mentioned in this text.

Note on transliteration

Throughout this book I have sought to transliterate phrases and terms in a way that best reflects their pronunciation in Khowar. I have sought to keep to a minimum the use of diacritical marks. Khowar is above all a spoken language, and whilst there is a Khowar alphabet, many Chitral people themselves claim to have a less than perfect knowledge of it. Many Khowar words are also used in Urdu, Persian and Arabic (e.g. *'alim, madrasa, izzat, buzurg*), yet there are differences in the way they are pronounced in Khowar, and Khowar also has several sounds and letters that are not found in Persian, Urdu, Arabic or Pashto. I have sought to reflect these differences in my transliterations of them.

Glossary of Khowar words used in text

adamzada	true human being, nobleman
aff	down
aih	up
'alim	learned man
'amal	practice
aman	harmony
andreni	inside
anparh	illiterate person
'aql	reason / intellect
asheq	lover
aurat	woman
azadi	freedom
azhelie	children
badikhlaq	person of bad morals
badmash	scoundrel
bahus korik	to debate
basheik	singer
batin	concealed/hidden
bazar	market
berie	outside
berozegarie	unemployment
buzurg	holy man
chit	choice
chogh	thief
chumutker	young unmarried woman
daf	large tambourine
damama	kettle drums
daq	boy
dar-ul uloom	mosque school
dashman	learned man

deh	village
demagh	brain
dor	home, household
dost	friend
drocho ogh	wine (literally, grape juice)
dunik	to think
duniya	the world
falsafa	philosopher
fikr korik	to contemplate
ghairat	honour
ghalamus	serf
gham	sadness
ghariban	the poor
ghazal	divine love song
ghot	deaf and dumb person
ghurbat	poverty
hadith	traditions and sayings associated with the life of the Prophet Muhammad
hardi	heart
hazir-e imam	the present Imam; the Aga Khan (see *imam* below)
ikhlaq	morality
ilm	knowledge
imam	for Sunnis: the person who leads prayers in the mosque. For Ismai'lis: the Aga Khan.
insan	human
insaniyat	humanity
intiha pasand	extremists
ishq	divine love
izzat	reputation
jam	good
jeer can	jerry can – used as drums
jezbat	emotion
jihad	holy war
kafir	infidel
kalam	Islamic theology
khoasht	hidden
khoshani	happiness
khulao	open
khuloose	affection

kimerie	lady, wife
kushik	to slaughter
lal	lord
lotoran	elders
lu	words, talk
madrasa	religious seminary
mantiq	Islamic logic
mashkulqei	gossip, conversation
mawlana	an advanced religious scholar
mazadar	enjoyable
mazhab	religion
mosh	man
muhabbat	love
mulla	man who performs Islamic rituals and teaches Islamic knowledge
musulmani	Muslim practice
nafs	carnal soul, passions
nan	mother
nau juanan	the youth
nimez	prayer
nishie	outside
niyat	intention
pereshani	confusion, anxiety
pornik	to dance
pyar	love
qahar	anger
qur'an	Word of God as revealed to the Prophet Muhammad
qur'an-e natiq	The speaking Qur'an, the Aga Khan
rigish	beard
rigishweni	the bearded-ones
shahar	city
shahzadah	prince
sharab	alcohol
shari'a	Islamic legal code and roles
sharif	polite
sharum	shame, embarrassment
sheili	beautiful
shirin	sweet
shum	bad, rude

sitar	four-stringed Chitral instrument
sooch korik	to think
sufi	person devoted to the mystical path
sukoon	peace
sunnat	customary tradition
surat	bodily shape
tahzibi yafta	sophisticated, cultured person
tait	amulet
tait korak	amulet-maker
talib-e ilm	religious student
taliban	religious students
talimi yafta	educated person
tara	alcoholic spirit made from dried fruits
tat	father
tazbeh	rosary beads
tsetsk	little ones (infants)
wereigh	open
zahir	revealed
zehn	mind

Map 1. Pakistan and neighbouring countries; shaded area corresponds to Chitral district
(see Map 2)

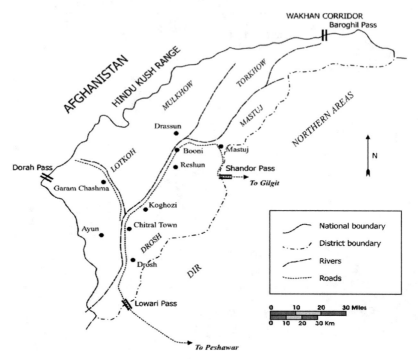

Map 2. Chitral district

CHAPTER I

Introduction

This book is a study of what it means to live a Muslim life in the Chitral region of northern Pakistan – a large Muslim populated area in one of the most turbulent regions of the Muslim world, yet virtually unknown in academic and popular literature. My fieldwork was conducted approximately fifty miles from the Afghan border, thirty miles from refugee camps where hundreds of Afghans lived during and after the Soviet invasion of Afghanistan, and a twelve-hour drive from *madrasas* (Islamic seminaries) and paramilitary training camps that are now widely known to have been connected with the emergence of the Taliban government in Afghanistan. The book's focus is on two localities in Chitral, a village and a small town. Its chief concern is with the commitment shown by many Chitral Muslims to the living of intellectually vibrant and emotionally significant lives in the region. By documenting this critical dimension of their everyday lives it seeks to illuminate aspects of Muslim life both within and beyond South Asia that are not fully accounted for in the otherwise sophisticated body of anthropological work on Islam and Muslim societies. Chitral people value verbal skill and emotional refinement to a very high degree. They are also people who think, react and question when they are called upon to change their ways or conform to new standards of spirituality and behaviour. The levels of commitment shown by Chitral Muslims towards the living of intellectually engaged lives is especially striking because it is maintained in the face of attempts made by Islamising Muslim reformers and purifiers from Pakistan and beyond to homogenise and standardise religious thought and practice throughout the region.

CHATTING, PLAYING AND PERFORMING: MUSLIM LIFE IN CHITRAL

I made my first visit to Chitral in 1995, and over the course of the next eight years my fieldwork among the Khowar-speaking people of this remote and beautiful mountain area took me to exuberant week-long polo tournaments played out on dusty poplar-lined polo grounds, and to night-time male-only public musical programmes at which delighted crowds cheered touring performers combining exquisite Persianate verse with penetrating contemporary satire. I first went to the region as an eighteen-year-old school leaver in order to teach for twelve months at a small fee-paying English-medium school in Rowshan village located in the north of the region: this village became one of the two field sites documented in this book. In September 1996 I started my undergraduate degree course in Cambridge, and over the course of the next three years, I made three further three-month visits to Chitral.[1] Between April 2000 and September 2001 I conducted eighteen months of 'formal' PhD fieldwork in Chitral. In addition, having completed my PhD I made three further visits to Chitral, between March and April 2002, February and March 2003, and June and October 2003.

Much of the material presented in this book was collected during my eighteen months of formal PhD fieldwork, yet it draws deeply on the experiences, memories and reflections of the earlier visits I made to Chitral. The relationships I established during my prolonged stay in the region were diverse: some of them were structured around my status as a foreign researcher, yet many of the people whose views, attitudes and lifestyles I explore in detail in this book had known me since my post-school days and corresponded with me for up to five years before I started the formal research on which this book is based. Many of my Chitral friends, indeed, had encouraged me to work on a PhD about Muslim life in their region, and we spent much time sitting in the houses and gardens of the village discussing which dimensions of Chitral society they thought it would be interesting for me to explore. Above all else they were concerned with the growing influence that an array of 'Islamising' forces were having on the nature of Chitral life. It was the Afghan Taliban, Pakistan-based Islamist political parties and their activists, and Chitral-folk who had themselves adopted strict interpretations of Islamic thought and practice, and were often referred to as the 'bearded ones' (*rigishweni*), who were the focus of many of these discussions.

During my initial stays in Chitral I also set about learning, with the help of village people, the Khowar language. Some of my friends claimed they

---

[1] During these visits I stayed with my friends in the region, conducted research for an undergraduate dissertation in social anthropology, and worked as a translator for a team of academics from British and American universities engaged in a research project on the geography of the region.

could not understand why I wanted to learn such a 'useless' (*faltu*) language, and that I would be much better off teaching them English. Yet when I did achieve a degree of fluency, I was also often told that the form of Khowar I spoke, like that of Rowshan people themselves, was its purest and most authentic form, and was unlike that spoken by Chitralis from other towns and villages in the region that were more influenced by non-Khowar-speaking 'outsiders' (*nagoni*). Indeed, I would often be asked by my friends in the village to repeat words, phrases and pieces of poetry before their friends from other villages and small towns in Chitral. They particularly appreciated when I, as they did, responded to their questions with pieces of poetry I had memorised from other friends and audiocassettes I had bought in the bazaar. My friends also sent long letters written in English, and sometimes Khowar, telling me of the goings-on in Chitral, and, after the introduction of a relatively reliable source of electricity to the region in 2001, we chatted on the World Wide Web and established email contact.

My long-established connections with Chitral people meant that I was able to interact with a wider array of people than usually possible for male anthropologists working in rural Muslim societies. During the early visits I made to Chitral, I lived with a family in Rowshan and I attended weddings, funerals and musical gatherings, not only in the village in which they lived but also in many other surrounding villages and valleys. By the time I returned to conduct my PhD fieldwork, I had come to be treated as a brother and son of the family with which I lived. As a result, I was able to sit and converse – alone and with other family members – with the wives, mothers, sisters, daughters and nieces of the household, as well as with young and old women in many other houses in the village. This unusual situation of being allowed access to women's worlds and conversations prompted me to make the gendered dimensions of Chitral village Muslims' responses to the teachings of 'reformist' Islam central to the arguments presented in this book.

Rowshan village itself is surrounded by high snowcapped mountains and mountain pastures which are green in spring – a time of year loved by many Rowshan people when they take their family and friends on 'picnic tours', at which they cook meals of rice and meat, listen to local and Indian music on cassette players, and challenge each other to games of cricket and 'polo without horses', a local variant of hockey. Rowshan's small and dusty village bazaar, with its concrete shops, old tea-houses and dusty minibus stand is described by most villagers as 'dirty' (*gandah*) and 'rubbish' (*bakwaz*). Yet villagers invest greater energies into beautifying the inner lanes of the village itself – they often plant rose bushes along the village paths, have a great love for cultivating 'delicate' (*nazuk*) flowers in their gardens, and, in the late spring months, delight in absorbing the 'intoxicating' perfumes of the Russian Olive tree (*shunjuur*), a much loved feature of Chitral's landscape. The beauty of the landscape is not lost on Rowshan villagers: my friends often told me how they were lucky to live in the most beautiful village not only in Pakistan but also in the world. Yet, for many Rowshan people, the mountains in which they live also have a darker and less appealing side. It is the dry mountains in whose shadows (*chagh*) they live, villagers often claim, that lie behind the negative features of village life that, as I explore in the following chapters, are a source of great anxiety to the villagers: 'We', I was often told, 'are mice in the world's darkest hole (*duniyo safan sar chui guch*); living in these mountains it is only inevitable that there are people who have thoughts that are narrow and bad.'

The villagers whose lives I document here also have extensive experience of city life in Pakistan, and frequently compare the merits and demerits of 'city' (*shahar*) and 'village' (*deho*) life. During my extensive stays in Chitral, besides living in the village, I also travelled in minibuses with migrant workers living in Pakistan's major cities, and stayed with young men from Chitral in hostels in Peshawar University, where they were studying for Masters degrees in subjects such as sociology, political science and international relations. Indeed, my friends and I from Rowshan especially enjoyed experiencing Chitral life in Pakistan's major cities, and we spent much time visiting groups of Chitral men and boys who worked in carpet shops in the five star hotels in Islamabad, Karachi and Peshawar. It is not only to Pakistan's cities, however, where Rowshan people like to travel – they enjoy making 'tours' and 'expeditions' to villages they describe as being even 'remoter' (*pasmandah*) and more 'traditional' than their own. My Chitral friends and I would often spontaneously decide to visit a village in the region known for being especially 'remote' and 'interesting' (*dilchaspi*): to reach such villages we would endure long and painful journeys on narrow mountain roads sitting in overloaded cargo jeeps atop bags of wheat and tins of ghee and listening to local music cassettes.

During my early stays in the region I thus came to recognise the important role that music, poetry and travel played in the living of a Muslim life in Chitral. There was rarely a minibus or jeep journey I made during which local music – usually comprising a solo male voice accompanied by the Chitral sitar and the deft beating of local drums – was not played loudly on the vehicle's cassette player. Indeed, often some of the passengers in the bus would sing along with the music. They would often translate and interpret (*tarjuma korik*) the songs for me. These were mostly about the simultaneous experience of the pain and delight of love, but my friends also compared their own understandings of the songs' deep (*koloom*) and complex (*pechida*) meanings with one another. Not all in the region, however, I soon discovered, were equally moved by the words and sounds of this music. Heated discussions often took place in the confined space of the minibus between men who wanted to listen to Khowar song, and the 'bearded ones' (*rigishweni*) who chastised their fellow countrymen for listening to music. These men claimed that it was un-Islamic and said that it should be replaced by cassettes of Qur'anic recitations. Yet what I recognised as critical was the flourishing of this musical life in the face of Islamisers' objections. Indeed, many of the evenings that I spent in the village itself were with young men of my own age who would gather in the evening to play the sitar, beat drums, sing and dance. We would also often travel many miles on dark nights, along precipitous roads and in battered jeeps, in order to attend musical programmes in other villages in the region.

My friends and I greatly enjoyed attending these musical programmes, and I had long wanted to experience first hand the performances of a particularly famous group of musicians who call themselves, in untranslated English, the Nobles. Their music was recorded on cassettes that were listened to with great enthusiasm in jeeps and houses throughout the region. When in January 2001 I was invited to attend a Nobles programme in Markaz, the small town that is the second locality I focus on in this book, I was excited, and, for the next eight months I became a regular presence at the Nobles' programmes – they even arranged and recorded programmes at which 'Mr Magnus from Britain, the researcher of Khowar culture and language' was the Chief Guest, and gave me the honour of being a life member of their group. I was always invited to attend their programmes, would make long journeys with the musicians of the Nobles to the many villages where they performed, and became close friends with many of the Nobles and their entourage.

Life in Chitral, though, was more than about music, dance and relaxing with friends. The importance of a good education and the struggle to learn was something very much on the minds of many village people, and in Rowshan I spent a great deal of time teaching my friends' children. Nearly all of the villagers wanted their children to learn English, and, over the years I spent in Rowshan, many parents sent their children to receive English lessons from me. I also gave English classes at schools in the village. It was not only the village's children and their parents who were interested in my knowledge of English – young Rowshan men and women also often asked me to help them with their education and thinking. Some of these folk were well educated, and they would often ask me to read the essays they were writing in preparation for their MA degrees and civil service examinations. These men repeatedly told me that they were worried that their writing was too critical for the 'narrow-minded' civil servants from Pakistan's major cities who would mark their exam scripts. Talk of such concerns took place not only in classroom situations but was, rather, a feature of everyday life: we would often go on long walks in the summer along mountain paths to nearby villages known for their sweet and juicy mulberries and apples. As we walked we would discuss the ideas of, amongst others, Rousseau, Kant and Adam Smith, and they would tell me about their reading of Islamic scholars and thinkers, including Ibn Khaldun and more contemporary Islamic scholar-politicians, such as the founder of the Islamist Jama'at-e Islami party Mawlana Mawdudi. Indeed, even my friends who lacked extensive formal education were always active in searching out people whom they thought I would find knowledgeable (*ma'alumati*) and witty (*namakin*), and such folk were themselves often poets who regularly read their poetry at formal recitals (*musha'ira*).

I also discovered that there was a great love for holding public events in the village, and that the performance of public disputation was an important feature of daily life. Yet whilst these gatherings were said to be 'fun' (*mazah*) by the villagers, they also had a serious dimension. I attended many public events – especially school 'programmes' – at which speeches were given; indeed, I was also often invited to speak in both Khowar and English about the importance of education. These speeches often initiated great discussion amongst my friends after the events when they went to the bazaar and returned to their houses.

Thus, a great deal of my time was spent in discussion with the villagers as I taught them English, played with their children, attended the weddings of their friends and relatives, helped them water their crops, went to their houses for meals and, in the long cold winter months, sat with them around wood fires nibbling dried fruit and, infrequently, enjoying a local glass of home-brewed red wine. Some of this discussion was part of a sociable exchange of views and ideas that took place when men gathered in shops, tea-houses and guest houses in the village. Cracking jokes, laughing loudly, and slapping hands were all part of these discussions. In the households of the village, women – old and young, educated and uneducated – also often vocally participated in conversation with their family members and relatives who visited their homes. Yet, many of the discussions I had were close personal exchanges with my friends, and with the men and women in the houses in which I spent much time. In the evenings after having watched television with the family with whom I lived, I would retire to my room or, in summer, to my rope bed placed outside in the cool orchard, to take a rest. There one of the brothers or sisters of the house would often join me, and we would sit and chat until I fell asleep. During these exchanges we spoke in hushed voices, made sure that nobody was sitting outside the room listening to our conversation, and the discussions we had were often about sensitive topics. These moments of hushed talk alerted my attention to a key theme explored in this book: the role played by anxieties about the status of the hidden and the open in the living of a Chitral Muslim life.

Most of my friends were serious about their faith – they prayed regularly, sent their children and relatives for religious education in schools in the village and religious colleges (*madrasas*) beyond, and they were knowledgeable about Islamic doctrine and teachings. Yet, at the same time, they often did and said things that both I and my Rowshan friends found surprising. Some of them enjoyed drinking locally produced alcohol, whilst others smoked hashish. They were also often critical of the region's 'men of learning and piety' (Khowar *dashmanan*; Arabic *ulama*) and of many politicians and public figures in Pakistan whom they associated with Islamising policies. Rowshan people's deep knowledge of Islamic doctrine and respect for Islamic practice convinced me that the wide spectrum of opinion and ways of being Muslim that I encountered in Rowshan were certainly not a result of some people in the village being ignorant of normative Islam or current Islamising trends. Nor were these village people just eccentric holdouts swimming against the tide of an inevitable trend towards the sweeping away of non-standard or 'liberal' forms of Islamic belief and behaviour in the Frontier, and my exploration of the active and critical intellectual life of Chitral people is intended to document this. Thus, the complex nature of Muslim subjectivity and thought that I found in Rowshan encouraged me to reflect on where Chitral Muslims locate religious and spiritual authority.

The diverse array of illiterate and literate small holders, operators of small businesses, as well as educated middle-class people with professional qualifications who are the focus of this study, are aware that they are living in a world where hostile stereotypic views of Muslims are pervasive and influential. Chitral Muslims have lively and creative minds, live emotional lives, and are deeply concerned about being swallowed up by an essentialising discourse that stereotypes Muslims as 'fundamentalists' driven by a desire to wage 'holy war', and precipitate a 'clash of civilisations' (Huntington 1993). The perceived threat has been further intensified by the events of 11 September 2001.[2] People in Chitral feel that they have ideas and approaches towards Islam that are novel and important, they think that their ideas and opinions should be heard by commentators in the wider world, and their awareness of hostile global stereotypes of Muslims sharpens the ways in which they reflect on being Muslim.

AIMS OF THE BOOK

My account of the critical responsiveness of Chitral Muslims to 'Islamisation' has two major goals. First, it seeks to contribute to the anthropology of Islam in the contemporary world by exploring the ways in which people lead a Muslim life in Chitral, and how they contribute in their daily lives to the form the 'Islamic tradition' takes in the region.[3] Second, it seeks to make connections between the anthropology of Islam and debates in anthropology concerning intellectual creativity, emotional modes, ethics and morality, and personhood. These are dimensions of Muslim life that have been only partially explored by anthropologists of Islam: it is often assumed that because Islam is a religion of submission that whilst the relationship between the intellect (*'aql*) and faith (*iman*) is important for Muslims there is little place for the expression of individual creativity in the living of a Muslim life, and that morality in Muslim societies is a ready-made and uncontested category simply deriving from a single set of scriptural codes.[4]

More generally, whist the term 'Muslim societies' is used a great deal in both scholarly and more popular works, and its usage is sometimes contested, there are real though very dynamic concerns involved for people in places like Chitral in conceptualising the settings in which they are living as 'Muslim societies'. This is not least because of the long tradition of Islamic scholarly debate concerning what is required of Muslims to make and keep their 'society' a 'truly Muslim' one, and the term society itself is certainly one with analogies in Arabic and Persian, and the word frequently used in to refer to the concept of society in Urdu, *mua'shira*, is the focus of many of the discussions I encountered in Khowar.

---

[2] For one anthropologist's reflections on 11 September 2001, see Tapper 2001.
[3] I employ the phrase 'Islamic tradition' following Asad 1986. Asad questions anthropological writing that either essentialises or disintegrates Islam (Starrett 1998: 7).
[4] On individuality in South Asian Islam, see Jalal 2000.

By focusing on the place that intellectual creativity plays in the living of a Muslim life in Chitral, I also seek to further the anthropological understanding of the relationship between 'local' and 'global' Islam.[5] A number of recent studies have sought to highlight the ways in which relatively recent converts of the Muslim world are resisting the Islamisation of their lives (see especially Masquelier 2001), and many studies have emphasised how conflict and debate is an inherent feature of Islamising processes (e.g. Kurin 1993).[6] Yet global Islam remains too often depicted as an irresistible force behind the homogenisation and 'perfection' (Robinson 1983) of Muslim identity and practice in both academic and popular accounts of the Muslim world (Kepel 2002; Naipaul 1981; Robinson 2000).[7] I therefore draw on recent anthropological accounts of cultural globalisation in an attempt to ask the degree to which Chitral Muslims defer to authoritative calls for commitment from purist, reformist or modernist Muslims.[8] I seek to argue against simplistic formulations treating local Islam as inherently vulnerable to global trends and forces in contemporary Islam. Moreover, I show that Muslims living in a village and a small town in a remote and poor region of Pakistan are critically engaged in debate on the shape of Islam and the current state of the Muslim world. Chitral Muslims are engaging in this culture of debate in a way that is regionally distinctive and builds on older social forms and institutions in Chitral.

My account is focused on life in Chitral, but it raises questions that bear on broader debates in anthropology and the social sciences. Social scientists are now documenting and theorising the importance of new and critical

---

[5] The historian Francis Robinson has argued that 'mass reform movements have emerged which shattered any sense that there might be equilibrium maintained between the high Isla-mic and custom-centred traditions' 2000: 5). For a critique of Robinson's historical formulations, see Das 1984. Anthropologists have long theorised how to write about Islam in a way that both reflects diversity but also captures the religion's universal features. See Abu Lughod 1989; Ahmed and Donnan 1994; Arkoun 2001; Asad 1986; Bowen 1998; Eickelman 1982; El Zein 1977; Geertz 1968; Gellner 1981; Gilsenan 1982; Donnan and Stokes 2002; Hefner and Horvatavich (eds) 1994.; Gilsenan 1990b; Lindholm 1995, 2001; Street 1990.

[6] I use the term 'Islamisation' to refer to activities by Muslim organisations, movements and persons which seek to promote changes at both the collective and individual level in Muslim thought and behaviour in line with their visions of the formal requirements and doctrines of Islam.

[7] Indeed, recent studies in the Arab-speaking Muslim world tend to assume that 'revivalist' Islam is the most powerful dimension of Muslim thought and identity in the contemporary Muslim world. On the 'Islamic revival' in Cairo for instance, see Hirschkind 2001; Mahmood 2001; Starrett 1998.

[8] For anthropological discussion of globalisation, see, especially, Appadurai 1993; Ferguson and Gupta 1992. On the study of contemporary globalisation in its historical context, see Hopkins 2002 (ed.), Hopkins 2002a, 2002b. The importance of recognising global processes in even the most 'out-of-the-way places' (Tsing 1993) has been an important focus of much recent anthropology, see Tsing 1993 and Pilot 1999.

debates in Muslim-majority states and Muslim communities in many parts of the world.[9] The intellectual life of village Muslims, however, has only very rarely been the focus of anthropological research.[10] Indeed, the predominantly rural societies in which much of South Asia's and other Muslim populations live continue to be stereotyped as intellectually barren, rendering Muslim villages as places of non-thought. These stereotypes partly reflect old tensions in anthropological work concerning the relationship between images of the city and village in the Islamic tradition. More specifically, they also reveal the widely held assumption that villagers are deficient intellectually, and, once educated, will inevitably 'Islamise' because Islam is a faith of codes, rules and book standards, which has further tended to narrow anthropological attempts to understand the intellectual life of rural regions of the contemporary Muslim world. Nowhere has this been more apparent than in both popular and academic accounts of Pakistan's Frontier province, where the use of the term 'Talibanisation' has conveyed a view that Muslims in the region do not think but, instead, just somehow become 'fundamentalist' and Taliban-like (Kepel 2002; Rashid 2000). This is why I focus on the ways in which village and small-town Muslims in my field sites think, reflect, and debate the circumstances of the world around them, and make active and varying decisions about what kind of Muslim life to lead.

Whilst some Chitral people described in this study are relatively wealthy and educated by local standards, many are illiterate or at best educated only as far as primary school level. Yet these folk often call themselves 'intellectuals' (*hushiyar*) and creative people of emotion, and do not think that it is only formally educated Islamic purists or 'modern' secular people who have the capacity to live rational, discerning, intellectually acute and morally sophisticated lives. At the same time, however, levels of education are rising in Chitral, and Chitral people are becoming more literate and more knowledgeable about formal textual Islam. Yet these changes are not leading to a one-dimensional progression towards a single, all-powerful

---

[9] See Eickelman and Piscatori 1996 on contemporary debates about religion and politics in the Muslim world. On these issues amongst Southeast Asian Muslims, see Hefner and Horvatich 1994. On 'political Islam', see Kepel 2002; Nasr 1999; Roy 1994; and for an anthropological critique of the concept, see Hirschkind 1997. On the shape of Muslim politics and identity in Muslim communities outside the Muslim world, see Kepel 1994, 1997.

[10] On anthropological writing on the importance of practice and ritual in 'village Islam', see, for instance, Bowen 1989, 1992b; Loeffler 1988. In the wider world it is often assumed that there is little intellectual activity in Pakistan. V. S. Naipaul has recently commented that Pakistan 'is not a book-reading country, it has no intellectual life. All you need is the Koran and a ruler with a big stick' (Naipaul quoted in A. Robinson 2002: 17).

model of moral and spiritual perfection based on behavioural codes derived either from Qur'anic texts or from the teachings of Islamic jurists and other authorities. So-called village Muslims are often said to be either straight-forwardly resistant or meekly submissive and uncritical in their responses to the calls of self-styled Islamic purists and reformers. The nature of Chitral Muslims' engagement with Islamising processes and the Islamic tradition is greatly more complex than this simplistic approach, and I found that my understanding of the ways in which Chitral people handle the pressures to 'Islamise' required a consideration of Chitral people's conceptions and experiences of the life of the mind, intellectual activity and emotional sensitivity.

Chitral people are knowledgeable about a variety of Islamic normative standards of belief and behaviour. Yet, rather than being either automatic-ally deferential or simply resistant to the figures of authority – the Taliban, mullahs and the representatives of 'Islamist parties' – who want to pre-scribe this kind of Islamic standard for all, they are active, reflective and thoughtful about how and whether to embrace these norms. Moreover, the variety of opinions that Chitral Muslims hold about how to live virtuous Muslim lives reflect more than simply the two competing Islamic doctrinal traditions powerful in the region. They are also about matters of greater complexity than any simple disjunction between scriptural Islamic norms and the nature of everyday Muslim behaviour and practical reasoning. Rather, Chitral Muslims take pleasure from experiencing the life of the mind through discussing and reflecting openly about these matters with fellow Chitralis and value the fostering of an intellectual life that involves the exchange of critical and contentious ideas. It is likely that Chitralis have long had this kind of village-based intellectual life, which thrives on the free-ranging and unceasing search for intellectual engagement, and it was certainly clear to me in my prolonged period of residence in Chitral that this continues to exist now in a dynamic and growing form, and, indeed, it is being stimulated by new developments in education, learning and literacy.[11]

The material presented here is all the more striking because the field-work on which this book is based was conducted between 1995 and 2003, precisely the point when Afghanistan's Taliban government and its

---

[11] The verbal skills and intellectual prowess of Chitral people was even something noted by British scholar-administrators in their earliest visits to the region. Having visited Chitral in 1894, Curzon, India's future Viceroy, commented that, 'there was a certain natural dignity in the speech and bearing of those untutored men; and I have rarely heard an argument more fluently expressed or more cogently sustained' (Curzon 1984: 139).

supporters in Pakistan were making a concerted effort to impose a radically puritanical Islamic lifestyle on the region's Muslims. Yet despite the pressures placed upon Chitral Muslims by an array of Islamist movements and organisations to 'Islamise' their lifestyles, Chitral Muslims should not be thought of as all accepting in the face of these demands. Some people in the region have embraced Taliban-style Islamisation enthusiastically; yet there are others who are hostile towards such forms of Islamic identity and thought: it is the form of relationships between Chitral people who have responded to Islamising pressures in very different ways that is central to the arguments this book seeks to make about the experience of the life of the mind in a Chitral village. What is critical is that Chitral Muslims are are not simply the passive recipients of Islamisation imposed on them by outsiders; instead they are active and make choices about the role that Islam plays in their lives.

So the specific historical moment during which I lived and conducted fieldwork in Chitral is of central importance for understanding the themes I address in this book. I am concerned with a period of time marked by the formation of the Taliban government in Afghanistan at the beginning of my field study in Chitral, and its defeat by the Americans as I completed it. Moreover, this period was one during which a number of critical global and South Asian events impinged on the lives of Chitral people, not least the terrorist attacks of 11 September 2001, the December 2001 terrorist attacks on the Indian Parliament building in New Delhi, and the political changes which they generated throughout the subcontinent. This is important because this changing historical context influenced not only the nature of the setting of this study but also the array of questions that I asked of it – most centrally concerning the ways in which Muslims in Chitral talked about and conceptualised the movements and values of so-called 'reformist' Islam. All this resulted in a particularly distinctive form of anthropological enquiry which entailed taking note of people's attentive responsiveness to international events, and registering the active process of observing and acting on change.

VILLAGE AND TOWN: 'LOCAL ISLAM' IN NORTHERN PAKISTAN

Both of my field sites are located within the boundaries of Chitral district, an administrative region of Pakistan's North West Frontier Province. The majority of the region's population are Khowar-speakers and refer to themselves as Chitralis. Khowar is an Indo-Aryan language which shows the imprint of both Central Asian and South Asian 'linguistic areas' (Bashir 1996: 196). It has a written script – a modified version of the Urdu alphabet – but few people in the region actually write in Khowar. Most use Urdu for correspondence both with fellow Chitralis and other Pakistanis, while official business is conducted in both English and Urdu. Khowar is unintelligible to Urdu and Farsi speakers including Afghanistan's speakers of Dari, another Farsi-derived language, but most people in Chitral speak other languages beside Khowar, often being fluent in Urdu, Pashto, English and Dari. Very few people in the region have spoken fluency in Arabic, although many are able to read and write parts of the Qur'an they have memorised at school and in religious education classes. Many of the older women in Rowshan who have not had formal education speak no language other than Khowar, and in Chitral's more remote valleys and villages many people have spoken fluency only in Khowar.

Chitral is a highly mountainous region: the Hindu Kush, Hindu Raj and Pamir mountain ranges all meet in Chitral. The region itself is made up of four major and several tributary valleys. The entire region was an independent monarchical state until the late nineteenth century, when the British negotiated a forced treaty with its hereditary ruler, the Mehtar, under which Chitral became a semi-autonomous princely state within the Indian empire. This realm inherited traditions of status, politeness, etiquette, and 'high culture' that were characteristic of the Mughal-Timurid states and khanates of South and Central Asia, despite the fact that Chitral was never fully integrated into the Mughal Empire.[12] So the region's political culture was shaped by traditions and dynastic styles originating in the Central Asian khanates and Mughal-Indian realms, and there are important ways in which its political culture differed from that of other constituent realms of Pakistan and the Frontier, most especially those of the neighbouring 'tribal' Pukhtuns.

Until its full incorporation as part of the Pakistan state in 1969, Chitral was ruled by a hereditary dynast (*mehtar*, literally owner), who belonged to the ruling family, known as the *katore*. The former ruling family remain powerful in the region today: the present elected Mayor (*nazim-e ala*) for the Chitral region is a prince (*shahzadah*) from this family, and, besides exercising powerful political influence, family members also own large tracts of land and have considerable business interests in the region. Thus, Chitral people must negotiate not only with Pakistan and Afghanistan, but also with the ongoing historical legacy that the Chitral

---

[12] See Parkes 2001a.

state (*riyasat*) and its rulers play in determining the nature of society and politics in the region.

Chitral as a whole is a predominantly rural region, and even in the biggest urban centre, Markaz, many families are engaged in farming. The Chitral region is remote. In the winter all passes to Chitral are blocked by snow and ice, and people must take an unreliable and expensive flight from Peshawar to Chitral, or travel by way of a dangerous overland route through Afghanistan. This often means that the seriously ill fail to reach the better-equipped hospitals of 'down Pakistan' in time to receive effective treatment. Even in summer, Chitral lies a hot, long and bumpy sixteen hours minibus drive from Peshawar over the Lowari Pass, which slowly winds to an altitude of 3,200 metres and connects the region via a poorly maintained and mountainous road to the rest of Pakistan. The many Chitral people who work elsewhere in Pakistan and the minibuses that daily ply the road between Chitral and Peshawar mean that the region is deeply enmeshed in the broader social changes that are important in other regions of Pakistan and the wider world.[13] So, the Chitral region's relative remoteness is an important concern, and the processes entailed in negotiating the physical and cultural boundaries that separate Chitral from the wider world is a further focus of great thought and reflection by Chitral people.

The total population of Chitral district is about 350,000. Most of these people are Chitrali although Pukhtuns dominate the southern valleys of the region. Most Chitralis consider themselves to differ culturally in profoundly important ways from the dominant Pukhto-speaking people of the North West Frontier Province and many regions of Afghanistan, even though Pukhtuns are fellow Frontier people. Khowar-speakers refer to themselves as belonging to an ethnolinguistic group (Chitrali), which they distinguish from the Pukhtun-speaking Pukhtuns. Chitralis say that their language is 'sweet' (*shirin*) and their 'people' (*roye*) are 'noble' (*sharif*) and 'sophisticated' (*tahzibi yaftah*) compared to the 'wild' (*jangali*) Pukhtuns who speak a 'hard' (*sakht*) language. Chitral people are widely known in Pakistan, and are thought to be different from Pukhtuns: they are said by many Pakistanis to be peaceful (*aman pasand*) and trustworthy, and, as a result of these qualities, are often sought out by wealthy businessmen to work in their shops and warehouses. Chitral people are especially famous in Pakistan for their love of music and dance, as well as horses, polo and other 'lordly' sports, especially duck and ibex hunting, and many

[13] Compare Didier 2001 on Islam in another 'isolated' Muslim society in South Asia, Lakshadweep.

Pakistanis from the cities of the Punjab flock to the region to attend its major summer polo festival.

The majority of people living in Chitral are Muslims; and there are two Islamic doctrinal traditions represented in the region: Sunni and Shi'a Ismai'li. Approximately thirty per cent of the population of Chitral are Ismaili, the remainder being Sunni.[14] While most Chitralis live in settled towns and villages, there are small populations of semi-nomadic Muslim Gujur-speaking herders (Gujars) who largely live in the southern valleys of the region. In the far north of the region there is also a small population of semi-nomadic Wakhi-speaking herders (Wakhik) who keep yaks and cows, which they graze on the high plateau of the Pamir mountain range that straddles the Pakistan–Afghanistan border along the Wakhan corridor (see Faizi 1996; Shahrani 1979). There is also a small population of about 3,000 sedentary non-Muslim Kalasha people, who have been the focus of considerable anthropological research.[15] A rich and diverse body of anthropological writing exists on the Pukhtuns of the Frontier Province;[16] this book, however, is the first substantial modern anthropological study of the Muslim-majority people of Chitral.[17]

Most of my fieldwork was conducted in the village of Rowshan in northern Chitral, about 80 miles from Markaz and 280 miles from Peshawar. The population of Rowshan is approximately 7,000 – all are Muslims. Both of the two Islamic doctrinal traditions which are important in Chitral are represented in Rowshan: Sunni and Shi'a Ismai'li Muslims.[18] Despite the important doctrinal differences that exist in Rowshan I use the

---

[14] On the history of Islam in Chitral, see Holzwarth 1998.

[15] On the Kalash people of Chitral, see Lievre and Loude 1990; Maggi 2001; Parkes 1987, 1991, 1994, 1996a, 1999, 2001a, 2001b; Roberston [1970] 1976.

[16] For ethnographic, historical and theoretical writing on Pukhtuns in the Frontier Province and in neighbouring Afghanistan, see Ahmed 1976, 1977, 1980, 1983; Anderson 1985; Asad 1972, Banerjee 2000; Barth 1956, 1959, 1969, 1981; Boesen 1980; Grima 1992; Hart 1985; Jahanzeb 1985; Kaiser 1991; Lindholm 1982, 1996, 1999; Meeker 1980; Shah 1999; Tapper 1983, 1984; Titus 1998; Watkins 2003. For two accounts on Pukhtuns by British colonial scholar-soldiers who served in the Frontier, see Caroe 1965 and Howell 1979. For the anthropology of Pakistan beyond the Frontier, see Ahmed 1986; Donnan and Werbner 1991 (eds), and Titus (ed.) 1997.

[17] There is a sizeable body of work on Chitral by British scholar-soldiers who worked and lived in the region when it was a semi-autonomous princely state in British India between 1895 and 1947. See especially Robertson 1899. See also Biddulph 1972; Curzon 1984; Durand 1899; Gurdon 1933, 1934; Kennion 1910; O'Brien 1895; Schomberg 1935, 1938; Thomson 1895; Younghusband and Younghusband 1895; Younghusband 1895. On present day Chitral and the Northern Areas, the Pakistani province on Chitral's eastern border, see Parkes 1996b; Staley 1969, 1982. For a popular account of the region's colonial history see Keay 1996. For a history of Chitral written by a local historian, see Baig 1994, 1997.

[18] On Ismai'li doctrine and history, see Corbin 1983; Daftary 1990, 1998, 2001; Hunsberger 2000, 2001; Nanji 1978.

terms Rowshan Muslims and Rowshan people throughout this book. My use of these terms reflects the views of most if not all the villagers: the term *musulman* (Muslim) is often employed by both Sunnis and Ismai'lis when talking about themselves, and when discussing the lives and moral standards of their fellow villagers. Living a Muslim life (*musulmanio zindagi*) is felt to be something that unites – albeit in a fraught and contested way – all Rowshan people (*Rowshaneach*), both Sunni and Ismai'li.

Pakistan's Ismai'lis have received very little scholarly attention, despite the important role played by Ismai'lis in the Pakistan movement in the 1940s and in the creation of the Pakistan in 1947.[19] Muhammad Ali Jinnah, the founder of Pakistan, came from Karachi's Ismai'li Khoja community, whilst a key figure in the pro-Pakistan Muslim League was the then Aga Khan, Sultan Muhammad Shah. Moreover, in the past twenty years the Aga Khan Development Network has become one of the world's most active non-government organisations (NGOs) promoting social and economic development in many 'developing' countries including Pakistan. There are, however, important differences between Pakistan's array of Ismai'li communities, and Chitral Ismai'lis distinguish themselves culturally and religiously from the wealthy Gujarati-speaking Khoja Ismai'lis who reside primarily in Karachi.[20]

The Aga Khan, or 'Present Imam' (*hazir-e imam*) is the centre of Ismai'li belief and cosmology – as the direct descendant of the Prophet he is imbued with a special 'spiritual power' (*ruhani taqeat*) and 'light' (*nur*).[21] This 'spiritual power' means that he can understand and interpret the Qur'an in a way that is impossible for ordinary humans: not only is he the 'Present Imam', but he is also the 'speaking Qur'an' (*qur'an-e natiq*). 'Catching a glimpse' (*deedar korik*) of the Aga Khan is a moment when Ismai'lis feel themselves to be in the presence of 'spiritual truth' (*haqiqat*); and it is a religious event that is without comparison for Ismai'li Muslims.

---

[19] Ismai'li Muslims form under three percent of Pakistan's population. Pakistan's Ismai'lis may be broadly divided into two categories. First, there is a substantial and wealthy population of ethnically Khoja Gujarati-speaking Ismai'lis who are mostly settled in Karachi. Second, there are Ismai'li communities living in Chitral and Pakistan's Northern Areas, and they distinguish themselves culturally from Khoja Ismai'lis (see ch. 6 below). These Ismai'lis are, however, themselves ethnically and linguistically divided. All Chitral Ismai'lis are Khowar-speaking Chitral people, and there are significant numbers of Khowar-speaking Ismai'lis living in the Northern Areas. However, other Ismai'lis in the Northern Areas speak Burushashki and Shina, and they also distinguish themselves culturally from Chitral people. On the history of Chitral's Ismai'lis, see Holzwarth 1994.

[20] See Daftary 1998.   [21] See Nanji 1995.

The religious plurality explored in this book is, then, not evident only in terms of nuanced differences existing between Muslims in the region with regard to the nature of their responses to the teachings of 'reformist Islam', or the styles of spirituality and Muslim identity that Chitral people inhabit and construct in their daily lives. There are also important and apparently more clear-cut doctrinal differences; the differences between Ismai'li and Sunni 'doctrinal clusters' (Eickelman 1992a) are great, and they have become a central focus of debate in present day Chitral. Ismai'li doctrine and practices are considered by many Sunni Muslims in Pakistan and beyond to represent a deviation from mainstream Islam. The question of whether Ismai'lis are truly Muslims is a contentious topic amongst Sunni Islamic scholars and religious authorities throughout the country. In Chitral, the boundary between Ismai'li and Sunni Muslims has hardened significantly over the past twenty years, with the hardening of these 'sectarian identities' manifested in a number of incidents of violent conflict between people in the region. In exploring the intellectual traditions and emotional dispositions important in the region, I ask how values of social harmony as well as discourses of difference are able to take shape in the minds and actions of Chitral people.

The shape of Ismai'li identity in Chitral has been powerfully formed by the wider geo-political context in which Chitral is situated. First, over the course of the past thirty years, Pakistan has experienced intermittent policies of state-led so-called 'Islamisation'.[22] Much of this Islamisation has been formulated in response to calls for commitment made by the country's Sunni *ulama* and Islamist political parties, many of whom have sought to impose Sunni legal codes and definitions of what it is to 'be Muslim' throughout Pakistan.[23] Second, Ismai'lis in Chitral have also felt threatened by hard-line Sunni-dominated governments in neighbouring Afghanistan. In particular the Taliban government in Afghanistan was greatly feared by many Ismai'lis in Chitral; it was widely thought of as especially hostile towards styles of Muslim religiosity that did not conform to the strict interpretations of Sunni Islam that this regime sought to impose in Afghanistan.[24] Afghanistan's close proximity to Chitral, and

---

[22] See Nasr 2001. See also Metcalf 1983, 1987. See Kurin 1993 for an account of Islamisation in the 1980s in a village setting in Pakistan.

[23] On the changing role of the *ulama* in Pakistan's politics, see, especially, Nasr 2000.

[24] For scholarly writing on the puritanical vision of Islam enforced by the Taliban in Afghanistan, see, especially, Edwards 1998, 2002; Kepel 2002; Maley (ed.) 1998, Marsden, P. 1998; Rashid 2000, 2002; Roy 1998. On the Taliban's treatment of non-Sunni Muslim minorities in Afghanistan, see, for example, Mousavi 1998.

the visible presence of the Taliban in Chitral itself (the Taliban had offices in Markaz, and some religious scholars in Chitral associated themselves with the movement) contributed further to the creation of a 'threatened' Ismai'li identity in the region. Moreover, Sunni people in my two field sites also gave much thought to the Taliban, though they were more divided in opinion about the negative and positive dimension of their influence than the region's Ismai'lis.

The fall of the Taliban in Afghanistan in December 2001 and the initial 'anti-extremist' tone of Pakistan's government in the wake of the terrorist attacks on 11 September 2001 in the USA, lifted some of the pressures off Chitral's Ismai'lis.[25] 'The *ulama*', I was told in telephone conversations with Ismai'li friends in Chitral during the month of Ramadan in 2001, 'are not even daring to come to the bazaar to buy food with which to break their fast. It's great fun. You must come – we can really enjoy now!' This brief experience of a respite from a Sunni-dominated and Islamising political regime in Pakistan by Chitral's Ismai'lis was, however, short lived. In Pakistan's October 2002 elections an alliance of religious parties, the Muttahida Majlis-e Amal (MMA), successfully contested elections for both Chitral's National Assembly seat as well as the region's two Provincial Assembly seats. More generally, the alliance was able to secure a majority in the Provincial Assembly of the Frontier Province, as well as increasing its influence in the country's National Assembly. The central commitment made by the MMA during the election campaign was to introduce the Islamic legal code (*shari'a*) in the Frontier Province. By the summer of 2003 the MMA government in the Frontier had passed an Islamic law bill that declared illegal, amongst other things, the consumption of alcohol by non-Muslim foreigners and the playing of music in public transport. Indeed, in 2004 the leaders of the MMA were seeking to introduce a 'Hisbah' bill that made full veiling and the performance of prayers compulsory for government employees, and stipulated that shops and businesses would have to close during prayer times.

This form of cultural Islamisation, close to that of the Taliban, is something that Chitral's Ismai'lis, as well as many Sunnis, regard as a threat to their way of being Muslim. Yet even the success of the MMA in the October 2002 elections has not resulted in any automatic narrowing

---

[25] In particular, the banning of a number of powerful Sunni paramilitary organisations in January 2002 represented a positive development in the country's politics for many Ismai'lis I spoke to in March–April 2002.

of the diversity of ways in which Chitral Muslims set to the task of living a virtuous Muslim life. Despite the attempts of the region's now politically powerful mullahs to ban the playing of music in public vehicles and discourage outdoor musical programmes in the region's villages, these dimensions of Chitral life continue to be a valued feature of life in the region by many if not all Chitral Muslims. Indeed, even with regard to the sensitive domain of women's veiling, the MMA's strict requirements have resulted in no simple process of unthinking deference by either Sunni or Ismai'li Chitral people. In December 2002 the MMA representatives in Chitral told the managers of NGO offices in the region's administrative headquarters that men and women should not work together in shared office spaces, and that women should arrive at work in the full Afghan-style *burqa*. Yet the employees of these organisations refused to comply with these requirements, and I was even told by one Ismai'li woman who worked at such an NGO that she now purposefully 'tied' an even smaller veil around her head than she had previously done. I was also told that two Sunni women had arrived at work wearing Western style trousers (*pantaloon*) in an act of defiance against the region's 'hardened' *ulama*. The larger political context of fluidity and flux in which Chitral is located is, then, something that is directly perceptible to the people living in the region; this book seeks to convey the experience of life in a world undergoing dynamic and often unpredictable political change.

More specifically, sectarian conflict is another dimension of life intimately connected to my wider arguments about the importance of reasoned contemplation in the living of a Muslim life in Chitral. The process whereby the boundaries between once fluid 'doctrinal clusters' are hardened and ethnic-like 'sectarian' identities become active is at the centre of much discussion in the anthropology of Islam. Education is a critical concern in many of these works. Eickelman has argued that religion has become 'objectified' in the contemporary Muslim world, a process by which 'religious beliefs are seen as *systems* to be distinguished from one another' (Eickelman 1992a: 646–7). In particular, Eickelman argues that modern styles of education, and the mass literacy they have resulted in, has meant that a new literature of mass-produced pamphlets that treats Islam as a 'system' has fuelled the creation of 'sectarian distinctions'. The 'systematic' approach to Islam in school and university course and popular pamphlets and books has made differences within the Muslim community more visible to Muslims, 'treating Islam as a system of beliefs and practices implicitly highlights differences within the Muslim community' (650).

These distinctions are important for a wider cross-section of people in the Muslim world than ever before.[26]

The emergence of sectarian distinctions in the Muslim world – partly generated by higher levels of literacy and mass-education – is especially important because sectarian conflict and violence is now a feature of life in many Muslim-majority states, and in Muslim communities elsewhere. Nowhere has so-called sectarian conflict threatened the lives of Muslims and future viability of the state more than in present day Pakistan. Over the last twenty years violence between Sunni and Shi'a organisations in Pakistan has 'polarized communities and undermined civic order and political stability' (Nasr 2000: 40). Between 1989 and 1994 alone, 208 people were killed in incidents of 'sectarian' violence and 1,629 people were injured (40).[27] 'Militant Sunni and Shi'a organisations have carried out assassinations and bombing campaigns that have killed political rivals as well as children and the innocent at prayer in mosques' (40).[28]

Yet, growing levels of literacy in Rowshan have not resulted in a straightforward increase of support for movements of Islamic purification in the village, and only very few Rowshan people I spoke to claimed that they were supporters of sectarian movements influential in other regions of the country.[29] Indeed, I seek here to refine the anthropological study of the relationship between literacy and religious thought and identity. I argue that Chitral Muslims make choices between modes and forms of Islamic life, play an active role in making and defining these styles of being Muslim, and, critically, making choices about education is one dimension of living a Muslim life that matters continuously to Chitral people. The importance of education and literacy is a source of incessant debate in the region, and a domain of life where Chitral people take great pleasure in verbalising their views. If reading and learning has not simply resulted in a one-dimensional process of the hardening of sectarian identities for these Muslims, neither is it simply about status nor a purely intellectual activity.

[26] On the ways in which Islam is taught as a 'system' in Pakistan's school textbooks, see Jalal 1995b. Compare Al-Rasheed 2002: 189–96 on history textbooks Saudi Arabia, and Mehran 2002 on school textbooks in Iran. On the anthropology of learning, knowledge, and education in Muslim societies, see, especially, Eickelman 1985a, 1992b; Brenner 2000; Horvatavich 1994; Starrett 1995, 1998.

[27] These killings continue: approximately 104 Shi'a were killed between June 2003 and February 2004 in the Baluchistani city of Quetta alone.

[28] See Zaman 1998 and 2002 ch. 6, for a further discussion of 'sectarian conflict' and the 'radicalisation' of Sunni and Shi'a identities in Pakistan.

[29] According to the 1981 Census of Pakistan the overall literacy level in Chitral was 14.4%, with only 2.93% female literacy and 24.12% male literacy. By 1998 in rural areas of Chitral there was an overall literacy level of 38.4% (female: 20.42%; male: 56.29%). In 1998 the overall urban literacy level in Chitral was 56.65% (female: 38.19%; male: 71.53%).

Rather, it is also about repartee and emotion, and the complexity of attitudes Chitral people hold about learning, education and literacy certainly convinced me that these village Muslims live neither simple and unthinking 'everyday lives', nor lives of 'the Book', but rather spoken lives redolent with thought and reflection.

Whilst I focus in large part on Muslim village life, I am also concerned with the all important setting of the small Muslim town. While historians especially have recognised how far small towns are an important element in the life of many Muslim countries, they have not received the attention anthropologists have invested in the study of so-called 'tribal' and village settings on the one hand, and big cities on the other.[30] Thus, additional fieldwork was conducted in the district headquarters of Chitral, Markaz, which has a population of about 20,000, and is located three hours drive from Rowshan.[31] Markaz contrasts in a number of important ways with Rowshan. Historically, the population of Markaz is entirely Sunni. The only Ismai'lis who live there come from places in Chitral where there are substantial Ismai'li populations, and work in the offices of government and non-government agencies established in the town. The population of Markaz is ethnically more diverse than that of Rowshan: there are significant numbers of Pukhtuns especially from the Swat and Bajaur regions of the Frontier Province, and Afghan refugees who have been settled there since the Soviet invasion of Afghanistan in 1979.

The town has the region's biggest and most important bazaar where Chitrali, Pukhtun and Afghan merchants have shops and small businesses. It is rare to see women from Chitral in this bazaar, and when women do visit the bazaar they are fully veiled and taken in vehicles in which they remain whilst enlisting the help of their husbands or close male relatives, who always accompany them, with the purchases they are making.

Keeping purdah is, then, a feature of daily life in Rowshan and even more so in Markaz: in both places women rarely visit the bazaar, or even make journeys outside the immediate confines of their hamlet without a close male relative. Yet, as in other Muslim societies, the past twenty years in this region have brought about 'changes in women's notion of self and appropriate conduct' (Eickelman 1985b: 138), and these changes have not always been focused on emergent and reformist styles of veiling and

---

[30] For an historical exploration of the key role played by small town or *qasbah* societies in the transmission of Islamic learning and provision of local Muslim leaderships in South Asia, see C. Bayly 1992: 189–93 Compare Meeker 2003 for a study of village and small town Muslim life on Turkey's Black Sea coast.

[31] For a more detailed description of Markaz, see ch. 4 below.

religious piety. In Rowshan, especially, women now actively seek 'modern' styles of knowledge: attending 'computer literacy centres' and travelling to the cities of 'down Pakistan' for nursing courses have become especially popular activities for women in the village. So, I ask how far Rowshan people consider women to be capable of critical thought and stimulating intellectual discussion.

Moreover, exploring purdah and women's lives allows reflection on a further dimension of the living of a mindful Muslim life in Chitral – the experience of concealed thought. Not all thought in Chitral is vocal and part of the sociable exchange of ideas and viewpoints; thought may also be concealed, and Chitral people distinguish between different types of thought, and bring complex value judgements to their understanding of the act of thought. A great deal has been written on the place of purdah in Muslim society and, more generally, in South Asia, yet much of this writing assumes that keeping purdah is important in the lives of women alone.[32] In both Rowshan and Markaz, however, keeping purdah is also an important dimension of male Muslim experience. Keeping purdah, I found during my stays in Chitral, is as much about concealing thoughts and emotions as it is about covering heads and bodies.

Much recent work in the anthropology of Islam has focused on the transformations that the Islamic tradition and Muslim identity have undergone through interaction with public spaces that, whilst reflecting the impact of modernity, also have deeper histories in Muslim majority societies (e.g. Eickelman and Salvatore 2002). Many of the ethnographic spaces explored in this book are also often located in the shadowy zone between the public and the semi-public: musical programmes in village guest houses, gatherings of men chatting at weddings, and events organised by the region's schools and attended both by women and men all furnished me with insights into the life of the mind in the region. Yet my analysis of how Chitral people conceptualise social living and the places in which they do so, also extends beyond such public spaces and forms of social action, and seeks to assess the importance of secret knowledge, everyday tactics of concealment and local conceptions of the inner self in the living of a Muslim life in Chitral. I therefore seek to achieve a new and different understanding of the relationship between Islam, everyday religious

---

[32] On women in the contemporary Muslim world, see Kandiyoti (ed.) 1991a, 1991b, 1992; Kandiyoti (ed.) 1991b, 1996; Mir-Hosseini 2000. On purdah practices and domestic life, see Abu Lughod 1986, 1990, 1993; Friedl 1989; Jeffery 1979; Mundy 1995; Tapper 1990a. On women in Pakistan, see Jalal 1991; Weiss 1992, 1994, 1998.

experience and interpersonal relationships in Muslim societies, which explores the role concealment plays in the thought processes, moral valuations, religious experiences and emotional modes of Chitral people.[33]

The relation between the open (*kholao, wereigh*) and the concealed (*khoasht*) brings us back to the underlying theme of the book: the interrelation between the intellect and emotions in our understanding of 'local' and 'global' Islam. The division between the open (*al zahir*) and the hidden (*al batin*) is a recurrent dimension of many classic Sufi texts (see, for instance, Das 1984). In Chitral, the division between the open and the hidden is not confined to the experience of spiritual reality (*haqiqat*) alone: it also infuses the ways in which Rowshan Muslims make moral judgements about the state of village life.

By exploring the ways in which Chitral Muslims make moral judgements, I seek to build on recent anthropological work which treat the making of ethical and moral decision as a conflictual and ongoing process.[34] Yet this emphasis on the importance of the conflictual in the making of ethical and moral decision-making is strikingly at odds with conventional understandings of Islam that see it as a book-centred faith that provides believers with a coherent set of doctrines and rules by which to live their lives. By exploring the complex thought processes through which Chitral people make moral judgements, this book seeks to contribute to long-running debates in the anthropology of religion about the interaction between religious text and lived religious experience.[35] It explores how the Sufi textual emphasis on the division between the hidden and the open, rather than simply structuring in a one-dimensional way the thoughts of Chitral Muslims, actually contributes to the critical and vibrant intellectual and emotional life of Chitral people. When Rowshan people make moral judgements they do so actively, in the context of critical debate, and in a multidimensional way that involves the deployment of the critical faculties and reflection on the conflicts and complexities of the society and broader political circumstances in which they live. However, the vibrant nature of village life, the emphasis on decision-making, critical thought, contemplation and discussion is also a source of deep anxiety for Chitral people.

[33] See especially Ferme (2001) for an account of secrecy and concealment in Sierra Leone, and Gilsenan 1982 ch. 6 and 1996, on the surface and the hidden in a Lebanese village. Compare Wikan 1982 on veiling practices in Oman.

[34] See Bayly, S. 2004; Laidlaw 1995; Lambek 2000a

[35] This debate has been important for South Asia specialists, especially in relation to the caste system: see, especially, S. Bayly 1999; Dumont 1980; Quigley 1993; Raheja 1988. Compare Southwold 1983 on the anthropological study of Buddhism. On textual and locally understood Islam, see, especially, Bowen 1992a, 1992b.

THE FRONTIER AND THE PAKISTAN STATE

The wider setting of this study is one that is politically volatile and unpredictable, characterised by high levels of anxiety and the sense of a need by Chitral people for urgent changes in the way they live their lives. This volatility is challenging to Chitral people, and it raises searching questions for them about personal morality, identity, choice, faith and religious commitment. In spite of the pressures they feel to display commitment to purifying visions of a world made perfect by Islam, and far from showing deference to powerful Islamisers, they retain striking independent critical spirit in reflecting on moral and religious concerns.

The political volatility of life in Chitral is itself a reflection on the great cultural and linguistic complexity of the region's broader setting. The negotiation of both national and international borders, as well as the states, provinces and ethnolinguistic groups they reflect and seek to divide, is an important feature of daily life for many Chitral people. A number of recent anthropological works have suggested that national, ethnic and gender identities in border zones are multidimensional, and their moral orders diverse and contested (Wilson and Donnan 1998: 26).[36] Chitral's location in a frontier zone, defined insightfully by Banerjee, as 'spatially extended regions with their own cultural processes' (Banerjee 2000: 28) poses a question of central importance for this book: how far are the striking levels of intellectual vibrancy documented here a reflection of Chitral's location within a unique frontier zone, or to what degree do they challenge assumptions about the nature of religious thought and identity in rural localities in Pakistan and, indeed, other Muslim countries, more generally?

Since its foundation as a nation state in 1947, Pakistan has had a troubled and difficult history: military coups, ethnic and linguistic conflict, growing levels of sectarian violence, intermittent policies of Islamisation, military conflict with India, and developments in war-torn Afghanistan have all impacted heavily on the lives of ordinary people.[37] The people of Chitral have had direct experience of this unstable world: this region lies sandwiched between Afghanistan to the west and Kashmir to the east. One of the two localities discussed in this book lies three hours (70km) drive from the Afghanistan border; and many Chitralis have fought with the Pakistan Army in undercover action

[36] See, especially, Wilson and Donnan 1998, and Banerjee 2000.
[37] For political histories of Pakistan, see Talbot 1998 and Ziring 1997.

within Kashmir. Moreover, the events of 11 September 2001 and the political upheavals that followed in the region have significantly changed its geopolitical landscape. In September 2001, for instance, there were reports in both international and Pakistani newspapers that American military forces were considering using the small airport in Markaz, the administrative headquarters of the region, as a base for attacks on Afghanistan. Moreover, in March 2003 reports in the international and Pakistani media claimed that high-level intelligence agencies were conjecturing the possible presence of Osama Bin Laden in Chitral: these reports were the subject of great discussion amongst the people I know in Chitral. The vulnerability of Chitral is further enhanced because this is a region of Pakistan that suffers from high levels of unemployment and rural poverty: educated young men in Chitral often have no choice but to migrate to Pakistan's cities in search of what they regard as demeaning work as household servants and construction labourers.[38]

Muslims in my two field sites do not, then, unthinkingly embrace calls to commit themselves to the many reform-oriented movements that are active in the region. Nor do they, in any one-dimensional way, turn to the Islamising Pakistan state as a source of legitimate Islamic law and morality. Yet, the state is an important feature of life in Chitral: the police, the Pakistan Army, and government departments are present in both the village and the small town, and many people living in these two localities are employed in these institutions. As elsewhere in the country, the Pakistan state has also impacted powerfully on the ways in which Chitral people conceptualise what it means to live a Muslim life in the region. Blasphemy laws, laws prohibiting extramarital sexual contact (*zina*) and the potential for non-Sunni Muslim communities to be labelled 'non-Muslim' and made subject to prosecution and capital penalties on this basis, are all concerns that form a key part of village debate.

An account of personal intellectual life and creativity in Chitral social life would be incomplete without this element of their concerns – the 'state' – and indeed Chitral people connect all these elements of life in discussion. Nasr has recently argued that state-led Islamisation policy in Pakistan has allowed the state to extend its hegemony in the country, and thus to blur the division between state and society (Nasr 2002). Nasr's discussion of the interaction between state power and Islamism is insightful, and throws light on the connections between Islamisation and current anthropological and social science literature on the South Asian post colonial development

---

[38] On economy and social 'development' in Pakistan, see Weiss 1999.

state.[39] This is a concern that has not, as yet, been addressed by Pakistan specialists in any substantial way. I am especially interested here in the role of the state and the machinery of state level politics in the 'routinisation' of communal and ethnic violence in South Asia (Tambiah 1996; Brass 1997). Yet, there is also no clear division between 'state' and 'society' (Hansen and Stepputat 2001), and where the Pakistan state does enter the lives of Chitral people, there is no simple interaction between Chitral society and a faceless external political entity. As a further window into the fragmentation of religious authority in the Muslim world, then, I document the ways in which Chitral people reflect on the institutions of both the Pakistan and Afghanistan states as a source of Islamic moral norms in their lives.[40]

EMOTIONS, THE INTELLECT AND DEBATE IN MUSLIM SOCIETIES

Living a Muslim life in Chitral involves the active experience of intellectual creativity, and the making of decisions and voicing of opinions about contentious issues in fraught social settings. Rather than documenting the degree to which religion is a disciplinary order (Asad 1986, 1993, 2003), or attempting to empirically assess the extent to which morality is about either religion or the making of practical judgements, this book seeks to explore the interconnectedness of religion and sociality in Chitral by tracing the 'particular conjunction of contemplative thought, reasoned action (praxis) and creative production (poiesis) characteristic of any given social setting' (Lambek 2000a: 309).[41] By exploring Muslim life in terms of its creative intellectual dimensions, I seek to contribute to the understanding of the experience of particular kinds of intellectual creative powers, and the role that the experience of emotion plays in this process. By arguing in these terms, I build on anthropological writing on the intellect, rationality and emotion, and I seek to connect these debates to broader philosophical and political concerns about morality, political violence and religious tolerance.

---

[39] On the South Asian post colonial 'development state', see, especially, Bose and Jalal (eds) 1997. On Pakistan, see Verkaaik 2001.

[40] Recent anthropological ethnographies of 'the state' both within and beyond South Asia include Gupta 1995; Hansen and Stepputat 2001; Navaro Yashin 2002; Verkaaik 2004.

[41] Some anthropological studies of religion generally and Islam more specifically have emphasised the degree to which religion is 'bound up in the naturalization of power' (Lambek 2000a). For an influential work that develops this perspective, see Asad 1993. I find helpful Lambek's argument that 'discussions remain merely cynical if they do not delineate the capacity and means for virtuous action as well as the limitations placed upon it' (Lambek 2000a: 309).

The intellect and rationality were the source of great anthropological debate in the 1970s and 1980s.[42] Whilst these debates did much to refine anthropological understandings of the relationship between orality, literacy, tradition and modernity, they said relatively little about the intellect as a category of analysis.[43] Thought and cognition continued to be conceptualised as having their primary source in the disembodied mind, and there was little recognition of the role played by emotions and feelings in the ways in which people in specific cultural contexts conceptualise the exercise and cultivation of the critical faculties. In the broader context of the history of ideas, the absence of an anthropological attempt to explore in a systematic way the interaction between intellectual and emotional processes is surprising. In *The Theory of Moral Sentiments* (2002 [1870]), Adam Smith systematically describes the shape of morally informed emotions, or sentiments, and also points towards the emotional dimension of the experience of the play of the mind. Smith emphasises the role played by pleasure in people's attempts to understand the thoughts and, importantly, sentiments, of others (399; Haakonssen 2002). So, for Smith, intellectual satisfaction has a powerful emotional dimension, and it is this dimension of the experience of thought that I seek to explore here in the context of present day Chitral.[44]

Some anthropologists have explored the role of feelings and emotion in cognitive processes. In particular, this dimension of the study of cognition has contributed to the anthropological understanding of ritual and memory, and social scientists, more generally, have recently explored the interrelations between cognition, belief and emotion.[45] Many anthropologists have explored how religious practices use states of heightened emotional susceptibility in constructing spiritual experience of the world.[46] They have also explored the ways in which emotions are socially constructed in specific cultural settings.[47] Yet rather than documenting how emotions are socially constructed by Chitral Muslims, my central theoretical concern

---

[42] See, especially, Hollis and Lukes 1982; Tambiah 1990; Wilson 1970; Overing 1985.

[43] On the interaction between literacy, orality and rationality, see, especially, Goody (ed.) 1968; Goody 1986, 1987; Street 1984. For ethnographic critiques of these works see, especially, Street (ed.) 1993; Parry 1985 and Fuller 2001.

[44] See Smith 2002 [1870]: 400. On the place of emotions in seventeenth-century philosophy, see James 1997.

[45] On emotional modes in the transmission of religious knowledge and ritual, see, especially, Mahmood 2001; Radcliffe-Brown 1964; Tambiah 1985, Whitehouse 1992, 1996, 1998. On the interaction between cognition, moral beliefs and emotions, see Elster 1998, 2000.

[46] For influential works, see Kapferer 1988 and Bennett 1990.

[47] See Abu Lughod 1986; Abu Lughod and Lutz 1990; Rosaldo 1980; Lynch 1990; Scheper-Hughes 1992.

here is with the ways in which Chitral people conceptualise the interplay between the intellect and the faculties of feeling and emotion. Ethnographically, then, I seek to demonstrate how it is possible to present an anthropology of the embodied experience of thought.

In order to achieve this broad theoretical aim, this book documents the ways in which Muslims in two localities in the Chitral region take pleasure in experiencing the free play of the mindful body by immersing themselves in a culture of joking, impersonation, music, dance, poetry and travelling.[48] By taking this approach, I seek to bring to 'attention to the role of feelings and emotions in the spread of ideas' (Stewart 2002).[49] The creative intellectual activity that forms a central focus of this study is not, however, based only on the embodied experience of the aesthetic dimensions of human life. At the same time, there is also a culture of public debate and intellectual activity that places high value on the exercise of the faculty of the trained intellect, the play of reason and the cultivation of intellectual acuity through education, learning and the acquisition of knowledge. In the context of a Muslim society that is strongly influenced by the ideas of reform-minded Islam, the content of this discussion is often surprising. Whilst Chitral people do pursue debates about religion, they also love to explore other causes of concern that many in the region see as being more critical and urgent. For these Muslims the current shape of society, what it means to be a 'true human being', the transforming potential of education, the role of religion in society, and the techniques required to understand the 'inner thoughts and intentions' of other people are the focus of much popular discussion.[50]

For many Muslims in Chitral a virtuous (*jam*) life is something that is spent in debate. Whilst a number of studies have explored the importance of debate and rational argument in the Islamic tradition, most of these have focused on the intellectual tools used by Muslims to debate complex religious concerns in well-known centres of Islamic learning.[51] Chitral Muslims rejoice in articulating thoughts, and they take pleasure in handling impersonal and abstract concepts that they apply to life in the region and to present day concerns and anxieties. It would, however, be wrong to

---

[48] See Toren 1993.

[49] See Stewart 2002 and Jackson 1983, 1989 for discussion on the interaction between emotional modes and cognitive processes in embodied subjectivity.

[50] The presence of debate and discussion on ethics and morality in pre-colonial India that was distinctly Indo-Muslim in shape is explored in Bayly, C. 1998. Ali 2004 explores the form of ethics, emotion and morality in early mediaeval Indian court society.

[51] See, especially, Eickelman 1985a; Fischer 1980; Mottahedeh 1985. On the Islamic sciences more generally see Bakar 1999.

imagine Rowshan as an isolated island in a sea of 'fundamentalist' Islam where people are remarkably 'tolerant' and consensual about issues that other Muslims see in puritanical or ultraconservative terms. What I seek to document, rather, is a very wide spectrum of opinion about the Taliban, purdah, women's education, the merit and demerits of religious education, the status of non-Muslims, and how far Muslims should be deferential to conservative 'men of learning and piety'. Whilst some Chitral Muslims visibly take pleasure in openly expressing surprising and contentious 'liberal', 'tolerant' and 'broad-minded' ideas, others, for instance, vocally support the Taliban and its vision of a world governed and made perfect by Islamic law (*shari'a*). What makes this diversity of opinion particularly important is that many Chitral people apply critical intelligence to these matters, and they expect to live among people who rejoice in debating deeply contentious issues.

Furthermore, the culture of debate (*bahus korik*) explored in this book does not entail fleeting moments when villagers sit in seminar-type gatherings. Rather, debate and the play of the mind are features of everyday life for Chitral Muslims. One component of this intense verbal activity in the village involves the solo voice, and entails strategising attempts by individuals to make a name in the limelight of public speaking performances or 'programmes'. Yet the voluble lives that many Chitral people live, throw light on more complex anthropological concerns than those of honour and reputation. Far from simply being isolated individuals of honour, Chitral Muslims – both men and women, educated and uneducated – are continually involved in a series of intensely social, crosscutting and ongoing conversations that articulate the present day concerns of the villagers. It is this ongoing conversation to which I refer throughout the book as debate, and as involving the play of the mind and the exercise of the critical faculties of the intellect.

Muslims in these two sites thus see themselves as intellectually active; they discuss thought a great deal, and what I also seek to emphasise is that this intellectual vibrancy is a reflection of broader trends across the Muslim world. The place of critical debate in a range of Muslim countries is the focus of a recent volume edited by Eickelman and Anderson (1999). Their introduction points to the ways in which new technologies, systems of education and the mass communication media are tending to dissolve traditional monopolies shaping the transmission of knowledge in Muslim societies. In particular, they see mass education, especially since the 1960s, as having created the conditions for dynamic change in the Muslim world by having formed a cadre of 'new people' who have 'benefited from a huge increase in mass modern education' (Eickelman and Anderson 1999: 10–11).

The importance of self-consciousness and self-examination in the study of Muslim thought has deep historical roots, of course, and is related in a complex way to the effects of colonialism, and to the role played by the printing press in the wider distribution, standardisation and translation of scripture into vernacular languages. This development in the study of Muslim identity and consciousness benefited especially from explorations into the place that Urdu has historically played in the thoughts and subjectivities of South Asian Muslims.[52] Yet what is new about current trends in the Muslim world is the fact that literacy and the media are affecting the lives of more people than ever before. As increasing number of people in the Muslim world have availed themselves of the opportunity to partake of courses of religious education over the past thirty years, the spectrum of people able and willing to participate in debate in the Muslim world has broadened in a novel way. Today's authorities on Islam are as likely to be engineers and doctors as they are students or teachers in mosque schools (*dar-ul uloom*) and colleges (*madrasa*). For Eickelman and Anderson, this has contributed to a 'fragmentation of political and religious authority' in the Muslim world, as 'multiplying the media through which messages can be transmitted diffuses political and religious authority' (Eickelman and Anderson 1997: 47). 'New Muslims' with multiple and varied educational backgrounds are approaching the doctrines and practices of Islam from new perspectives, and in new spaces. This is a key feature of the past decade because of the central role of the Internet, the telephone and satellite broadcasting, and their role in worldwide cultural globalisation.[53]

My aim, then, is to account for and document the distinctive intellectual vitality of Chitral people, noting in particular that it takes place in a wider context of the globalisation of Muslim identity, thought and debate. The debates and discussions over Islamic doctrine and practice in the mini-buses, orchards, shops and male guest-houses of my two field-sites take place in a space that is neither 'public in an official sense nor private in a personal one' (Eickelman and Anderson 1999: 15). What is important about

---

[52] See, especially, Jalal 2000, Metcalf 1982, Robinson 2000. Compare Edwards 1995 on print and religious revolution in Afghanistan, and Huq 1999 on texts, literacy and piety in Bangladesh.

[53] On the expanding role of the Internet in the Middle East, see Anderson 2000, and on the telephone and national identity in Turkey, see White 1999. On television serials in Egypt, see Abu-Lughod 2005. For the writings of one of Iran's most influential 'new' Muslim intellectuals, Abdolkarim Soroush, see Buchta 2002: 293–9.

them is the ways in which 'new Muslims' are adapting 'existing cultural practices to new communicative environments' (ibid.).

The distinctive ways in which Chitral people go about living a Muslim life also invite reconsideration of widespread ideas about the shape of contemporary Muslim identity. Many studies have suggested that there is only a narrow range of definitive ways of 'being Muslim' in the contemporary Muslim world, and that the boundaries between these styles of Muslim identity are clear-cut and discrete.[54] 'Islamist', 'modernist', and 'neofundamentalist' are the conceptual categories often used to label styles of Muslim identity that are considered active and potent in the Muslim world today.[55] Muslims not seen to fit these categories are sometimes assumed to be lax about faith, secular or simply indifferent towards religion.

In contrast, this book shows that Chitral Muslims inhabit multiple identities, which they work hard – emotionally and intellectually – to create in the face of powerful constraints. Recent anthropological works have argued that Muslim identity is much more fluid than the systematising and typifying approaches of earlier scholarship suggest.[56] Living a creative and enjoyable life in Chitral is maintained in the face of criticism voiced by those who are seen by local people as being 'narrow-minded', 'bored', 'extremist', and unable to derive any pleasure from the short life that God has given to them. 'The world', I was often told, 'is one of two days (*ju baso duniya*); tomorrow God may take you from this world to another existence – why spend your life in worry and anxiety?'[57] Criticism made by 'hardened' (*sakht*) men of piety in Chitral of Muslims who are said to have stepped outside the fold of 'correct' Muslim behaviour is injected with a very real potency in present day Pakistan, and especially Chitral. This was particularly the case during the five years of Taliban rule in Afghanistan. The Taliban, and the strict Sunni interpretations of the Islamic tradition that they sought to impose, were conceptualised by

---

[54] Geertz, for instance, sought to define the array of ways of being Muslim he encountered in Java as discrete types (Geertz 1960). See Robinson 1998 for the use of the categories 'modernist' and 'Islamist' in the analysis of Muslim identity in British India, and compare Werbner 2002.

[55] On the differences between 'Islamists' and 'neofundamentalists', see Roy 1994 and Kepel 2002.

[56] In a discussion of Islam in Java, Beatty has argued that there is a great 'blurring of the boundaries' between styles of Muslim identity and practice there (Beatty 1999: 156). See Bowen 1998; Ewing 1998; Manger 1999; Wilce 1998 on multiple identities in Muslim societies.

[57] Of course, it is important to recognise that the same notion is used by the region's many Taliban supporters to underwrite a very different ethic – one that encourages Muslims to fight 'holy war' (*jihad*). This ethic is also a feature of thought amongst some of Chitral's Muslims: the main road in the region is daubed with graffiti telling believers that 'holy war is the one road to heaven (*jihad jana'at ka sirf rasta hai*)'.

many Chitral people as a very perceptible threat to the continuing possibility of fluid and multiple Muslim identities in Chitral. The setting for my account of Muslim life contrasts starkly with contexts such as Cairo where anthropologists have increasingly explored Islamic revivalism as a 'response to the problem of living piously under conditions that have become increasingly ruled by a secular rationality' (Mahmood 2001: 830).[58]

Many Chitral people – including ordinary Muslims, as well as musicians, poets and men of learning and piety – combine styles of spirituality and Muslim identity that are often assumed by social scientists to be irreconcilable. Men who are associated with and committed to the policies of reform-oriented Islamist parties in Pakistan, are also known by people in the region to be 'masters' (*mahiran*) in the writing of forms of love poetry that have deep intellectual roots in the 'mystic strain' of Islam, Sufism. This is important: Sufi-oriented Islamic traditions in South Asia have come under intense attack and criticism from Muslim reformers for at least the last two centuries. Sufi practices and ideas are represented by Muslim 'purists' as being 'illegal' accretions from Hinduism, and as distorting 'correct' Islamic doctrine and practice that must be based entirely on the Qur'an and the sayings of the Prophet (*hadith*).[59]

The study of Sufi Islam has long sought to engage with the intellectual and emotional dimensions of the living of a Muslim life, and this book seeks to refine further the understanding of the ways in which Muslim identity and thought are influenced by Sufi texts and practices. As Arkoun puts it, Sufism (*tasawwuf*) is Islam's 'mystic strain' the 'ultimate purpose' of which is the 'unifying encounter between believer and his or her personal God' (Arkoun 1994: 81).[60] The ways in which this 'unifying encounter' can be experienced and imagined are diverse and complex, however, and there is a rich body of anthropological writing that explores

---

[58] See also Hirschkind 2001 and Starrett 1998.

[59] See Metcalf 1982 on opposition to Sufi practices and ideas in the Sunni Deobandi school of thought in India, and Eaton 1996 on the historical role of Sufis in the 'Islamisation' of India. On 'Sufis and anti-Sufis', see Sirriyeh 1999. On historical opposition to Sufi Islam, see Baldick 2000. On the nature of this debate in the contemporary Middle East, see, especially, Gilsenan 2000. On Sufi Islam in contemporary South Asia, see, especially, Werbner 2003; Werbner and Basu 1998: 17–21; van der Veer 1992. On the continuing vitality of Sufi Islam in Yemen, see Knysh 2001.

[60] Of course Islamic mysticism and Sufism are in no sense interchangeable terms. Sufi Islam is a complex phenomenon, and the many types of Sufism entail varying degrees of both the mystical imagination and conformity to Islamic doctrine and law. However, in relation to the ethnographic material presented in this book, Islam's mystical dimension – 'something mysterious, not to be reached by ordinary means or by ordinary effort' (Schimmel 1975: xvii) – appears as prominent as Sufism a straightforward Islamic path to human perfection.

this. Sufi Islamic traditions are often associated with 'shrine-centred worship' and recognised affiliation with organised Sufi 'brotherhoods' (*tariqa*) and 'lodges' (*zawiya*). There are also more ecstatic and individual ways of feeling the personal presence of God, and these often involve the use of drugs and renunciation approaches to the world.[61] Yet other Sufi orders and traditions, most especially the Naqshbandiyya, advance a reform-oriented intellectually motivated vision of Sufi practice and thought, which calls upon followers both to reform their lives according to the *shari'a* and to follow Sufi paths (*tariqa*) and teachings.[62] Such forms of Sufi Islam are critical of the role played by mediating saints and shrine worship in other types of Sufi orders; instead they follow more sober forms of religious devotion revolving around repeatedly reciting the names and qualities of God (*dhikr*). Finally, the devotional power of Sufism is a powerful feature of the institutions and practices of great movements of Islamic revival and purification, such as the worldwide preaching movement the Tabligh-e Jama'at, and Muslims in South Asia have not had to make stark decisions between Sufism and an emphasis on prophetic teaching (Metcalf 2004: 11).[63]

The power of Sufism is strong in Chitral, but visible in areas of religious experience other than shrine worship – indeed there is no pronounced tradition of the worship of saints at shrines in the region.[64] People from Chitral who visit shrine complexes 'for fun' (*mazah kokobachen*) in Pakistan's major cities, are often shocked at what they say are the un-Islamic goings-on inside. Nor do most Chitral people claim to belong or to have been influenced by *shari'a*-oriented Sufi brotherhoods such as the Naqshbandiyya. Indeed, whilst the word *sufi* is a part of villagers' vocabulary, it is largely used to identify men in the village who are strict about faith, pray regularly, grow their beards and do not drink or 'look at girls'.[65] Moreover, whilst some men claim to be followers of the Naqshbandiyya brotherhood, on the whole few people in the region claim affiliation to the

[61] On the anthropology of Sufi brotherhoods see especially, see Eickelman 1976; Gilsenan 1973; O'Brien 1971. On Sufi worship in Lahore, see Ewing 1984, 1997 and Werbner and Basu (eds) 1998, and Edwards' 1996: ch. 4 on Sufi thought and practice in Afghanistan. For an early attempt to define diverse forms of Sufi Islam, see Trimingham 1998.
[62] See, for instance, Gladney 1999: 448–57; Metcalf 1982; Nasr 1996; Robinson 2000.
[63] See also Werbner 2002.
[64] There is one shrine near the village in which I stayed at which villagers offer prayers whilst walking or driving past on their way to other villages in the region. However, there is no tradition of gathering at the shrine for communal forms of worship or picnicking. Compare N. Tapper 1990b.
[65] Villagers rarely use the Arabic word for Sufism, *tassawuf*. Indeed, I was once asked to write an essay for a Chitrali friend that would explain for him exactly what this concept meant.

'brotherhoods' and 'orders' of Sufi Islam that are powerful elsewhere in South and Central Asia. Yet they do draw in a knowledgeable way on Sufi thought in their daily discussions, and they themselves produce poetry that is deeply infused with the themes of classic Sufi texts, and recite it at musical gatherings (*mahfil*). 'Islam', I was once told by a man from Chitral working in a carpet shop in Karachi, 'is the knowledge of the heart'.[66] Many young men in Rowshan spend hours sitting with the few families of Dari-speaking Afghan refugees in the village learning Persian, as they say they want to be able to read for themselves and understand the Sufi writings of Khayyam, Rumi, Sa'di and Hafiz.[67] They also seek out religious scholars and other learned men in the village who are known to have a deep knowledge of these classic Sufi texts. Thus, there is an important intellectual dimension – manifested in the learning of the languages, the reading of texts and the writing of poems – in the way Chitral Muslims experience a form of Sufi Islam that is active and important in their region. In the context of a sophisticated body of anthropological writing on both the more ecstatic and reform-minded forms of Sufism, this book's contribution to the study of Sufi Islam is to explore the life of Sufi texts and concepts in the minds of village Muslims. This is something that it aims to accomplish by exploring the interaction between the intellectual and embodied dimensions of Islam – what Gellner called the 'religion-of-the-flesh' and the 'religion-of-the-book' (Gellner 1981) – in the living of a Muslim life in Chitral.

There remains a lingering assumption in anthropological writing that Islam, above all else, is a religion of the Book, a faith of exceptional coherence and normative guidance for adherents, and hence that it provides the only acceptable standard of proper life and faith. This book is concerned with Muslims living a life of critical engagement within a world of dangerous national and local events – especially sectarian conflict – and international upheaval, especially the 11 September 2001 terrorist attacks and the presence of the Taliban government in Afghanistan. By focusing on the life of villagers, what emerges requires us to question much that is still assumed about the way Muslims think in times of international political upheaval, and about the impact of mass education, religious learning in religious colleges, the status of women, and sectarian conflict.

---

[66] The notion of there being 'knowledge of the heart' and the heart as being a 'seat of the mind' is an important feature of much Sufi philosophy: see Corbin 1997: 221–45.

[67] These Afghans speak the Dari – an Afghan dialect of Persian. Yet they and Chitral people say that their language is Persian (Farsi), and, so, when referring to Dari, I use the word Persian throughout the course of this book.

More generally, the expressive lives of Chitral people refine our understanding of the nature of thought and the experience of emotion. Chitral people think, value reasoned contemplation, respect the mindful, enjoy the emotionally infused experience of the play of the mind, and actively make complex and multidimensional decisions about the moral standards by which they live their lives, and so this book focuses on the act, nature and experience of thought.

PLAN OF THE BOOK

In a setting of economic uncertainty, sectarian division, growing levels of education, and anxieties over wealth and status, my concern is with thought, emotion, and how village Muslims engage critically and reflectively with the politically and morally volatile world in which they live. My six major ethnographic chapters explore the key dimensions of these issues in the following ways. After an introduction of Rowshan village in chapter 2, chapter 3 asks what a village is in northern Pakistan, and examines the place that affection and emotions play in the living of a moral Muslim life in Rowshan. It connects these two themes by exploring a moralising discourse important in present day Rowshan that emphasises the 'upside-down' role that affection plays in structuring the relations between Muslims living in the village. These moral discourses are constructed through critical discussions that go on apace between Rowshan people, and chapter 4 explores daily discussion in the village and asks how villagers take pleasure from the play of the mind and the voicing of critical and new ideas. Intellectual activity is also an important dimension of chapter 5, which turns its focus to the urban setting of Markaz, in order to explore the role that creative intellectual activity plays in the living of an intellectually significant life in the region. An exploration of music and creative performance is central to the concerns of chapter 4 about what the process of 'being Muslim' means and entails in Markaz.

The music discussed in chapter 5 is the focus of considerable opposition from religious-minded folk in Chitral, and chapter 6 returns to Rowshan, in order to explore the lives and ideas of the village's 'men of learning and piety'. Many of these 'men of learning and piety' (*ulama*) have studied in religious colleges (*madrasas*), and this chapter asks how the *ulama* contribute to the intellectual climate of village life. They also often hold deeply anti-Ismai'li views; so, therefore, Chapter 7 focuses on 'sectarian' relations, and on conflict between Rowshan's Sunnis and Shi'a-Ismai'lis. It asks how Rowshan people construct the sectarian divide during the course of their daily lives, and then analyses moments of heightened sectarian tension when violent communal conflict was a distinct possibility and asks why it was avoided.

CHAPTER 2

Rowshan: Chitral village life

ORIENTATIONS

Rowshan, in summer, is a beautiful and verdant village surrounded by the peaks of the Hindu Kush and Hindu Raj mountain ranges. In winter its frozen streams, muddy village paths, and smoke-filled houses make life difficult even for the most resilient of its inhabitants. It is flanked by the fast flowing Chitral River, brown with glacial melt water in summer and deep blue in autumn, which cuts a gorge around the perimeter of Rowshan. On the steep banks of this gorge men and boys spend many an afternoon and evening sitting in discussion, reciting love poetry, studying for exams, talking about Islam, playing with children, smoking cigarettes and gazing at the mountains surrounding them.

The village's men and boys largely dress in sombre colours in the loose trousers and long shirt (*shalwar kameez*) worn across Pakistan. Older men often wear woollen Chitrali caps (*pakol*), waistcoats and long coats (*chugha*), made by Chitrali tailors (*darzi*) who skills are renowned across Pakistan. The village's more fashion conscious boys (*fashnie daqan*), however, prefer American-style baseball caps, and often say that they are embarrassed to wear the older types of Chitrali clothing preferred by the village elders. The women and girls of the village, in contrast to the men, wear colourful patterned outfits, and, on special days, such as the two main Muslim festivals, Eid-ul Fitr and Eid-ul Azhar, the two major occasions of the year when they are able to freely leave their homes, they wear outfits they have lovingly sewn and embroidered both with Chitrali style patterns and new 'down country fashions' they have seen on the television and in magazines brought to them by their brothers and fathers from Pakistan's cities. All women in the village cover their heads with scarves (*petek*) when they leave their homes, for instance, on trips to the hospital and schools. Yet there is great diversity of veiling forms in Rowshan: some women 'tie' (*botik*) them around their face revealing only their eyes, others drape them loosely around the back of their heads leaving their face and hair exposed, and some women even wear the all enveloping Afghan-style *burqa*.

Rowshan is connected by metalled road to the administrative head-quarters of the region, and minibuses, trucks and jeeps frequently ply this road. Households (*khushun*) in Rowshan are evenly dispersed, and between them lie fields (*chetur*) of wheat (*gom*), barley (*sirie*) and rice (*shali*), kitchen gardens (*khar*) of vegetables (*shakh*), and orchards (*shan*) of apple, pear, apricot, mulberry, peach and plum trees. The houses of the village, mostly separated by narrow fields and orchards, are connected to one another by village paths (*deho rah*), lined with poplar trees, hawthorn and rose bushes and flanked by irrigation channels. These paths are used mainly by the villagers, and the sight of a stranger (*nagoni*) on them results in great comment amongst Rowshan people. There is also a net-work of smaller and more hidden (*khoasht*) paths through the village fields, and these are mostly used by women and girls when they visit other households, go to school, and make trips to the one of the two hospitals in the village.

Rowshan is a large village by Chitral standards stretching about 3 km alongside the banks of the Chitral River, and is composed of about twenty-three hamlets. The village is also divided physically by a metalled road (*pakka rah*). Along most of this road shops owned by villagers intersperse road-side houses and fields, whilst at the centre of the village this road becomes the bazaar, where there are about eighty shops and eight tea-shops (*hotels*) serving cooked food, baked bread (*tanoori shapik*) and tea. Most of the village shops are general purpose and sell daily household items as well as clothes, shoes and 'gifts' (*tuhfa*) such as jewellery and make-up. These shops are also the focus of much male socialising outside the context of the home: in the early evening (*namazdigar*), before prayers, men join one another and sit and talk in the shops owned by their friends and relatives. There are also some more specialist shops in the village: two shops sell music cassettes, three books and stationary, three hardware, two provide photocopy services, and there are also three bakers and sweet makers.

The majority of Rowshan people are small-scale subsistence farmers. Small plots of land are cultivated on which are grown crops of wheat, rice, vegetables and fruit largely for household consumption. Most households also keep a few cows, sheep and goats for the daily production of milk, and for meat that is consumed on ritual occasions such as marriages, funerals and at other times of happiness (*khoshani*). Yet the village is now firmly embedded in Pakistan's cash economy; subsistence agriculture is no longer a viable basis for the village's economy. High levels of population growth, a pressing shortage of agricultural land and a high unemployment rate makes it impossible for households to survive on subsistence agriculture alone, and so many Rowshan people aspire to join the Pakistan Army or secure posts in the local administration or police.[1]

OUTSIDE PEOPLE

Rowshan's permanent residents are without exception Chitral people who speak Khowar, yet the village is not simply an ethnically and linguistically one-dimensional world. Rather, Rowshan people experience the cultural complexity of the frontier region in which they live not only in their visits to the region's small towns but in their everyday lives in the village itself, and this awareness of and ability to engage with diversity is itself a significant dimension of what it means to be a Rowshan villager.

Most of the village's shops are owned by Rowshan people, but Afghan refugees (*mohajiran*) – mostly Sunni Persian-speaking Tajiks from the Panjshir valley and Badakshan – have in the past six years opened bakeries and butcher-shops (*qasab khana*) in the village. There are five permanently settled Panjshiri Afghan families in the village. They live in rented houses inside the village and in rooms in the bazaar, and they are now amongst the wealthiest 'business people' (*karubari roi*) in the village; they all have anti-Taliban sympathies.[2] Most Rowshan people are on close and friendly terms with these Afghans, and the Afghans often attend the marriages and funerals of the villagers. There has been no case of intermarriage between Sunni Rowshan people and the Afghan refugee families, however. Whilst preferring to liken themselves to Persian speaking Afghans as opposed to Pashto-speaking Pukhtuns, most Rowshan people claim that they are far more polite than these folk who they say have angry brains (*bad dimagh*) and can think of little else than money and fighting.

In addition to these long-term Persian-speaking refugee families, there are also some Pukhtun-speaking Afghans from the Jalalabad region of

---

[1] On Chitral's incorporation into Pakistan's cash economy, see Staley 1982. See Kreutzmann 1991 on economic change in Pakistan's Northern Areas. According to the Census for Pakistan the Chitral's population was 106,000 in 1951; 159,000 in 1972; 209,000 in 1981; 319,000 in 1998.

[2] Some of these Afghans had fought beside the leader of the Northern Alliance leader Ahmad Shah Masoud against the Taliban.

Afghanistan, and Pukhtun-speaking men from other regions of the Frontier Province – especially Bajaur, Dir and Swat – who set up temporary summer stalls in the bazaar. These hawkers (*alghani*) live mostly in small unused shops at the edges of the bazaar, and are seen by many Rowshan villagers as a new and unwelcome feature of village life. They are accused by many villagers of polluting the village's water supplies, encouraging the village boys to smoke cigarettes and hashish and causing the women of the village to waste scarce household resources by encouraging them to buy the cheap jewellery that they peddle from house to house.

Finally, in the summer months, Wakhi-speaking Wakhiks from Afghanistan's Wakhan corridor and sometimes Gorno-Badakshan in Tajikistan also migrate to Rowshan, and they are employed by many Rowshan families to harvest and thresh the wheat crop. Afghan Wakhiks are said by Rowshan people to come to the village as thoughtless, simple and uneducated folk, prepared to work in the fields for low wages. Yet they soon show the imprint of Rowshan life and become cunning (*chalak*) and intellectual (*hushiyar*). This is something that creates problems for Rowshan people when the Wakhiks start to demand higher wages for their toils in Rowshan's fields. Wakhik-speakers who come from Tajikistan, however, are held to be able to contribute in more complex ways to the intellectual life of the village.[3] They have taught phrases in Russian to some Rowshan people, painted pictures inside the tea-houses and homes of the village, and their descriptions of life in Tajikistan, Moscow and other Russian cities are often the source of evenings of discussion for the villagers.

In their daily lives Rowshan people speak in Khowar, but many villagers are multi-lingual. Besides speaking Urdu and sometimes English, both official languages in Pakistan, which they have learned at school, many of the villagers speak Pashto which they learn whilst study-ing or working in Peshawar. With growing numbers of Afghans living in Rowshan, increasing numbers of young people in the village also speak Afghan Persian. On the one hand, Pashto is often associated with low-status and inferior forms of work and employment such as driving and labouring, and, by some at least, seen as a force that potential threatens ideally cultured and sophisticated Chitrali selfhood. One man I knew

---

[3] Civil war and poverty in the Gorno-Badakshan region of Tajikistan during the mid-1990s resulted in considerable numbers of Pamiri Tajiks migrating to Chitral. On the civil war in Tajikistan, see Akiner 2001.

who had lived for many years in the Pashto-speaking heart of the Frontier, Peshawar, proudly claimed that he had not picked up a single word of Pashto and had no interest in doing so. On the other hand, speaking Persian is said to invest the person with special thought, tenderness, and politeness. 'Persian', I was often told, 'is sweet (*shirin*) and the language of paradise (*jannato zaban*)'.

THE OUTSIDE WORLD

The village is connected to the major cities of what is referred to by local people as 'down Pakistan' (*aff pakistan*); and this connectedness with the world 'outside' (*berie*) is a further important feature of the experience of Rowshan life.

A high proportion of people leave Rowshan to work in the district headquarters, Markaz, 70 miles away, and in Pakistan's major cities, especially Karachi, Islamabad and Peshawar. Much of this 'going down' (*affote bik*) is seasonal, and men from the village leave their homes in early winter (*yomoon*) in order to 'labour' (*mazdoori*) in the cities of 'down Pakistan' until spring (*bosoon*) and the reopening of the road to Chitral. However, there are also families and individuals who are permanently settled in cities in 'down Pakistan' where they are engaged in paid employment, and they return to their homes in Rowshan usually only for two months in the summer. In addition, many boys and young men leave the village in order to attend schools and colleges. These men travel 'down' either to seek admission in institutions that teach 'worldly studies' (*dunyavi sabaq*), or to religious colleges and seminaries (*madrasa*) that teach the Islamic sciences and train 'men of learning and piety' (Arabic: *ulama*; Khowar: *dashmanan*). Over the course of the past five years, increasing numbers of girls and young women have also left the village to study nursing and attend academic courses in colleges in cities such as Karachi, Islamabad and Peshawar.

Historically the village also has deep links with places beyond the confines of the present day Pakistan state, and these historical connections continue to occupy the horizons of the villager's imaginations. Five households in the thirty-household hamlet in Rowshan I lived in, Gurzen, are the descendants of families who moved to the village from Afghanistan about 100 years ago. Three families told me their ancestral grandfather (*lot bap*) had come from Herat, and two families had close maternal relations in Afghan Badakshan. Men from each of these families had visited their relatives in Afghanistan since the victory of the

Mujahidin in 1989, and the stories of the long journeys they had made on donkeys and horses through the Pamir mountain range were often the source of discussion in the village. With the fall of the Taliban in Afghanistan in November 2001 and the prospect of greater peace and stability in the country, the senior member of one of these households even talked about returning to his ancestral home (*lot bapo door*) in Afghan Badakshan.

A further dimension of the village's connections with the world 'outside' is television: many houses have satellite dishes on which they watch TV channels from around the world, especially the BBC and the Indian station Zee TV. There is also a television booster tower in the village, which allows those without satellite dishes to watch Pakistan Television (PTV). Rowshan people particularly enjoy watching Indian dramas and films broadcast by popular Indian satellite stations, and watching the evening news (*khabarnama*) on PTV is an important evening routine for most Rowshan people. Many Rowshan people also read newspapers. The more educated villagers prefer to read one of Pakistan's respectable English dailies such as the *Dawn* or *The News*, and they say they do so to allow them to improve their English 'writing power' (an English phrase often used in Khowar). Those with less education read Urdu papers such as *Nawa-e Waqt* and *Aaj*.

Rowshan is the headquarters of a 'subdivision' within Chitral (sub-division Payeen), and, as a result, there are a number of government offices and institutions in and around Rowshan's small bazaar. There is a court for civil cases (*tarikh*), and the offices of several advocates (*wakilan*). The subdivision's government hospital is located in Rowshan. There are also several primary schools and a government high school, as well as a degree college that teaches boys from this village and others in 'upper Chitral' studying for higher secondary (FA, FSc) and bachelors (BA) degrees. People from this region of Chitral see Rowshan as a prosperous settlement, and many people I spoke to from villages elsewhere in upper Chitral told me how they dreamed of buying land in Rowshan and settling per-manently there.

Rowshan's perceived prosperity has indeed encouraged significant levels of in-migration into the village from poorer and more remote villages in 'upper Chitral' (*aih chitrar*). Yet Rowshan is conceptualised by most if not all people who live there as a village of long-term inhabitants, and even those families who have been living there for the past century are often referred to condescendingly as 'outsiders' (*berieo roi*) and sometimes even as 'the homeless' (*gadai*).

Migrants from elsewhere in Chitral into Rowshan are both Sunni and Ismai'li and the sectarian dimensions of migration into Rowshan is something much commented on by Rowshan people. Plots of land had been bought for the construction of houses by six families in the hamlet where I stayed in Rowshan, and many people from this hamlet commented that three of these houses were Ismai'li and three Sunni. Many Ismai'lis in Rowshan complained that the influx of Sunni families into the village over the course of the past ten years from *jangali* (wild), 'frontier' (*sarhad*) and Sunni-dominated regions of Chitral has changed the atmosphere (*mahaul*) of Rowshan life. In particular, they complain that greater numbers of 'outsiders' mean that households must practice stricter *purdah*, and that a significant increase of Sunni households in the village has also perceptibly heightened sectarian tension in the village. Yet Rowshan is also seen by many Ismai'lis living in Sunni dominated 'upper Chitral' as a place where it is easier to be Ismai'li than other regions of Chitral. Two Ismai'li men I knew who are now living in the village had moved to Rowshan from Sunni-dominated villages where they say that life is made impossible for Ismai'lis. In these villages, Ismai'li-owned shops are boycotted by Sunni families, Ismai'li weddings and funerals are not attended by Sunni neighbours, and Ismai'li places of worship have been burned and destroyed. I suggest in later chapters this contrasts greatly with the form taken by the sectarian divide in Rowshan.

Rowshan has also benefited from the activities of various branches of the Aga Khan Development Network (AKDN) that have been working in the region since 1982.[4] In 1997 a maternity home and women's hospital was established in the village, and Rowshan also has a 'Field Unit' of the Aga Khan Rural Support Foundation. The Aga Khan Education Services (AKES) built a hostel for girls in the village in the early nineties. This hostel is located at the very centre of the bazaar, and AKES have also facilitated the construction of a fee-paying English-medium school for girls. The Aga Khan Development Network employs considerable numbers of people in the village, and its activities in Rowshan have had an important economic impact on life in the village. Many Rowshan people are employed by the AKDN both in professional and non-professional positions: teachers, drivers, economists, social organisers, cooks and researchers all receive comparatively handsome salaries from the organisation. In Gurzen,

---

[4] The AKDN is one of the world's richest and biggest international NGO aid organisations, see Daftary 1998.

for instance, 10 people had professional jobs in the various branches of the Aga Khan Development Network. The money that comes from the Foundation has allowed people to build conspicuous new houses, finance shops, and send children to school and university in other regions of Pakistan. But this new money has itself caused considerable friction and tension in the village, of the ten people employed in the AKDN in Gurzen eight were members of one extended family. The distribution in the village of employment by the Foundation is also the focus of considerable comment by villagers: 'why is it', I was often asked, 'that in one house everybody has received employment in the Foundation, whilst in another house none have been successful?'

VILLAGE LORDS

Rowshan people, then, frequently express deep concerns about divisions emerging in the village that are based on wealth and income that is largely generated by the Aga Khan Development Network. Yet these tensions themselves build on older forms of status divisions which have been important in the Chitral region since before the British colonial period. As I discuss below, open discussions that involves making assertions about the relative status of Rowshan's residents are considered distasteful by most village people. Yet such comments are an important feature of hushed talk in the village, and the broader theme of the relevance that such status distinctions have for life in the 'modern era' (*tajdid-o zamana*) is a source of great debate in the village.

British scholar-soldiers described a society in which concerns over hierarchy and status were an important feature of the Chitral state (*riyasat*) and its court (*darbar*). They said that Chitral society was divided into four categories of people: the ruling family (*kartore*) from which the Mehtar or ruler of Chitral was descended, a lordly class of nobles (*adamzada*, literally, 'true humans'), peasant farmers (*yuft*) and serfs (*cheermuzh*).[5] As is the case with much colonial writing on caste and social structure in British India, these works essentialse status difference in Chitral in ways that reflect the internal logic of colonial rule (Cohn 1987). Yet they are also echoed in the way many Rowshan people talk about and describe status difference today, and the ways Rowshan people make status distinctions highlights how far the capability to think is an

---

[5] On colonial categorisations of status groups in Chitral, see, especially, Biddulph 1972, and on traditions of lordliness in South Asia more generally, see S. Bayly 1999.

important dimension of leading a Muslim life in the region. While Chitral's lordly folk are often said to be 'true humans', the descendants of *cheermuzh* in the region are often described as being something less than complete human beings. The descendants of *chermuzh* families are often said to be animal-like (*haivanghonie*) by Rowshan's gentry families: they lack intellect (*'aql*), are unable to control their tongues (*tan liginiean khabaar giko no boynian*) and this means they speak 'dirty words' (*gandah lu*).

There are a number of households of lordly families in Rowshan, and, importantly, these families are both Ismai'li and Sunni. The houses of the lords (*lalei*), number about eight in Rowshan, and are mostly located on small raised hillocks that stand out on the gently sloping alluvial fan on which Rowshan is sited. Like all other houses in the village, they are one-storey constructions made from mud plaster, and comprise of a central living quarter that is supported by five wooden beams (*thoon*). Households in Rowshan consist of this central living quarter (*dor*), where women cook meals on a wood-fired hearth (*daang*) below a hole in the roof that serves as a chimney (*kumal*), a feature of the house that often makes it smoky in summer and damp in the winter months. Indeed, in winter snow must quickly be removed from the roof (*istan*) of the house to stop melt-water dripping (*chotiko*) onto the beds inside. The family sits around the hearth in the central seating area (*pheran lasht*) for meals of bread and tea at lunchtime (*granish*), and rice with vegetables or occasionally meat for the evening meal (*boto shapik*). Children and young unmarried adults sleep in beds placed in designated sleeping areas (*nakh*) in the house. Many married couples often now have their own private rooms (*angutie*), although poorer families may still sleep together in the house.

The houses of Rowshan's lordly families, sited on hillocks (*dok*), have commanding views of the village. Having a house sited on raised ground (*osniru zamin*) is a mark of status for the beautiful views (*nazara*) which these houses command. But power and status are also embedded in the physical landscape of the village, and Rowshan's lord's often proudly state that nobody is 'above' them (*ma sura kaa di nikie*). Yet 'raised land' is also at the centre of considerable tension in present day Rowshan. Many villagers complain that those living in high places break the purdah of the households that lie in their shadow. Young men and boys, especially, are told not to walk to Rowshan's hillocks for this is likely to provoke fights with men in the village who claim they visit these revealing places in order to 'look at girls' in the houses below.

Lordly houses are also often distinguished by having large orchards (*shan*) and grassy areas (*gaz*) where outdoor musical performances are held at times of happiness (*khoshani*) such as the marriage of one of the family's sons, or after the victory of the village team in a polo tournament. Large Chinese plane trees (*chinar*) in front of houses also mark out the households of high-status families: the tree's deep roots symbolise the families long and known genealogy, and their big leaves are said to create a cool shade (*sharu chagh*) worthy only of reputable men. Horsemanship, cool shade, luxurious orchards, and expansive views are the standards set by lordly families for the living of a truly significant human life of respect and value.

Villagers are also aware of which households in the village were once those of the 'serfs' of the Rowshan's lords; and some Rowshan people call hamlets in the village where there are many such houses 'the hamlet of the slaves' (*ghalamusandeh*)[6]. Yet men who speak like this are themselves said by other villagers to be rude (*shum*) and unrefined (*weshirau*) for talking about others in such a disrespectful way. Rowshan people also claim that they are the most 'progressive' (*taraqi korak*) people of the entire Chitral region: in other villages, I was often told, lordly men continue to boast about the number of households of serfs they have serving them. Rowshan's lordly families are not immune from this criticism: they are also said to have lost touch with the era (*zamana*) in which they are living, and their love for polo and falconry and their penchant for self-praise (*ishtikhik*) are the subject of much joking by many Rowshan people. They are said by self-styled 'progressive thinkers' in the village as having been unable to benefit from modern education, and this is something that makes them stagnant and stupid: their minds (*zehna*), I was often told, are preoccupied with an outdated ancient era (*qadimo zamana*) now gone (*hate zamana baghai*). Lordly families' interest in maintaining their position as landowners has meant, in the minds of many villagers, that they live materially deprived lifestyles in comparison to families in the village who work for a living and 'do business'. The lords' one-time serfs, I was often told, are now wealthy because of their willingness to leave the village and work as labourers in Pakistan's cities, whilst the lords themselves are still proudly (*tsarak biti*) playing polo on Rowshan's dusty polo ground (*jinali*).[7]

---

[6] On the category of 'serf' in Chitral, see Parkes 2001a.

[7] On power and status in a feudal region of Lebanon in the 1970s, see Gilsenan 1996, especially chs. 15–16.

Concerns of status and pedigree are, thus, a focus of much thought and debate for Rowshan people. Yet this is also a domain of village life that is deeply sensitive and a source of great pain for many villagers. Indeed, whilst I was able to explore family life I Rowshan in a way that is not usually possible by male anthropologists working in other Muslim societies, I found it considerably more difficult to explore the role that status distinctions played in the everyday religious and social lives of villagers. Whilst I do seek to allude to the importance of these distinctions for the ethnographic material presented in this book, this is a dimension of Chitral life that for ethical reasons have I decided not to make a central theme of the present book.

HOUSEHOLD ECONOMICS

All households in Rowshan rely on the village's small bazaar where they purchase expensive (*qimati*) requirements for day-to-day life: especially ghee (*don*), rice (*grinj*), tea (*chai*) and sugar (*shokor*). Many families in the village describe themselves as being poor (*gharib*). Average household size in the village is about fifteen persons. Poor families have little or no regular source of cash income, and rely on loans taken from village shopkeepers for the purchase of their daily household requirements. Some households are said to be in debt by as much as 300,000 Pakistani rupees (about £3,000). At most, such households receive an income of 3,000 Pakistani Rupees (about £40) per month – a very small amount by local standards. This cash may come from one of the male family members' employment in the Chitral police force, or the local branch of the Pakistan Army, the Chitral Scouts, and some Rowshan people are soldiers in the Pakistan Army itself. In the hamlet I lived in, for instance, one man was employed in the police force, five were retired non-commissioned officers of the Chitral Scouts, three were retired soldiers from the Pakistan Army and three young men were selected as fresh recruits (*rangoot*) in the Chitral Scouts. Several men and women were also employed in other government jobs, especially in banks, agricultural and social welfare departments, and district-level clerical jobs, both in the village and beyond.

Poor households in the village have only small landholdings of about half an acre, and this allows them to produce supplies of rice and wheat that last for, at best, three months of the year. Such households often rely on the migration of their sons to Pakistan's cities. In particular, poor 'sons of the village' (*deho zhizhou*) work as factory labourers, household servants and drivers in Karachi, Islamabad and Peshawar. Some households have successfully earned some income from small businesses, most especially shopkeeping (*dukandari*) and driving (*driverie*). There were eleven shops owned by people from Gurzen, and four men owned vehicles – minibuses and jeeps – which they used for commercial purposes. Such businesses are reliant on the debt-ridden local economy and they often go under shortly after being established. Loans are ideally hidden and secret, and in order to avoid the shame of asking for money themselves, shopkeepers often send their children on missions to persuade their fathers' debtors to repay long outstanding loans.

The family with whom I stayed in Rowshan were Ismai'lis, and the household comprised twenty-one persons. Two members of the household were in regular employment, and, as a result, this family was said by other villagers to live a comfortable yet difficult life. The eldest brother – in his mid-thirties – worked as a field assistant for a government department after having completed training in a vocational course from Peshawar University. He earned about 2,500 (£35) Pakistani Rupees per month, although a significant proportion of this was immediately 'cut' by his bank to pay off a loan he had taken to build a guesthouse for his family. The eldest sister in the household, Shabnam, who had a Bachelors degree for which she had studied privately with the help of her younger brother, Farhan, was aged about twenty-seven years, unmarried and employed as a field assistant for another government department active in Rowshan. Her salary (*tankha*) was also about 2,500 Pakistani rupees per month. Thus, the family had a stable income of about 5,000 Pakistan rupees per month (about £60) which was comparatively little by local standards.

These two regular cash incomes were supplemented by farming: the household sold apples, dried fruit and turnips for cash to traders from 'down Pakistan' and to shopkeepers in the bazaar. Each month about 1,600 rupees was spent on rice, 1,500 rupees on flour, 750 rupees on ghee, 500 rupees on tea, 400 rupees on sugar and 100 rupees on salt. Thus, on basic items alone 5,000 rupees were spent each month. Luxury items such as meat (*pushur*) and seasonal fruit (mangoes, husk and watermelons) freighted in by truck from down country Pakistan were occasionally purchased for especially 'respected guests'. The bulk of the family's expenditure, however, went on educating the elder brother's seven young children. Four of these children studied in a private English-medium school in the village that charged fees of 250 rupees per child per month. In addition to these school fees, school uniforms, textbooks and stationary were frequently required, and who got 'new things' was a source of great anxiety for the little ones (*tsetsek*). Financial constraints meant that this man had to send his other children for education in free Urdu-medium government schools.

A monthly household income of 50,000 rupees (about £550) allows a family to live a very privileged and grand way of life. One household in the hamlet where I stayed had such an income. All children in such a household are encouraged to study in English-medium schools in the village, and some travel to schools and colleges in Pakistan's major cities for prestigious education in reputable institutions by village standards. These households are also often able to own a vehicle, and this means that they and the female members of the household are able visit other villages, relatives and go to the hospital in great comfort. Wealthy families also employ Afghan refugees living in the village as wage labourers during the wheat harvest and threshing season, these men are paid about fifty rupees a day to harvest the crops. Over the course of the past two years wealthy families have also started purchasing computers and connecting themselves to the World Wide Web: in the hamlet in which I lived three households now own computers and have access to the Internet. Poorer families in Rowshan, however, find it hard even to afford the cost of having a telephone, and if they do buy a telephone their more wealthy neighbours often tell them how they are wasting their precious money on unnecessary luxuries.

CONCLUSION

People in Rowshan talk about the world as being divided between the home (*dur*) and village (*deh*), and the outside (*berie*). From the perspective of this schema, the home is ideally meant to be the locus of affection (*khuloose*) and security (*tahafuz*) that Chitrali men can always return to after their travels to the outside. The world outside – be it the factories of Karachi, the bazaars of Peshawar, the largely Sunni neighbouring valleys, or the even just Rowshan bazaar – is one of *tensien* (tension) and anxiety (*pereshanie*).[8] On trips 'outside' the Chitrali men, and increasingly also women, will be expected to deal and interact in a calm and respectable fashion with 'all sorts' of people whom he will 'bump into' (*qesma qesma roi ta roi tu doynie*). The home provides, ideally, a haven from the complex and fraught social arena of the outside world. Noise (*havaza*) in the home should ideally be kept to the minimum. A house in which arguments

---

[8] Compare Beeman 1986.

(*janjal*), fighting (*eeghodik*), and noise (*havaza*) are a frequent element of day-to-day life is said not to be a home, but, rather, a den of cats and dogs (*reinie-pushie mali*). Moreover, a person who lives in such a house can never be expected to compete successfully (*muqabila korik*) with the outside world. The next chapter explores how Chitral people negotiate and experience the division between the hidden and the open.

CHAPTER 3

Emotions upside down: affection and Islam in present day Rowshan

Having put on a pair of glasses, it turns out that she has a good look beneath her veil (*aynak tchackei chardaro muzhen jam lolak birai*).

(Modern Khowar love song)

INTRODUCTION

This chapter explores the complexities of village life (*deho zindagi*) in Rowshan. What is a village (*deh*) in this region of northern Pakistan, and what constitutes village life? It addresses these questions by exploring the moral complexity of village life. In particular it discusses the ways in which Rowshan people make moral and social judgements about the state of village life, and it examines the ways in which the making of moral valuations is concerned especially with maintaining proper levels of emotion and affection. Ethnographically this chapter deals with 'devilish' children, parental affection, illicit cross-gender friendships, human–animal relations, cleanliness, education and migration. In all these areas of village life a discourse of moral valuation is continually constructed by Rowshan people (*Rowshanech*) in debate, and a recurrent focus of this debate is the current state of the villager's emotions. This discourse is itself structured by broader concerns about secrecy (*khoashteik*) and revelation (*khulao korik*), the inside (*andreni*) and the outside (*berie*), as well as the interaction between the village (*deh*) and the state (*sarkar*).

I am here concerned with village life because it is so often just assumed to be stagnant, backward and static: intellectually just waiting to be enlightened or Islamised.[1] Despite the importance of movements of people, finances, ideas and technology, discussed in chapter 2, local people do

---

[1] For discussions of the Indian village, see Dumont 1980 and Pocock 1973. For a critique of conventional anthropological writing on the village as a social unit in South Asia, see Fuller 1989. On the transformations in the study of the village in India, see Madan (ed.) 2002.

think of the village (*deh*) as an important social unit, and use it as a primary source of reference in their daily lives.[2] Above all for Rowshan people, as anthropologists have argued in their discussions of the village in other regions of South Asia, the village is a bio-moral unit (Daniel 1984) where an array of social relations is supposed to consist of distinct forms of sentiment and affection.[3] Even the most ordinary daily activity is judged by villagers to have a moral (*ikhlaqi*) quality, and to involve a specific form of emotional attachment and interaction. Ideally the village is a community of shared happiness (*khoshani*), difficulties (*mushkilat*) and sadness (*gham*)

Yet Rowshan life is also characterised by a feeling of disorder on the part of villagers.[4] Villagers conceptualise the village as part of the wider world, and see themselves to be actively responding to the complex array of forces acting on their lives. Many Rowshan people talk of the need to change the way they lead their lives in order to meet the challenges of the 'fast era' (*tez zamana*) in which they conceive themselves as living. Yet there are also deep anxieties about unattainable desires that originate in watching the television and the high expectations placed on returning migrants. The ambiguity of contemporary village life is expressed in a moralising discourse that represents the village as being at once a space of special and authentic affect and emotion and at the same time a place that is morally corrupt (*shum*) and dirty (*gandah*).[5] Yet there is no simple rejection of village life by Rowshan people, and the Rowshan of the mind takes on very different moral qualities when villagers leave their homes for education and work in Pakistan's major cities.

The moral valuations that Rowshan's Muslims make about the state of village life, however, are not causally located on the immoral outside in a way that relieves Rowshan people from moral responsibility. There is no single consensus of opinion in the village on the desirability of 'Islamisation' of village life to reform and purify the moral standards of Rowshan people. Nor are villagers deferential to the Islamic authority of Rowshan's religious notables or the authority of government officials.

---

[2] Daniel (1984) emphasises the extent to which being nurtured on the soil of the village enhances personhood, whilst I show that for Rowshan people being brought up in the village can also entail distinct moral problems. Compare Raheja 1988. Much recent anthropology has sought to question conventional ways of thinking about the interaction between sociality and space and scale (Barth 1993: 172, see also Barth 1987, 1992).

[3] Recent anthropological writing on kinship has focussed on ways in which affect shapes relations by people in different cultural contexts. See, for instance, Carsten 2000; Lambert 2000.

[4] Murphy 2000 explores the moral ambiguities of social representation in the Pakistani city of Lahore.

[5] See Hansen 2001: 171 on notions of moral decay important among Mumbai Muslims.

My concern here is to ask how Rowshan people actively live through, debate and make moral judgements about the transformations they are experiencing in their everyday lives.[6] Of particular importance here is Laidlaw's work on the ethical complexities of the lives of urban Jains in north India (Laidlaw 1995). Laidlaw shows how people can 'live by' without necessarily 'conforming to' ethical and religious values that are highly ascetic and otherworldly. The religious tradition Laidlaw discusses is obviously different from Islam's emphasis on the need for Muslims to lead worldly yet pious lives. Yet, as will be seen here, Rowshan's Muslims must also work hard to find consistency in their daily actions and the moral judgements they make about the state of village life. This is partly because, as Laidlaw argues, 'religion is not ever all there is to ethics' (Laidlaw 1995: 12). At the same time, however, it would be to oversimplify the moral reasoning and work of Chitral people to suggest that what is constitutive of 'true' Islamic norms in the village automatically has the consensus of all villagers.[7] It would be wrong to assume that all actions that are seen to transcend these are beyond Islam and thus subject to a different set of moral evaluative criteria. This chapter challenges any lingering notion in the anthropological study of Muslim societies that the daily thought and actions of Muslims is best understood in terms of what falls within the domain of the Islamic and what lies in the realm of 'practical reason'.

Possessing affection (*khuloos*) and love (*muhabbat*) for others is an important feature of living a virtuous (*jam*) and emotionally legitimate Muslim life in Rowshan.[8] Yet in the specialist literacy on contemporary Muslim societies, piety and conformity to textual Islamic doctrines and practices are often depicted as the key features of emergent styles of Muslim identity and religiosity in the modern era.[9] Emphasising the conflictual dimension of the making of moral judgements, and drawing on recent developments in the anthropology of emotion, I ask how Rowshan people subject emotions to 'normative assessment' (Elster 2000: 202).[10] It is often

---

[6] Compare Taussig 1980.

[7] In particular, I find Lambek's recent discussion of morality helpful: 'morality is not a coherent, imposed system a specific set of rules . . . but the forms and acts by which commitments are engaged and virtue accomplished' (Lambek 2000a: 315). See also Laidlaw 2002.

[8] On morality, responsibility and affection in the living of a Muslim life in Bali, see Barth 1993: 190.

[9] On the place of emotion and affection in the anthropology of Sufi Islam, see Werbner and Bassu 1998, and compare Abu Lughod 1986 and Tapper 1990a. On morality, piety and 'revivalist Islam' in Egypt, see Hirschkind 2001.

[10] Moral philosophers have long sought to classify the virtues of contrasting emotions, see Smith 2002 [1870], especially section II. On emotion and worship in South Asia see, Lynch (ed.) 1990 and Bennett 1990. On the social construction of emotions, see, for instance, Abu Lughod and Lutz 1990. Of greater relevance to the approach taken to emotion in this chapter is Csordas 1994.

assumed that moral judgement in Muslim societies is dominated by a clear-cut binary schema that defines action and thought as being either lawful (*halal*) or forbidden. Another prevalent view is that moral judgement locates actions and thoughts on a four-part spectrum of mandatory (*farz*), permitted (*mubah*), disapproved (*makruh*) and forbidden (*haram*) acts. Morality in Muslim societies is thus widely thought of as being an uncontested and ready-made category.[11] Islamic doctrines and teachings certainly are a key reference point for the ways in which Rowshan's Muslims live their lives and decide on their daily actions, and Rowshan people themselves use the words *jaiz* (permitted) and *najaiz* (forbidden) when talking about their conceptions of morality. Yet there is no simple formula emanating from puritanical Islam which establishes what people think in Rowshan.

MY MOTHER! SHE CARES FOR HER COWS, BUT HAS NO LOVE FOR ME

In what sense is Rowshan a moral unit, and according to what standards do Rowshan people subject everyday activities in the village to moral verification?

There are two sets of moral and ethical standards in the village, and these two sets of standards are a source of much conflict in the minds of villagers concerning what is moral (*ikhlaqi*) and virtuous (*jam*). There is one set of open and publicly recognised general norms about how to lead a moral, good-humoured, civilised, cooperative and civil Muslim life with one's fellow villagers. Yet there is also a secret underside to this ideal of sophis-ticated civility that involves the use of tricks, ploys and hidden devices.[12] The division between the open (*al zahir*) and the hidden (*al batin*) is, of course, an important dimension of Islamic doctrines and standards, but villagers also conceive of there being something distinctively Chitrali about these categories of thought and action.[13] My friends in the village would often comment to me that being Chitrali means 'being one thing on the surface and another thing on the inside' (*sura khur mula khur*).

---

[11] See, for instance, Peletz 1996: 148–54. On the historical complexities of Islamic moral thought, see Cook 2000.

[12] See Ferme 2001 for an ethnographic account of secret tactics amongst the Mende of Sierra Leone.

[13] See Das 1984 on the division between the open and the hidden in Islamic thought and practice. See Beatty 2000, and Parkin 2000a, 2000b on the importance of the open and the hidden in Islamic prayer. The outer and the inner is also an important dimension of late twentieth-century develop-ments in Islamic philosophy, especially in the writings of one of Iran's most popular yet controversial religious thinkers, Abdol Karim Soroush, see Buchta 2002: 293–9.

The open and the hidden are two sets of moral standards for the judgement of village life, and these standards are an important dimension of much Islamic philosophy and Muslim thought. Yet Rowshan Muslims do not cognitively separate them, and these parallel sets of values do not instrumentally structure villager's conceptions of what it means to live a virtuous (*jam*), proper (*sahi*), moral (*ikhlaqi*) and clean (*pazgah*) life. Rather, Rowshan people constantly make decisions about which parts of their lives they should keep concealed, and about the things they should allow to be made open and part of the known knowledge of the villagers. This ongoing decision-making process is a great cause of anxiety for Rowshan people. The open dimension of morality is not in any simple sense more Islamic and Muslim than that which is secret and concealed: both making things open and keeping things concealed creates moral and ethical problems in different contexts. There is a constant concern that the ideally hidden dimension of life will 'come to the surface' (*sura nisir*). The danger of the underside of life emerging in public discussion has the potential to bring shame and disrespect, and disrespect affects not only individuals but also families, and, importantly, the moral unit of the village itself. At the same time, allowing things to 'come to the surface' is also conceptualised as diluting the aesthetic delights of that which is concealed.

My friends in Rowshan often told me that true Muslims (*sahi musulmanan*) are not those who are regular in their prayers or strict in keeping their fasts. Rather, it is those who have 'souls that burn for others' (*zhan pulu'ak*) and whose 'hearts are full of love and affection' (*hardi muhabatochen khuloos tip*) who are true Muslims and real human beings. Compassionate self-sacrifice for others is seen as being central to what it means to be a 'good Muslim'. There is a general level of consensus amongst the villagers that balanced and compassionate emotions lie at the heart of fully realised Muslim selfhood.

This idealised vision of compassionate Muslims who have souls that burn for others is widely seen as unobtainable for most if not all Rowshan people. Sociality, which should ideally be based on warmth and love, is, in the context of present day Rowshan, pervaded by mistrust, jealousy and hatred. 'Rather than loving and cooperating with one another', I was often told, 'the people of this village are more fond of creating hatred, anger, and mistrust of one another' (*eegho soom tavawun koriko zhagha eegho no khosheinian*). Rowshan's Muslims say that they are living in an era of expense (*mengaieo zamana*) and that poverty (*ghurbat*) has made people greedy (*lalichi*). Moreover, the degraded state of the villager's moral and emotional health is also conceptualised as having an effect on the bodily health of Rowshan people. The conditions of present day life are said by many Rowshan people to result in high levels of mental and bodily illness in the village: headaches (*kapal chameik*), depression (*tang bik*) and anxiety (*pereshani*) are said to plague the lives of Rowshan's Muslims.[14] Indeed, antidepressant and anti-anxiety drugs are amongst the most commonly prescribed medicines by Rowshan's doctors and medical-store owners, and the region's newspapers often carry articles and letters relating what they perceive as Chitral's high level of heart disease to the tense nature of people's lives.

Rowshan is composed of several smaller hamlets (*deh*) which themselves have specific names known by all the inhabitants of the village, and often people from other villages in Chitral. These hamlets vary in size, but the hamlet I lived in, Gurzen, contained thirty households. People in Rowshan take much pride from belonging to the hamlet in which they have been born and brought up; and the moods (*tabiyat*) of the people who live in these hamlets are said to be contrasting in striking ways. Some hamlets are said to be particularly pious or Islamic, others are said to be especially civilised (*tahzib-i yafta*), polite (*sharif*), and welcoming to guests (*mehman nawazi*), whist there are hamlets where life is conjectured as being fun-loving and free (*azad*), if a little devilish (*sheytani*). Gurzen, for instance, is said to be dominated by religious-minded families who support the Islamist Jama'at-e Islami political party, founded by the scholar-journalist Mawlana Mawdudi in 1940. The Jama'at-e Islami party has been a powerful force behind reformist Islam in Pakistan and elsewhere in the Muslim world. In particular it has sought to remove the 'encumbrances of cultural accretion and tradition', reconstruct the 'pristine faith of the Prophet', gain political power, enforce Islamic law (*shari'a*), and construct the ideal 'Islamic state' (Nasr 1994: 7).[15] Yet, rather than being said to be pious and pure, many people from Rowshan, and indeed from Gurzen itself, would say that of all Rowshan's hamlets it was this one that had become the dirtiest (*safan sar gandah*) and the most morally degraded

---

[14] Anxiety and confusion (*pereshani*) are seen as having pathological potentials for people in Rowshan. In the context of Bali, Wikan shows how anxiety and confusion have the potential to shatter the ideal place that 'calm' plays in a person's life (see Wikan 1990).

[15] On the Jama'at-e Islami, see Ahmad 1994, Nasr 1994. On Mawdudi, see Nasr 1996. For a comparative discussion of the Jama'at-e Islami in Kashmir, see Sikand 2002. An important dimension of identity in Rowshan is being a known supporter of one of Pakistan's major political parties, especially the Pakistan People's Party, the Muslim League, the Jama'at-e Islami, and the Jama'at-e Ulama-e Islam. For an ethnography of party affiliation in the urban setting of Karachi, see Verkaaik 2004.

(*safan sar badikhlaq*). As a Sunni man from the village once told me, 'you should know one thing about Jama'at-e Islami folk, they are always ready to point the finger of blame at others, but if you knew the immorality that goes on in their homes it would make you scared'.

Thus, in the mind of this man, rather than imputing purity and morality, the strict observance of Islamic standards allows people to conceal the immorality of their own households behind the façade of fraudulent Muslim austerity. Moreover, this man was also thinking critically about where Islamic moral authority comes from, and who has the right to enforce it. He is engaging in debates which have long been important in the Islamic sciences about how Muslims should go about 'preventing vice' and 'promoting virtue'. This was particularly important for Rowshan people at the time because the 'prevention of evil and promotion of virtue' police (*al-amr bi'l m'ruf wa'l-nahy 'an al-munkar*) in Taliban-controlled Afghanistan had a high profile in both the Western and Pakistani mass media at the time. By objecting to what he sees as the way in which self-styled Islamists in the village interfere in Rowshan people's 'personal lives' (*zati zindagi*), this man is critically engaging with an important dimension of Islamic moral philosophy. Moreover, he is also voicing contentious ideas about the sensitive issue of what form a so-called Islamic state should take.[16]

It is not only the religious persuasions of people living in particular hamlets that differentiate them in the minds of Rowshan people. Concerns about class, status, tradition and modernity also infuse the morally complex visions Rowshan people have of their village. Different hamlets also take on specific cultural characteristics in the minds of Rowshan people, and these are connected to villagers' experience of modernity, globalisation and social change. The householders of one hamlet, for instance, are said to be *schokh* (snobs) *maghrur* (proud) and *takabur* (arrogant). Lordly people from another hamlet, Dok, are known for being overly rigid, traditional, and unable to meet the needs and requirements of the modern age in which they live. These lordly families, who have historical connections with Chitral's court culture, are often accused by villagers who represent themselves as being educated and modern as living in a bygone age and living their lives according

---

[16] The phrase 'promotion of virtue' and the 'prevention of vice' was used by Afghanistan's Taliban government for the department that checked lengths of beards and sizes of veils, and punished people for listening to music.

to outdated moral standards. As one Ismai'li man in his late twenties commented:

Oh my brother, what is lordly about them. Look at the way they waste their time playing polo dressed in dirty clothes and swearing at one another. They are living in an ancient age (*qadimo zamnan*) – they have not been able to benefit from education and they are still rigidly (*rau rau*) talking about traditional things like polo, falconry and how many serfs (*chermuzh*) they have.

Far from unthinkingly embracing the lordly styles of Rowshan's gentry classes, or remembering a golden age of emotional warmth when society was properly ordered around social status, many Rowshan people seek to question and contest the relevance of these moral standards to the present day era.

Yet, at the same time, there is no simple attempt to embrace modern (*jadid*) values associated with the outside world (*berieo duniya*). The folk of yet another hamlet are said to be especially 'free' (*azad*) and 'relaxed', particularly with regard to the moral propriety of their women. The people of this hamlet were said to have become so 'free' that they had converted their area into a 'little India' (*tan deho tsek india ghereiasuni*). Visions of India that are conjured up by television programmes and films make India into a kind of fantasy land of freedom in the minds of many of Rowshan people. Yet Rowshan people are said to be capable of bringing India to the village, and thus of making the fantasy come real – all too real, in fact. In this 'small India' (*tsek india*) purdah was said to have ceased to matter, and the women and girls of the hamlet were spoken of as morally loose. It was said that they even danced, with their unveiled hair flowing in locks (*gheluchi phooran*) around their 'milk-white necks' (*cheer golan*), to the music of Indian Bollywood films. The girls of this hamlet were said to have *bad characters* (in English) be 'immoral' (*badikhlaq*) and, the worst insult of all, to be *sexy* (in English). They were thought to have illicit love relationships, and to be unable to control their dangerous and destructive sexual passions. If Rowshan people are not willing to embrace the lordly and traditional styles of the village's gentry or the pious styles of the Islamists, then neither are they willing to accept unconditionally the introduction of un-Islamic styles of life from outside the village. Thus, in the minds of Rowshan people, the village is seen as encompassing a very high degree of diversity, and this diversity itself reflects the moral conflicts that lie at the heart of village life.

Besides bearing the imprint of bygone eras, Islamic revivalism and dynamic globalised modernity as depicted in Indian films, village life is also said to be fractured by 'village politics' (*deho siyasat*). If there is a certain aesthetic in the creative ability to imagine Rowshan as the film set for an all too real Indian film, then 'village politics' is one dimension of village life that many villagers consider to reflect more problematically on their current state of emotional and moral failure.

The pretence of friendly relationships between villagers – performed through prolonged greetings in the bazaar and village alleys – is said to conceal a more unpleasant 'reality' (*haqiqat*).[17] I was often told by my friends that whilst Rowshan people embrace when they meet in the bazaar and exchange long strings of polite greetings (*basharawal*), the thoughts that they keep in their souls (*kiya sooch ki het tan zhana lakhoynian*) are far more sinister. People claim that life in the village is dominated by jealousy (*hasat, zid*) and 'bad intention' (*bad niyat*) towards others. In August 2000 when it had not rained plentifully for three years and the village was suffering from acute water shortages, Rowshan people often commented to me:

Are you surprised, the intentions of the villagers are bad, everybody wants their neighbours to fail not to succeed, why should it rain? This, my friend, is our punishment. You people are good and have clean intentions, and so that is why it rains every day in your beautiful country.

At the same time, however, this jealousy is often said to be a result of new money being brought to the village by Rowshan people employed in powerful NGOs, such as the Aga Khan Rural Support Programme. Poorer families complain that rather than being helped by the rich they are 'stood on' (*sora chunik*) by them. If some men from the lordly families are depicted as living in a bygone era, then many of the employees of foreign-funded NGOs are said to be selfish (*matlabi*), and to be interested only in filling their own stomachs (*ishkamaho tip korik*). They are accused of having forgotten their commitments to their fellow villagers, and of having become self-seeking 'saints of money' (*paiso qalamdar*), interested only in accumulating money (*paisa*) and wealth (*daulat*). At the same time, families that have prospered in recent years complain that jealousy (*hasat korik*) enjoins people to 'speak against' them (*khilafa lu dik*), and try to damage their 'position' in the village.

One elderly man who is the father of nine children, has only a little land, and no stable source of monetary income, told me that above all village life is characterised by jealousy and mistrust:

Magnus, a man doesn't like you because you are wearing a beautiful pair of glasses, a man doesn't like me because I wear a new set of clothes. We don't like one

---

[17] On Persian linguistic conventions concerning etiquette (*ta'aruf*) in Iran, see Beeman 1986.

another (*eegho no khosheisian*): our village is full of jealousy (*hasat*) and mistrust (*beihtibar bik*). All this jealousy has cut my heart from Rowshan.

For this man jealousy has come to dominate the villagers' thoughts about even the most minute things, and he makes direct connections between the immoral state of the villagers emotions with the probity of personal economic transactions. Moreover, if a Rowshan person's relationship to the village should ideally be structured through the heart and compassionate affection, then when emotions become immoral, this relationship is severed.

The climate of mistrust that is said to be so powerful in Rowshan today generates a perpetual anxiety about what people 'say about others' (*eeghoten kia reik*): *stausik* (back-stabbing) and *kos sora hosik* (laughing at others), are often said to be the favourite past-time of Rowshan people. Rowshan people exert considerable energies trying to discover what their fellow villagers are saying about them behind their backs. Moreover, people living in the village also claim that their enemies (*dushmanan*) and those who speak against them use black magic (*seher, jadoo*) in order to make their lives even more difficult and painful. Rowshan people are said, even by those with 'secular' and Islamic education, to employ sorcery in order to break up families and make others ill (*lahaz*) and depressed (*tang*). Family arguments and sometimes even domestic violence are blamed on jealous neighbours turning to sorcery in order to weaken the position and reputation of their fellow neighbours.[18]

There is, however, a powerful dualism in the way in which Rowshan's Muslims talk about and experience life in the village. Rowshan people also pride themselves on being polite (*sharif*), civilised (*tahzibi yafta*), peaceful (*aman pasand*) and welcoming to guests (*mehman nawaz*). They also claim that despite the fact that their community is composed of both Sunnis and Ismai'lis, there is little ill feeling between them. The very same man who had told me about the jealousy and mistrust that pervades life in the village had also praised the village and its people to me on many occasions.

The people of Rowshan are polite (*sharif*) and honest: in this village there is no theft, there is no adultery (*zina*) and there is no violence (*eegho dik niki*). The people who live in Rowshan are affectionate (*pura khuloos*) and the lovers of peace (*aman pasand*).

---

[18] By many Chitral people sorcery is seen to be the product of jealousies resulting from access to new money. Compare Comaroff and Comoroff 1993.

Living a virtuous life requires the person to live in a virtuous village, even if this means exercising the imagination to its limits and having thoughts and saying things that appear to be deeply incompatible.[19] In other villages, I was told, it is impossible to walk freely over a man's land (*zamin*), or across a family's orchard (*shan*): there is a danger of being insulted by 'angry' (*qahri*) and impolite (*weshirau*) men in these villages who are likely to accuse you of 'looking at girls' (*kumoro lolik*). Within Rowshan, however, people say that if you pass a man's house he will invite you to sit and take tea, and, if the season is right, will share his fruit with you. If one discourse emphasises the jealousy and mistrust that pervades the state of village life, another presents Rowshan as a place of peace (*sukoon*) and affection.

Rowshan people must thus make judgements about how to live their lives in the gaze of other villagers, and in a general atmosphere of emotional failure that is both painful yet also conceptualised as unevenly affecting the villagers. One of the most sensitive areas of ethical decision-making in the village is the handling of money and the making of economic transactions. Great efforts are made by Rowshan's Muslims to disguise the degree of poverty in which they live. Even the poorest households build special tin-roofed guesthouses in which male guests sit, sleep and are entertained when visiting. Many families also use fertile land and scarce water resources to cultivate beautiful gardens (*bagh*) with dense flowerbeds and grassy lawns, where they sit on expensive metal garden chairs and entertain their honourable (*ghairati*) and respected (*izzatman*) guests. Even these gardens are the cause of village dispute: instead of carefully rationing scare water resources for the good of the village, some families are accused of secretly leaving their taps on overnight to water their beloved flowerbeds, thus depriving others in the village of drinking water.[20] Here, then, an aesthetic of surface form is stripped of its moral legitimacy by the underhand tactics of those who work to create it.

The guesthouses themselves are decorated with woollen *qalin* (rugs) woven by the women of the house and the walls are covered with home-sewn embroideries and wall hangings. The *mehman* (guest) will be offered

---

[19] Compare Yamba 1995 on the 'virtues of rural life' as conceptualised by West African pilgrims living in the Sudan (Yamba 1995: 71).

[20] A love for cultivating gardens (*bagh*) and orchards (*shan*) is something for which Chitral people have long been famed. The British scholar-soldier Kennion, after having visited Chitral in the first decade of the twentieth century, notes that Chitral people 'have a great love for flowers: young and old bind blossoms in their rolled caps' (Kennion 1910: 8), and that, 'Chitrali gardens are famed all over the Western Himalaya. It is in reality more of an orchard than a garden, but one with exquisitely kept turf.' (3).

tea in a special china tea set reserved for special occasions, and food will be served on plates kept aside for respected visitors to the house. As one young man who owned a small shop in the village commented to me:

We Rowshan people are really stupid (*bewarkoof*). If a guest comes to a man's house the host runs out and buys – on loan – expensive things like chickens and meat from the bazaar rather than just giving the guest what he has in his home already. He is trying to imitate people who have money, but he thinks he has to live up to their standards.

There is much pressure on households to maintain a fraudulent (*dookahbaz*) image of respect and dignity at all costs, even at the cost of falling into serious debt. The handling of money and the probity of personal economic transactions are areas of village life where the making of ethical and moral judgements are painful for Rowshan people. They throw into all too stark relief the division between what is on the outside and what goes on in the inside.

The 'civilised' and 'polite' values of Rowshan's lordly elite families remain a powerful source of faith and values for many in the village, and living up to these difficult norms of hospitality and courtly life of the one-time elite is a cause of much anxiety for Rowshan people. This is despite the fact that many Rowshan people accuse the lordly families of living in a by-gone era and of failing to adapt to the 'modern era' (*jadid zamana*) in which they are now living. At the same time, the wealthier families in the village say that poorer families show their lack of ability to make sensible decisions about how to spend their money. By trying to live up to the difficult norms set by the village's wealthy and high-status few they show that their 'intellects are closed' (*hetan 'aql basta*). Living a moral life is something that requires the deployment of the critical faculties, and unobtainable desires have the potential of 'tying the intellect' and making reasoned and moral thought impossible.

Moreover, this area of ethical decision-making also has the potential to produce public humiliation, showing that the division between the hidden and the open is all too fragile in the minds of many Rowshan people. On one occasion, a shopkeeper in the village was so irritated at waiting for his fellow villagers to repay their loans that he posted a large sign on his shop naming the villagers who were in debt to him, and listing the amounts they owed him. One man was showed as owing no less than 100,000 Pakistan rupees, despite the fact that he was educated and worked as an advocate (*wakil*) in the village. For many in the village, the shopkeeper had gone a step too far. He had released secret information (*khoasht ma'lumat*) about the current financial difficulties of his neighbours that resulted in their public humiliation. I was even told that one debtor was so racked by shame he left the village altogether for a number of weeks and went to stay with his in-laws (*ishpashur bolo*) until the dreaded sign was taken down. Other villagers argued, however, that the poor shopkeeper was right to release this sensitive information. He was teaching the mindless (*khaka kyagh noshiru*) villagers a lesson – they should be more careful in the way they spent their money and should not burden others as a result of their own love for 'wasteful spending' (*fuzul kharch*) and 'showing off'. Deciding when things should 'come to the surface' and when they should be concealed, is an ongoing feature of Rowshan people's moral lives, and the poison of a damaged reputation is something that results in the experience of heightened levels of anxiety.

All households in the village keep livestock, which provide meat and milk and are used for agricultural work such as ploughing. Yet even this seemingly mundane dimension of village life is the focus of complex moral judgements by Rowshan people. At one level, the good qualities of Rowshan life are spoken of in terms of the keeping of animals and the growing of produce on the village's rich soil (*paidawar korak zamin*) and not having to depend on alien, bought and non-Chitrali commodities.[21] Many people in the village claim that the height of luxury (*ayashi*) is to eat a plate of 'home-grown rice' (*duro pakhti*) along with especially nutritious (*takatwar*) village eggs.[22] One summer, for instance, Pukhtun traders from Peshawar brought a freight load of 'fat chickens' (*thool kahak*) from 'down Pakistan' to the village. These chickens were said to be *mashini* (the product of machines) by many of the villagers, and it was rumoured that one Rowshan man who had eaten too many of them had died from a heart attack at a young age. The fat (*ghep*) of these *over-weight* (in English) birds was said to 'sit on the heart' and result in death for the foolhardy and greedy folk who loved to waste their money on them. Compared to village chickens (*batani kahak*) factory chickens were described as being *wekhal* (tasteless) and without enjoyment (*bemazah*). Many men in the village complained that in some years past the village had been full of chickens but that nowadays women were unable to rear and care for chickens in a good

---

[21] For comparative anthropological discussion on food, substance and morality in South Asia, see, Appadurai 1981; Tapper and Tapper 1986; C. Bayly 1998 especially ch. 1.

[22] Rice is seen as so intrinsic to personhood and the living of a good Rowshan life that even elderly men in the village on finding that they have to put up with a rice-free evening meal (*bot*) have been reduced to tears and 'turned into children'. On rice in the 'culinary cultures of the Middle East', see Zubaida 2001.

and proper manner. Chicks (*kuluchi*) died days after they hatched thanks to the carelessness (*bekhial*) of the village women.

At the same time, however, women's responsibilities for tending animals is not simply a matter of loving nurture for the benefit of the household, but is also seen as a matter of selfish indulgence that involves love for animals instead of the giving of warmth and love to children. For instance, elderly mothers are often accused of caring more about their cows than their children: women are said to go to the animal quarters (*shal*) in order to escape from the *havaza* (noise) and *pereshani* (disturbance) of their children. At several school parents' day meetings I attended, mothers were told that whilst they kept the animal quarters spotless they failed to notice the dirt behind their children's ears.

One man aged about thirty-three years old told me that as a boy his mother had left him crying in the house while she had gone off to tend for her cows.

When I was a child, my mother would leave me wrapped up in the orchard so I couldn't move whilst she went to look after her cows. With a mother like that isn't it amazing that I even managed to get educated?

These women are said to squander their affection on undemanding animals, instead of putting up self-sacrificingly with the more emotionally demanding claims of their clamouring children.

The concern with the emotional dimensions of motherhood in village life was made particularly visible to me after my own parents visited me in the village. When I returned to Rowshan after seeing my parents onto their home-bound flight from Peshawar, a young woman told me how lucky I was to have an 'educated' (*talimi yafta*) and 'affectionate' (*pura khloose*) mother who knew what was in my heart and what troubled me.

Oh brother, if only our mothers were like yours. Our mothers are illiterate, they have not seen anything (*kia no poshie asuni*). They know nothing of what is in our hearts, they think only about going into the animal quarters and feeding their cows. They can never help us.

Good mothers are thus expected by the village's younger generation to have particular insight and engagement in their dealings with their children, and motherly relations with children are a recognised feature of living a Muslim life in the village.[23] Mothers are said to know the hidden thoughts and

---

[23] It is often assumed that in many Muslim societies it is the fatherly figure who is associated with running the house. For a rather essentialising discussion of the patriarchy a in Turkey, see Delaney 1990.

emotions of their children in a way that is never possible for fathers. Whilst Rowshan people are concerned with the place that authentic affection plays in the living of a Muslim life, education and literacy – rather than weakening natural motherly emotions – are often said to heighten the special nature of a woman's attachment with her children.[24] Cultivating the intellect is conceptualised by some Rowshan people, then, as also having the potential of refining the emotions, and this is one area of village life where there are considerable differences of views between older and younger people.

It is not only the daily activities of women that are subject to detailed processes of moral valuation by villagers. How men go about contributing to the wellbeing and enrichment of the village land is also a source of much comment and concern. In years of drought (*khushk*) irrigation water is allocated by the 'village elders' (*deho lothoroan*) on a rota basis (*sororgh*), but people reach different conclusions about the decisions made, and there is considerable competition for scarce water resources. Ideally the elders of the village should agree about the time and duration of each house's access to water for irrigation. There are, however, a number of ploys and secret devices that men use to get more than their fair share. Some men are accused of using unfair tactics in order to procure water for their dried out crops: lanterns are left as decoys by the water channel at night in order to deceive (*fan dik*) people into thinking that men are guarding the water. One man in the village who was known to do this even used to ride his motorbike silently around the water channels in order to allow him to cut water supplies to his neighbours' houses.

The conflict between the ideally civil and compassionate shape of village interactions and the secret underside of tricks and ploys is not one that is always maintained. Indeed, if revealing the hidden can make morally illegitimate the aesthetics of surface form, then releasing the secrets of the underside of village life is something that can itself have a creative and aesthetic dimension. Sometimes tensions run high and the cunning ploys of villagers come to the surface when men hurl accusations of unfair play at one another, and young boys rejoice in watching the supposedly polite elders of the village losing their tempers, swearing and threatening one another with spades. The most 'devilish' (*sheytanghonie*) of boys in the village even enjoy telling lies to these men with the hope of making them angry (*qahar angik*) and seeing them losing their temper. Moreover, many

---

[24] Najmabadi explores the interaction between education and nurturing in modernist discourses about motherhood in Iran at the turn of the twentieth century (Najmabadi 1998). Compare Shakry 1998.

men and boys in the village have a reputation for being skilled in 'starting' (*shurugheik*) village fights, and riling their 'hot-headed neighbours' (*khaka phech grambeshan*). Men are told that their neighbours have recently stolen the water and taken it to their own fields. The occasional physical fights that take place are described minutes later with a great amount of glee to the women and girls sitting in the safe confines of the house.

The village, then, is not a moral unit in the simple sense that people living there share a set of fixed categories prescribed by the village's religious authorities or the Pakistan state about what constitutes proper, correct and 'Islamic' behaviour. Nor is Rowshan the self-contained village republic of traditional anthropological accounts of South Asia (Dumont 1980; Pocock 1973). Rather, villagers themselves actively participate in moralising discussions that go on apace in the village, and these discussions are often about the current state of the emotions and affections of Rowshan people. The ways in which people make these valuations reveal the divisions in the village today that many Rowshan people find morally troublesome. It is divisions between people who are seen as being rich and poor, young and old, and high status and low status that are widely seen as disrupting the state of the villagers' emotions. The complex way in which the villages' hamlets are each said to have particular moral and cultural essences, also reflect on the ways in which Rowshan people conceptualise the village as being connected to the wider world. Rowshan people bring multidimensional value judgements to the complex array of influences acting upon their lives. If morality is not an 'unequivocal code' but, rather, about the 'practical judgements people make about how to live their lives wisely and well' (Lambek 2000a: 315), then Rowshan is a contested moral space where villagers take ethical decisions and make moral judgements that are often conflicting and a source of anxiety.

The village is said to suffer because of the upside-down emotions of Rowshan people. Even more problematic for the villagers are the ways in which immoral emotions are seen to be eroding the nature of the villagers' relations with one another, and it is to this issue that I now turn.

'DIRTY ENVIRONMENTS', 'IMMORAL BOYS' AND FLIRTATIOUS GIRLS

How do Rowshan people bring their processes of active moral verification to their understanding of the relations between villagers, and where do they locate the origins of what they see as being the village's current state of moral decline?

Rowshan people are deeply concerned about their village's rapidly expanding population, debt-ridden local economy, and high unemployment rate. And there is a general level of consensus in the village that these are features of life in the village that are the breeding ground for immoral (*badikhlaq*) behaviour and dirty thoughts (*gandah sooch*). An important dimension of the moralising discourse in the village is about the network of relations, within and beyond the household, open and secret, that make up the village. The range of relations that form the focus of this moralising discourse is wide and complex. The proper and improper, and real and ideal, nature of relations between mothers and children, fathers and children, children and children, brothers and brothers, boys and girls are all the subject of extensive discussions between Rowshan people. These relations are themselves further superimposed with concerns regarding the shape of relations and interactions between Sunnis and Ismai'lis, rich and poor, educated and uneducated, city and village, and young and old. In particular this moralising discourse focuses on imputations of bad behaviour and morals to the village youth, and the role that defective parenting in the village has played in this.

The social tensions and conflicts that lie at the heart of village life are the topic of continual discussion by Rowshan people. This discussion shows that Rowshan people are engaged in an active process of moral valuation, and they must work hard to 'create, reproduce and maintain' a 'logical consistency' in their lives (Laidlaw 1995: 21). This critical discussion is particularly important in the lives of young people living in the village; and there is a recognised generation gap between the village 'youth' (*nau juan*) and 'elders' (*lothoroan, lilotan*). Many of the young people in the village talk about the pressures and strains of living a life that can both make them happy (*khoshan*), as well as living up to the standards set by their elders. The category of 'youth' is a broad one in the minds of many Rowshan people, and I was often told that a man remains young until he is thirty-five years old. Yet, on the most part, the term youth refers to young men aged between eighteen and about twenty-eight. This age group is referred to in Khowar as the *nau juan* (the youth). Young men are also referred to as being *deho daqan* (the village boys) – a somewhat pejorative term that is applied mostly to unmarried young men living in the village, and suggests dependency on the extended family as well as unemployment (*berozegarie*). The age of marriage in the village can vary considerably, but usually for men it is in the late twenties and for women in the late teens or early twenties. Some women are 'given to men' (*moshanta dik*) at a much younger age, but nowadays many families are reluctant for their daughters to marry until they have completed their secondary school education.

Young and unmarried women in the village are *deho komoran* (the village girls) and girls of marriageable age are the *chumutkheiran* (the mature ones). They also play a vocal part in the moralising discourse about village life. The moralising discussions in which women partake are similar to those of men in the village, yet they are also a reflection of different anxieties and concerns.

Most of the village's youth are educated and literate in Urdu, and some also literate in English. The majority of them have attended school until the age of sixteen, many of them have completed degrees in the village's college, and some of them have studied for Masters degrees in Peshawar University. Many of the younger women in the village have also received an education up to the age of sixteen, and growing numbers of women leave the village in order to train as nurses and health workers in Pakistan's major cities.[25] Despite the high levels of education and the great commitment to learning in the village, one of the defining features of Rowshan's youth is unemployment.

Unemployment and having spare time (*ghosh*) are seen by many in the village to have contributed to the moral weakening of village life. The village boys (*deho daqan*), I was often told by young men themselves, 'show a lack of interest in receiving education', and many were unemployed and said to be a *boorch* (burden) on their families. What is striking is that perceived deficiencies in village morality were only rarely accounted for in terms of 'irreligion' or failure to conform to 'Islamic' values. Rather, it was poverty (*ghurbat*), unemployment (*berozgarie*) and too much spare time that were widely identified as the crucial factors behind the morally degraded shape of village life.

According to both younger and older people in the village, the village boys had become *badmashan* (scoundrels) and their *kamzoor* (weak) and *amphal* (uneducated) parents were seen as being unable to control and unable to understand the minds (*zehna*) of their now mature children. In particular, the sexual needs of the village's youth were the cause of great discussion, and the younger and more self-defined 'open-minded' members of the village often said that 'sexual frustration' lay behind many of the problems with village life.

On one occasion I was travelling in a jeep with an educated Ismai'li friend, Zulfikar, from Rowshan, and a Sunni man in his forties who was a

[25] See ch. 3 below for an in-depth discussion of education in Rowshan.

medical doctor from Markaz. Zulfikar had studied for a Masters degree in Urdu literature in Peshawar University. He told our Sunni friend and myself that parents were cruel (*zulm korak*) to their children in the village.

A man has a daughter, she is grown up and mature. Her father is sleeping with his wife every night and he is happy and content. Yet he is unable to see that his daughter also has desires [*arman*] and needs companionship. Even if she talks to a boy she gets shouted at. Is it not surprising that all in this village are upset and troubled?

The doctor sitting in the vehicle nodded his head in agreement, and commented, 'What good does a quick kiss in the bushes do anyone, and even that in the fear of being spotted by someone?' Zulfikar saw himself as 'open minded', and his thought free from normative Islamic moral constraints. Indeed, he told me that he had studied Urdu literature when he was younger because he had 'for long been fed up with religion' (*mazhabar zhot bezar hotam*). For his degree studies in Urdu literature, he had read Urdu novels and poems, and he often sought to bring the cultured and sophisticated ideas in the books he had read into his understanding of village life. Zulfikar told me that he had especially enjoyed the writing of the great Persian and Urdu poet Mirza Assadullah Khan Ghalib (1797–1869). Ghalib is renowned by scholars of South Asia and ordinary Muslims in Pakistan alike, for his 'irreverence towards established religious norms', and 'his rejection of social closure based on religion' (Jalal 2000: 2–3).[26] My Rowshan friends often told me that Ghalib was 'the biggest alcoholic (*sharabi*) of them all', and portraits of him were often posted on the walls of the villagers' houses.

Zulfikar was discussing a deeply contentious dimension of village life and he was breaking the taboo of talking about women's sexuality in a way that went beyond issues of honour and reputation and, instead, broached the issue of emotional, bodily and psychological needs. Moreover, he was not simply doing so for his liberal English friend, but, more importantly, he was showing his educated Sunni friend that the way he thought and made moral judgements was different from that of other Rowshan people. In doing so, he was bringing his understanding of Islamic mystical poetry into the way he made moral valuations about villagers and the state of village life. Some Rowshan people have a diverse array of knowledge about Islam; this is something that reflects their own personal experience and

---

[26] 'Ghalib went to the extent of saying that even a Brahmin true to his faith could die in the idol house and qualify for burial in the *kaaba*' (Jalal 2000: 2–3).

views, and they bring different perspectives to the village in a way that makes processes of making moral verification an active and multidimensional process.

Young men in the village also spoke scornfully of men who created houses full of children and then had little idea of what to do with them. As one Ismai'li man in his mid-twenties and with a Bachelors degree in commerce commented to me:

These illiterate men just sleep with their wives on cold winter nights, produce children, and then say that God will take care of them. They don't think that about their lack of land, lack of money and that there is no hope of anybody taking a job.

Living a virtuous life requires foresight and a cultivated mind. Belief (*yaqein*) without reasoned contemplation (*fikr korik*) on the part of the village's elders is seen by many Rowshan youth as something that has contributed to the difficulties of the present era, and having a cultivated mind entails thinking about the consequences of one's actions. The result of the lack of foresight of Rowshan's elders is clear and plain for everybody to see. The little ones (*tsetsek*) running up and down the alleyways of the village were said to be *no chichiru* (untaught), and they had been left to live a life according to their own choice (*tan chita lakieasuni*). These young children lived lives devoid of fatherly guidance (*rah namaiee*) and discipline (*disiplin*), as fathers had failed to acknowledge the moral responsibilities that having children requires. Thus, if adults do not live thoughtfully, then children retain animal-like and morally deficient qualities.

It is not only Rowshan youth who are a source of anxiety for the villagers, small children raise particular anxieties in relation to the judgements people make about defects in village morality, and a critical factor that explains why this is so is the economic uncertainty of present day village life. Ideally, small children should be *ma'asum* (sinless, infallible), yet the mature *badmashan* of the village were also accused of being responsible for leading them astray. Boys as young as twelve, I was told, had picked up the habits of truancy from school, cigarette smoking (*cigaretti bik*), and shirking from work at home. The degraded nature of the society in which they were living was said to be shaping the minds and ideas of the young children living there. Efforts needed to be made in order to save (*bach korik*) the little ones from the bad setting in which they were being raised.

The only way that was seen to be possible was the educating of these youngsters in a civilised way, ideally the little ones had to be removed from the dirty atmosphere of the village and given the hope of having a future in the world outside. So, wealthier villagers send their children for education in 'down Pakistan', and the decision of one bank manager from Rowshan to send his five-year-old son to an English-medium school in a small town near Peshawar resulted in considerable comment in the village.[27] Could these children survive without motherly love and affection? Was there not a danger that this woman would die of 'heart explosion' (*hardi phat*) as she yearned for her beautiful and rose-like (*gulaboghon*) son? Indeed when this boy's mother did fall ill and was taken to hospital, many in the villager blamed her illness on the fact that she was missing her children. Educated young men in the village told her that she must learn to tolerate (*bardasht korik*) the pain of separation if she wanted her children to have a clean and respectable future. If the outside is seen as a source of immorality, it is also conceptualised as playing an important role in the development of proper and mature human beings. The process of making clean and mature humans entails cleansing young minds of dirty and jealous village thoughts by sending them to respectable, clean and often English-medium educational institutions away from the village.[28]

Rowshan children not only raise anxieties in the minds of village elders about thought and morality, but they are themselves active participants in discussions about the current state of village life.[29] Children have a privileged access to the secrets of the village, and they are able to use this in order to turn 'upside-down' the shape of village relations. They have the ability to shame people as a result of the information they acquire during their daily lives and social interactions. These children sit 'like simpletons' (*nachar biti*) in houses as they listen to the secret conversation of their elders: when they return to their own houses their families try and coax them into telling them the 'talk' (*lu*) in other houses by offering them small rewards of money and sweets.[30] They provide their mothers, sisters and aunts who are largely confined 'inside' the

---

[27] Whilst both Urdu and English are 'official' languages in Pakistan, English is often held by Pakistanis as the language of social and economic uplift. This sentiment is particularly strong in Rowshan, and villages would often tell me that being educated in Urdu is the same as having no education at all. On the language controversy in Pakistan, see Rahman 1996. On English as a language of social and economic uplift for Mumbai Muslims, see Hansen 2000a.

[28] The intellectual and emotional dimensions of a further form of education that takes place beyond the confines of the village – religious learning and training – is discussed below in ch. 5.

[29] See Toren 1993: 462.

[30] Carsten explores the importance of the mobility of children between houses in a Malaysian village, and identifies the 'in-between' place of children in that rural setting (Carsten 1991). For Carsten children are 'agents of transformation' regarding kinship and relations in Malaysia. My focus is on children as moral and ethical agents in village life in Rowshan. On childhood and kinship in China, see Stafford 1995 and compare Viegas 2002.

house with greatly valued knowledge concerning life on the 'outside'. Indeed their female relatives often carefully differentiate between children who are simple (*sada*) and able to keep a secret, and those who are devilish and have tongues that will not keep still. I was even told that a child of five years old with whom I spent much time was dangerous, and that under no circumstances should I talk to him or let him hear about any sensitive conversation I was having with my friends. Rowshan's children are the carriers of potent information about the village and they have the capacity to destabilise between the secret and the open dimension village life. If making moral judgements requires reasoned contemplation, then Rowshan people see children as particularly dangerous because they are unable to mindfully distinguish between which dimensions of life should remain concealed and which revealed.

So, unemployed, unwilling to study and skiving off work at home, the village boys and young men had 'got into bad habits' (*shum adat korie asuni*). Their lives had become *bemaqesad* (meaningless), and they were said to have few interests and pastimes other than *istausik* (back-stabbing), sitting and gossiping (*masqeulgi*) in shops, looking at girls (*kumoro lolik*), drinking illegal 'foul-smelling' (*kherdar*) home-brewed spirits (*tara*) and smoking hashish (*bong*). In particular, the village boys' penchant for smoking hashish, I was often told, meant that they had dirty and sexual thoughts about the village girls. Moreover, smoking hashish, I was told, had made them blind of their 'bad position', and the fact that villagers were looking at them with 'wrong perspectives' (*ghalat nazria*). These were all things that their blood-shot eyes and clothes burned by falling ashes from their 'full' (*tip*) cigarettes clearly illustrated. The physical segregation between men and women in the village not only had the potential of being disturbed by illicit and hidden meetings between boys and girls, but purdah of the mind could also be dissolved by hashish-induced erotic thoughts. The boys of the village had become aggressive and violent (*janjali*) and were guilty of picking fights when drunk and of arguing at night when they were bringing water to irrigate their crops. That their parents were 'always ready to beat them with a hot stick' (*hamisha pech band dikoten tayar*) did not help matters, but only made them worse.

It was not only the village boys who were accused of having become immoral and out of control. I was also frequently told that the village's girls (*deho kumoran*) were devoid of affection and love for their families, parents and even husbands; and it was both older and younger Rowshan people who held these views. For the elder women of the village, the village girls had become *soost* (lazy, weak) and were *bosmukhie* (impertinent). The elderly mother of four *chumutker* (mature) daughters in the family I lived with told me of the problems her daughters gave her.

My two elder daughters are good – I can't say anything wrong about them. They work hard, they help in the home, and they have love and affection for me and even their father. But my other daughters, oh my sweet son (*ma shirin zhou*), they are worthless (*khiobash no*) they just sit in the fields chatting, reading books and reading digests [magazines]. You yourself have seen them. They sleep until late in the morning and then they sleep all afternoon. They don't care about me (*ma khialo no lakoynie*), about what happens to their father or their elder brother. They have become *tan chita baig* [live life according to their own choice]. You ask me when they will get married, my nightingale son (*ma bulbul zhou*), who will marry these creatures (*makhluqeu*)?

When she spoke to me, her sons and her nephews, as well as other village men who visited her house, this elderly woman would often use this poetic vocabulary in order to emphasise the amount of love and affection she felt for her fellow village people. The use of such 'sweet' (*shirin*) poetic language is characteristic of the way many elderly women in Rowshan speak. Thus, 'village sons' are addressed as nightingales (*bulbul*), pearls (*durdana*), pieces of their mother's souls (*zhano nas*), and their mother's hearts (*hardi*). Yet the younger women of the village were accused of being 'devoid of affection' (*berakhum*), and an important domain of life where this manifested itself was their inability to speak using 'polite and fully affectionate words' (*narum pur khuloos alfaz*).

Even younger women in the village talked about the lack of affection and warmth they sensed in the hearts and minds of the girls of the village. One young, unmarried, educated and employed woman in her late twenties, Shabnam, told me that she was astonished (*hairan hotam*) by the behaviour of the girls of the village. Not only did they have no loyalty for their parents – they were also increasingly showing themselves to be devoid of affection and commitment when it came to the amorous connections in which they were becoming more involved.

My sweet brother Magnus (*ma shirin brar magnus*), you do know that all the girls in this village have secret friends [boyfriends]. They used to hide these secrets from their parents. Now they feel no shame, they tell everyone and they don't even feel scared if their fathers find out. There's nothing wrong with having one friend, loving one person. But these girls have one friend here, one friend there. They have no real love or affection for anybody, they just like to play around with people's hearts and affections.

Shabnam was the eldest sister in the house in which I lived, and she made this remark to me whilst sitting alone at the foot of my rope bed while we were sitting out in her family's cool orchard. As will be seen in chapter 7, Shabnam is in many ways an exceptional Rowshan woman; however, many other women – educated and uneducated – made comments like these to me during my stay in Rowshan. The conversation that I had with Shabnam on this occasion was characterised by secrecy – she spoke in hushed tones and giggled quietly. Yet she thought critically even about this sensitive domain of village life, and was prepared to vocalise such thoughts in discussion with me, her 'adopted brother' (*brar ganiru*). For Shabnam, then, the girls of the village were guilty of leading on (*chaleik*) the boys of the village, making them worried and confused (*pereshan*) and diverting their attentions from their studies. She told me that they wore bright (*rosht*) clothes and laughed out aloud in a way that 'stirred up' (*kiteik*) and 'cooked the hearts' of the easily flattered 'sons of the village'. At one level, then, there is something wrong with any form of flirtatious tie between a boy and girl, and girls are imputed agency in forming illicit unions with boys.[31] At the same time, however, she is also suggesting that if such relations involve true love and affection then they are, at a deeper level, permissible and acceptable. This young woman's comments suggest again the complex nature that the division between the secret (*khoasht*) and the open (*khulao*) plays in the moral judgements made by Rowshan's Muslims.[32] On the one hand secrecy is disparaged as it leads to falsity and concealment. It is secrecy that allows girls to be able to have more than one boyfriend, and it allows them to deceive and cheat their supposed loved ones. Secrecy, then, breeds hypocrisy (*munafiqat*). Yet at the same time she disparages the failure of these girls to conceal their relations with boys as being brazen and even as being more immoral than concealing them. And there is also the sense that there is something spiritual and special about entering the domain of the hidden by falling in love.[33]

For others in the village, however, the immoral thoughts of the villagers were dissolving the moral heart of the village. The village should be conceptualised I was told by one Ismai'li man in his thirties, as one house (*ee dur*), and all those living in the village should consider themselves as being the people of one house (*iduro roi*). In the current state of village

---

[31] The teachings of revivalist Sunni Deobandi scholars who see the woman's place as being in the home are clearly evident in this Ismai'li woman's thinking. See Metcalf 1990.

[32] Compare Jalal 2000: 71 for a discussion of contradictory Muslim thinking in British India that depicts women as both 'jewels' and 'prostitutes'. Compare Osella and Osella 1998 for a discussion of pre-marriage flirting in rural Kerala, South India. See Jeffery, Jeffery and Jeffrey 2004 on living a pious Muslim life in present day Uttar Pradesh, India.

[33] Compare Ask 1993 for a discussion of women and love in North-East Pakistan.

immorality, however, boys and girls rather than considering themselves to be brothers (*brargini*) and sisters (*ispsargini*) were, instead, bent upon 'making friendship' with one another. As one of my friends, who had studied for a Masters in political science, put it to me, in English, 'the very fabric of our village is being ripped apart the incestuous-like tendencies of its inhabitants'. Not only were these relations wrong in that they crossed the sexes but they were seen as being even more pathological because they also had the potential of partially dissolving the boundary between Sunnis and Ismai'lis living in the village.[34] Girls were seen as being particularly susceptible to the amorous advances of boys from the different Islamic doctrinal tradition: 'women', I was often told by both men and women, 'have no religion' (*aurato mazhab niki*). Given a proposal of love, girls were often said to be prepared even to abandon (*petsik*) their religion for a boy from another sect.

The debate on parenting and affection peaked when the sense of moral degradation and decline in the village took a criminal form. There were a number of criminal incidents in the village over the course of the winter months: shops were broken in to, money stolen from houses and satellite dishes whisked away from rooftops under the cover of darkness. There were also accusations made about sexual contact outside of marriage – a criminal offence in Pakistan since General Zia's introduction of the Hudood Ordinance in the 1980s. It was rumoured that the village's young thieves had been stealing packets of shampoo and brightly decorated veils in order to lure the daughters of the village into having sexual relations with them. These incidents of theft were a new feature of village life: no one could remember a time when thieves (*chogh*) had actually entered the village before. What few incidents of theft there had been had taken place in shops in the bazaar and had largely been blamed on the Pukhtun-speaking traders and hawkers from 'down Pakistan' who had set up business there. These men had also been accused of supplying hashish and even heroin to the young men of the village, and of dirtying the village water supply with the scrap metal, animal skins and old tyres they collected for recycling purposes. It was the presence of these strangers (*nagonie*) at the periphery of the moral unit of the village that had first alerted villagers to the unpleasant and dirty dimensions of village life.

This winter's incidents of theft suggested, however, a knowledge of the village and people's houses within the village; and the finger of blame was pointed towards the 'boys of the village' who had already cultivated a

---

[34] For a discussion of intracommunal love marriage in present day India, see Mody-Spencer 2002.

reputation for being scoundrels. The discourse of village criminality, having found its starting point on outsiders living at the peripheries of the village, now turned to the hidden heart of village life itself and villagers had to confront moral responsibility themselves.

These incidents of theft brought great shame on people in the village, especially as the police decided that they had to conduct night patrols along the very inner alleys and paths of the village. In the end it was one of the village's most notable scoundrels who released the information 'to the surface' that it was, indeed, some village boys who had been responsible for the criminal activities. This telltale (*lu kaseik*) scoundrel had already eloped and married one girl, divorced her, eloped with another and married her, been jailed for theft, and been accused of smuggling hashish and alcohol. Being himself a man without reputation (*beizzat*), he sent a report to the police saying that he had evidence that it was the son of his own father's brother (*micky*) who was behind the thefts. The supposed enforcers of law and Islamic morality were invited into the village by a person who, in many Rowshan people's minds, was its most immoral and outrageous (*apakar nisiru*) son. It took a man who no longer sought to maintain his personal respect and dignity by upholding the division between the open and the secret to bring village tensions to the surface and bring disrespect to the villagers. At the request of this man, the police filed a first investigation report (FIR) into the thefts and accusations of adultery in the village.

Four boys aged between fourteen and sixteen were arrested and taken to the Rowshan police station, where it was widely rumoured by villagers that they ate the 'hot stick' of the police. One of the arrested children was the son of a man in the village known as a *gaderie* (madman): he was known for sitting in his orchard and swearing at people who walked by. Rowshan people thought that this man was mentally defective rather than just bad tempered, especially because of the incestuous insults he would shout at his daughter. He not only had a lack of affection for his children, but also seemed to be unable to recognise them as being his own 'bones and blood' (*kolochen lei*). He was poor (*gharib*) with little land and no regular source of cash income. When his son was accused of theft few in the village were surprised: the son of such a poor and mentally infirm man could only be expected to 'turn out' to be a thief.

However, when the child of one of Rowshan's 'respected men' was arrested on the charge of breaking into shops the villagers were shocked and surprised. Not only had this man been a soldier in the Pakistan Army with a regular source of income and a decent pension, but he was also from a respectable family. When this man was told that his son had been arrested on the charges of theft he was reported, according to discussion in the village, to have told the police:

Keep him. I have no interest in my so-called son. If he comes back to my house I'll beat him. I've given him all he's ever needed – shelter, food, education. What else could I be expected to do. If he comes home he'll just eat from my hot stick.

Young men in the village argued that it was the very attitude of this 'hot-headed' (*khaka pech*) man that was the root cause of his son's alleged wrong doings. The father was said to have no ability to deal with the sensitive issues he was having to face. His background, as a *fauj* (army man) in the Pakistan Army, had given him only a sense of discipline and order: like other army men, when it came to matters of family and village life he was a 'donkey' (*gordogh*). He could walk with a straight back with his face pointed up, his chest out and his arms briskly moving by his side, but he was unable to care for and be responsible towards his children. The model of fathering this man presented his children was out of balance: he may have been a man of discipline but he had none of the special insight that accompanies a father's affection for his children. The place of heat and anger – so often characterised by the father brandishing his hot stick (*pech ban*) – ideally needs to be balanced with the warmth of sincere affection (*mukhlis khuloos*) and the ability to forgive (*mu'af korik*). As another man once advised me, 'Boyhood (*daqi*) is a time when all sorts of things happen; when I was a boy I did things that I now regret – these things should always be forgiven.' The father of this young man had, however, a heart that was 'empty' (*khali*) of 'love and affection'; and the alleged criminality of his young and otherwise *sharif* (polite) son were the product of a lack of fatherly emotional nourishment.

During my time in Rowshan the police were always a looming presence over village life: the police station (*thana*) is located on barren land (*chuchu zamin*) directly across the river from the village. Yet mostly the activities of the police had been confined to the open and public spaces of the bazaar, and the main metalled road that ran through the village. Villagers had been prepared to use their array of hidden ploys and tricks to erode the authority of the region's agents of law and order. On one occasion an Ismai'li man in his mid-twenties who was a soldier in the Chitral Scouts, took me to the riverbank that faced the police station, and he pulled out a glass bottle of home-brewed wine from the concealed pocket (*khoasht jip*) in his *kameez* (shirt). We sat on a small piece of grass only meters away from the village path, and drank the entire contents of the bottle in full view of the dreaded police station. I was rather nervous, and so attempted to drink my share (*zhira*) of this scarce commodity as quickly as possible, as I feared that someone would notice us and disapprove of my moment of un-Islamic behaviour. My friend noticed my ill-concealed nerves and told me what an 'easily scared' (*bukhtuak*) person I was; he told me not to worry, for the policemen could never get a hold of his penis (*ma puchi ka dosiko no boni*).

Now, however, the terms of the game had changed as the police began to penetrate the intimate and secret confines both of the physical layout of the village, and the economy of knowledge concerning the relations between the villagers. The police had come to the village on one dramatic occasion and gathered the villagers together and told them, 'You are hiding things, very bad things, about life in this village; from now on we are going to change the situation.' In this context the police had the potential to shatter village calm by forcing unwelcome and hidden truths about village life to the surface.

The state's invasion into the lives of the villages, far from being faceless and external, took a distinctly personal form. The then Senior House Officer (SHO) in the village police station was a Chitrali man from a nearby village who was known to take great pride in being a 'man of principles' (*usuli mosh*). This man's sister was married to a man in the village, and his family had many other relations with villagers. He was a short and rotund man with a beard and always to be seen fingering rosary beads. Late each afternoon he would walk along the main road through the village wearing his police uniform consisting of pale trousers and a large blue overcoat while brandishing his police stick (*vertuk*). He was usually also accompanied by two police orderlies (*sipahi*) walking either side of him. The uniforms and walking styles of these showy (*tsarak*) policemen was a cause of great mirth and amusement by many of the village girls. One twenty-one-year-old woman commented to me, 'Look at their shape (*hetan shikilo lo*), how ugly (*wedachu*) they look in their uniforms; but I bet they think how great they look.'

Two years previously the SHO had shocked people in the whole of Chitral by stopping the vehicle of Chitral district's Superintendent of Police, a sophisticated man from 'down Pakistan', and searching his vehicle. In the glove box of his superior's plush police jeep he discovered a bottle of illegal home-brew mulberry spirit. The SHO seized the bottle and poured its contents onto the road. The secrecy of the glove compartment had been penetrated and its illegal inside displayed for all to see. For some Rowshan Muslims this man was admirable: he lived his life by open principles (*usul*), and he was even prepared to bring his seniors to book by the rule of the law. But being a man of open and clear-cut principles also made him dangerous (*khatarnark*): having been brave enough to bring disrespect to an officer senior to him in the police force, he could now be counted on to great to lengths to get to the hidden truths about village life.

The Pakistan state, taking a highly personal form in the shape of a religious-minded and dogmatic policeman, was seen as having the capacity to disturb the balance between hidden and open knowledge in the village by opening up the secret goings-on of Rowshan life. Yet by shattering the division between the secret and the open, and holding people up to public humiliation, the state was not seen by all villagers as being a source of authoritative and Islamic moral categories to the immoral village. For, as one man told me, 'the police are the biggest scoundrels of them all' (*safan sar lot badmashan*). Moreover, the fact that they were invited into the village by Rowshan's biggest scoundrel of all did little to invest them with moral authority in the minds of Rowshan people. Yet the state was no faceless entity imposing itself on the village (society) from the outside. What made it all the more potent and intrusive was the fact that it had a personal and known face, and was entering intimate zones of village life from an all too intimate starting point. It was one of the village's own scoundrels who had grassed on the hapless boys of the village, and the policeman determined to reveal the secrets of village life was himself a 'son of the village'.[35]

Balanced and morally informed emotions are conceived as structuring an array of relations between villagers, and the current 'upside-down' and immoral state of village life means that emotions have been corrupted and relations are formed between the wrong people for the wrong reasons. How does the experience of migration add to the moral valuations Rowshan people make about the current state of village life?

'THE VILLAGE' AND THE 'OUTSIDE'

The experience of migration furnishes Rowshan people with another set of categories and comparisons for reflecting about the current state of life in the village, and the role that emotions play in the leading of a Muslim life. Drawing on recent ethnographies of migration, I now ask how migration may be 'integrated and fed into local frameworks' (Osella and

---

[35] I am here drawing on Herzfeld's discussion of 'intimacy', see Herzfeld 1997. For an account of Islamisation and the state in Turkey, see Navaro Yashin 2002. On these themes in Pakistan, see Verkaaik 2001.

Osella 2000: 117), in particular those concerning morality, thought, emotion and personhood.[36]

Rowshan's Muslims do not live lives that are confined to their homes and the moral unit of the village. The village, rather, becomes part of a larger moral universe where relations and action are also the subject of complex systems of valuation and judgement. As I discussed in chapter 2, people in Chitral talk about the world as being divided between the home (*dur*) and village (*deh*), and the outside (*berie, nishie*). Yet the world outside is generally not seen as a one-dimensional threat to the integrity of the Chitrali household or self, as it has been argued is the case in other South Asian societies (Kapferer 1988). The fluid nature of migration in Chitral reflects Rowshan Muslims' willingness to confront and embrace the diverse array of influences that the life of a South Asian migrant inevitably implies. My friends in Rowshan often told me that a person is 'made' (*sauz*) by living outside the confines of his home and village. In particular, separation (*judaiee*) from kin and friends and the experience of loneliness (*tanhaiee*) were said to make a person. Young men I spoke to living and working in Pakistan's major cities often told me that they were only able to grow up and become adult if they left the security of their homes. Undertaking labour (*mazdurie*) is at once seen as both character building yet also demeaning and painful. I was informed by one twenty-five-year-old man, who had recently left Rowshan to set up an internet café in Peshawar, that it was motherly affection in the home that made people in the village unable to make decisions (*faisala korik*) about their own lives.

In the village we spend our days sitting in the home by the hearth (*dango gucha nishik*), and we become dependent on our mothers. We never learn how to make decisions (*faisala*) that benefit our own lives and our own happiness. Instead, the affection we feel for our mothers ties us to the home and the decisions of our parents (*nan-taat*).

Leaving the village and experiencing the world outside, then, is considered by Rowshan people an important way in which the critical faculties are cultivated. If motherly affection is deemed as an important dimension of

---

[36] In doing so I share the Osella's scepticism towards recent anthropology of migration as embodying a 'wider contemporary condition in which binarisms and essentialisms are replaced by an appreciation of hybridity, dislocation and multiplicity' (Osella and Osella 2000: 117). See Gardener 1993, 1995 and 1999 for the impact of migration on the shape of Muslim identity and village life in the Syhlet province of Bangladesh, and compare Hansen 2001: 167–71 and 2000b on the anxieties created by labour migration to the Gulf in Mumbai.

parenthood, then it also conceptualised as having the potential of suffocating independent mental activity.

Rowshan people are at once anxious that the situation in their village has become so bad that people have to leave, yet they also invest much energy in advising young males to leave the village because they see things going wrong in the intimate and crowded setting of the village. Migration is seen by many Rowshan people as a corrective to the failings of village morality. Many a young boy in Rowshan was advised to tie his bags (*bageno botie*) and head down country (*aff*). After the events described above, a number of young men left the village for fear of becoming involved in the accusations of theft that were so prevalent at the time. One man in his mid-thirties, who was uneducated and worked as a postman in the village, told me how he had persuaded an uneducated young man to leave the village in the wake of the incidents of theft and arrests.

After all the incidents of theft I told Akhtar that he should leave the village and go down to the cities as soon as possible. He was always wandering around the village paths, smoking hashish and mixing with the village scoundrels. I had heard rumours that the police planned to arrest him. You known how poor his father is, and it would have been too much for him to cope with if his son had been put in jail. So one early morning he went down, and nobody has heard from him since.

Many young men saying that they are fleeing from life in Rowshan to Pakistan's cities later complain of suffering from the pain of *hardi phat* (heart explosion) as they yearn for the delights of village life at home. They say they long to return to the beautiful setting of Rowshan with its green mountain pastures, abundant fruit, cool water, musical programmes and affectionate people. They complain that life in the city is *bemakhsad* (meaningless), and that the people living there are interested only in themselves and in making money. Village life is transformed from being troublesome, worrying and immoral to being a seat of authentic emotion and affection. Yet at the same time the experience of being separated from one's loved ones in the village is also said to help turn boys into men and immature (*nafakhum*) children into mature (*fakhum*) and complete humans (*sahi insanan*). Migration, then, is an important dimension of the active construction of selfhood, morality and mental activity for many Rowshan people.

The arrival of the first few hundred rupees from a son's pay packet resulting from his labours in 'down Pakistan' is welcomed publicly and with great happiness.[37] Even a son who was previously a disowned (*nabehel*) and naughty boy becomes a man (*mosh*) when he hands his father a direct contribution to the household's expenditure (*kharcha*). The act of giving money to the head of the house has the potential of putting right child–parent relations. Receiving money from down (*aff*) country is news that quickly becomes relayed throughout the village. The boy's father or uncle proudly makes a trip to the local shop and buys a month's supply of ghee (*don*) and rice (*gringe*) as well as some clothes (*zap*) for his young children. This he is now able to do without having to ask for a further humiliating loan (*wam*) from one of the nearby shopkeepers. Ismai'li families, indeed, often greet the first pay-packet sent by a son working in down Pakistan with such enthusiasm and delight that part of it is used to prepare food (*khodaiee*) for the congregation that gathers each evening at the Ismai'li place of worship – the Jama'at Khana.

The experience of *shaharo zindagi* (city life) by many of Rowshan's Muslims heightens the sense of current ambivalence concerning the current state of village life. On the one hand, time spent in the city encourages people to reflect on what is said to be the special affection and love that characterises village life. On the other hand, experience of city life that is held as being free of the constraints and pressures of village life also makes many of Rowshan's Muslims discontent with the lives they have to lead in the village.[38] The product of this ambivalence is that the very boundaries between the city and the village are dissolving in the minds of Rowshan people. Content neither with the constraints of village life nor the alienation of life they discover in the city, many dream of the day when Rowshan will itself become a city, but a city on their terms. The fantasy world of freedom they construct for the future is one that transcends even the boundaries of the Pakistan nation-state. As one love-sick Rowshan boy is reported to have told his beloved in what is now one of Rowshan's most popular poems, 'Rowshan is also a city, no less so than London.' (*Rowshan bhii ek shahar hai london se kia kam nahi.*)

CONCLUSION

An important component of being Muslim in Rowshan is to possess authentic affection (*khuloos*) for one's fellow villagers. Yet for many of

---

[37] Osella and Osella 2000 explore the complexities of migrant earnings in their discussion of migration in Kerala, south India.

[38] On experience of 'home' and 'away' by Turkish guest workers in Germany, see Mandel 1990.

Rowshan's Muslims the role that affection plays in the living of a Muslim life is being corrupted by sentiments of jealousy (*hasad*), greed (*lalich*) and suspicion (*shak korik*). Unreasonable desires and economic compulsions are depicted as having polluted the villagers' affection and love for one another, and the upside-down (*ulta pulta*) nature of the villagers' emotions is seen, in turn, as having deformed the shape of the relations between the villagers.

There is a much consensus in the minds of Rowshan people to the effect that emotions which should define and construct the relations between the villagers have become inauthentic and insincere. Boys and girls who should see one another as brother and sister fall in love and have improper sexual desires. Rather than devoting their love and affection to their children, mothers prefer to escape from their noisy children in the house to expend their emotional energies on undemanding animals in the cow shed, whilst fathers are angry and hot-tempered with their children and prepared to leave them languishing in jail rather than showing them love and affection.

In order to resolve these problems, villagers do not turn in any one dimensional way to the village's religious authorities for purifying Islamic moral standards that will serve to rescue them from their current state of immorality. In later chapters, especially chapter 6, I explore the ways in which even those who are supposed to be the very guardians of village morality and purity – the men of learning and piety – are now said by many villagers to be guilty of 'playing with' the villager's love and affection. Nor do Rowshan people locate proper morality one dimensionally in the offices of the Pakistan state.

The moralising that is such a key part of village life is not, then, a simple dualistic schema in which people interpret things as being either allowed (*halal*) or forbidden (*haram*). Rather it is highly perspectival in shape, and this perspectivism is a product of the complex and highly fraught relationship between types of knowledge and understanding that are open (*khulao*) and those that are ideally more hidden and secret (*khoasht*). Yet it is not just that the secret world is an alternative to that of the open, and distinguished cognitively in the minds of Rowshan's Muslims. The knowledge of the secret always has the potential of bursting through onto the surface and destroying the surface-level peace of the village; and both the hidden and the secret are conceptualised by villagers as having inherently moral and immoral dimensions.

In the same way, villagers' conceptions of the relationship between the outside (*nishie*) and the inside (*andrenie*) are complex and multidimensional. If the outside is seen as a potent source of immoral thought and action in Rowshan, then it is also seen as a domain that Rowshan people must live in and learn in if they are to develop into fully fledged persons capable of independent thought. At the same time, the interaction between the outside and the inside and the hidden and the revealed is fraught and complex. Forces that have the potential to rupture the village's economy of knowledge are not simply those of the outside but, rather, people that either no longer respect the division between the secret and the open or those who are unable to grasp the subtle ways it needs to be nurtured. And it is often outsiders with an impartial knowledge of the inside or insiders connected with the outside that are the most dangerous folk in the village's moral landscape. Thus, Pukhtun traders, zealous policemen, young village scoundrels, crazy old men, devilish children and brazen women all have the potential of fracturing the division between secret and open knowledge and bringing shame and disrespect to Rowshan people, their families and the moral unit of the village itself.

Affection, then, is not simply the binary opposite of the intellect but, rather, has a form of logic and rationality of its own, and emotion and affection are themselves always the subject of active and conscious processes of moral verification by Rowshan people. It is the interaction between the intellect and emotion in the intellectual lives of Rowshan people to which I now turn.

CHAPTER 4

The play of the mind: debating village Muslims

Love: higher even than thoughts, lower only than the sky (*ishq khialar zhrang asmanar past*).
(Modern Khowar love song)

INTRODUCTION

This chapter explores the place that thought and discussion play in the living of a Muslim life in Rowshan. It seeks to refine anthropological analyses of the shape of intellectual activity and critical thought in the lives of village Muslims, and to examine what thought and the living of a 'mindful' (*zahin*) life entails for Rowshan people. 'Village' Muslims are often wrongly thought to be either unreflective, or to think solely in 'religious' terms. Rowshan people, on the contrary, value the intellect and the play of the mind, and base their claims and arguments on a strikingly wide range of different sources, both 'secular' and 'religious', and not just unthinking references to the Qur'an or to addresses made by the village's religious authorities. Far from being confined to the discussion of Islamic doctrine and practice, the intellectual life of Rowshan's village Muslims broaches sensitive issues that are important in the present day, and Rowshan people see the village as both having and needing to sustain an intellectual life. Making contentious remarks, debating (*bahus korik*), and saying surprising things, are all ways in which Rowshan people enjoy the play of the mind and experience thought in their daily lives. For Rowshan people, thought (*dunik, sooch korik*) and contemplation (*fikr korik*) are elements of daily life that are recognised as critically important to the leading of a Muslim life; and many Rowshan people take pleasure in the handling of abstract concepts drawn from a variety of sources and intellectual traditions and applying them to village life.[1]

---

[1] There have been historical explorations of the life of the mind and the importance placed upon intellectual creativity in Muslim modernist educational endeavours, but these concerns have rarely been the subject of anthropological exploration. For a discussion of intellectual creativity and the life

The chapter asks what it means to be a 'person who understands' (*hushiyar bandah*) in Rowshan, and explores how people in the village judge intelligence and intellectual ability. It documents a spirit of critical debate, which pervades village life and explores the extent to which this spirit of debate values the considering, testing, rejecting, and challenging of people's ideas and viewpoints. What I found in Rowshan is that it is possible to lead a lively intellectual life in a rural setting where some people are educated and others uneducated. A further question is how far both women and uneducated males in the village are thought of as contributors to intellectual activity and critical discussion.

There is a sophisticated body of writing exploring the nature of logical discussion and reasoned argument in the Islamic sciences, and much of the work documents how these dimensions of Islamic learning are taught in religious colleges.[2] A key theme in more recent works is the ways in which the employment of styles of reasoned argument have come to be deployed in the form of televised and recorded discussions and debates involving religious scholars Muslim world.[3] This chapter draws on this work, but shows that debate in Rowshan is not an attempt to emulate the styles of debate as taught in religious colleges or displayed by well-known men of religious learning and piety on television and radio programmes. Its concern is with the standards that Rowshan people themselves employ to judge the mindful activity of villagers and the extent to which they see people as capable of engaging in worthwhile discussion and debate (*bahus korik*).

This chapter has two main aims. First, it explores the place of critical thought and exchanges of ideas in the lives of 'ordinary Muslims' in Rowshan. Anthropologists of Islam have tended to focus on the political and religious outcomes of mass literacy and education in the contemporary Muslim world.[4] Few have focused attention, however, on the ways in which growing levels of education in rapidly changing Muslim societies have an impact on the ways Muslims employ the critical faculties in their

of the mind in the Aligarh University, established by Sir Sayyid Ahed Khan in nineteenth-century British India, see Lelyveld 1979, especially 204–52; and compare Troll 1978. On debates between Muslims and missionaries in India in the first half of the nineteenth centrury, see Powell 1993. On intellectual creativity in Arabic thought between the eighteenth and early twentieth centuries, see Hourani 1997.

[2] On reasoned argument and logical discussion as taught in the Islamic sciences, see Hirschkind 1996; Roff 1996; Mottahedeh 1985; and Fischer 1980: 61–76. On the Islamic sciences more generally, see Mahdi 2001.

[3] On the application of these styles of debate in the television channels of the Arab-speaking Middle East, see Eickelman and Anderson 1999. On the use of radio by religious scholars in Yemen, see Messick 1996.

[4] See, especially, Eickelman 1992a, 1997, 1999; Eickelman and Anderson 1997, 1999; Mottahedeh 1985; Meeker 1991; Starrett 1998.

daily lives.[5] The second aim is to advance the anthropological understanding of the interaction between emotion and intellect. Chapter 3 demonstrated how Rowshan people actively make moral valuations about the emotional dispositions of the villagers. Here I focus on how Rowshan people conceptualise the ways in which feeling is an important dimension of thought and intelligence.[6] A key concern of this chapter is, thus, the ways in which Rowshan Muslims conceptualise the interaction between feeling (*ihsas korik*) and thought (*dunik*) and it documents where villagers think thought has its source.[7]

I was often surprised when my friends in Rowshan commented to me, and to one another, that 'to be a Muslim means to be a liar and a fraud'. Moreover, when people made contentious remarks like this, those listening would often laugh and nod enthusiastically. In this chapter I seek to make sense of why people make such remarks. I focus on formal and semiformal public gatherings and special occasions, and informal discussions among villagers in their houses and orchards. Rowshan people – educated and uneducated – spend much time sitting and discussing the intellect (*'aql*), the psyche (*nafs*), the soul (*zhan*), the nature of emotion (*jezbat*) and the current state of Pakistan and the Muslim world. Therefore, I now document the intellectual traditions they bring to these discussions, and the emotional modes they stimulate.

STOP THINKING! YOU'LL BECOME THIN

Rowshan people have much to say about the interaction between the intellect and emotions and their comments about this throws light on their understanding of the interaction between thought, emotion and feeling. At one level, they make a division between the rational intellect (*'aql*) and the emotional carnal soul (*nafs*). One man in his forties – who was a well-known supporter of the revivalist Jama'at-e Islami party in the village – told me that it was the intellect that distinguished humans from animals.

---

[5] There are a number of anthropological attempts to explore the leading of a Muslim intellectual life in the context of religious education, see, especially, Eickelman 1985a.

[6] For important anthropological studies on cognition, see, especially, Bloch 1992, 1992; Boyer (ed.) 1993; Sperber 1985. On recent work that seeks to explore the interaction between cognition and feelings, see, especially, Csordas 1994; Stewart 2002; Toren 1993.

[7] There is a tendency in anthropological discussion of the relation between the intellect (*'aql*) and the carnal soul (*nafs*) in Muslims societies, to locate one in the reasoning mind and the other in the passionate heart, see, for instance, Anderson 1985.

I see a girl walking before me and I want to sleep with her, I am driven by my passions (*nafs*), but I stop and think no, this is wrong. My intellect (*'aql*) stops me from behaving like an animal. It is my *'aql* that makes me a human and a Muslim.

Reasoned intellect, then, is in the mind of this reform-minded Muslim, something that is juxtaposed to emotional and animal-like instinct. The notion that it is the intellect that is the source of rational and moral thought is widely held by Rowshan people. When fathers scold their children for behaving badly by failing to respect their elders or guests in the house, they often ask angrily, 'What has happened to you? Has your *'aql* become closed (*ta kia 'aql basta biti shera*)?' The intellect, then, should be open, allowing it to be a paramount dimension of people's thoughts, and a source of rational and moral beliefs and action.

Yet, at another, deeper level, for Rowshan's Muslims the most important source of a person's genuine thought is the heart (*hardi*), and not the mind (*zehn*) or brain (*dimagh*). There is no simple correlation between animalistic emotions located in the carnal soul, and the proper feelings of human love and affection that have their source in the heart.[8] For whilst a person's brain can be *chalak* (cunning) and produce speech and ideas (*lu*) that can deceive, a person's heart always tells the truth, and the only way to understand somebody is to come to know what their heart speaks (*hardio lu*). If the 'fully affectionate' (*pur khuloos*) person speaks the truth, then cunning people not only disguise their inner thoughts (*khiyal*) and intentions (*niyat*) in 'pretty words' (*sheli alfaz*), but also conceal their more animalistic emotions and feelings that are located in the carnal soul (*nafs*).[9]

The interrelation between the heart and the mind, and the carnal soul and the intellect, is also said in Rowshan to influence a person's level of intelligence. The ability to understand others' thoughts requires not only a 'fast brain' (*tez dimagh*), but also a highly developed sense of feeling (*ihsas korik*). Sensitive humans (*ihsas korak insanan*) can understand people's hidden thoughts and feelings in a way that those who are simply 'able' (*qabil*) cannot. A Sunni friend of mine, a man in his mid-thirties, often told me that he was a 'sensitive human' (*ihsas korak insan*), and that when he walked into a house he would instantly be able to understand who was thinking what about him. Thus, one way Rowshan people take pleasure in

---

[8] On knowledge as 'inscribed on the heart' of the Muslim believer and scholar, see Messick 1993.

[9] Wikan refers to the double-anchordness of the person in Bali: the 'face' which is the template for appearance, performance and act, and the 'heart' which is identified as the source of impulse and passion, see Wikan 1990. For Rowshan people, the heart is not simply the source of animal-like emotions and passions, but the feelings and emotions that well-up in the heart are themselves a complex form of thought.

experiencing the play of the mind is by seeking to understand the real thoughts and feelings of others, and this again raises issues of the surface and the hidden. He told me how he could register even the slightest of bodily movements such as a blinking eyes or an upturned lip, and he could understand exactly what these movements meant. He was, he often told me, something of an 'expert of the psyche' (*nafsiyato mahir*), a term that many people in the village use to describe someone who has heightened senses of intuitive perception. Being an 'expert of the psyche', however, was not something that came without cost: this man often told me how he was always confused (*pereshan*) and 'in tension' because he knew what people really thought about him.

As I noted in chapter 3, this man's comments show how, rather than being about the bodily concealment of women, purdah is about the concealment of thoughts and feelings. He felt his faculties of feelings and perception were so highly developed that he had broken the conceptual purdah of village life – not because he had seen women unveiled, but, rather, because he constantly unveiled the thoughts of others himself. And it was this unveiling of the village and the thoughts of the villagers that meant that he lived a deep yet anxious life. His comments show, then, how thought is itself deeply located in perceptions and feelings. This man evinces a deep concern with the presence of secret and inner (*batin*) knowledge – knowledge that he conceptualises as located in the concealed parts of the body. Along with many other Rowshan people, he spends much time and devotes much emotional energy in seeking to understand the hidden (*khoasht*) realities of life.[10]

Thought reveals, then, and this is something that makes it painful but also valuable. But thought is not necessarily always valued as a creative and positive activity; it has a dark and dangerous side too. Rowshan men and women complain of becoming weak (*kamzoor*) as a result of thinking too much. 'Thought', I was often told, 'eats a human' (*sooch korik insano zhiboyen*), and people often advise each other not to think too much, for thinking about troubling things is said to make a person become thin (*zhogh*) and weak (*kamzoor*). When I went to the bazaar looking worried or upset, my friends would often tell me that I 'appeared thin' in their eyes (*ma ghechi zhogh gosan*), and they would advise me, as a friend, to stop thinking (*dunie mo la yar*).

Indeed, one man in his late fifties, with eight young children and little income, told me that thought could do nothing but make a man weak and

---

[10] Compare Gilsenan 1982, 1989, 1996 on rural life in the Lebanon.

sick (*lahaz*). The only way for this man to avoid being 'dragged down' (*aff zhingeik*) by troubling thoughts, he told me, was to smoke hashish – a substance said to relieve thought, and bring on an appetite (*shapik zhibaru angoye*). On the other hand, somebody who is happy and free of troubling thoughts is likely to be fat (*tool*) and content. The person with a 'love of life' (*zindadil*) is often said not to think, and not to be troubled by the words of others. Yet not thinking in this context does not mean living a life devoid of ideas and intellectual rewards. Those who are free from the pains of inward thought and who do not worry about the criticisms of others have the potential to experience a free mind and to use tongues that are not 'locked' by sadness and worry (*ghamo qulf no korie*). Thus, thought is made up of differing degrees of intellectual and unreflecting activity, and if some thought is reasoned then other thought is not.

So, Rowshan people distinguish between different types of thought, as well as the ways in which thought is expressed, and the proper and improper use of the intellect. Thought that is verbalised in social and sociable settings is valued and seen as an important marker of a person's intelligence and ability, whilst internalised and inward thought has the potential to endanger a person's bodily and mental wellbeing. Yet even positive thought modes are viewed ambivalently by many villagers. People who have fast minds, who 'speak like the wind' (*lua tofan*), and are gifted with God-given intelligence (*khudadaud zehniyat*) are also said to be skilled at leading on and deceiving their fellow villagers. There is a form of deeper and more sincere intelligence that is associated with highly developed faculties of feeling and bodily sensitivity, and possessing such intelligence allows people to get beneath surface-level words so as to speak and understand the true (*frosk, horsk*) sounds of the heart (*hardio hawaz*). Yet having a capability for entertaining such thoughts also makes life complex and painful.

VILLAGE DEBATERS AND VILLAGE EDUCATORS

Being intelligent, cunning, and emotional are all categories which people use to discuss one another's characters. While Rowshan people talk about 'people of respect' (*izzatman roye*), they also value 'people of thought' (*sooch korak roye*). Maintaining a respectable public face or damaging the respect of another are often assumed to be the most important and constraining features of conversation in Muslim societies.[11]

---

[11] Charles Lindholm's ethnography (1982) of the Swat Pukhtuns of Pakistan's Frontier Province gives the impression that the majority of conversation amongst men in the region is made of attempts to

Rowshan's Muslims are also deeply concerned with esteem and pride in the self, and these concerns are the cause of considerable levels of distress and anxiety in their daily lives, as was seen in chapter 3. Yet rather than tending towards patterns of social consensus, Rowshan's Muslims rejoice in the voicing of ideas that generate heated discussions in the village. Rowshan people set much store by skills they deploy in being polite and civilised humans, but they also recognise that they can use these skills in a distinctly non-consensual way. They are aware that voicing contentious ideas is likely to result in public criticism from their fellow villagers, yet this is something they are prepared to face and from which they derive distinct feelings of emotional pleasure.

Rowshan people often categorise villagers as being either 'open-minded' (*khulao-dimagho*) or 'narrow-minded' (*trang-dimagho*), regarding their capability of critical thought and intellectual activity. Yet people's mental qualities are not thought to be fixed and unchanging; individuals can and do change the ways in which others classify their qualities of the intellect. Those represented as being narrow-minded also think that they too are knowledgeable and active participants in the intellectual life of the village. Far from being the passive recipients of Islamic or other sources of authority, they also conceptualise themselves as being thoughtful and of having ideas and expressing opinions that are interesting and important. There is the sense that people in the village who self-styled folk label as being 'narrow-minded', and often call themselves 'traditionalists' (*riwaj-pasand*), are able to benefit from and enjoy critical discussion and the exchange of different ideas and opinions.

Far from being the taciturn and deeply tactful Muslims described by Barth in Sohar, many villagers enjoy injecting formal social occasions with an element of unpredictability by voicing contentious ideas in order to test the mental faculties of their fellow villagers. Anthropologists working in Arabic-speaking contexts in the Middle East have explored 'verbal duel-ling' (*jaqmara*) or 'mock fighting with words' during which male performers compete 'to outdo each other in linguistic subtlety, metrical skill and poetic representations of their own or their communities' glories' (Gilsenan 1996: 208)[12]. Rowshan's Muslims also use speech (*lu*) to 'assert the primacy of their personal view against rivals' (211) yet there is also an

slight the reputation of village rivals and enemies, whilst Barth's study of sociality in Sohar suggests the all-importancerole of male public esteem and pride in the self circumscribes free conversation. See also Bowen 1993.

[12] Gilsenan analyses 'fighting with words' in rural Lebanon in the 1970s. See Caton 1990 for the analysis of *jaqmara* in Yemen.

intellectual dimension to these verbal fights that is distinct from and complementary to this competitive dimension of speech. Rowshan people do employ their intellectual capabilities in complex attempts to shame others in the village, but they also love exploring intellectual matters for the sake of lively debate and discussion.

Few of the Muslims who are discussed in this chapter are 'intellectuals' in the strict sense of the word, but they do refer to themselves in ways that indicate dedication to thought and intellectual pursuits. They use the word *hushiyar* (one who thinks, understands) to talk about people whom they see as being clever and well informed about a diverse array of themes pertaining to the world in which they live. One of the most complimentary things said of a person in the village is that they are 'very much an intellectual person' (*bo hushiyar insan*). Whilst such folk may have written theses for Masters courses in social science subjects, none of them are full-time academics in Pakistan's universities, nor have they published books or pamphlets, although they do typically enjoy such pursuits as writing poems (*shahir*), essays (*mazmoon*), and sometimes articles for English language newspapers.[13] Neither are these village intellectuals the local producers and transmitters of knowledge like the poets, musicians and comedians who are the focus of the chapter 5.[14] Yet many of Rowshan's self-defined intellectuals say that they are committed to learning and thinking, and to the transmission of knowledge (*ilm*) to their fellow villagers. Many of them are unemployed or earn little, yet they spend money on buying scholarly books that they find on their trips to 'down Pakistan', and these books, along with stacks of newspapers, are proudly displayed in the cupboards of their rooms and guesthouses.[15]

Many young people in the village say that they become bored (*bor*, from the English) by village life, and one way of relieving this boredom is to exercise the mind and listen to thought-provoking ideas so as to acquire interesting knowledge. Exercising the mind is seen as having the potential

---

[13] There are lecturers and writers living in the more urban setting of Markaz, the focus of the chapter 4. In Markaz launches of books written by local scholars are always popular and well-attended events. A 'society for the promotion of Khowar' (*anjuman-e-taraqqi-e-khowar*) was established in Markaz in 1943, and is active in the publishing of Khowar works today (see Faizi UPMS; Rahman 1996: 221–5). Few people in Rowshan regularly read Khowar works, however, and their attitudes towards the value of written Khowar are ambivalent. For Khowar volumes that include comical anecdotes (*mazarq*), essays (*mazmoon*), love poems (*ghazal*) and poems praising the Prophet (*naat*), see A. Chughtai (ed.) 1997; Mir 1994; Naji 2001; Zakhmi (n.d.).

[14] Compare Feierman 1990.

[15] See Eickelman and Anderson 1997: 53–4 for a discussion of books currently popular in Pakistan's cities.

to transform the emotional modes of Rowshan people: interesting and fast-moving discussion relieves boredom and replaces it with enjoyment (*mazah*) and heat (*garmi*). Unlike the hot stick of the aggressive and angry father, heat is here enjoyable, healthy and good. There is a feeling amongst the villagers that thought and creativity are the essentials of village life, and Rowshan people living away from their village often complain about the lack of entertaining discussion (*mazadar mashqeulgi*) in their lives. Yet, as was seen in chapter 3, villagers' views about Rowshan are often distinctly ambivalent, and the realities of village life mean that villagers must also go to great efforts to separate everyday village life from the life of the mind – the latter serves to relieve the monotony and anxieties of the former.

Many Rowshan people exert considerable social energy, and expend substantial economic resources, on cultivating a suitable environment where they can experience the joys of the play of the mind. Men actively seek out particular individuals in the village and beyond who are thought to be knowledgeable (*ma'alumati*) and to give good value in conversation (*mashqeulgi*). In particular, they enjoy visiting men who are renowned for making outrageous, alarming and witty comments, and, at great expense by local standards, my friends and I would often book jeeps to take us to the houses of such men who lived in distant villages.

A key feature of Rowshan life is the critical discussions that take place in both formal and informal settings as well as in more public and private domains of social life in the village. Organised school functions and impromptu discussions in the village bazaar can quickly take on a contentious form. Even comparatively impromptu discussions have an element of planning about them: people choose to visit friends or village personalities whom they recognise as having interesting ideas and the ability to engage in lively discussion. There are also more informal teacher–student interactions. Young men in the village who are enrolled in colleges and universities elsewhere in Pakistan often visit older folk in order to take advantage of the deep knowledge that they are said to have. And the younger people often say that these men are much more knowledgeable than their better-educated teachers and lecturers in 'down Pakistan'.[16]

Many of the young men in Rowshan visit each other's houses in the late afternoon in the summer months for the purpose of debate and discussion. They often choose to visit friends who are known for their ability to make

---

[16] On peer and outside class learning in Morocco, see Eickelman 1992a, Hammoudi 1997, and, on Afghanistan, Edwards 2002.

interesting 'chat' (*gap*). Such meetings would usually involve taking tea and biscuits whilst discussing a variety of topics including politics, religion, the state of village life, and even the sectarian divide in the village. Many of these occasions saw Sunni and Ismai'li men gathering in the same room and discussing matters of mutual interest.

These occasions in which people planned to get together to talk and think aloud were sometimes structured into more formal invitations (*da'awat*). A man would choose two or three of his friends whom he felt were 'good for discussion' (*mashqeulgio bachen jam*) and invite them to his house for a meal. Indeed, when I was given an invitation my host would often say to me 'come to my house and we'll sit down and have some food and a discussion (*mashqeulgi*); it will relieve the boredom (*boriat aff doye*)'. The guests (*mehman*) would arrive in the early evening and talk for an hour or two in a room in the guest house where the elders of the home were not encouraged to enter. Young men said that they felt bored, irritated and nervous sitting in the company of their elders who had 'nothing on their minds but cows and watering their crops'. Such discussion was not only said to be boring, but also had the potential of causing the brain to go crazy (*dimagh aspa boyen*). Many Rowshan people differentiate, then, between discussion that is worthwhile and about abstract ideas, and 'useless gossip' about everyday life that invades peoples' personal lives.[17] Whilst some elderly men in the village are said to be deep thinkers, older people's brain activity is also thought to be feebler than that of the young.

Rowshan's educated folk often style themselves as thinkers (*sooch korak*) and intellectuals (*hushiyar*), and they take great pride in being referred to as *falsafaran* (philosophers) by their fellow villagers. If the last chapter showed that a person who is sincere and affectionate is valued in village life, then the intelligent person also has a special standing in the village. Having a good education, being successful in competitive academic examinations, and showing a fluent grasp of languages other than Khowar – especially English and Urdu – are all seen as being important indicators of a person's intelligence.

Despite the emphasis on education and literacy, enjoying the play of the mind and exercising the critical faculties are not seen by villagers as being the preserve only of those who have followed courses in the Islamic sciences

---

[17] For contrasting treatments of gossip in the anthropological literature are, compare Bailey 1971 and Brison 1992. Compare Bailey 1997 for a discussion of an Indian village in the 1950s where life was about 'cultivating one's own garden and letting people get on with cultivating theirs' (Bailey 1997: 168).

or have gained from an education in 'worldly' subjects at college and university. Even illiterate (*anparh*) and uneducated (*betalim*) villagers are widely seen as having the potential to contribute to the vibrancy of intellectual life in the village, and some villagers emphasise the different perspectives that the village's different minds can bring to conversation. Uneducated people who are recognised as being intelligent and able are often described called 'local philosophers' (*watani falsafan*), and such people rejoice in voicing contentious ideas that become a focus of much discussion amongst Rowshan people. Moreover, villagers also distinguish between those who are clever because they study hard and read many books (*sabaq rak*) and those who have God-given intelligence (*khudadad zehniat*): some of the most respected villagers have had no formal education but are regarded as 'philosophers' because they are thoughtful about abstract issues including religious, secular and political matters.

Israr is the caretaker (*chaprasi*) in one of Rowshan's government primary schools; his duties include running errands in the bazaar for the teachers, and serving them their tea and lunch. Israr is in his mid-forties, is unmarried and lives with his one surviving brother, and his deceased brother's wife and children. At one level, Israr is seen as being the ideal householder, and as capable of spending what little money he has in a sensible (*sanjidah*) and beneficial (*fidaman*) way for his family. Israr has managed, on his small salary of 2,000 rupees, to send the all the children of his deceased brother to fee-paying English-medium schools, and he has built a guesthouse with a beautiful garden, as well as a large and well maintained house for his family members (*doro roi*). He is known to be an affectionate man who takes care (*khiyalo lakik*) of his family members. Many Rowshan people marvel at how generous Israr had been with his money: instead of spending what little he has on himself, he has, rather, in a self-sacrificial way, helped the poor and fatherless children of his dead brother.

Yet there is also a more intellectual dimension to Israr's lifestyle. Whilst Israr is educated only as far as primary level, he is nevertheless known as being one of the village's 'deep thinkers' (*kulum dunak*), and he also has a reputation for making contentious and highly alarming comments. He keeps his small room in a state of immaculate tidiness, and his aesthetic sensibilities are clearly shown in the colourful pictures of deer and mountains painted on the white-washed walls of his room by an artist from Tajikistan who had visited Rowshan some years previously. If Israr is only barely literate, the power of the written word is something that is an important part of his worldview. Along with the beautiful paintings of landscapes, there are verses, in Urdu, from the poetry of Iqbal, Pakistan's national poet, painted on the walls of his room, and the poet's portrait is also painted on the walls. Israr does not simply revere the script: he knows the verses and chose to have specific ones painted on his wall. Israr is also known to live an unconventional life by village standards. He is one of the few men in the village who drinks alcohol and smokes hashish openly, and is even known to wander into the bazaar and the lanes of the village in a 'state of intoxication' (*nasha asika*).

Israr loves to quote Khowar and Urdu poetry and explain the deep meanings of the lines to those sitting with him, but in particular Israr enjoys expressing critical views about what living a Muslim life entails. On one occasion a friend and I had visited Israr in his home, and he had given us a glass of home-brew mulberry spirit along with some walnuts (*birmogh*) and fried meat. My friend, Ali, is an educated Ismai'li man who is also known by villagers as being a man with 'God-given intelligence': he is fluent in English, Persian, Pashto, Urdu and Arabic, is knowledgeable about the writing of Islamic philosophers, and able to translate the Qur'an into Khowar. Our host, Israr, having first persuaded the young sons of his deceased brother, whom he called his *commandos*, to show what good dancers they were, then made the following remark to us in the context of a conversation we were having about Islam, and the current state of Pakistan, 'Where there are Muslims there will be lies (*changik*), fraud (*dookah korik*), and terrorism (*dashardgardi*). Seeing Muslims makes me want to run away (*musulmanan poshie ushturaru goyan*).'

This comment immediately made my friend and, indeed, myself, fall about in hysterical fits of laughter, and Ali's laughter was not of shock or discomfort but of real amusement. Israr, with a glass of alcohol in one hand and a hashish filled cigarette in the other, was not only prepared to flout Islamic doctrine and norms, but to question the very value of being Muslim in the contemporary world. Israr, then, cherishes his ability to display his individuality, and many Rowshan people rejoice whilst watching him do so.

Israr had made a name in the village for himself for making such contentious comments. Not all in the village were happy, however. One educated Ismai'li man in his mid-thirties, Sabbah, told me that he was fed up (*bezar hotam*) with the drunken Israr coming to his home each evening, sitting in his garden and making 'stupid' (*bakwaz*) remarks about Islam. Yet, for Ali, Israr's contentious comment was not something that was designed to make others laugh or even make them angry, and he did not treat him like the drunk village buffoon. Indeed, the educated Rowshan school teachers with whom Israr worked would also often visit Israr's house, and invite him to their homes for meals and evenings of discussion. It was not, then, just an provoking comment made for the sake of it, and, despite the disparities of wealth, Israr is treated by many educated folk in the village respectfully and as a man of thought and ideas.

Importantly, though Ali felt that he himself was intelligent and open minded enough to understand Israr in a way that other Rowshan people were not – he often told me that Israr was wasted (*israf*) on Rowshan people. Having dramatically puffed his cigarette and sipped from the clear white spirit in his glass, Ali, with his finger pointing skywards, told Israr to tell us, what, then, his philosophy of life was (*di lu det, ta zindagio kia falsafa sher?*). After leisurely taking a sip from the glass before him, Israr distinctively shook his shoulders and tightly pursed his lips thoughtfully and replied.

My philosophy is my heart (*ma falsafa ma hardi*). There are two things. One is a believer (*maumin*) – somebody who has faith in God, and believes that God watches him twenty-four hours a day. The other is a Muslim – a liar, somebody who believes by tongue only. They pray and have beards just to show things to other people, but their thoughts are different. They are ready to eat bribes (*rishwat*), and let poor people be poor. In Pakistan there are many Muslims but no believers.

Ali now looked at me, and said to me, 'Did you see (*porshtawa*)? He's a Sufi. Find me somebody able to think like that in your Cambridge.' In the mind of Ali, Israr was not only able to make contentious and provocative comments, but his thought was shaped also by his knowledge and under-standing of broader Islamic intellectual traditions, and, the weight of Ali's words were invested with even greater importance because they came 'from his heart'.[18] Ali thinks then that Israr was distinguishing between the open display of personal piety and the inner nature of a person's spiritual relation with God. Like many of the great Sufi and Ismai'li philosophers, he was saying that religion requires inward thought on the part of believers in order that they may recognise their own affinity with God. But, it was the second phase of the conversation that proved to the educated and well-informed Ali that his friend's thinking was about more than about making remarks calculated to offend the village's 'religious-minded' folk

---

[18] Making 'ecstatic sayings' (*shath*) that embody truth because they have their origin in the deep recesses of the heart has for long been an important dimension of Sufism. Al-Hallaj's exclamation on attaining spiritual truth, 'I am the truth' (*Ana al-Haqq*), which played a major role in his execution, is the most dramatic instance of this in Islamic history. Rowshan people often told me this story, and they frequently said that after al-Hallaj's execution the blood that flowed from his severed head repeatedly whispered, 'I am the truth'. See Ghomi 1999.

(*mazhabi dimagho roi*). Israr's comments were not simply casual remarks made by an alcoholic (*sharabi*), eccentric, and uneducated (*betalim*) villager, who was not serious about Islam. They represented both for him and many others in the village, rather, the intellectual work of someone who spent his life in thought (*dunik*) and reflection (*fikr korik*).

Ali went on to tell me that although Israr never went to the Jama'at Khana, and was a drinker of alcohol, he was one of the village's few real Ismai'lis because he understood the real meaning of his religion (*tan mazhabo sahi matlabo hush koyen*). He did not care what people thought of him or what they said about him. In short, he was not religious just to show people (*royan pasheiko bachen*) – rather, he had religion in his heart. Living a life of deep thoughts (*kulum sooch*) was also said to be a great source of anxiety for Israr. His body was tiny and thin, and many in the village commented that there was sadness (*gham*) at the root of Israr's penchant for thinking and reflection. When people said this they often had a wry grin on the faces, and conveyed the unspoken assumption that Israr was in love. But Israr was not a lover (*asheq*) like the immoral boys of the village who had 'dirty thoughts' about any girl who 'crossed their paths'. He was a lover like the Sufi poets, for his love was honourable and respectful because it was hidden – no one knew whether the object of Israr's love was a woman or a man, or God himself. And, importantly, in hiding his love Israr was, once again, showing himself to be a man of affectionate self-sacrifice: he was prepared to tolerate (*bardasht korik*) the pain of love in order to uphold his and his beloved's dignity. Inward thought, then, also has a creative intellectual potential. But it is not something that comes easily: living a life of thought and morally legitimate emotion has the potential of damaging bodily health and mental wellbeing.

Rowshan people go to great lengths to rejoice in the play of the mind. They differentiate between different kinds of intelligence and the uses to which intelligence and thought can be put. They value people who are seen to be capable of making sensible decisions for themselves and their families on the basis of reasoned thought, and those who are said to be deep thinkers and who make witty, humorous and daring comments. When people do make provocative remarks, they generate complex thoughts in the minds of villagers and they foster lively discussions in the village. Israr combines both of these forms of intelligence, and, importantly, he does so in a way that also proves that he is a man of affections (*pur khuloos insan*). Whilst both ways of being intelligent are valued, many villagers see the second as being superior – it has the potential for injecting a dimension of mindful activity into village life and making life enjoyable.

'IRON LADIES'

Up to this point the way in which Rowshan people experience of the life of the mind has been a male activity. It is men gathered in guest houses, young men visiting learned men in the village and the alcohol drinking and hashish smoking man who seek to earn reputations as 'intellectuals' and 'local philosophers'. I now explore in greater detail the extent to which Rowshan people conceptualise women as having a potential to contribute to the intellectual life of the village.

A further dimension of Rowshan people's concern with mindfulness and the intellect is the question of how women should be educated in the village. Like young men, many of Rowshan's young women complain about the 'boredom' of village life, and the constraints that are imposed upon their 'personal freedom' (*zati azadi*). The majority of the village's young women are educated – most of them having attended school until the age of sixteen, and, in the absence of a secondary college for girls during fieldwork, some of them have completed further education privately or in girls' colleges in Peshawar and Karachi.

Educated women in the village aspire especially to train as nurses and health workers for which they must attend courses in the cities of 'down Pakistan'. Receiving such training is no simple task for Rowshan's young women: fathers who send their daughters 'down' to the nursing colleges in the cities are often asked by their neighbours if they realise that their sexually mature daughters will have to conduct 'night duty' with male staff and colleagues. But some young women and their families take daring steps, and become engaged in these projects in the face of considerable criticism from other villagers and family members.

At one level women's education in the village is narrower and more focused on skills training than the social science degrees pursued by many young men in the village.[19] There is the sense here that Rowshan women are less capable of critical and creative intellectual activity than Rowshan men. As one Sunni religious scholar (*dashman*) in Rowshan told me, 'A woman can become a nurse or a teacher, but she can't become an engineer; these are the professions (*kasp*) of men.'[20] Yet, at another level, the division between creative intellectual activity and professional training does not reflect the gender divide in any simple binary way. There is also the

---

[19] Compare Rostam-Kolayi 2002 on the distinction between teaching 'domestic science' and more 'academic' courses to Iranian women in Reza Shah's new Pahlavi state (1925–41).

[20] The extent to which women are capable of intellectual activity is, of course, a long-standing source of debate in Islamic sciences and jurisprudence. See Sachedina 2001.

pervasive feeling that families who send their daughters for professional training as nurses to 'down Pakistan' are compelled (*majboori*) to do so for the wages (*tankkah*) and free accommodation that these institutions provide for their students. Like the religious colleges (*madrasas*) I discuss in chapter 6, these training centres are considered by many in the village to provide a rather low-status form of education that is unable to cultivate minds and refine the critical faculties. Thus, whilst women could be educated in social or other professions like engineering and medicine, the lack of facilities in Rowshan and the financial issues are the key concern and not the girls' inability.

Some families and individuals in the village do encourage women to undertake academic courses, and when they do so it is always a source of great discussion. Marrying an educated woman is for many young men in the village an important marker of status, but it is also a reflection of deeper concerns about what it means to live an intellectually significant life and how this can be achieved in a village setting. Farhan, an educated Ismai'li man in his early thirties had recently married Nabila. Farhan had chosen to marry Nabila having 'fallen in love' (*asheq bik*) with her after seeing her from a distance when she was attending her higher secondary exams in the village high school. Her striking red clothes and voluptuous 'big body' (*body wallah*) had caught his heart (*hardi chokitaiy*) and, for Farhan, there was no looking back. Farhan's choice of wife had caused many arguments in his house: his parents complained that the woman was 'lazy' (*soost*) when it came to work in the home, and that she was habitually 'angry' (*qahri*) and the cause of fighting (*janjal*) in her father's home (*tato dor*). If high-pitched intellectual discussion between men is a valued and sought after feature of village life, then family arguments (*doro janjal*) involving women are unseemly moments when passions go out of control and shameless folk bring disrespect onto their household. Great efforts must be made to ensure that a house does not become a 'den of cats and dogs' (*reinie-pushie mali*), and choosing a suitable 'daughter-in-law' (*rozhayu*) is an important dimension of this. Yet, despite his parents' opposition, after two years of relentless persistence, Farhan eventually persuaded them to arrange his marriage with Nabila. Farhan told me that if his marriage was to be a success, he needed a wife who could talk about more interesting things than the health of her cows or the goings on inside the home, and this is why he had chosen to marry the educated and 'bold' Nabila.

Even though Farhan had married the woman he wanted, he was nervous about their relationship. He told me that his wife was younger than him, and only had an education until the age of eighteen. 'It is very difficult', he told me, 'for an educated man like me to share my life with such a young and uneducated woman.' He said that the way to cultivate his relationship with his wife was by educating her, and by teaching her to have thoughts 'higher' than those confined to the house (*dor*) and the village (*deh*). Farhan set high standards for his wife, and, in the absence of a degree college for women in Rowshan, encouraged her to study privately for a BA in the social sciences – this would mean that she would be able to sit exams and receive a degree without attending a college. Having studied a social science subject himself, he would sit with his wife each day and teach her from a university textbook written in English. He also encouraged me to help teach his wife, and I would sit alone with Nabila, aged about twenty-three at the time of my fieldwork, in Farhan's private room. The book from which Nabila studied covered Western theories of the state (including the writing of Hobbes and Rousseau), democracy and the nature of Islamic political systems (focusing particularly on the writing of Ibn Khaldun). Nabila would write 'difficult words' (*mushkil alfaz*) in a small notebook, and memorise model essays (*mazmoon*) provided in the textbook; in the evenings Farhan would ask her the meanings of English words from her textbook. At one level, cultivating the mind of Nabila involved a vision of knowledge that is 'fixed and enduring' (Eickelman 1998: 289), and entailed the perfect memorisation of the written word, and it was a process initiated by her better-educated husband.

Importantly, though, Nabila had played a role in the decision for her to prepare for the social science examination. She had told her husband that she did not want to study Urdu or Islamic studies, subjects, she said, that were 'easy', 'boring' and studied by all the unable (*nalaiq*) women of the village. If she passed her degree in the social sciences, she told me, she would be the first woman in the village to do so. The thought of examination success and intellectual fame in the village had caught her imagination, and she was conscious of the fact that she was doing something new and was actively involved in changing village standards. The final success, then, was going to be passing an exam based on memorising set essays. Yet what is important for my analysis here is not the extent to which Nabila fully understood the English textbooks she was reading, but, rather, that she was embarking on this difficult task having only been schooled in Urdu up to the age of sixteen, and for two years in English until she was eighteen.[21]

Other members of the family were sceptical about Farhan's decision to teach his wife a social science degree. His elder brother, for instance, asked

---

[21] On the English–Urdu language controversy in Pakistan, see Rahman 1996.

me how this woman could possibly be expected to understand social science and write complex exam questions in English. Farhan himself often commented to his wife that if she did not pass the examination then they would both be the laughing stock of the village. His friends had already told him that his wife would never be able to pass the exam, and that it would be better if she did a Pakistan open-university degree in education. If she did this, they told him, he could do the coursework for her, and there would be no possibility of her failing. Farhan and Nabila were therefore making a risky and fraught decision in the context of villagers' perceptions of the intellectual capability of Rowshan women.

The couple clearly recognised the pressure placed on them to conform to more conventional expectations held by the villagers about women's intellectual activity, and the now battered textbook was the cause of numerous arguments between the couple. Nabila frequently threw her books away in disgust when her husband scolded her for not having studied hard enough, and on more than one occasion she locked her husband out of their room to protest about how he became angry over the slow progress of her studies. Indeed, I too received a telling off from Nabila on more than one occasion for failing to help her in studies in a sufficiently committed way. She told me that I would leave the house having failed to write an essay for her, and after having done so on one occasion Nabila refused to speak to me for a week. Farhan and Nabila sensed that they were doing something new in the village, and that there was pressure on them to conform to village expectations that Rowshan women were unable to be successful in learning English and studying academic subjects. Yet they were determined to disprove the views of their detractors both in the village and in their household.

Besides throwing light on Rowshan people's divided thoughts about women's capability of intellectual activity, the decision of Farhan and Nabila to study the social sciences also brings into focus the ways in which Rowshan people conceive the thought of Ismai'lis and Sunnis as being different. Farhan is an Ismai'li, and, importantly, all the women who had gone for training in 'down Pakistan' in the hamlet in which I lived were Ismai'li. Ismai'lis broadly represent themselves both as being more 'open-minded' (*khulao dimagho*) and flexible in their thought processes than the village's Sunnis; and an important dimension of this is their willingness to educate their women. As is shown by the comment of the Sunni religious scholar mentioned above, some Sunnis in the village conceive of the Ismai'lis desire to educate their women as being something that is un-Islamic and improper (*najaiz*).

Yet other Sunnis in the village admire Rowshan's Ismai'lis for being more open minded in their attitudes to women's education than the village's Sunnis. One wealthy and educated Sunni family in the village had decided to educate all their girl children, and they sent them to a fee-paying English-medium school in the village. The father one of these girls told me that he hoped to send his daughter, along with his sons, to an English-medium school in 'down Pakistan' so that she could study science subjects and eventually qualify as a doctor. The activities of Ismai'lis in the village has provoked a complex array of intellectual and social responses from Rowshan's Sunnis: some families seek to emulate and compete with the 'open minds' of their Ismai'li neighbours, others argue that Ismai'lis are involved in un-Islamic activities.

At the same time, however, many Rowshan people also say that a concern with 'reputation' (*izzat*) is a feature of village thinking that unites both Sunnis and Ismai'lis. Yet, rather than being Islamic and proper, this concern with purdah practices and the concealment of women is also conceptualised by many Rowshan people as something that is unhealthy and that narrows thought processes. Women and girls in the village are now also undergoing computer training in 'computer literacy centres' which have recently been opened by young male villagers. Some women find it hard to persuade their male relatives to allow them to attend such courses within the village, let alone to seek admission to nursing colleges in Pakistan's major cities. There were two 'computer literacy centres' in Rowshan at the time of my fieldwork, and one of them had gained a 'bad name'(*bad naam*) in village discussion because it was said that men and women not only sat in the same room whilst undergoing their training, but also used the same computers. For some in the village, even shaking hands with a woman was deplorable, and the thought of sexually mature boys and girls sitting together in front of the same computer screens had almost pornographic connotations both because of students' physical proximity and because their gazes coincided so closely.

One young Ismai'li woman, Abida, was attending classes in this computer-training centre in the village. Both her uneducated mother and her educated father had encouraged her to go to the centre. This girl's mother's brother (*mama*), and her father's uncle's wife (*betchie*), however, had tried to persuade the girl's parents to stop their 'mature' (*chumutker*) daughter from making her daily trips to the computer centre. 'It looks bad with the family' (*ispa soom shum noyuko*), the man had told his sister. 'People are saying bad words (*shum lu*) about our daughter, and your daughter wanders around the village with her scarf falling off her head (*sasiri biti kasiran*).'

Abida had also been shouted at by her uncle for having been seen walking back from the computer centre with some of the boys from the village, and for several days had refused to go to the computer centre despite the attempts of her parents to persuade her otherwise. Abida's mother told me that since her brother had made these remarks she had stopped encouraging him to visit her home: 'Such low thoughts (*past sooch*) have turned him crazy. Why should he inflict such things on my daughters? They should encouraged to be happy not worried.' For this Ismai'li woman, then, thinking about purdah and family reputation was itself something could act to limit mindful activity, lowered thoughts, and was so unhealthy that it had the potential to cause mental illness. Importantly, having these 'bad thoughts' was something of which both Ismai'lis and Sunnis, men and women, were capable; she assumed that people with cultivated minds would never have such thoughts and it was they who would be able to get through life happily.

Yet Abida not only protested at her uncle's comments in an unspoken and bodily way by sulking and refusing to eat with them at meal times. She told me, on several occasions, that her uncle had told her that she had 'become big', and that no longer could she do the things she loved to do when she was a child, such as running around the village and playing football and cricket. Thus, for many Rowshan women, purdah is not in any one-dimensional sense a type of bodily comportment that women in the village automatically learn as they grow older, and which operates below the level of consciousness as a habitus, a 'system of durable, transposable dispositions' (Bourdieu 1990). Purdah is, on the contrary, a process that is verbally taught to young Rowshan women. This process is experienced by them through thought, and stimulates reflection about the life changes they experience. Abida, however, was not ready to defer in any simple way to her uncle's dictates: she continued going to the computer centre, and she would often tell me how she wanted to be a *career woman* (in English) and not just 'get married, cook bread, have children and grow old'.

Women's education, then, is a source of much discussion and conflict in the village, and reveals much about the ways in which Rowshan people's conceptions of women's intellectual capabilities have been undergoing considerable transformation in recent years. Moreover, this transformation is something in which women are themselves playing a major role. As will be seen below, it is not only male, alcohol-drinking 'local philosophers' like Israr who have the potential to add to Rowshan people's experience of the life of the mind. Women too are active if indirect makers of Rowshan's intellectual vibrancy.

Women do not actually participate in the public discussions that take place in all-male spaces of the village, such as guesthouses and the bazaar. Even in the home women are often excluded from conversation by men in the household who comment, 'what voice does a woman have?' (*aurato kia lu biti sher*) and label all conversation involving women as *faltu mashqeulgi* (useless gossip). Rowshan people distinguish between conversations that are meaningful and about abstract ideas, and 'rubbish talk' (*faltu lu*) that invades into the 'personal' (*zati*) live of individual villagers, and this type of conversation is often associated with women. What makes these types of conversations particularly unhealthy and immoral is that they take place 'behind the backs' of the people they are about. One young and uneducated Sunni man who worked as a carpenter asked me what I thought about the traditions of the village. I replied politely that I liked the village very much. He disagreed and told me that he was not happy with the state of village life.

The people in this village are not good. They are all like women (*auratananghon*) – they sit in corners and complain about other people. They are too weak to say anything in the open (*wereigh*) but can only go into little corners and talk about people behind their backs.

Proper and worthwhile conversation, then, should be open and up-front, not hidden, cowardly and concerned with people's personal lives; and for this uneducated man the pursuit of mindless gossip reduced men to a state which for him was like that of the intellectually weak, shy and sly women of the village.

Yet, despite this pervasive dismissal of women's speech as being meaningless and unhealthy, many women do play an active role in intellectual discussions in the village. Both old and young women exchange views with brothers and close relatives in their households, and engage regularly in discussions they have with other girls at school and in places of religious instruction. Women are often judged by men, and by each other, as being *qabil* (able) and *laiq* (intelligent), and when the annual school examination results come out, the issue of who achieves the best results is a great source of discussion in Rowshan. Villagers also told me that men trying to marry women with reputations as being *bold*, *social*, and intelligent rather than shy (*sharumdar*), simple (*nachar*) and like a deaf and dumb person (*ghotghonie*) is a new (*nogh*) feature of marriage practices in Rowshan. Farhan's marriage, and the conflicts that it has generated, is one such example. Women earn reputations for being *social* and *bold*, both English words frequently used in Khowar speech, by greeting men who visit their homes rather than 'hiding' (*khoashteik*) from them, and by being prepared to speak and voice their opinions in conversations in which they become involved. In seeking such reputations they also tread a delicate path: in the minds of some villagers a woman who is *social*, often means a woman who is of bad morals (*bad ikhlaq*) and of *bad character* (in English).

Despite the accusations of bad morality, it is not only in the confines of the household where women seek to earn reputations for being independent and active. Women in the village pursue complex strategies to earn local reputations for being able and intelligent, and these strategies are the focus of complex and multi-dimensional discussions by Rowshan people.

Thus, there are women in Rowshan who have earned a reputation both locally and beyond the village for being powerful and independent intellectual actors. One woman aged about forty-five years had completed a Masters degree in education in Karachi and is now the headmistress of Rowshan Girls' Government High School. This woman was often invited as a chief guest (*mehman-e khusoosie*) to formal 'programmes' held at schools in the village. At these programmes she would be invited to address those gathered and share her thoughts and ideas with them, and she was known and referred to as able and intelligent.

During such public occasions, people are expected to say something with content, and not just to utter predictable set-piece remarks of welcome and thanks. At one school parents'-day programme in an English-medium fee paying school in the village, attended by the female and male relatives of the school's children, invited guests saw children display the life of their and their teachers' minds. All present – including a religious scholar (*dashman*) – laughed loudly and clapped in appreciation when they saw young Sunni and Ismai'li children aged between five and nine sporting false beards and imitating the region's *ulama*, by giving speeches and quoting from the Persian verses of Rumi and Alama Iqbal. They also performed in political satires that depicted Pakistani politicians as liars and the makers of impossible promises to Chitral's poor, impressionable and uneducated folk. Other children sang the words of Indian film songs that were well known to those in attendance, and impersonated the dancing styles of famous Indian film actors. There were also dramas that were critical of village life, and these showed bossy elderly men drinking alcohol and ordering their wives about in a rude and 'uncivilised' (*badtamiz*) fashion.

The owner and headmaster of this school of about 150 students, told me that he wanted to show people in the village how he was teaching his students to be *active* and *critical* (he used the English words). He said he wanted his students to become bold and confident, not like what he said were the 'bored' and 'dull' children of other schools in the village who just sat in their schools rocking back and forth memorising texts and being beaten by their teachers. He had even fixed a poster on the wall, in English, on which was written, 'The beating of children results in confusion rather than ease.' There was a great deal of consensus in the minds of those who had attended the programme that it had been a great success and that the children of this school were active in a way that students in other schools were not. Unlike other such programmes where they remembered sitting uncomfortably for hours listening to predictable speeches by village personalities, the children in this programme had been amusing (*namakin*) and had shown how able they were by speaking in English and boldly dancing before the village's respected elders. If, as I discussed in chapter 3, children are expected to respect their parents and do as they are told, then in other settings fathers love to display the intelligence, independence and creative minds of their children. Many men in the village ask their little children – sons and daughters – to 'sing' (*chulei*) their comical and beautiful (*choost*) words before their respected guests. There is then an important tension here, and this tension reflects the different ways in which Rowshan people conceptualise the intellect, and the uses to which it should be put. On the one hand, the intellect should be a force for the control and discipline of animalistic emotions. On the other hand, the intellect should also have the potential of instigating creative and critical thinking, and this is something that is often manifested in free bodily activity.

At the end of this particular programme and following on from the satirical displays, the programme's chief guest – the headmistress of the Girls' school – was invited to address those attending. Her comments engaged with the diverse and often contrasting ways in which Rowshan people conceive of how intellectual activity should be displayed. Her ideas and comments were listened to attentively by the large audience, which was composed of men and women of all ages sitting separately in the school's small playground. The headmistress told the audience gathered that for a child's education what was even more important than schooling was the environment (*mahaul*) at home and in the village. She said that the environment of the village and the home needed to be changed. Children needed to be disciplined by their parents and unless parents did this, their children would never succeed in life whoever their teachers were and whatever books they studied.

This woman, then, was prepared to debate and even disagree with men who had addressed the gathering. The headmaster of this private school had already told parents that it was important that children were encouraged to be active. Another man who had spoken had told parents not to 'defeat' (*shikast korik*) wills and minds by beating them their children they did not do their homework or were naughty at home. 'Becoming social' (*social bik*), he had told them, required parents to have 'broad minds' (*wasigh dimagh*). This woman had ideas and arguments that she wanted to voice to her listeners, and her tone was at odds with the headmaster's speech. Speaking without a text or notes, she went on to tell the gathering that they needed to think more carefully about how they managed their household expenditure. She told them that she was able to send her six children to fee-paying English-medium schools on the small salary she received as a teacher in a government school.

All of you have vegetables, rice, tea and bread in your houses. Yet when you have guests you go to the bazaar and buy plates of curry and chickens to feed to them. Then you say that you are poor and cannot educate your children. You are not poor and can educate your children but do not think about how to spend your money. First, improve the atmosphere in your houses and then sort out the way in which you manage your expenditure if you want to give your children a future.

This woman's speech was the subject of considerable male discussion after the programme. Some men said that they were impressed by her bold and serious style: she had spoken non-stop for twenty minutes in a loud voice without displaying shyness in front of all those gathered. This was an achievement, they said, that they thought even many men could never hope to achieve. Yet, at the same time, one man questioned the extent to which this woman was really 'open-minded' (*khulao dimagho*) and held genuinely liberal views about girls and education. This Sunni man, in his thirties, said that all she was interested in was discipline, and was 'at heart' very conservative in her attitudes towards education and women. Rather than encouraging free ideas and thinking, she was interested in discipline alone. Indeed, some of the other women who had been present at the programme told me that this woman was the most 'closed minded' of all. When they had been her students, they told me, she had been opposed to even the slightest display of *fashen* (from the English word fashion) such as wearing earrings (*karineni*) or colourful hair bands (*phur band*).

There was a paradox in the opinions voiced by this woman, of which other Rowshan men and women are themselves aware. The headmistress was seen, and indeed viewed with approval, as bold, freely spoken and assertive, with a strong mind, and prepared to voice decisive and critical opinions. Yet the views she was voicing were not in defence of limitless freedom for students and their parents, but were seen, rather, as somewhat harsh and authoritarian. In effect: cleanse yourself of the luxurious excesses of Chitrali village life, be disciplined and subjugate your will to rote learning and modern, austere values. She had not approved of the almost licentious displays of free thought and activity – embodied in the sight of five-year-old boys thrusting their hips to the sound of Indian music – that she had seen, and she was not afraid to tell people. What is especially interesting is the complexity and diversity of other people's reactions to all this. Rather than simply complaining that an unveiled woman had given a speech before a gathering of men, they commented in detail and with much thoughtful reflection on the actual content of her address. They were mostly admiring and well disposed to the fact that she was an assertive and strong-minded woman, and they expressed approval for the seriousness (*sanjidahgi*) in her voice and her commitment to education. But at another level, some, though not all, found her out to be out of step with their attitude to intellectual creativity – she was held to be narrow, puritanical and, importantly, boring (*bor*), which suggested that she was unable to elicit any real emotional response from people sitting in the audience.

Thus, villagers in Rowshan value the voicing of ideas, and they enjoy being involved in conversations that they themselves feel have an intellectual dimension, but, at the same time, they also recognise the constraints that stop the village from being a place of free discussion and action. Moreover, Rowshan people conceptualise these constraints as being partly those of their own creation: low thoughts about purdah, authoritarian schooling techniques, argumentative houses, and narrow-minded village gossips all have the capacity to limit the extent to which the ideal Rowshan of the mind takes a real form. In response, Rowshan people must themselves take active and often daring steps to foster intellectual discussion and creativity. Some women are encouraged to study the social sciences despite familial opposition, children are told to dance 'boldly' in front of their village elders, and other women chose to disregard the low thoughts and gossip of their narrow minded fellow villagers.

Educating women, children and the village boys is an important part of how Rowshan people conceive that minds can be cultivated and discussion in the village improved, and it is this dimension of living an intellectual life in Rowshan to which I now turn.

READING MINDS AND REACHING THE TRUTH

The impact of growing levels of literacy and education have had surprising effects on what Rowshan people consider to be the experience of the life of the mind. There are a number of detailed studies on education in the contemporary Muslim world. Recent studies have show shown how growing levels of education in Muslim societies facilitate not only the rise of 'scriptural', 'systematic' and 'fundamentalist' styles of Muslim thought and practice, but also the ways in which they have resulted in growing levels of debate in the Muslim world.[22] There has, however, been relatively little attention paid to transformations in the intellectual lives of village Muslims brought about by rapidly expanding levels of literacy and education.

A 'reintellectualisation' of life is taking place in Rowshan, and 'new Muslims' from a diverse array of backgrounds are playing an important part in the process (Eickelman and Anderson 1999). Yet what I encountered in Rowshan differs from Eickelman and Anderson's recent focus on the ways in which new Muslims are specifically rethinking and transforming the shape of the Islamic tradition: Rowshan Muslims discuss things that are about religion, but also many things besides. The outcome of now widespread mass literacy programmes in newly educating regions of the Muslim world has an intellectual dimension that generates an interest in abstract thought and critical debate.

Whilst being civil and polite, the participants in these discussions are not deferential to one another but, rather, are often decidedly critical and argumentative; and the process of taking sides in these interchanges is an important dimension of their structure. There is indeed a powerful element of competition and sparring in discussions in the village, and this is recognised and enjoyed by those present. As was seen in chapter 3, Rowshan Muslims pride themselves for being *sharif* (polite) and cultured (*tahzibi yafta*), but they also say that they take pleasure in making others *qahri* (angry) and *pereshan* (confused). Vehement and competitive discussions have the capacity to arouse emotions, and much pleasure is to be had if one of the discussants leaves in a sulk (*kruik*). The debates are given further potency in that there are often critical and discerning audiences whose members subsequently discuss the intelligence of those involved after the event.

Whilst Rowshan's Muslims do not always talk about religion, when they do they often say things that might be thought of as surprising in the context of village life in northern Pakistan. The village discussions taking place about Islam often broach contentious and sensitive topics. Who is it permissible to call a 'Muslim' (*mussulman*)? What is the status of the

---

[22] See Eickelman 1992a; Eickelman and Anderson 1999, 1997; Hansen 2000a; Messick 1993; Starrett 1998.

Prophet (*paighambar*) in Islam? Should purdah be a focus for bodily practice in Muslim societies or is it, rather, something 'inscribed on the heart' (*hardio teka niveshi sher*) and manifested in lived and experienced morality? Are the soul (*zhan*) and spirit (*ruh*) really an empirical component of human life and existence? What is *jihad* (holy war) and how should Muslims use violence in their struggles in the world today?

On one hot summer late afternoon I was sitting with three of my friends: Zulfikar, Aftab and Farhan. All three had Masters degrees from Peshawar University: Zulfikar had studied Urdu, and the other two social science degrees – at the time of my fieldwork in Rowshan all were teaching in English-medium fee-paying schools. Aftab is Sunni and married to an uneducated woman, whilst both Zulfikar and Farhan are Ismai'lis and married to educated women. At one level, the fact that they joined to sit and converse with one another shows how one arena of village life where interaction between Sunnis and Ismai'lis is seen as being proper and healthy is in intellectual discussion, meaning talk that is abstract and not about personal or mundane matters. Moreover, unlike the people Barth worked on in Sohar, these men did not try and avoid having sensitive discussions about religious doctrine, but, rather, as we shall see, were prepared to broach such issues. At another and deeper level, however, the shape the conversations took resulted in the men rethinking conventional ways in which Rowshan people conceptualise the characteristic features of Ismai'li and Sunni thought in the village.

The discussion began with the way people in the village talked about spiritual power (*ruhani taqeat*). The Sunni man, Aftab, told his friends that he had ambivalent (*muzharmuzhie*) thoughts about spiritual power.

Sometimes I become very spiritual. I think that there is a spirit (*rooh*) within me and I become driven to do things for God. One day I heard Arkhon Sahib [the village's most important Sunni *'alim*] and on listening to him, I became moved to go down to the river and carry heavy wooded beams (*toon*) to the mosque we were building. On other occasions, however, I think that it is all rubbish (*bakwaz*), if we do not see such spirits then how can there really be such a thing? Where is the proof (*suboot*)?

Aftab, then, recognised that there were certain dimensions of his thought and activity that were spiritual, and other dimensions that were rational and required him to think in terms of scientific evidence and proof. What is especially interesting about his comments in relation to the concerns raised here, is that he spoke in terms that showed that he wished to be seen as reflective and questioning about his personal beliefs. Moreover, he considered this to be a special feature of his thinking in relation to less 'mindful' (*zahin*) village folk.

One of the Ismai'li men present, Zulfikar, who had studied Urdu, continued the men conversation.

I also think like this. Look at the case of the Prophet. People say that he was a special man, that he could do special things. But I think that he was just an ordinary man like you and me. He may have been a great character, or a social reformer, but why do people say that he could do miracles (*mo'jiza*)?

For Zulfikar the very spiritual power of the Prophet himself presented problematic intellectual concerns. Zulfikar's comments are complex. Some reform-minded Muslim organisations that are active in Chitral and across Pakistan, especially the Ahl-e Hadith, teach that the Prophet was an ordinary man who acted as a conduit for God's word.[23] They say that all Muslims can live a life as pure and as pious as that of the Prophet, and they hold up the Prophet's lifestyle as something that all Muslims should attempt to follow in their daily lives. Yet the man making these remarks was an Ismai'li; and the importance of the spirit and spiritual power lies at the centre of Ismai'li belief and cosmology. The spiritual leader of the Ismai'lis – the Aga Khan – is direct descendent of the Prophet and is therefore conceptualised as having access to a special spiritual power that allows him to interpret the Qur'an in a unique way.[24] In saying that the Prophet was just an 'ordinary man', then, this Ismai'li man was coming close to questioning the very central beliefs of his faith. This was certainly the view of Farhan, the other Ismai'li participant in the discussion.

I don't know how you are saying such things. If you can't understand the spiritual power of the Prophet then it means that you don't believe (*aqida korik*) in it properly. Have you not read Islamic history or studied the Qur'an? This is the word of God, and if you are Muslims you must take it as being the truth.

For Farhan, Zulfikar's remarks had gone beyond the limits set by strict Ismai'li norms for permissible debate or speculation about spiritual matters. The men present told him that he misunderstood what they were talking about. Unable to think in an abstract and self-reflective way, Farhan had lowered the tone of the conversation and was told that he had 'lost his temper like a child' (*tsitsekan ghon qahri biti asoos*), and this reflected the unsophisticated (*behuda*) nature of his thoughts. They reprimanded their emotional (*jezbati*) friend, telling him that they were talking not about their personal beliefs (*zati yaqein*) but, rather, about ideas (*khiyalat*).

---

[23] On the Ahl-e Hadith, see Metcalf 1982.   [24] See Daftary 1998.

For the other men present, Farhan had failed to understand that they were talking about abstract ideas in a rational and distanced way, and his narrow mind had brought a halt to their free-flowing and critical conversation. He was ruining the conversation by acting in a clumsy and calf-like (*bacholeghonie*) way that resembled not the educated and liberal young Ismai'li man he should have been but, rather, the region's hardened (*dang*) men of learning and piety (*dashmanan*). 'It turns out', they later told me, Farhan 'is not a man yet ready for free and critical conversation.'

What was particularly important for Aftab about Farhan's clumsy contribution to the conversation was the fact that he had proven himself to be something of a religious 'extremist' (*intihai pasand*); and this was particularly important because Farhan was Ismai'li. Aftab later commented to me, 'Farhan is just as much as an extremist as any Sunni in the village; he can't accept anyone else's ideas, and if you say something against religion he at once (*yak dam*) becomes angry (*qahri*) and emotional (*jezbati*).' Despite the fact that Farhan had gone against the wishes of his parents by having a love marriage, educating his wife, allowing her to walk the lanes of the village and teaching her a BA degree, he had failed to meet Aftab's ideal vision of an open-minded person. And it was because Farhan was emotional about religion and was not prepared to carefully listen to the ideas of other people that made him something of an intellectual 'donkey' (*gordogh*). Farhan was an educated man who had studied social science, but, unfortunately for Aftab, even this had not furnished the cultivated mind and the balanced levels of emotion that it should have.

Thus, education and literacy in this village in northern Pakistan do not result automatically either in Islamic conformity or 'fundamentalism' or in the acquisition of 'liberal' attitudes. Many Rowshan people, though, conceptualise the experience of education as being something that should ideally cultivate minds, promote critical thought, and importantly, result in the cultivating of sensitive emotions.[25] Villagers scrutinise Islamic doctrines in contentious ways, and many Rowshan people have an idea of a type of open-mindedness (*khulao-dimargo*) that involves the ability to listen to others' arguments in a detached way; and being able to do so requires a degree of detachment from their own personal (*zati*) religious beliefs.

[25] Other studies of the experience of education by village students in the urban universities of the Muslim world have emphasised its disorientating dimension, something that is often argued to result in the formation of peer groups and radical Muslim politics. As Hirschkind has noted, such analyses of revivalist Islam are problematic in that 'they reduce these movements to an expression of the socio-economic conditions which give rise to them' (Hirschkind 1997: 3). For an account of Kabul University in the 1960s–70s, see Edwards 2002: 203–5. On radical student politics in Pakistan, see Nasr 1992.

Many Rowshan people display, therefore, complex and multifaceted ideas that are rooted both within and beyond the Muslim world.[26] Those who have completed higher education in the village frequently discuss the ideas of Rousseau as well as Ibn Khaldun, writers whom they have studied during their degree courses in Peshawar University, in their efforts to explore and understand the world in which they live. Farhan, who had studied the social sciences, used to refer to Ibn Khaldun's concept of *assabiya* to explain the qualities of different hamlets in Rowshan in a way that is remarkably reminiscent of Ernest Gellner's writing on Ibn Khaldun (Gellner: 1981). In one hamlet, he told me, there was a great degree of group feeling and cooperation (*tavawoon korik*) whereas the hamlet he lived in was characterised by division. Whilst the people of the former hamlet had been successful in helping each other to secure lucrative posts in the Aga Khan Development Network, the people of the latter had been determined more to 'bring each other down'. Whilst Zulfikar, who had studied Urdu at Peshawar university, had read about Rousseau in an Urdu book about his ideas, and he used to tell his fifteen-year-old pupils in the school about Rousseau's belief in the existence of an underlying value of humanity (*insaniyato qadr*). He told them that they should forget about their religion (*mazhab*) and lineage group (*qawm*), and 'first learn how to be humans' (*pisa nast insaniyato chichelik*).

Rowshan's educated Muslims, then, seek to bring complex and abstract ideas into their understandings of contemporary life in the village, and the intellectual models that they use to think about the village are not confined to the teachings of reform-oriented and purist Islamic scholars. Not only are attitudes towards village life shifting and open to challenge and debate, but so too are attitudes towards Islam multidimensional, and this is one powerful factor behind the failure of movements of Islamic reform and purification to homogenise the thought and identities of Rowshan people. Most young men in the village are unwilling to be labelled as *mazhabi dimagho* (religious-minded), and the symbolic markers of strict religious identity in the region – keeping beards, wearing shawls and fingering rosary beads – are adopted by very few of the village's youth.

Discussions over the shape and form that the 'Islamic tradition' should take in Chitral are not confined, then, to questions that address the extent to which life in Chitral is 'Islamic'. Moreover, the contours of the debates reflect very clearly the 'current experience' of believers (Eickelman and

---

[26] Compare Marr 2000 for an account of the diverse intellectual traditions discussed by Vietnamese intellectuals in the first decades of the twentieth century.

Anderson: 1999), and one important dimension of this experience is the access villagers have to diverse intellectual traditions. The contrasting educational experiences of Rowshan people contribute to the lively intellectual climate of the village, as will be seen from the following discussion.

Majid is Sunni, in his mid-thirties and educated in Peshawar University in sociology. Majid now divides his time between his family home in the village and Peshawar's bazaar where he works in a printing and word-processing shop. Majid is also a friend of Aftab, Farhan and Zulfikar. His sociology course in Peshawar had focused on the study of social norms and mores and the problems of life in contemporary Pakistan, and the course contained an Islamic component that labelled drug abuse and prostitution as 'social evils', to be cured by the introduction of *shari'a* law in Pakistan. Majid agreed with this, and at the height of Taliban power in Afghanistan in 1999–2000, Majid used to tell his friends that the Taliban was the true example of an *islami nizam* (Islamic system) free from corrupt Western influences. The problem with Pakistan, he often said, is that it is neither Western nor Islamic but, rather, a hybrid that has no hope of succeeding in its present form. Majid is a reader of the Islamist anti-Western journal *Takbir*, and the son of one of the village's most respected *'ulama*. He does express feelings of shock at the controversial comments made by his both Sunni and Ismai'li liberal-minded friends and 'class fellows' in the village. But while we might expect someone like Majid to cut himself off from those who do not share his views, or people who belong to different Islamic doctrinal traditions than himself, he still has friendly relations with them, and enjoys discussing sensitive issues including religious matters with them.

On one day I went with three friends from the village to congratulate a Sunni man whose daughter had been married that day to a young Sunni man from a nearby village. Having eaten the specially prepared rice (*pakhti*) served at weddings and other occasions of happiness (*khoshani*), we sat on the chairs arranged in the man's orchard. Two of the visitors were Sunni, the other man present was Ismai'li. Both of the Sunnis had studied in Peshawar University. Aftab and Majid had gained Masters degrees in the social sciences. The Ismai'li man, Farhan, had not been able to afford to go to university in Peshawar but he had studied privately in the village for a degree also in social sciences. This meant that he read the books and notes for the course in Rowshan without getting admission in Peshawar University and attending the lectures there, and it allowed him to sit the exams and gain a degree. All three were 'class fellows' and had attended the village primary school together from the age of six. This shared experience of education allowed them to discuss highly sensitive issues about Islam and doctrinal differences within the village with one another, despite belonging to different doctrinal traditions. Such discussions, they told me, would never take place between *nagoni* (strangers), as strangers would be afraid of insulting one another.

Most of the guests had now left the wedding place, and, over a final cup of green tea (*och chai*), a lively debate started between the three young men present when Majid declared that the Taliban government in Afghanistan was a perfect Islamic political system. Farhan immediately took offence at this remark and told Majid that the Taliban had been responsible for killing thousands of Ismai'lis and had thrown their bodies into the rivers of Afghanistan. He angrily demanded of Majid, 'where does it say in the Holy Qur'an that killing people is acceptable?' The conversation had now become tense, and some less educated boys sitting on the grass around the men were visibly enjoying watching these educated 'sons of the village' lose their tempers. The watching boys winked at me to suggest that there was fun in the making as these men started to lose their tempers and take their ideas seriously. I heard these boys comment that the discussion between the three men had now 'become hot' (*garam biti asuni*), and they slapped each other's hands in excited anticipation of what was to come. If the headmistress discussed earlier in this chapter had been described by villagers listening to her speech as 'boring', then these men were certainly more successful in their attempts to incite heated and emotionally rousing discussion.

Aftab, who was generally respected as a reasonable and level headed young man, tried to reduce some of the tension between Majid and Farhan. He told them of the time he had been travelling from Peshawar to Chitral through Afghanistan in 1999 and a Talib had noticed that he was clean-shaven. This was at a time when the Taliban government made all men in Afghanistan grow their beards. The division of the Taliban police force responsible for the 'prevention of vice and the promotion of virtue' (*al-amr bi'l m'ruf wa'l-nahy 'an al-munkar*) strictly enforced this law in the regions of Afghanistan they controlled. Having noticed this clean-shaven man sitting in the vehicle, a Taliban fighter had opened the window, reached his hand into a snuff box, and smeared black soot over Aftab's face. Aftab felt shamed and dishonoured (*beizzat hoye*), and when the news reached Rowshan people found it hilarious: one of Rowshan's most committed Sunni Muslims, regular in his prayer and a onetime member of the Jama'at-e Islami party, had fallen foul of the famously strict policies of the Taliban.

Aftab told his friends that the Taliban were only interested in surface level interpretations of Islam, and they were not concerned by what a person was really like on the inside. Aftab was careful not to dismiss the

Taliban in the way Farhan had chosen to, yet was, at the same time, prepared to suggest that their version of Islamic governance was far from perfect in the way that Majid had suggested. He sought to mediate a position between the two men who had taken sides against one another. The debate that had started as a political discussion on the Taliban government in Afghanistan had now shifted towards a debate about truth and honesty. Aftab, looking in the direction of Majid, started to contest the notion that Islamic governance (*islami hokumat*) was opposed to notions of morality in the West.

In London the boys and girls meet up (*mulaqat korik*) in the streets; in Chitral they do the same but in the thorny bushes at the edges of darkened riverbanks. People say that they fall in love, but all they want to do is kiss, and then something more. Our so-called (*bara-enam*) Muslim society is one that is dominated by lies, concealment, fraud and hypocrisy. We can't do anything truthfully (*haqiqata ispa kiagh koko no bosie*).

The comments Aftab makes here are complex and multi-dimensional. At one level they represent the ideas of the purist Muslim, a Jama'at-e Islami party supporter. He calls for the purification of Muslim thought and sees this purification as something that can be achieved only through more transparent practice. He labels the domain of the secret as immoral and corrupt: there is nothing spiritual about love, for its cause is sexual desire like that of animals. Yet his comment also has a surprising twist. Islamic regimes do not rid society of concealed immorality – the beards of the Taliban conceal what lies beneath the surface – and if humans have sexual desires they should have them in public in the streets of London and not the darkened bushes of Rowshan. Moreover, whilst deriding the domain of the secret, Aftab uses the word *haqaiqat* (truth) – an important concept in many of the great Persian Sufi texts. A modernist education in the social sciences far from instrumentally directing Aftab to think either in a 'secular' or Islamic 'revivalist' way, here creatively interacts with a knowledge of the concepts of the Persian Sufi canon. This interaction can be seen in the theories of human thought and action which Aftab frequently advanced in the village, and which I now explore.

For Aftab, it was local notions of politeness and civility that needed to be reformed, and the Jama'at-e Islami's attempts to Islamise Pakistan society from the top down could never work. However hard people tried to introduce Islamic government and law in Pakistan, he felt, hypocrisy would remain until people changed they way they thought and behaved. Aftab told his friends that the men and women he respected in the village were the honest (*froski*) who spoke 'from their hearts' (*hardiyar*), the kind and affectionate (*khuloos korak, rakhum dil*), and even those who were known as 'hot heads' (*khaka pech*), emotional (*jezbati*) and angry (*qahri*). Such folk, he argued, are true Muslims and human beings in that they do not try to conceal their thoughts and feelings in wily and greedy (*chalak ochen lalichi*) socially constructed styles of polite behaviour. Rather, they are honest to their natural (*qudrati*) emotions. It is emotions (*jezbat*), he believed, that lie at the heart of all human behaviour, and it is more honest to let emotions come to the surface than mask them in polite behaviour. Veils, beards, purdah, politeness – these are all things, for Aftab, that conceal natural emotions and authentic thoughts, and make living life a pack of lies. Aftab believed he had ideas about emotion that were not confined to the lives of the village's Muslims; and that he had an abstract notion of the role that emotion plays in human experience. His thinking combined some of the key concepts of the textual Sufi canon – especially the heart as a seat of truth (Corbin 1997: 221–45) – with a desire to construct modernist and social science generalising theories to explain human thought and action.

It is important to note here that Aftab had not always been thought of in the village as a man of critical and daring ideas. His ideas were seen as daring because at one level they questioned the extent to which traditions valued by some villagers were truly Islamic in nature. At a deeper level, they doubted even the very ideal of a state powered by a pure and perfect vision of Islamic law. Many in the village told me that they were unable to understand Aftab: 'At one glance he appears to be through and through religious; at another glance he seems to be free and relaxed (*ee loliko katar mazhabi, ee loliko azad*).' As a young man he was said to have been, like Majid, very religious-minded: he had never 'looked at girls', always opposed the drinking of alcohol and had been regular in saying his prayers. During this period of his life he had cultivated a name for being a 'through and through' (*katar*) supporter of the Jama'at-e Islam party. Aftab had actively sought to acquire a reputation as being 'religious-minded' and had, to a large degree, succeeded. Some Rowshan people had even accused Aftab of having become a 'man without religion' (*la din*), and others even said that he had become 'like a communist' (*communistghonie*). The views currently being expressed by Aftab, then, were the product of a transformation in the way that Aftab thought about his village and his religion, and this transformation was recognised by the villagers. Importantly, they show that there is a dimension of considered intellectual activity involved in the processes by which Rowshan people seek to acquire reputations in the village, and also in the way in which reputations are bestowed on them by others.

Aftab recognised that his 'thoughts had changed', and was also determined to change the minds and thinking of his friends. He told me that he visited Majid every evening in order to try and 'broaden his mind' (*dimagho wasigh korik*), and bring him over to his style of thinking. Aftab had even tried to persuade Majid to drink alcohol with him – although his attempts fell on deaf ears. Farhan was more sceptical. He told Aftab that his attempts to change the mind of Majid would never succeed: 'he is a calf at heart', he had told Aftab. 'Look at how strict his house is; however hard you try he'll never change the way he thinks.' The women of Majid's house had a reputation for keeping strict purdah. Majid's mother, in particular, was known as being a *rupush*: a woman who never left the compound of her house and was careful to ensure that no stranger ever cast his eyes upon her. In addition, Farhan told me, Majid read the Urdu-language Islamist magazine *Takbir*, and had similarly rigid opinions about Islam: not only did articles in this magazine criticise the West, but they also attacked the spiritual leader of the Ismai'lis, the Aga Khan. Writers in *Takbir*, apparently, had accused the Aga Khan of being a non-Muslim who drank alcohol and gambled. Farhan, then, imputed a form of power to the written word: this 'extremist' (*intiha pasand*) journal was seen as having the potential of stopping people from thinking critically, freely and independently. 'Wherever you find *Takbir*', he told me, 'you'll find people who are extremist and anti-Ismai'li.'

Rather than chaotic or disorganised, discussion in the village is concerned with a number of underlying themes – rationality, abstract thought and secrecy and revelation, and villagers think about these in relation to strikingly different dimensions of village life. Moreover, rather than avoiding fraught and contentious topics, many Rowshan people deploy their intellectual faculties to discuss the most sensitive of issues important in the village today. The changed emotional modes induced by such conversations, is one way in which villagers experience the joy of the play of the mind.

CONCLUSION

Many Rowshan people value the place that critical discussion and creative thought play in their lives, and they are critical of those whom they represent as being narrow-minded and emotional about religion. Indeed, the division in the village between those who are 'open-minded' (*khulao dimagho*) and those who are 'narrow-minded' (*trang dimagho*) is one that is highly significant to many Rowshan people. Moreover, this division is one that transcends – in certain contexts, and at particular moments – other important systems of categorisation in the village, such as uneducated and educated, Ismai'lis and Sunnis, young and old, and, in a complex, fraught and textured way, men and women. Yet the division between the open and narrow-minded folk in the village is not based on any crude set of standards, or an essentialising opposition between the West and the Muslim world. Even women who appear in public, and men who educate their wives, are accused of being, at heart, closed-minded. Indeed, open-mindedness and the leading of a serious Muslim life are not incompatible projects in the minds of many Rowshan people. Rather, villagers conceptualise critical conversation as something that requires a certain detachment, and a degree of momentary indifference, from what they talk about as 'personal' religious beliefs.

Gaining a reputation for being 'broad-minded', then, does not come easily, and nor does it come without its fair share of stress and anxiety. Not only are the standards that villagers set for 'open-minded' thought and behaviour complex and subtle, but so too are there many forces in the village that work to constrain the degree to which people can think and behave 'freely'. For many in the village, this array of forces is considered to be intellectually unhealthy, and to have the potential to disrupt the bodily and mental health of Rowshan people. It is folk who have low thoughts about women and purdah, people who read too many religious books, and villagers who are over-emotional about religion, who constrain the degree to which Rowshan is a place for the experiencing of the play of the mind. And rote systems of learning in school are accused of making 'bored' rather than mentally 'active' children.

I also found that women's acquisition of 'modern' knowledge is rapidly changing the definitions and standards regarding intelligence and the creative use of the intellect by women and, in some cases men, in the village. Acquiring education or seeking professional qualifications are partly a result of the economic difficulties being faced by the village's households. Yet they also have important intellectual outcomes, and new value judgements are emerging in Rowshan concerning the proper use of women's intellect. Women are not, then, only a focus of all-male debate and discussion in the village, but themselves exert a powerful influence on the intellectual life of the village. Moreover, the contribution of women to the intellectual life of the village does not manifest itself only in debates between women. Women also express their views and ideas in heated discussions with their male relatives, and discussions involving women.

are similar in content to those between males in the village, yet they are also often a reflection of different anxieties and concerns.

In addition to exploring the climate of intellectual activity in the village, this chapter has also sought to show that being intelligent in the minds of Rowshan people requires not only a fast mind and an ability to use words poetically, but also a heightened sense of bodily feeling and intuition. In order to understand the inner thoughts and intentions of others, people in the village must have the ability to go beyond the surface-level words and get to the sounds of the heart, for it is in the hidden depths of the heart that true thoughts are to be found.

It is the heart, and the sounds of the heart, which provide the focus of the next chapter. This will involve a discussion of music and poetry, and an exploration of the diverse ways in which people in Markaz set about the task of being Muslim.

CHAPTER 5

Mahfils *and musicians: new Muslims in Markaz*

My most respected and able listeners: love's name is the blossom of
the rose garden of the heart. With love's perfume life's hope is bright;
the garden of hope is green and related thoughts are allowed to fly
high and freely. Love is such a blessed thing that there is no
alternative.

Introduction to a commercially produced tape of one of the
musical programmes discussed in this chapter

INTRODUCTION

The audiocassette has a bad name in present day Pakistan. Religious organisations, movements and political parties in Pakistan have used audiocassettes to spread hatred and violence amongst Pakistan's Muslims. Recordings
of addresses by the leaders of Sunni and Shi'a religious paramilitary organisations call on people to identify those belonging to other than their own
communities as *kafirs* (infidels). They are told that it is their duty as Muslims
to wound their opponents so that they 'bleed for centuries'.[1] It will come as a
surprise, then, that the most popular audio cassettes in Chitral talk of the
'garden of the heart' (*ishqo gurzen*) and the 'high thoughts induced by love'
(*ishqo zhang khial*).[2]

This chapter seeks to document and theorise the power of music and
music-making in Chitral. By focusing on musical gatherings known as
mahfils and the commercial music recordings of these gatherings, I explore
the complex attitude towards the 'Islamic' displayed by Chitrali performers
and their audiences.[3] In a recent article on the so-called Islamic revival in

---

[1] On Sunni–Shi'a sectarianism in Pakistan, see Nasr 2000. On Sunni Ismai'li conflict in Chitral, see
chapter 7 below.
[2] On cassettes and popular music in North India, see Manuel 1993.
[3] On music and the anthropological study of Islam, see Stokes 2002. Anthropologists have explored
emerging musical styles in the Muslim world especially in their attempts to understand the processes

Cairo, Hirschkind argues that listening to tapes of Islamic sermons induces a 'moral state' that is articulated within the 'traditions of Islamic self-discipline' (Hirschkind 2001: 632). This state, Hirschkind suggests, has 'more to do with embodied capacities of gesture, feeling and speech than with obedience to rules or belief in doctrine' (632). He contrasts heightened moral states induced by the practice of listening to cassette recordings of religious sermons to the state of calm that his male informants said they experienced when listening to 'non-religious music'. In contrast to Hirschkind's work on Muslim morality in Egypt, this chapter documents the importance of music and dance in Chitral people's ideas of what it means to live a virtuous (*jam*) and intellectually significant (*hushiyar*) Muslim life in the urban setting of Markaz. It explores musical performance as an emerging and contested site where Chitral Muslims debate the relationship between local and global visions of a world made perfect by Islam.[4]

By focusing on a group of musical performers, this chapter identifies how musical life is an arena for the display and enjoyment of creative skill, and this is both surprising and important in a region of the world where religious authorities are often deeply hostile to music and dance.[5] Markaz lies only a two-hour drive from the Afghan border, and at the time of fieldwork the Taliban controlled over eighty percent of Afghanistan. The Taliban had offices in Chitral; their aims and goals were also supported by known 'men of learning and piety' influential in the region's mosques. Being Muslim in Chitral in a way that digresses from the calls to commitment towards these 'hardened' styles of Muslim identity is a statement that can evoke criticism and opposition from Islamists movements, organisations and figures that are powerful both in the region and beyond. Moreover, this criticism is itself invested with greater intensity and force by Pakistan's current political and religious culture. Blasphemy laws, introduced by the Islamising military government of General Zia ul Haq in the 1980s, are increasingly deployed against Muslims who question the purifying visions of Islam held by deeply conservative sections of the country's religious authorities.

Yet Chitral has a distinct musical tradition, which is unique to the region, and the sound of local music is an ever-present feature of life in

---

of urbanisation, nationalisation and migration. J. Bailey 1987, 1994 explores these themes in relation to music in the 1970s in the Afghan city of Herat. See Stokes 1992, 1994, 2002 for analyses of urbanisation, music and migration in Turkey.

[4] For a study of the interrelation of local and the global in Islam through the study of music, in the context of rural Egypt, see Zirbel 2000. Compare Goodman 1998.

[5] On poetry and poetic performance in the Middle East, see Caton 1990, Gilsenan 1996; Meeker 1979; Mills 1991; Shyrock 1997.

Chitral. Cassette players playing Khowar music are found in houses, mini-buses, and shops in the bazaar, and attending the musical programmes where these cassettes are recorded is a memorable moment for many men in the region. At the same time, the significance of the findings of this chapter should not be understood as being confined to Chitral alone: other Frontier peoples, including Pukhtuns, also have rich musical traditions, and, as in Chitral, one of the central components of such musical traditions is the love song (*ghazal*). Yet the anthropological study of the intersection between musical and literary creativity and religious life remains undeveloped by scholars of present day Pakistan, and this has had serious implications for our understanding of the form of the Islamic tradition in the region.

So, it is through an analysis of music that I provide insight into the much-debated phenomenon of how Muslims handle and respond to the pressures to 'Islamise'. What I seek to show here is that this process entails active 'resistance' to puritanical visions of Islam. However, the musicians and performers in Chitral who engage in this 'resistance' cannot simply be categorised as Sufis fighting anti-Sufis, or traditionalists resisting reform-minded Muslims, or secularists objecting to the aims and goals of politically oriented Islamists.[6] Rather, in Markaz, many Muslims show a deep – if informal – knowledge of a rich literary heritage of classic Persian Sufi texts.[7] This knowledge is pervasive and visible in what they say and do: in particular, the music they perform and listen to is deeply influenced by this dimension of the Islamic tradition. Their love and respect for this body of textual knowledge is also clearly evident in the many ways in which they are engaging with the forces of scriptural and purifying Islam powerful in the region today. The literary knowledgeability of many Chitral Muslims has played a major role in directing the uneven impact that movements of Islamic reform and purification have had on the region. Yet, whilst the music performed at these gatherings is deeply influenced by the writings of the great Persian Sufis, especially Sa'di, Rumi and Hafiz, the gatherings themselves are not easily compared with other important South Asian manifestations of Sufi Islam such as worshipping at shrines, or adherence to Sufi brotherhoods.[8] Indeed, many of the performers we meet in this

---

[6] See McKenna 1998 for a complex account of resistance among the Moros Muslims of the Philippines, and on resisistance to orthodox Islam in Niger, see Masquelier 2001. On resistance and women's lives in Egypt, see Abu-Lughod 1990.

[7] Compare Andreyev's (1999) account of knowledge of Sufi concepts in 'highly illiterate' Pukhtun tribal society in the sixteenth century.

[8] On music and Sufi worship at shrines in India and Pakistan, see Qureshi 1995, 2000. For historical accounts on the intellectual dimensions of the experience of Sufi Islam in South Asia, see, for instance, Eaton 1996 [1978], especially ch. 6.

chapter are themselves supporters of parties and movements of Islamic reform and purification, and it is the significance of these complex concatenations of Islamic knowledge and ways of being Muslim that I seek to document and analyse here.

SMALL TOWN ISLAM IN NORTHERN PAKISTAN

The population of Markaz is about 20,000. Markaz is an old and important settlement: at the bank of the Chitral River that runs around and through the town is sited the impressive fort (*noghor*) where the hereditary dynast (*mehtar*) of Chitral once lived and presided over his court. Indeed, the former rulers wealthy and politically influential descendants, the princes (*shahzdagan*) continue to inhabit this fort today when they return from their houses in Pakistan's cities during the summer months. Next to the fort is the Chitral region's largest and most elegantly decorated mosque, the *badshahi ma'jid* (royal mosque), built by Chitral's ruling family in the first half of the twentieth century. The long-term inhabitants of Markaz are entirely Sunni. The only Ismai'lis who live in Markaz come from Chitral's northern regions and villages, and work in the offices of government and non-governmental agencies established there.

The population of Markaz is more diverse than that of Rowshan. There are many male, short-term Pukhtun traders especially from the Swat and Bajaur regions of the Frontier Province, and Afghan refugee families who have been settled there since the beginning of the Afghan resistance to the Soviets in 1979. There is some intermarriage between Pukhtun, Afghan and Chitrali Muslims living in Markaz, although most Chitrali families prefer to 'give' their daughters to other Khowar-speaking families. For many Khowar-speaking people in Markaz the rapid influx of Pukhtuns and Afghans into the town over the past twenty years has been a negative development. It is these 'outsiders' (*berieo roi*) who have been accused of bringing violence, theft, drugs and 'hardened' (*sakht*) Islamist views and values into what is remembered by many in the town as being a peaceful and relaxed 'village' (*deh*).

The town is also an important trading centre for the Chitral district and neighbouring regions of Afghanistan, especially Badakshan, Shughnan and Nuristan. As a result it has Chitral's biggest bazaar where Chitrali, Pukhtun and Afghan merchants have shops and small businesses. Those who visit the bazaar are mostly men, and it is rare to see a woman there. There are Afghan-owned 'hotels' (eating-houses) selling Afghan-style rice and grilled kebabs. Some shops deal in cloth brought to Chitral by truck from Lahore and Karachi, whilst others sell locally made woollen (*schoo*) products such as waistcoats, the local cap (*pakol*), and long winter coats (*chugha*) and shawls (*zhil*). Small hotels provide accommodation to travellers (*musafiran*) and traders (*karubari roi*) from Chitral and other regions of Pakistan visiting Markaz. These hotels do a thriving business: Markaz's small bazaar is always packed full of people from the region's remote villages who are trying to complete 'some small piece of work' (*phuk korum*), usually getting permits and national identity cards, in the government offices located in the town. Whilst there is no major manufacturing industry in Markaz, there is a thriving Pukhtun-dominated transport business, several mechanical businesses, and a small airport: people come to Markaz from all areas of Chitral when making the long trip to 'down Pakistan' (*aff pakistan*).

The presence of the bazaar and the merchant *bazaaris* who work there is an important feature of life in the town, and one that distinguishes it from 'village life' (*deho zindagi*) elsewhere in Chitral. The bazaar, in the eyes of both people from Chitral and my friends from Rowshan, is 'hot' (*garam*), and full of 'strangers' (*nagoni*) making it a dangerous (*khatarnark*) and unpredictable place. It is also often said by townsfolk and by villagers visiting the town, to be dominated by the 'religious-minded' (*mazhabi dimagho roi*) and as the place in which 'malicious gossip' (*shum lu*) is incubated and spread. The town's *bazaaris* are known for being particularly strict in the ways they go about leading a Muslim life they lead. Even men driving their vehicles through the narrow bazaar lanes are always careful to turn off any music they have playing in their vehicles so as to avoid incurring the wrath of the bazaar's 'bearded-ones' (*rigishweni*) and 'men of learning and piety' (Khowar: *dashmanan*; Urdu and Arabic: *ulama*).

It is particularly the 'religious scholars' (*ulama*) who control the bazaar's mosques (*ma'jid*) who have cultivated a reputation for being 'hardened' (*sakht*) and 'extremist' (*intihai pasand*) in their approaches to Islam. Men who are said to be 'drinkers' (*sharabi*) are named in the sermons of the bazaar's mosques and publicly denounced for having 'stepped outside the fold of Islam' (*islamar nishienisie asuni*).[9] Even households in which musical gatherings are held are described by religious scholars in their addresses as having 'reached infidelity' (*kufra torie asuni*). These religious scholars have had considerable success in imposing their power and

---

[9] See Gaffney 1994 for an account of Egyptian mosque addresses, and Antoun 1989 on sermons made in rural Jordan.

authority on life in the bazaar, and those who act against their dictates are the focus of critical comment.

In the 'fraught environment' (*tez mahaul*) of Chitral bazaar, townspeople engage in subtle strategising projects in order to navigate a path through the dictates of Chitral's 'bearded ones'. However, despite Chitral Muslims' carefully calculated efforts, the threat of dishonour and violence remains for those who fail to abide by the pronouncements of the *ulama*.

In the days leading up to Eid in December 2000, for instance, a number of men had decided that the best way of buying clothes for their daughters, wives and sisters was by taking them to the bazaar under the cover of darkness. Shopkeepers (*dukandaran*) were telephoned and told to keep their shops open until late at night in order to allow women to enter the bazaar in privacy and under the veil of darkness. The next day, however, the *imam* (prayer leader) of one of the bazaar's mosques delivered a sermon in which he told worshippers that 'bad things are reaching my ears; women have been seen in this bazaar'. He told the men assembled in the mosque that they should forcibly marry (*zoro sora nikah korelik*) any women they saw in the bazaar in the future. Marriages where women appeared in public, he told them, are *najaiz* (illegitimate) and the breaking of purdah means the ending of a marriage. Chitral's more 'relaxed' (*azad*) men were once again forced to make tiring and repetitive trips to the bazaar in order to cater to the complex clothing requirements of their 'fashion-minded' (*fashnie*) sisters, daughters and wives. Markaz's *dashmanan* were said during these days to be men of 'empty words' (*khali lu*), and were said to be saying such things in order to 'make the lives of Markaz people even more difficult'. While annulling the marriages of the townsfolk was largely conceptualised by Chitral people as being beyond the capacities of the *ulama*, they were thought to be capable of even dirtier (*gandah*) criminality (*badmashi*). Many of the shopkeepers obeyed the dictates of the mullahs. Those who did not feared that their stores would be burned by scoundrels (*badmashan*) given money by the mullahs if they opened up for women in the evenings. Indeed, during my fieldwork a number of shops and houses with satellite dishes were burned, and it was widely rumoured that the *dashmanan* were behind these attacks.

Yet, even in Markaz, there is no rigid and irresistable 'Islamisation' requiring deference to strict, Taliban-style norms. Markaz dwellers actually live amid a wide range of different degrees and versions of 'Islamic' norms. Outside of the bazaar (*bazarar nishie*), women are able to visit their relatives and attend school by walking along secluded paths through village fields that men should avoid. A man seen walking along one of these paths is in danger of being shouted at by village people and accused of being there to 'look at girls'. This is something that would be the cause of deep 'disrespect' (*beizzat*) and 'shame' (*sharum*) for any self-respecting man living in the Town. These paths are certainly out-of-bounds to 'strangers' (*nagonie*) and 'outsiders' from other villages in Chitral district and other regions of Pakistan. Some of the villages and hamlets that make up the residential areas of Markaz lie only a two-minute walk from the bazaar. It is in the guesthouses of these villages where the musical gatherings that are discussed in this chapter are performed and recorded before the cassettes are sold in the bazaar.

THE NOBLES

What is a musical gathering (*mahfil*) in Markaz, how do Markaz dwellers go about hosting such an event in the highly charged atmosphere of the town, and why is music such an important part of living a creative Muslim life in the region?

It is certainly notable that in a town in Pakistan so close to the Afghanistan border music and creative performance are central to village and town life. When the Taliban took control of Kabul in 1996, images of their destruction of music cassettes and displays of unreeled video and audio tape on roadside trees and bushes were disturbing for many observers in the West.[10] Yet music continues to be an ever-present feature of life in Chitral: audiocassettes of music play in buses, jeeps, and in the region's households. There is also a vibrant and varied culture of public musical performance in the region: this involves frequent outdoor and public musical programmes (*general ishtok*), as well as semi-public and private household performances (*mahfil*).

As was seen in chapter 3, being 'noble' (*sharif*) and 'polite' (*jam*) is an important feature of selfhood and day-to-day life in the region. Yet being polite and hospitable is also a morally fraught domain of Chitral life, and Chitral people complain of experiencing a high degree of anxiety (*pereshani*) and tension (*tensien*) in their daily lives. By documenting musical programmes attended by one of Chitral's most popular musical groups, I show how such gatherings constitute one especially important arena in which the constraints and worries of life in Chitral are dissolved. The men who attend these gatherings enjoy an atmosphere less saturated by concerns

[10] Of course, *ulama*-led opposition to musical performance has for long been an important dimension of debate in Muslim societies. See, for instance, Newman 1999.

of status, politeness and etiquette, and experience a momentary break from the stressful daily lives they lead.

There is also, however, an important religious dimension to these gatherings – the men sitting at the gathering experience moments of peaceful (*sukoon*) and trance-like 'intoxication' (*nasha*) induced by the relaxed atmosphere (*amano mahaul*) of the event and the 'beautiful words and sounds' (*sheli alfazochen havaz*) of the music being performed.[11] This is important to the general argument of this book: Islam's 'mystical strain' (Arkoun 1994: 81), Sufism, remains a vivid feature of life in a context where Islamic reform movements and organisations that are deeply hostile towards Sufi styles of Islamic practice and thought are influential. But there are many different ways of embracing Sufism in Islam, and while these entail a spectrum of both more and less 'textual' devotion, Islam's mystical strain in the subcontinent often takes concrete form around worship at the shrine complexes of holy men (*pirs*).[12] Where reform-minded Muslims have sought to combine the intellectual traditions of Sufi Islam with the need to purify Muslim practice according to Islamic law (*shari'a*), they have usually done so within the framework of a Sufi brotherhood.

In Markaz, unlike other neighbouring regions of the Frontier and Afghanistan, there are no major shrine-cults, and no major tradition of adherence to Sufi brotherhoods (*tariqas*).[13] Most Sunni Muslims in Markaz claim that they are Deobandi, and most of the town's influential *ulama* have received formal religious training in Deobandi religious colleges (*madrasas*). At its inception, the Deobandi 'school' of Islamic theology, established in India in 1867, had close connections with Sufi brotherhoods important in South Asia, such as the Chishtis. By the 1920s, however, its style (*maslak*) of Islamic theology became increasingly hostile to what Deobandi scholars saw as Hinduised Sufi practices such as the worship of saints at shrines, as well as more localised traditions (*rewaj*) which they denounced as illegal innovations (*bid'ah*).[14] These dimensions of Deobandi teachings have been further intensified over the last thirty years as Deobandi *madrasas* in Pakistan have received much funding from organisations and governments seeking to promote strictly purist visions of

---

[11] Compare Racy 2003 11–13 on ecstatic responses to musical performance in an array of Arab settings.

[12] The *pirs* of South Asia have, of course, often sought to use their mystical influence and power for political ends. On the role played by *pirs* in Sind at the time of partition, see Ansari 1992. On political decisions made by *pirs* in the Punjab in the same era, see Talbot 1996 and Gilmartin 1988. On Sufism and 'the state' in present day Pakistan, see Ewing 1983 and Verkaaik 2004.

[13] See Edwards 1996 for a discussion of Sufi practice in eastern Afghanistan.

[14] See Metcalf 1978, 1982 on the Deobandi style (*maslak*) of Islamic theology. Compare Sanyal 1996 on the Barelwi Islamic movement.

Islam powerful in Gulf countries such as Saudi Arabia (Kepel 2002; Metcalf 2004; Zaman 2002). Moreover, with the rise of the Taliban in Afghanistan, many Deobandi scholars vehemently decried music as 'infidelity' (*kufr*), and musical performance and dance as *najaiz* (impermissible) in Islam. In this setting of profound 'Islamisation' I seek to explain the significance of music in living a Muslim life in Chitral.

The musical group discussed in this chapter call themselves, in untranslated English, the 'Nobles'. The Nobles are a musical group of performers and poets based in the headquarters of Chitral district, Markaz. The composition of the Nobles is fluid, but they usually number about eight performers, five poets and a further four other 'members'. Whilst the performers (*fankaran*) of the group have been playing with each other in various combinations for many years, the group adopted the name Nobles in January 2001. The Nobles are amateur musicians (*shauqin fankaran*) who perform because of their own 'interest' (*shauq*) in music not because they are to make any financial reward. They do not receive money for their performances. They play for those who invite them to private and semi-public musical gatherings in their homes only as a result of their love of music, and they would often tell me that their main reason for performing was to 'make others happy'. Indeed, when not playing in the guesthouses of their friends, these musicians worked as shopkeepers, farmers, medical assistants, forestry officers, telephone exchange operators, and in the police force. Moreover, it is critical to note that despite the groups' name, whilst some of the performers come from lordly backgrounds many of them do not, and this self-parody is a further dimension of the Nobles' distinct identity in the region.

The Nobles are Chitral's most popular group of performers of local Khowar-language music, and their success has made them local celebrities known throughout the district. There are two other popular groups of musicians in Markaz who, like the Nobles, record their music on audiocassettes for sale in the region's bazaars. There is great competition between these groups, yet, during my stay in Chitral, the Nobles were the most popular group of performers in the region. Their songs are known to people living in even the most remote villages of Chitral: the songs of the Nobles are recorded onto audio cassettes and sold in the small music shops in the towns and villages of the Chitral region, and aspiring groups of musicans play the music of the Nobles in their own impromptu programmes in the winter months. Moreover, Chitralis living far away from their homeland (*watan*) in cities like Karachi are always sure to tell friends or relatives visiting them to bring with them a copy of the Nobles' latest cassette. The music of the Nobles, I was told by music shop owners, sells faster than even the recordings of India's Bollywood film industry. The Nobles mostly sing *ghazals* (love songs) recently written by members of the group who are experts in the art of both composing and performing love poetry.

Those who enjoy listening to the music of The Nobles are not confined only to Chitral's 'village boys' (*deho daqan*) and 'college students' (*colliget*). The region's influential politicians, high-placed Chitrali civil servants, doctors and medical workers, engineers, wealthy lawyers, and even the occasional 'broad-minded' Chitrali *'alim*, also often want to be associated with the group and its activities. Many women and girls in Chitral also keep in touch with the music of the Nobles, through the cassettes and sometimes videos of the group's musical programmes. And after I had made a video recording of a Nobles programme, when I returned to Rowshan the women of the village would be particularly keen for me to show them my recording on their television sets.

Gatherings (*mahfil*) attended by the Nobles are ideally 'civilised' (*muhazab, tahzibi yafata*) and polite (*sharif*). There are other musical programmes popular in Chitral at which professional musicians play a reed instrument (the *surnai*) and beat large drums (*dol*). These programmes are known as 'plays' (*ishtok*) and have a reputation for being rowdy and raucous (*weshirow*) events where drinking and fighting are part and parcel of the evening's entertainment. The *dom* (Chitral's professional musicians) play at this kind of event, and they are most often called upon to play at marriages and in celebration of the victory of polo teams in local tournaments. The musical programmes at which they perform are attended by hundreds of men and boys who descend on the 'place of happiness' (*khoshanio zhaghar*) in jeeps and on foot from villages often many miles away. Respectable men are often enjoined not to venture to such 'plays': sitting on the floor and watching men dance in the company of drunkards (*sharabi*) and hashish-smokers (*bongi*) is not something a 'man of respect' (*izzatman mosh*) should be seen to enjoy.

The Nobles are always keen to emphasise that the programmes at which they perform should be referred to by those involved as *mahfil* meaning 'gathering' and not as unrefined (*behuda, weshirau*) 'plays'. They go to great lengths to ensure that their musical programmes have a reputation for being civilised, cultured and proper. Many Nobles members and supporters frown upon those who drink alcohol before a 'gathering'. Indeed, now when one buys a Nobles cassette in the bazaar before the music starts there is always an announcement saying that the Nobles seek to promote the playing of Khowar music in 'an environment free of the curse of intoxication' (*nasha'ar pak mahaula*). Such ideals are not always strictly followed – on more than one occasion, 'free' (*azad*) Noble friends of mine enjoying a pre-performance drink in secrecy and behind closed doors, received dirty looks (*dish poshak*) when their stricter (*sakht*) friends stumbled in on their closed gatherings. Drinking alcohol, then, is a further fraught domain of living a virtuous life in Chitral. For those in the drinking circle, men who are ready to conform to the anti-alcohol strictures of Chitral's *ulama* are often said to be unsophisticated, anti-social and donkey-like (*gordoghonie*) men unable to understand the deeper pleasures of life.[15] There is, then, no simple division between having fun and being pious in the context of the *mahfils* of Markaz, and taking part in creative intellectual and bodily activity can here combine with an emphasis on God-fearing Islamic self-discipline.

The form a *mahfil* or *ma'jlis* attended by the Nobles Group of Chitral takes is fairly standardised. Gathering in the early evening, the members of the group and their entourage usually numbering about twenty travel to the evening's destination by the usual mode of transportation in Chitral – the jeep. Before setting off there are usually debates about who should have the honour of sitting in the front seat of the vehicle: taking the front seat is a mark of considerable status in Chitral. Self-respecting men never dream of sitting in the dusty rear section of the vehicle: clothes especially washed and ironed for the evening's programme will become soiled (*schute*) and creased (*krenj*) in the cramped seats in the back of the vehicle. By the same token, you cannot push yourself forward too obviously as a front seat passenger. Men pull on each other's arms and clothes in order to persuade them to take the prized front-seat, and politely refuse to sit down until all are seated in their places.

The Nobles almost always perform inside private houses, as they say that it is impossible to play good music in the open. On arriving at the house where the programme is due to be held the performers and other guests, sometimes numbering as many as fifty, will be met by their host (*mezban*), and will then be ushered in to a large room (*hall*). As purdah is observed strictly by all households in Markaz, the men visiting the house will not meet, see or hear any of the girls or women living there, unless they are related to them. Some of the women in the household, however, may take a quick peep at these local celebrities through windows covered in mosquito netting or from the tops of distant walls.

---

[15] See R. Tapper 2001 on drinking in the Middle East.

The early stages of the evening are characterised by the concerns of politeness, respect and etiquette that are a central feature of daily life in Chitral. Barth, in his study of sociality in the Omani city of Sohar emphasises the 'fantastic "tea party" politeness of all social interaction in town'. The importance of politeness in Sohar seems in many ways similar to the emphasis on etiquette and self-control explored in this chapter. Barth describes a code of politeness in Sohar that 'demands self-control rather than the control of others' and that 'appropriate behaviour towards others is a tactful and constructive attentiveness to their situation and their susceptibilities' (Barth 1983: 98–9). This self-control is an important dimension of the early stages of a *mahfil.* As chapter 4 demonstrated, however, conversation in the village setting of Rowshan is about more than the formulaic exchange of polite utterances. So here I document how despite the emphasis on etiquette the musical gathering is a further domain of life where Chitral Muslims experience the play of the mind. The play of the mind in this context is enriched by the intellectual traditions brought by the region's Muslims to Chitral music and poetry, as well as the experience of altered bodily states.

The guests and host must now decide who to invite to take the position of honour as the chief guest (*mehman-e khusoosi*) and sit at the 'upper side' (*turi nishik*) of the fireplace (*bukhari*). Yet being the evening's chief guest is more than an indication of a man's respect, and the man asked to take a seat in the special place will be required to make good conversation (*mash-kulqei*), recite interesting tales (*qissa*) and tell comical jokes (*qafiya*). An enjoyable gathering must begin with lively conversation, and the onus on initiating this falls on the chief guest. The discussion now beginning, however, is also punctuated by displays of politeness, and each time a man enters the room those assembled will stand and try to persuade the newcomer to sit on the floor 'above' them. Even if a man leaves the room to wash his hands or perform ablutions before prayers, as he enters the room all will stand up. The man will tell his friends, 'Why are you going to such trouble? Sit down, sit down, you are making me feel shy.' If a man stands up to pour himself a glass of water others in the room will reprimand him for not having asked them to do it for him, and before he drinks from the glass he will offer the water (*sat korik*) to all those sitting around him.

If the *mahfil* is to be successful this polite behaviour that is a routine and exhausting feature of everyday life in Chitral must come to an end: no *mahfil* can ever be successful and 'hot' (*garam*) if the people in attendance are feeling 'bored' (*bor*), 'serious' (*sanjidah*) or 'troubled' (*pereshan*). If the men now sitting in the guesthouse do not start to feel 'free' (*azad*) then the musical gathering is likely to be a disappointing failure.

Before the music can begin, however, the men present who want to say their prayers are encouraged to do so by one of the more 'religious-minded' (*mazhabi dimagho*) men present. With so many men and boys present it means that prayers must be said collectively, and that they must be led and recited aloud by one of the *mahfil*-goers. Most men stand to say their prayers. I always had some company at this stage of the evening, however. Despite the fact that men dress up in washed and newly ironed clothes for the evening's music, some gave the standard excuse (*bahna*) that their 'clothes were not fit for prayer' (*zap benamaz sheni*), and these men sat and chatted with me as we watched the others at prayer.

The men in attendance always made sure that they chose a man who was sufficiently 'religious-minded' to lead the prayers. Thus, a man who was always fingering his rosary beards (*dazbean hosta ganie*), kept a beard (*rigish*), and often ushered the phrases *allah tu ee*! (Allah you are one!), *allahu akbar*! (God is Great!), and *ya allah! ya mohammad*! (Oh Allah! Oh Mohammad!), will often be asked out of respect for his deep faith and religiosity to lead the prayers. Even the choice of man to lead the prayers will often result in a long and protracted debate: should a younger and educated man lead the prayers, or should he leave it to a more elderly and pious man to stand up before the assembled worshippers?

That men play and pray in the same room is in stark contrast to the account that Werbner presents of the ways in which British Pakistanis 'frame' spaces so as to separate 'the profane from the sacred, the pure from the impure' (Werbner 2002: 191). Werbner shows how 'music, dance, humour and sensuality are distanced from the religious activities focussed upon the mosque or the sobriety of Pakistani national commemorations' (Werbner 2002: 191). In the *mahfils* of Markaz the framing of space and time is complex. Islamic piety meets Islamic fun in the same room over the textured and changing course of an evening gathering. *Mahfil*-goers do not make any simple binary distinctions between the enjoyment of the experience and display of creative intellectual prowess, on the one hand, and bodily activity and sober Islamic thought and practice, on the other.

Having attempted to mark the stamp of Islam on the *mahfil*, those gathered now try to make relations with one another more intimate: this they do by sitting together and sharing in Chitral people's favourite food item – rice (*pakhti*). The men sit cross-legged in a square around the *dastarkhan* (a colourful piece of material), which is spread on the floor and laden with pots of curry and dishes of rice. The men and boy have their hands washed by boys who carry the *chilim chin* (a metal water pourer) to each of the guests in turn. In an act of deep respect and servitude for his guest that reflects court etiquette, the boy pours water onto the guest's hands holding a dish beneath to catch the dirty water that runs off. The evening meal is then served quickly, and eaten speedily and largely in quiet. Men sitting next to each other may murmur quietly to each other, and comment on the tastiness of the rice and the deliciousness of the chicken. The concern with public shows of politeness and deference remains important and visible: the host will usually not eat, instead standing above his guests and ordering his young sons and nephews to make sure that pots of food are delivered to the guests' empty plates. He reprimands the young boys if they fail to recognise that one of the guests' glasses has become empty of water or a plate short of food. The guest chosen to receive the chicken breast (*paz*) knows that he is one of the most respected men in attendance.

Hospitality is a source of considerable friction and conflict in Chitral. Many men in Chitral spend much time trying to persuade their friends to give them an 'invite' (*da'awat*) for a meal at their house. 'We are waiting for your invite and your kind offer to slaughter a chicken and cook some of your home-grown rice', is the usual tactic employed by a man to test a friend's sincerity and patience.[16] The man who never invites his friends quickly gets a reputation for being 'stingy' (*kanjoos*), whilst a man who is seen only to invite people whom he thinks he can 'get something from' is known as *matlabi* (selfish) and a snob (*schokh*).

The preparations for the meal will have been going on inside the house. The women of the house will be under intense pressure to ensure the food they are cooking is both tasty and ready at the right time. The house will be in a state of *kitigin* (chaos) as women desperately try to cook food on the large and smoky wood fire in the central hearth (*dang*) of the house. These women will be informed by the evening's tense host that the guests have arrived and are sitting and awaiting their meal. The host's reputation is now at stake: he will tell his household members that their 'close and respected' relatives are present, that a particularly 'important' (*aham*) influential man is in their house, and that men from Chitral's most respected families (*khandani roye*) are amongst those gathered and awaiting their food. Nobody wants any of the guests to leave their house 'in a sulk' (*kruee bik*) having felt insulted by his hosts, and all must be sensitive to the needs and moods of their guests. Guests will be constantly asked if they are

[16] As I showed in ch. 2, the expense of hospitality is a deeply stressful domain of moral decision-making for many Chitral people. See Lindholm 1982 on hospitality in the life of the Swat Pukhtuns and Ortner 1978 on the dilemmas of hospitality and 'getting something' amongst Nepali Sherpas.

'sitting comfortably or in pain', 'if they are feeling bored', or 'whether they are tired'.

Even a slip-up in the food presented to the guests has the potential of igniting tempers inside the house. The women preparing the food in the house will be most concerned that their rice is 'eatable' (*zhibiko bash*), that it is sufficiently salted (*troup biti sher*), and that the oil poured over the rice at the end of the cooking process (*dagh korik*) gives the rice the desired texture. They know that rice that is insufficiently salted (*wetroupo pakhti*), served with tough and unpalatable meat (*dongu pushoor*), and burned bread (*puleiru shapeek*), will all be the subject of sly comment by the evening's guests. The women in the house send the children on frequent visits to the guesthouse to make sure that the food they have worked hard to prepare is being enjoyed by the evening's guests. They will be anxious to know if the men are able to eat the meat, whether they want more rice, or if they are complaining about the burned vegetables. The women who cooked the meal themselves usually see little of the evening's feast, and little or none of the musical proceedings.

The assembled men, with stomachs full (*ishkamah akhti biti*), and more relaxed in one another's company, are now creating an atmosphere (*mahaul*) less strained with concerns of polite behaviour (*suluk*) and conversation. They lie stretched on the carpeted floor, some perhaps 'pulling' (*zhingeik*) on a cigarette, and conversation is more spontaneous and less focused on the occasion's 'chief guest' (*mehman-i khusoosi*).[17]

The *mahfil* is now set to begin. The evening's proceedings commence with the *comparer* (announcer), a member of the Nobles, welcoming the guests to the evening's event and naming especially respectable men seated in the audience. The *comparer* reminds the audience that the *mahfil* is taking place in 'an environment pure and free from the curse of intoxication' under the auspices of the Nobles Group of Chitral. He introduces the performers one by one by their names and nicknames, and the musicians are asked to start to play their *hardi chokonu havaz* (heart catching sounds). The Noble's main singer, for instance, is announced as the *bulbul-e chitrar* (the nightingale of Chitral). Before the first song is performed it is usual that the poet who wrote the lyrics will be named and introduced, and a few *band* (lines) from his work are also recited. This introductory part of the programme is recorded onto audiocassettes along with the musical performance itself that will eventually be made available for sale in the many shops in the region that specialise in the sale of music.

---

[17] See R. Tapper 2001 on 'pulling' tobacco in Muslim societies.

The musicians now begin playing. One or two men play the Chitrali sitar, one moves his fingers and palm across an empty petrol container (*jeer can*) that has been especially selected for having melodious sounds, another beats gently with two small sticks on small twin drums (*damama*); and a further taps a large tambourine (*daf*). The sitarists slowly pluck the strings of their sitars, and the percussionists rhythmically tap their instruments, whilst the singer sings in thin (*bariki*) and delicate (*nazuk*) tones. The singer changes the sound of his voice, sometimes singing deeply and at other times in such high-pitched tones that those listening are often 'amazed' and say that he sounds 'just like a girl' (*kumoroghon tan*).[18] The audience sits and gently rocks to the music, click their fingers, quietly clap their hands, and sometimes sing along underneath their breath with the musicians.

After a particularly moving or evocative line many sitting in the room will reflect on the words and the music with deep sighs (*shar istonik*) or exclamations of *wah wah, hai hai* and *ah ha*. Most people in the audience will sit in silence gazing raptly at the musicians and totally involved in the music. At the end of a *ghazal* (love song), however, the more confident men in the room will often repeat their favourite lines, and show their depth of understanding of the words by telling the audience the meanings encapsulated by the 'complex' (*pechidah*) and 'deep' (*kulum*) poetry. Listening to the music requires, then, a subtle combination of thoughtful reflection and honed sensory capacities.

Love poetry is an old and famous feature of Chitral culture and draws on a widely shared knowledge of classical Persian verse and literary material, and the existence of a large body of Khowar poetry dating back at least two centuries.[19] This poetry remains an active living tradition of poetic and musical composition and performance, and poets in Chitral today both write new versions of old poems as well as totally new works. The poetry and songs themselves are rich in the words and images of classical Persian Sufi poetry, and Chitral's poets themselves compare their writings to the works of the great Persian poets, especially Rumi, Sa'di and Hafiz.[20] The profane and spiritual worlds are juxtaposed, and the beloved's power over the poet is explicitly conveyed in

---

[18] In their 'feminising' colonial depictions of Chitral people (Nandy 1990) scholar-soldiers often noted the 'high-pitched' singing of the region's boys. '[T]wo boys sit down by the fire to sing, beginning with one high-pitched, long sustained note, and then continuing with the shakes and quavers so admired in the East ... The two boys press together and comport themselves like shy little maidens, whom they frequently resemble also in being pretty and feminine looking' (Robertson 1998 [1899]: 8–9).

[19] The British colonial scholar-official Kennion notes, 'The passion these people have for music and dancing is extraordinary, and this is not as a spectacle, but as a pastime' (Kennion 1910: 8).

[20] On the interregional role played by Persian language in South Asian Muslim religiosity, identity and thought, see, especially, Alam 1998; Cole 2002; Lawrence 1999; Robinson 1991, 1997.

terms recognised as close to the power of God himself.[21] This is how spiritual powers (*ruhani taqeat*) are conventionally represented in Persian and Urdu verse, and this use of religious metaphor is what makes the verse so powerful and moving to many Muslims in Chitral.[22] Persian phrases and words that are said to be especially 'sweet' (*shirin*) are frequently incorporated into the Khowar poetry. For instance, the Persian phrase *bad-e saba*, meaning morning breeze, is often used in Khowar love poetry, as are references to the 'orchard of love' (*ishqo gurzen*). Listeners often comment how beautiful (*sheli*) they find hearing such Persian phrases. Whilst many Chitral people do not know the meaning of the more complex Persian phrases, when listening to the cassettes of the Nobles they often ask 'intelligent' men sitting with them to translate them into Khowar. The love of Persian language and poetic form in Chitral is important: as early as the eighteenth century Sunni revivalists scholars in India called upon Muslims to identify themselves with an 'Arab'-derived religious orientation, and to purge their literary and cultural traditions of 'corrupt' and 'un-Islamic' Persianate influences.[23] Yet, known and often loved, this material forms a key part of Chitral's cultural heritage, and many Chitral Muslims, especially those in groups like the Nobles, cherish the place that Persian literary forms occupy in their lives.

In what follows I translate a number of hitherto untranslated love songs composed during my stay in Chitral by members of the Nobles from Khowar and performed at the programmes documented in this chapter.

Ju baso ta dostio muzhi
Haiya ulfatio mastio muzhi
Anwazo gan paighamo alai
Bedardohe salaamo alai
In the two days of your friendship
In the intoxication of this love
The breeze of spring carried a message
It carried a salaam devoid of your love

[21] Colonial scholars also noted that much Khowar song focused on love and the experience of love. '[A] sitar-player will sing of love, begging someone or other "speak so low for *her* heart is tender", and declaring that his beloved one is so ideal and rare that she cannot bear the weight of even one diamond!' (Robertson 1998 [1899]: 7).

[22] On the dissemination of Sufi teachings and Persian phrases in India through local languages, see Schimmel 1999: 418–19. On Persian and Urdu mystical poetry, see Schimmel 1975, 2001. Persian poetic form underwent considerable development and change during the sixteenth and seventeeth centuries in the 'syncretic and unconventional atmosphere of India' (Cole 2002: 20). Many Persian poets, considered trivial by Iran's Safavid ruler's, migrated to India where they developed a style of poetry that combined in complex ways classical Persian potery and Indian literary norms, see Cole 2002: 21.

[23] The 'outstanding leader' of the 'Islamic revival' in India, Shah Wali-ullah, called upon Indian Muslims to recognise their 'Arabic genealogy' (Robinson 2000: 216–17).

Another popular and new *ghazal* written by a Noble member in January 2001 and regularly sung at the programmes they attend, begins:

Chan chorio sharana ee chan ma zindagi
Katibe taqedire no zhan ma zindagi
Tu umre aziz ju bas birai resan
Ju baso prazghara no zhan ma zindagi
In the orchard of autumn one fallen leaf is my life
Oh the writer of my destiny how you have turned my life upside down
You are saying that this great life is of only two days
Even morning dew of two days turns my life upside down.

These love songs draw, then, on a fairly standardised of images and phrases in Persian and Khowar, but listeners (*sami'eenan*) are also critical of the words they hear, and there is great emphasis on the importance of using novel rhetorical devices in Khowar poetry. Listeners often comment on the extent to which the writings of Chitral's love poets are the product independent intellectual work, or, merely, translations of famous Persian and Urdu poems into Khowar. During my stay in Chitral, one poet was accused not only of plagiarising the great Persian mystical poet Rumi, but also of copying the works of other Khowar poets. There are often highly sophisticated discussions among listeners of this complex issue of intellectual authenticity: one man told me that whilst it was acceptable to derive inspiration from other poets and their work, a poet's writings should always be the product of his own thought (*sooch*) and struggle (*mehnat*). Indeed, many of the musicians and poets told me that their work was deeply influenced by the real life experience of love relationships. As a result of this intense environment of intellectually informed criticism and analysis, many poets also seek to incorporate novel phrases and images into their poems. One especially popular and recently written love song, for instance, begins with the phrase, 'having put on her glasses it turns out she has a good look beneath her veil' (*aynak chackei chardaro muzhen jam lolak birai*).

The programmes at which the Nobles perform are often recorded onto audio and sometimes video cassettes by the owners of one of the three music shops in Chitral's bazaar. Copies of these cassettes are then made and sold in music shops throughout the region at the affordable cost of thirty Pakistan rupees (forty pence). In the early stages of the performance in order to ensure that the cassettes are filled (*tip korik*) successfully, there is usually no dancing or excess joviality. The early stages of the *mahfil* focus, rather, on the words of the *ghazals* sung and the beauty and complexity of their meaning.

When both sides of the cassette have been recorded, the young boys in attendance are encouraged to take the floor and dance to their favourite songs.[24] 'My sons' (*ma zhizouan*), a confident man sitting in the room will often proclaim, 'now it's your opportunity to dance' (*di ponoor*). Men and boys dance individually in the centre of the room. They gently lift their heels to the plucking of the sitar and shake their shoulders and arms to the beat of the drums. The best dancer will move perfectly to the music but in new and exciting ways: his dance will be varied, sometimes moving slowly to the music, sometimes spinning around quickly. And a dancer who introduces subtle new movements to his performance will be the focus of much praise by those in attendance. Dancers start slowly but pick up the tempo of their performance throughout the song until reaching a final and sometimes frenetic climax.[25]

The evening's atmosphere now becomes more light-hearted and less introspective than the earlier stage: whereas the earlier *ghazals* were listened to largely in silence, now more people engage in discussion and comment on the dancers as they perform. Moreover, the music is now becoming faster, the clapping louder, and the sighs of appreciation for the lyrics turn into whoops and hisses of encouragement for the dancers: the delicate sound of the sitar is increasingly drowned out by the beating of the drums.

In addition to proficient players and singers, there are the jokers in the group and they too play a key role in the *mahfil*, for the refined musical and poetic performing has another key element: joking. This too is a key element of the complex phenomenon that is the *mahfil*, and it is full of remarkable things, above all playful humour directed at mullahs and super-conservative Islamists. Now the atmosphere of the *mahfil* is relaxed, the jokers and impersonators in the group start to lighten up the evening's proceedings. The jokes they tell and impersonations they perform are always successful in reducing the audience to ecstatic states of laughter and even tears of joy. A favourite of Chitral audiences are the jokers waggling their handlebar moustaches, making impersonations of Geoffrey Boycott's cricket ground inspections, and

---

[24] Compare T. Ali 1981 for a contrasting account of hierarchical and ceremonial dance performance in Hunza, Pakistan's Northern Areas.

[25] Colonial scholar-officials were often surprised by the importance of dance for Chitral people. Kennion noted that dance was a particularly important feature of Chitral life. 'Chitralis of even the highest rank are not excused, and officials holding appointments corresponding to those of our own Prime Minister and Commander-in-Chief may on occasions be seen capering about for the edification of the crowd' (Kennion 1910: 17).

mocking English-speaking doctors examining their 'illiterate' (*anparh*) and 'simple' (*sadah*) Chitrali patients, and even imitating men at prayer.[26]

One member of the Nobles, Irshad, had become a particularly versatile and dynamic comic during the time he had spent performing in Chitrali *mahfils*, and no programme is complete without his jokes. Unlike other members of the Nobles, Irshad is 'illiterate' (*anparh*) and has received little of a formal education. Irshad makes no bones about being identified as being one of Chitral's poor (*ghariban*): speaking in 'made-up' (*tan pazar*) English and Urdu, he delights at making others laugh at his attempts to copy Pakistan's rich and educated. One of his favourite acts during my stay in Chitral was his impersonations of Punjabi *qawwali* devotional singers from Pakistan's major cities. The *qawwali* genre is distinct from the *ghazals* performed by the Nobles; *qawwali* lyrics often include *sura* (verses) from the Qur'an, and are accompanied by instruments not found in Chitral, especially the accordion. Irshad would sing amusing lyrics in Khowar in the high pitched and quivering vocals of the *qawwali* singer. In a version of this act that *mahfil*-goers found particularly hilarious, Irshad sings about the trials of life during the Muslim month of fasting, Ramadan. Watching hungry and tobacco-deprived men losing their cool and 'beating one another' (*eegho donian*) is one activity that helps the long days of fasting pass by more quickly in Markaz's small bazaar. Irshad makes fun of dim Chitralis and their weak faith in a way that reduces audiences to fits of laughter for several minutes:

I went to the bazaar; the month was Ramadan.
I forgot about that and put some mouth tobacco in my mouth.
They beat me in my face oh what shall I do now!

This joking about Chitralis as people of 'weak faith' says much about the way in which many Chitral people distinguish themselves from other Pakistan Muslims. For some at least, this is something worth preserving and rejoicing over rather than lamenting and reforming. Moreover, Irshad's choice of the *qawwali* genre of Sufi musical performance to accomplish this task is also striking. The *qawwali* genre is associated with ethnic Punjabis and the Punjabi language. Many commentators have recently emphasised the trend of 'Punjabification' in present day

---

[26] This trope of Chitral people being weak in faith is something that appears to have been long important in the region. Kennion also gives accounts of comical routines in which Chitrali jokers imitated and poked fun at 'pious' 'Pathan' traders (Kennion 1910: 19).

Pakistan (Jaffrelot (ed.) 2002; Jalal 1995b; Verkaaik 2001). This trend
includes the expanding linguistic, cultural, political and economic influence of the Punjab, Pakistan's richest and most populous province, in
present day Pakistan. So we see here how the Nobles not only contest
puritanical Islam, but they also connect this project with resistance to the
homogenising cultural trend of 'Punjabification'.

The *mahfils* attended by The Nobles are, thus, the focus of considerable
social, emotional and economic investment by their Chitrali hosts. Feeding
up to forty guests a luxurious meal is an expensive task even for Chitral's
wealthiest families who mostly invite the Nobles to perform in their
houses. Even more difficult is rallying the household members to prepare
delicious food fit for the 'respectable' gentlemen who have been invited.
Hosting a gathering attended by the Nobles is also full of 'extrinsic' dangers
and risks (Howe 2000: 68–9): what if the 'religious-minded' neighbour
decides to try and bring an early end to the programme?[27] What if the
imam in the village mosque decides to decry the member's of the household for allowing un-Islamic music and joking routines to be performed in
the house? What if the musicians sulk because they do not consider the
arrangements (*bandobast*) made in their honour to be a fair reflection of the
trouble to which they have been put to perform? What if too many people
unexpectedly 'invite themselves' to the programme and there is neither
enough space for them to sit, nor enough food to feed them?

During the course of the programme, men's minds turn away from
'managing the self' and being sensitive towards others. These are important
dimensions of Chitral life but they are especially evident during the early
stages of a *mahfil* that sees gatherings of Markaz's most respected men. At
later stages of the evening, however, it is the words of the music and the
jokes being made that catches the attention of the *mahfil*-goers. This is
experienced intensely by those in attendance because it results in momentary break from the emphasis on politeness and etiquette that Chitral
people usually have to live through in their daily lives. The *mahfil* is an
arena in which people in Chitral experience an intense feeling of 'calm'
(*sukoon*); and it is this momentary break from day to day anxiety and
individual decision-making (*faisala korik*) that makes the experience of the
mahfil so intense and valuable for the *mahfil*-goers. Yet the state of calm-
ness experienced by the *mahfil*-goers is also religious and about what it
means to live a virtuous (*jam*) Muslim life. Alcohol is prohibited, prayers

---

[27] See Howe 2000 on the place of risk in ritual, particularly his distinction between risks that are
'extrinsic' as opposed to 'intrinsic' to rituals (Howe 2000: 68–9).

are performed, and rosary beads fingered. Moreover, the words themselves are rich in an Islamic imagery that likens the beloved to God's angels and talks about the garden of love as the ultimate paradise. The skilled *mahfil* participant is one who can both contribute to making the evening 'hot' by exciting the senses through dancing, joking and clapping, and also comment in an informed way on the words that are sung.

This rejoicing in experiencing and making of music and poetry takes place in the absence of a tradition of Sufi shrine worship, of recognised affiliation to Sufi brotherhoods and orders, and in the presence of Deobandi men of learning and piety in Markaz's bazaar. There is an intellectual awareness of the concepts and ideas of Sufi Islam in Markaz, and this is demonstrated by the intellectual activity by the poets and performers of the Nobles. Their knowledge of the concepts and values of classic Persian Sufi writings is clearly evinced in their ability to write poems and love songs which use idioms and phrases from these great works. At the same time, they are also competent at adding to this rich repertoire of evocative language about the powerful experience of love and devotion. Moreover, it is not only the few men who sit in the gatherings attended by the Nobles who acquire this intellectual awareness of Sufi-oriented Islam. And it is not only Islamist reformers and purifiers who feel confident enough to use the technologies of modernity to disseminate their ideas and visions of a world made perfect by Islam. The popularity of the Nobles' audiocassettes across the region means that the ideas encapsulated in their songs gain a far wider coverage. By putting their poems to a musical genre much enjoyed by Chitral Muslims, they play an important role in generating and fostering an interest, knowledge and awareness of a dimension of the Islamic tradition that is more mystically oriented than the Deobandi school.

THE PERFORMERS

As performers (*fankaran*) the Nobles are important because they add a further layer of diversity to the texture of the Islamic tradition in Chitral, and because they are independent minded and un-deferential towards strict and purist Islam. Yet even the Nobles represent a broad range of opinions and attitudes, and this is something that further reinforces the arguments made in Chapter 4 in the context of Rowshan about the important role played by debate and creativity in the living of a Muslim life in Chitral. What type of Muslims in Markaz join the Nobles, and what does this tell us about the place of intellectual creativity in the living of a Muslim life there?

The Nobles group is made up of men who hold deeply contrasting visions of Islam, and who inhabit very different styles of Muslim identity and spirituality. They are not an esoteric group of Sufi-minded poets who conceptualise themselves as fighting a last stand against Deobandi scriptural Islam. Whilst there are known styles of spirituality and religiosity in Chitral these styles are not the rigid and hardened 'types' that some anthropologists have depicted them as being in other ethnographic contexts. The styles of Islam and personal spirituality available to Muslims living in this newly urban setting are more numerous and compatible or, at least, interactive than is often considered the case to be in other Muslim societies. And Muslims exercise an important degree of what they themselves call 'personal choice' (*zati chit*) in constructing the styles of Muslim spirituality they adopt.

The diversity of viewpoints upon which I now focus is not, however, something that just *is*, but, rather, it is a feature of life that members of the Nobles cherish and work hard to foster and maintain. The gatherings attended by the Nobles are also used as an arena in which men vocally criticise and contest styles of Muslim identity they talk about as being 'extremist' and 'narrow'. The musical gatherings attended by the Nobles are, then, an 'alternative site' (Eickelman and Anderson 1999) in which Muslims in Chitral seek to contribute to debates concerning religious representation and discourse important in the region, in Pakistan and elsewhere in the Muslim world. In an atmosphere that is free from the constraints of 'managing the self' and where creative performance is valued, Muslims voice ideas about Islam and styles of Muslim identity powerful in the region that would be impossible to express in other 'public' spaces in Chitral.

Most of the Nobles are in their mid-thirties to forties, although the lead singer is about twenty years old. Yet the Nobles is made up of a remarkable assortment of men. Clean-shaven men who are known as being 'drinkers' sit beside bearded men who refer to alcohol as being the 'shit of the devil'. There are men who have actively campaigned for the success of the Jama'at-e Islami party in Chitral and who support that party's campaign to introduce a version of the Islamic legal code (*sharia*) in Pakistan. At the same time, there are committed activists of the Pakistan People's Party who remember fondly having sat and drunk whisky with Zulfikar Ali Bhutto before giving stirring election speeches. The lead singer of the Nobles is a young Ismai'li, whilst the Nobles most popular poet is a Sunni who regularly joins preaching tours organised by the worldwide movement of Islamic purification, the Tabligh-e Jama'at. This movement encourages largely Sunni Muslims to be stricter in their practice of the faith's daily rites.[28]

These men gather and sit together (*ee biti nishik*) in the face of criticism led by the more 'hardened' sections of Chitral 'religious scholars' (*dashmanan*). They are aware that some of Chitral's 'men of piety' tell Muslims living in the region that even sipping water from a glass used by an Ismai'li is *haram* (forbidden) in Islam. The very status of members and friends of the Nobles as 'Muslims' in the eyes of the 'bearded ones' (*rigishweni*) is something they throw into doubt by attending the *mahfils*. The more religious-minded men who sit with the Nobles worry that their friends accuse them of having forgotten their religion and their commitment to living a pious and proper Muslim life. The Nobles love for the long tradition of musical performance, dance and joking is something which purists in Chitral are eager to wipe out. There is a danger that becoming associated with the Nobles may result in old friends and family members describing friends of the Nobles as people who are 'lost' (*tonj*) to the 'flippant' (*ghair sanjidah*) lifestyles of Chitral's musicians and love poets. 'Being Muslim' in Chitral involves the continual making of decisions under the gaze of public criticism and comment, and the decision to 'sit with' the Nobles is one such decision, and an important one that counts.

The Nobles' *radio engineer* is Mufti: brilliant, outspoken, and a well-known poet who is never far from public controversy in Chitral. Mufti is a Sunni Muslim, whose home lies in a poor and drought-stricken village in a valley in upper Chitral. Mufti says that he is a follower of the Pakistan Jama'at-e Islami party. He had studied for a masters degree in Urdu literature at Peshawar University, and there, his friends told me, he played a very active role in Jama'at-e Islami student politics.[29]

Yet in the *mahfils* attended by the Nobles, Mufti is an important person for the evening's entertainment, and ensures that the proceedings are kept *garam* (hot) – meaning exciting, fast moving and full of laughter. He is not only a renowned poet in Chitral, but also a famed teller of comical stories (*namakin qissa*), jokes (*qafiya*), and an expert imitator (*ongolak*).

---

[28] Many Sunni Muslims in Chitral regularly join the Tabligh-e Jama'at on their preaching 'tours' (*gasht*) both within the region, to other regions of Pakistan as well as elsewhere in the world. In August 2000 the Tabligh-e Jama'at held its annual gathering (*ijtima*) in Markaz – an occassion that over 100,000 Muslims from Chitral and other regions of the Frontier Province attended. Amongst this gathering were many members of the Nobles. On the history and aims of the Tabligh-e Jama'at see Metcalf 1993, 1994, 1999.

[29] The student wing of the Jama'at-e Islami, the Jama'at-e Tuleba-e Islam has played a major role in the Islamisation of Pakistan's university campuses. On the Jama'at-e Tuleba, see Nasr 1992.

Mufti is best known for his imitations – his most popular being that of one of Chitral's widely known and most out-spoken and pro-Taliban *'alim*. This imitation has got him in a good deal of trouble: imitating such a holy and pious man, he has often been told, is a great sin in Islam (*gunah*). Some Muslims in Chitral told me that any form of imitation is 'forbidden' in Islam: 'Only a bad and evil man can derive pleasure from making fun out of others.' Yet Mufti told me that he never felt threatened by the region's *ulama*, and even informed me that he was in fact a very close friend of the religious scholar whom he was so famed for imitating. Mufti likes to imitate the way this scholar attempts to Arabise his speech, something the *'alim* tries to do by emphasising the guttural nature of the Arabic letter *ain* (ع). For instance, whilst most people in Chitral pronounce the Arabic word that means religious scholar *'alim*, Mufti enjoys impersonating the way this religious scholar pronounces the first sound of the word with a pronounced Arabic accent. Mufti is here stripping off this religious scholar's attempt to 'show himself' as a man of great learning and piety, by revealing that if he can make such a perfect imitation of the man then his reputation must be based on style and not substance. He is showing that this *'alim* is one of those men who is best described as being *sora khur mula khur* (one thing on the top, something else underneath). This is a project that is participated in by the ecstatic members of the audience when they comment to each other that Mufti's voice is an 'exact mimicry' (*hoo ba hoo*) of the *'alim*'s.

Mufti's imitation of this *'alim* is often the high point of any musical programme attended by the Nobles. Having transformed himself into the *'alim* Mufti, sitting cross legged and flailing his arms with a finger pointed in the air, is now ready to answer questions from the *mahfil*-goers. One man stands up and, as a joke, asks Mufti if he could tell the people gathered whether such a gathering of men where music is being played is a sin (*gunah*), an act of religious merit (*sawab*) or a permissible act (*mubh*). Mufti leans back and strokes his non-existent beard in the style of the *'alim* he is imitating: 'My brother', he replies, 'so long as there is nobody praying, there are no women in attendance and there is no alcohol, everything is permissible in Islam (*islama har kia jaiz*).' His audience is now falling around the floor in uncontrollable fits of laughter. But Mufti continues his impersonation: 'When I was a boy', he tells them, 'I danced, I sang, I was beautiful, I've done everything, let the young boys do what they fancy.' Mufti even makes up some verses of the Qur'an that sound like they are Arabic to give his *fatwa* on the musical programme greater weight and power.

Mufti, then, is saying things that for many people in Pakistan are unsayable, and he is doing so in a creative and intelligent way that involves him displaying his individual brilliance as an 'imitator' (*ongolak*). Yet the men present were not only rejoicing because they were participating in these daring displays of creative individuality. They were also laughing because they realised the world they lived in and experienced outside the room, as I showed in previous chapters, is one of intense anxiety, and, for a few moments at least, Mufti had prised off the lid and the pressure had been released. Moreover, Mufti's impersonation was all the more amusing to watch because, as I show in the next chapter, the man whom he was imitating, a known religious scholar, and others like him, is someone who is deeply feared by many Chitral Muslims. On their trips to the bazaar, seeing such a man may provoke some men to hide in a shop, whilst others would often stop, kiss the man's beard, and respectfully greet him as their 'sweet scholar' (*shirin dashman*). In this room, then, the *'alim*'s authority was dissolved, but the way in which this was made possible was both fleeting and hidden. The experience of the secret has the potential of being joyful, but it is also the source of moral and emotional anxieties. 'Back stabbing it is said in the Qur'an', I was often told, 'is like eating the dead flesh of one's own dead brother.' Further, as I showed in chapter 4, talking about someone 'in the hidden' (*pachana*) renders men 'weak, sly and shy women'. So during Mufti's comical imitations, joking, fear, the momentary dissolving of authority mixed, the experience of the play of the mind, and the nervous recognition of masculinity reduced to impotency and emotional failure combined, and this resulted in ecstatic laughter.[30]

Not all, though, are equally appreciative of Mufti's imitations of Chitral's religious scholars. Some of these men regularly attend the Nobles' performances, and that they do so points to the continuing ability of Chitral Muslims to share and exchange a wide array of views about deeply contentious issues. After one Nobles' gathering I had attended I stayed with a man who had been a senior figure of the Jama'at-e Islami party in Chitral for many years. He was driving the jeep and his younger cousin was sitting next to him. They had both enjoyed that evening's programme and they chatted to each other saying that whereas once they had been opposed to such gatherings on the grounds that they drew people's attention away from prayers and Islam, they could now see how they were an important feature of life. Yet the younger man objected to Mufti's impersonation of the *'alim*: not only was he imitating a respectable

---

[30] On laughter in rural Lebanon, see Gilsenan 1996.

and religious man of the region, but he was also insulting Islam's holy book by making up his own verses with the purpose of making people laugh. He had, this man said, overstepped the boundaries of decent Islamic behaviour (*islamar nishie nisie asour*).

Mufti's poetry is well known throughout Chitral. Some of his poems have been published in written form in volumes of Khowar poetry and he also reads his work at poetry recitals. Yet Mufti would often tell me that it was above all else thanks to the beautiful music of the Nobles that his name had become 'popular' (*manshur*) across all of Chitral. Mufti's poetry has also come under attack from certain sections of Chitral's *ulama*. In one *ghazal* Mufti compares the beauty of his beloved to an angel (*farishta*), and claims that the depth of affection he has for his loved one has given him the power to do what only God is able: delay the day on which his death has been appointed (*ajalo anus*):

Farishto ponga parim
rem tan ajalot achi boghhe
Hase wa kia zindagi
Ta sheli surat ki no hoye?
Reclining at the feet of an angel
I will say go back the day of my death
For what life is there
If your beautiful form is not to be there?

For some of Chitral's Sunni *ulama* Mufti had committed a grave sin (*gunah*) in that he conjured up images of angels having a bodily form. He was guilty, he was informed, of having led the region's Muslims astray from Islam's 'true path' (*frosk rah*). The *ulama* who had objected to Mufti's writings had threatened to take him to court on a charge of blasphemy. As in other countries of the Muslim world, Pakistan's blasphemy laws have been increasingly used by certain sections of the country's religious and political authorities to label their opponents as non-Muslim, and being convicted of blasphemy carries the death sentence.[31] That some of Chitral's *ulama* had been on the verge of taking Mufti to court shows the extent to which they consider the songs of the Nobles to have power and influence over the minds of Chitral Muslims. Moreover, it also shows how far the

---

[31] The making of Islamic legal injunctions (*fatwas*) is an important source of religious authority for the *ulama* across the Muslim world, see Masud, Messick & Powers (eds) 1996. On a high-profile blasphemy trial in Egypt, see Hirschkind 1996. Compare Bowen 2000 for an account of a similar legal case in Indonesia.

ulama see the activities of groups like the Nobles as threatening to their authority on the transmission of religious knowledge in the region.

Mufti was not shaken by this opposition to his writing, however. He told me that he could understand the meaning of the Qur'an better even than his *ulama* detractors. The comments he made to me reflect the ways in which education and literacy are an important force behind the 'fractured' (Eickelman and Anderson 1997) nature of religious authority in the region. When I asked him about this controversy, he recited a verse of the Qur'an that he interpreted as saying that the 'angels of paradise' (*jannato farishta*) had a bodily form. Far from being an 'ordinary Muslim' unable to participate in complex theological debate, Mufti was convinced that his education in Peshawar University and his understanding of Islam gave him a voice that was equally authoritative as the region's officially recognised religious scholars. Indeed, being a poet (*shai'ir*), Mufti considered that his understanding of Islam and 'the world' (*duniya*) was deeper and more complex than that of Chitral's 'narrow-minded' religious scholars:

Magnus, a man can go to school, go to college, attend university and study for a PhD and even higher forms of education, but not every man can become a poet (*har ivaloo shai'r biko no boye*). Being able to write poetry is a God-given gift (*shai'r bik ee allaho diru ishnari*). It is not an ordinary person's work to understand the ideas and thoughts of the poet (*aam roi shai'ro khialat hush no koynie*).

New Muslims who have benefited from growing levels of mass-education in Pakistan, like Mufti, are actively resisting these attempts, and the setting in which they do so is one where a very different vision of Islamic morality is sedimented in the bodies of *mahfil*-goers. Yet when they do resist those they themselves label 'hardened' Muslims, they do not do so because they are lax about faith or indifferent towards religion. Rather, the form of resistance they are engaged in builds on older social forms important in Chitral, on a complex knowledge of a body of Sufi texts, on the active and creative use of the intellect, and through displays of intellectual prowess. The work and activities of Mufti in Chitral, and the Nobles more generally, suggests that the boundary between the '*shari'a*-minded' and the 'mystical-minded' Muslim is in no sense rigid and inflexible in the identities and styles of spirituality inhabited by Muslims in Markaz.[32] Mufti is a supporter of the Jama'at-e Islami party – a party that supports the introduction of Islamic law in Pakistan. Yet, at the same time, he is a love poet

---

[32] The idea of rigid boundaries between *shari'a*-minded and mystical-minded Muslims is especially pervasive in treatments of West African Islam, see Brenner (ed.) 1992.

and he is known for his impersonations of known Chitrali religious scholars. Therefore, Mufti creatively combines deeply contrasting ways of being Muslim that are often held to be incompatible. Yet this process of creative combination does not only involve individuals managing and negotiating 'multiple identities from the specific images and metaphors they use to articulate their negotiations and experiences' (Ewing 1998: 266). Rather, the way in which Mufti combines contrasting ways of being Muslim must be understood in the context of the attempts made by some of the region's 'religious scholars' to 'universalise' and standardise Muslim thought and practice in the region.

THE NOBLES AND CHITRALI HIGH SOCIETY

Who attends the Nobles' *mahfils*, and what does this tell us both about the nature of the Islamic tradition in contemporary Chitral and the ways in Markaz's Muslims are responding to the pressures to 'Islamise' placed on them by powerful movements of Islamic reform and purification?

Powerful men with political aspirations consider the Nobles as being an important group of people to be associated with, and the ways in which programmes arranged for the Nobles involve a high degree of public competition renders them similar to what Appadurai has labelled 'tournaments of value' (Appadurai: 1986).[33] I now explore how the Nobles in no sense feel that they are on the back foot in the face of global movements of Islamic purification and reform. Like the organised parties and movements of Muslim reform and purification with whom they are interacting, the Nobles also have a vision of the world made perfect by the power of Islam. And they see themselves as being engaged in a project of 'making' (*sauzeik*) better Muslims of people living in Chitral. Yet this alternative model of Islamisation is not one that is missionising and has the goal of the purification of Islamic practice at it core. The Nobles, rather, are seeking to 'broaden the minds' and 'civilise' their fellow Muslims in Chitral in a way that makes them both intellectually more significant and emotionally more legitimate persons.

The musicians feel that they have the ability to transform and refine people's behaviour and thought; and this is a belief that they share with many of Chitral's refined (*sharif*) and educated (*talim-e yafta*) men. It is groups of poets and musicians like the Nobles, I was often told by such

---

[33] For a comparative discussion of public displays of wealth and generosity in 1970s Afghanistan, see Azoy 1982.

folk, who are a key force in stemming the tide of change towards, what people in Chitral themselves told me were 'extremist' 'narrow-minded' and 'animalistic' ways of being Muslim. One of Markaz's 'intellectuals' (*hush-yiar*) who was an advocate in his early fifties proudly told me that 'there are at the gatherings of poetry societies and local history clubs in the town ideas expressed that I don't think one could hear anywhere else in Pakistan'. Like Rowshan, then, Markaz is also ideally conceptualised by many townsfolk as a vibrant intellectual environment, and this is something that makes it different from other regions of Pakistan and, in the minds of many Chitral people, explains why 'hardened' visions of Islam have failed to take root there.

The kinds of people who host the musical programmes are relatively affluent, but they include both old elite families and members of Chitral's 'new rich'. Thus, I have attended *mahfils* hosted by a forestry commissioner, an advocate, a man who worked as the King of Saudi Arabia's personal bearer and driver, and by a headmaster in a village government school. The *mahfil*, then, is a place where the members of Chitral's 'high society' meet and talk with one another, and, as such, is a significant marker of a man's social status and prestige. Whilst it is usually relatively affluent people who host the gathering, the array of people who sit and listen to the music is much greater. Carpenters, subsistence farmers, shopkeepers, and young unemployed boys are often eager to make their way to a guesthouse if they hear the Nobles are to perform.

It is often assumed that Pakistan's emerging rural 'middle class' are those most likely to find visions of reform-oriented Islam attractive, and, as Nasr has illustrated, the ranks of the reform-oriented Jama'at-e Islami party has been swelled by such people over the past two decades in particular. Yet in Chitral, as my account of Mufti showed, association with the Jama'at-e Islami does not necessarily entail the adoption of a purifying and reform-oriented vision of Islam. Moreover, an emerging 'new elite' in Chitral of businessmen, shopkeepers, advocates, government contractors and migrants are seeking to convert their wealth into respect by investing in and becoming associated with the 'high society' that revolves around the Nobles.[34] At the same time, the Nobles, their work and the men associated with them are playing an important role in debating the shape the Islamic tradition should take in 'the local' context of Chitral.

---

[34] On the complexities of the role of Sufism in the so-called Islamic revival in Indonesia, see, for instance, Day 2001 and Hassan and Mufid 2002.

One of the Nobles most active and prominent supporters is a business-man based in Markaz itself – Afzal Khan. Afzal Khan is a Sunni Muslim who hails from a Chitrali village whose inhabitants are known for their 'strict and serious' (*dang*) approach to Sunni Islam. Afzal Khan himself is a very pious Muslim man – unlike other members of his profession, he never drinks any of the region's home-brew alcohol and is punctual in carrying out his five daily prayers. Indeed, until recently, he was a key party leader in the Chitral Jama'at-e Islami party. Afzal comes from a poor family back-ground, and was one the first members of his family and his village to gain a higher education. He no longer lives in the village in which he was born and raised, but, instead, he has bought land in Markaz, and the earnings from his profession have allowed him to build an impressive two-storey (*ju manzilah*) house there. Afzal Khan's house is one of Chitral's most com-manding and impressive new buildings, and is only rivalled by the fort (*noghor*) of the former ruling family that is also located in Markaz. The house combines South Asian ostentation with a local Chitrali architectural and design repertoire. Thus, a marble-laid second-floor veranda, in the style of the villas of Pakistan's rich city folk, provides his guests with sweeping views of Markaz's small airport, whilst inside the guest house even the sitting-room is made in the style of a traditional *khowar khatan* (Chitral room).

Why, then, does a man so seemingly pious and reform-minded in his approach to Islam chose to become involved with a musical ensemble in Chitral that is a focus of criticism by Chitral's 'religious-minded', and that has members who are famous for their parodies of a known Chitrali *'alim*? Indeed, some of the core members of the Nobles themselves sometimes tell me, in private, that they are rather baffled by Afzal's new-found love and passion for their jokes and music. Moreover, I was often informed, it was because Afzal is 'religious minded', and a '*shari'a*-lover' (*shari'a-pasand*) at heart, he is not really a man 'fit for the *mahfil*' (*mahfilo bachen fit mosh no*). Afzal was supposedly too often guilty of 'speeding up' (*tezeik*) the group's proceedings, and forcefully (*zor korie*) making the *qafiya korak* (jokers) start their jokes and impersonations at too early a stage of the evening's proceedings.[35] There is a proper pace and tempo for the sequences and stages of an evening's performance and the vulgar bigwig was accused, in private, of repeatedly getting it wrong. Moreover, Afzal is not the sophis-ticated and polite 'man of the *mahfil*': he too often uses a loud voice (*dol*

---

[35] See Racy 2003 37–40 on the listening manners expected of audiences of 'traditional' musical performances in the Arab world.

havaz) and enjoys being bossy and issuing commands and orders. For many people I spoke to, programmes attended by Afzal are often 'tasteless' (*wekhal*) and 'without enjoyment' (*bemazah*). If the *mahfils* arranged for the Nobles are 'tournaments of value' money alone is insufficient to guarantee that a man is at ease in the culture of the mahfil, and ensuring that a programme is tasty (*shiradar*) and hot (*garam*) is a skill possessed only by an elite few.

It was clearly recognised by other members of the group that much of the motivation for Afzal's interest and commitment to their programs lay in his own political and social ambitions. The connections Afzal had built up with the Nobles group allowed him to be regarded in a more favourable way by Chitral's liberal and relaxed folk, and it would enable him to present himself as a sociable and active member of Chitral's new elite. Afzal could never hope to enjoy relationships with such people if he continued to be associated purely with Chitral's 'through and through' (*katar*) and 'strong' (*pin*) religious-minded men. The advocate, at the time, was planning to stand for the newly created position of the Chitral district Mayor (*nazim*). Winning this position would involve much more than securing the support of the region's religious-minded.

Afzal, though, was not himself unaware of the rather dismissive ways in which other Nobles members thought and talked about the nature of his relationship to this prestigious musical group. He was sufficiently perceptive to understand that the Nobles and probably many of the other people, particularly those of the 'high society', present at the musical gatherings he organised or hosted were wise to his ulterior motives of social and political ambition. Yet Afzal also believed with some justification that his behaviour, thanks to conventions of politeness, civility and reciprocity so powerful and important in the social lives of many Chitral people, would nevertheless bring him benefits in the form of access to information, reciprocal hospitality and inclusion in communication networks, as well as, by his association with the Nobles and others present on these occasions, a reputation, especially further afield, that would give him an appeal to people with a wider range of moral, religious, political and social opinions than he would otherwise have. This was all especially important for Afzal during the time I attended Nobles gatherings in the winter of 2000–1 because the local government elections in which he intended to stand were only months away, and it is significant that this wealthy businessman with one-time Jama'at-e Islamic connections was convinced that his association with the Nobles musical group was an important and potentially politically profitable move.

If Afzal thought he would be simply able to use his money to ensure the support of Chitral's popular musicians to change his reputation or at least his public image, then the musicians themselves were playing a much more complex game. Many of the Nobles had deep reservations at the advocate's sudden upsurge of enthusiasm for Khowar poetry and song, and asked why they should put up with the rather vulgar and demeaning form of patronage he offered. The reason they decided to is important. Many in the Nobles felt that Afzal was not a lost cause. Afzal as a host was clearly rather fraudulent. Neither did the musicians turn to Afzal because they were weak, poor and in need of patronage. Rather, it was because they see themselves as able to transmit a kind of improving influence to this man. It was the hope of the musicians that as Afzal spent more time with them he would become better accustomed to the relaxed and free way of life they enjoyed. As one of the singers in the Nobles once told me, 'At present this Afzal is causing us a lot of problems Magnus, you know better. But with time we'll bring about changes in him and we'll make him in a way that will be better for all of Chitral. With time he'll even out (*waqto soom justa bara bar boye*).'

The musicians believe, moreover, that they have something to transmit not only on individuals in need of refinement, but onto Chitral society in general. On one occasion Afzal was very determined that the group should perform at the wedding of one of his cousins – the wedding was to be held at his home village. The musicians debated and strategised the dangers and benefits of performing in this village. From early on, group members were sceptical: weddings were usually disastrous places to perform – too many people would gather and there would be no hope of holding a respectable performance amidst the inevitable crowd and rush. Perhaps of even greater concern was the fact that the village Afzal intended to take them to was known for the high percentage of *dashmanan* (men of learning and piety) found there. How would the *rigishweni* (bearded ones) react to their music and joke routines? Was there the possibility that they could be shamed by being asked to stop playing their music? Despite the voices of concern the Nobles agreed that the programme should go ahead. Not to attend would risk upsetting Afzal and causing rifts and fighting within the group.

As had been predicted, too many people were present to allow the Nobles to perform in the small guesthouse made available by the host. The musicians were reluctantly cajoled by Afzal into playing for the huge crowd not in the guesthouse but in the grassy garden area outside. This was something they all intensely disliked, as the acoustics inside the room, they said, were far superior. The Nobles played their songs, and they did not come under attack from the 'bearded ones' sitting in the crowd. The imitations were toned down in order to adjust the performance for this potentially dangerous locality, and certainly Mufti kept his impersonation of the *'alim* to himself.

Thus, despite the unsatisfactory proceedings of the evening, some members of the group, at least, were pleased that they had taken successfully their music to a village so renowned for its *tablighi* (the worldwide movement of reform and purification, the Tabligh-e Jama'at) culture, and that so many young boys and men had turned out to watch and enjoy the performance. Indeed, the lead singer of the Nobles told me when I stayed in his house that evening that they had always intended on performing in this village, and that they had known that as a *mahfil* the programme would be a failure. Yet they had agreed with Afzal that his village people needed to have their minds 'broadened', and that it was in this spirit that they had performed.

CONCLUSION

What we see from the material presented here is that 'local Islam' far from being static and quiescent in the face of powerful 'global' Islamic movements is deeply injected with an intellectual energy and the sense of having its own message to deliver. As we see from the Nobles' active attempts to 'civilise' (*tahzibi yafata korik*) their fellow Muslims in Chitral by performing love songs and poetry that is deeply infused with the poetic forms of classic Persian Sufi texts, Islamisation is something other than a one-dimensional process of purification or standardisation. The assumptions challenged in this chapter can be summed up as follows: the creation of India and Pakistan resulted in a 'turn inward to local traditions' and a weakening of the importance of intra-regional languages such as Persian (Cole 2002: 31). I have demonstrated here, however, that local styles of Islam are themselves injected with cultural force and potent linguistic power that are distinctly global in origin and spirit, and that these are harnessed by Chitral Muslims in order to contest both religious and cultural homogenisation.

Members of the Nobles go about being Muslim in ways that entail combining visions of a world perfected by Islam that are profoundly contrasting and often held by academic Islam specialists to be incompatible. This is a dimension of the lives of the musicians, performers and poets that is not something that just *is*. Rather, it is something that they cherish, and have to work hard to foster in their daily lives. They perform their music and write their poetry in the face of considerable criticism. So when intellectual creativity does take place, it takes place in the face of very real constraints: blasphemy laws, organised Islamist parties and powerful men of learning and piety are all forces with which the Nobles have to confront in their daily lives. Yet Markaz's intellectually creative Muslims are themselves willing to employ the technologies of modernity (audio and video cassettes), and draw upon styles of Islamic knowledge that are themselves global in nature (classic Sufi texts). Moreover, they do so not because they are secular or indifferent to religion, but, rather, so that they may present an alternative vision of a world made perfect by the power of Islam to their fellow Chitralis.

The Nobles, then, play and pray in the same spaces, and this is important because it questions the assertion that Islamic morality is, above all else, about piety (Hirschkind 2001). I have argued in this chapter that, in the context of Markaz, an emphasis on self-discipline and conforming to Islamic standards combines with an emphasis on bodily and intellectual creativity. It is only by exploring bodily experience, creative intellectual activity and sensory modes in contexts that appear to be something other than 'religious', that the full complexity of the ways people construct Muslim personhood, and create and respond to revivalist visions of the Islamic tradition is fully illuminated.

Chitral's 'men of learning and piety' (the *ulama*) occupy a powerful and complex place in the minds of the Nobles and their friends – they are imitated, yet they are also deeply feared – and it is Rowshan's *ulama* who are the focus of the next chapter.

CHAPTER 6

Scholars and scoundrels: Rowshan's
amulet-making ulama

My brother – however long a man grows his beard, no matter how
religious he says he is his heart can never be empty of thoughts of love.
(Twenty-three-year-old Rowshan woman)

INTRODUCTION

I have demonstrated in chapter 5, then, that Chitral has a rich tradition of
intellectual and creative life embodied in the popularity and sophisticated
appreciation of the music and poetry of groups like the Nobles. In this
chapter we see something equally striking: the ways in which the region's
ulama think and act, and the ways in which villagers think about them, is far
from simplistic or straightforward. The statement above, made by a twenty-
three-year-old woman, shows that there is, for some Rowshan people, more
to the village's *ulama* than their beards (*rigish*), rosary beads (*dazbeh*) and
overtly pious lifestyles suggest. Men who have received recognised and
certified training in the Islamic sciences are known in Khowar as the
dashmanan (singular, *dashman*) – a word that derives from the Persian *danish*
meaning 'knowledge'. It is critical that we explore the lives of region's
dashmanan given their importance in Chitral life, but also because of how
easily one might assume that they are perceived as one-dimensional founts of
puritanical 'Islamic' authority, either universally deferred to, or 'resisted' in a
simplistic sense.[1] An exploration of how much more complex the reality is
reveals much about both Islam and Chitral, and the very active ways in which
Chitral people think about the act of thought and the nature of emotion.

In previous chapters I have sought to show that the lives of Chitral
Muslims are shaped in complex ways by a division between knowledge that
is open and knowledge that is secret. This division between secret and open

---

[1] See Roy 1990: 31–3 on the division between village mullahs and religious scholars in Afghanistan.
Werbner 2002 distinguishes between saint jurists and reform jurists in present day Pakistan.

knowledge is also an important dimension of the role of Rowshan's Sunni *dashmanan*, and this throws light both on the thought processes and religious practices of the *dashmanan*. Anthropological accounts of non-Islamic religious traditions have explored the importance of hidden knowledge in their analyses of the status and role of religious specialists.[2] In the study of Islam the importance of hidden knowledge has been given greatest focus in the analysis of Sufi figures of spiritual power (*baraka*). In Chitral there is little or no ecstatic worship at the shrines of saints, yet as I demonstrate in this chapter, the division between the hidden and the secret is an important feature of the thought processes and practices of Rowshan's *dashmanan*.[3]

A particular concern of this chapter is the use of amulets made by religious scholars to allow lovesick men and boys to marry the girls they love. My focus, then, is on something unexpected in the activities of 'men of religious learning' – the dispensation of amulets. Far from treating this as a departure from the 'proper' conduct of an *'alim*, I seek to show that this is compatible with both the villagers' and the *ulama*'s commitment to creative thought in and about faith. Making amulets requires the use of secret knowledge (*khoasht ilm*), and so the concern with the secret and the open is crucial to the way Rowshan people experience and reflect on these complex matters. The chapter has two central analytical concerns.

First, it seeks to illuminate the interaction between Sufi-centred and reform-oriented types of Islamic knowledge and practice. It is sometimes assumed by specialist scholars of Islam that secret knowledge is less important in the lives and practices of reform-oriented Muslims adhering to schools of Islamic thought that take a hostile stance towards 'un-Islamic' forms of Sufism.[4] At a more complex level, many reform-minded Muslims, rather than rejecting Sufi traditions out of hand, have sought to reduce its teachings to their visions of purified Islam.[5] I ask here in what ways do *dashmanan* in Rowshan conceptualise a domain of esoteric knowledge, and how does this shape the way Rowshan people perceive them?

Secondly, this chapter explores the ways in which the thought processes of Rowshan's *dashmanan*, the experience of *madrasa* education, and Rowshan people's reaction to the thoughts and actions of men returning

---

[2] For comparative treatment of secret knowledge in other religious traditions, see Barth 1987, 1990.

[3] See, for instance, Gilsenan 1982 ch. 6 on hidden secrets and sheikhs in Lebanon.

[4] On the division between esoteric and rational knowledge in Muslim education in Mali, see Brenner 2000.

[5] For the scholar-journalist Mawdudi who founded the Jama'at-e Islami party, for instance, 'Sufism was not an esoteric dimension of Islam, but merely a standard by which to measure "concentration" and "morals"' (Nasr 1996: 123). See Bledsoe and Robey 1986 on the interaction between new knowledge of Arabic and the indigenous elite's use of secret knowledge in Sierra Leone.

from spells of religious education in 'down Pakistan', illuminates local people's ideas about the interaction between thought and emotion. Thus, this chapter also documents the ways in which young men returning from *madrasas* seek to bring new Islamic standards to their villages and households, and how Muslims in the village respond emotionally and intellectually to these men and their Islamising projects. Anthropological discussion of the status and role of the *ulama* in Muslim societies have tended to portray them as figures of strong authority, and the possessors of text-centred knowledge of the word of God, the Qur'an.[6] Studies of Islamic education have also emphasised memory and deference to authority as a central feature of the transmission of Islamic religious knowledge (see, especially, Eickelman 1985a; Brenner 2001). Moreover, where rational thought and argument are said to be important they are often depicted as rooted in standardised and unchanging traditions of what proper debate entails in the Islamic sciences.[7] The implication, then, is that neither the *ulama* nor ordinary believers, especially 'villagers', value or cultivate the means to exercise independent critical thought as a feature of Muslim life and virtue.

These assumptions are particularly visible in the study of Islam in contemporary Pakistan. Kepel has recently argued that the experience of religious education in religious colleges (*madrasa*) 'brainwashes' students and gives them 'retrograde' worldviews (Kepel 2002). This style of education he argues has played an important role in creation of 'jihad-centred' visions of Islam in the country.[8] Such work takes as self-evident that the messages emerging from *madrasas* are homogeneous and that their reception is uncontestable, especially in poor and geographically remote regions of the Muslim world where *madrasas* are often assumed to be the focus of enthusiastic allegiance or even armed militancy. Yet there are few detailed ethnographic studies of this process of reception, and what models there are tend to represent the nature of village Muslims' reception of 'reformist' Islamic teachings either as reflecting ignorance of normative Islamic

---

[6] See: Gilsenan 1982. Compare Robinson 1984 for a historical discussion of the *ulama* in South Asia, and on Iran's clergy and their role in the revolution of 1979, see Fischer 1980. When anthropologists have noted the complexity of Muslims' views on religious specialists, they have tended to focus on saint-like religious figures who are 'ambiguous' because of the position they occupy in 'tribal' social structures (Lindholm 1996: 230), and not on trained religious scholars as I focus on here.

[7] Compare Fuller 2001 and Parry 1985 on priestly thought and education in contemporary India. On the practices of memory in Christianity, see Carruthers 1990. On styles of reasoned argument employed by religious scholars in Iran, see Mottahedeh 1985 and Fischer 1980.

[8] Nasr argues that a new genre of *madrasas* have emerged in Pakistan that are 'equally if not more concerned with *jihad* (holy war) than with religious scholarship' (Nasr 2000: 145). For a contrasting study on the importance of change and creativity in the thought processes political activities of Pakistan's *ulama* more generally, see Zaman 2002.

doctrines in rural settings, or in terms of straightforward resistance or submission to forms of religious authority emerging from supposedly more sophisticated urban centres. It is in this global context that I ask how far Rowshan people think, consider, reflect and exercise independent judgement in matters of faith, and how far they are uncritically deferential to men of religious authority on these issues.

MOSQUE SCHOOLS AND JAMA'AT KHANAS: EDUCATING THE 'LITTLE ONES'

How do Rowshan people conceive of religious education, and what do they think of the experience of being taught by the *ulama*? How do they regard *madrasa* education's effects in the functioning of the mind, and the cultivation of the critical faculties? Having a mind, and showing a capacity for deep critical thought are highly valued by many Rowshan people, and there is great emphasis in the village on the way in which education has the potential to refine both mindful activity and the rational experience of emotion. Now, as a further distinct window into Rowshan people's conceptions of the mind and the emotions, I explore how religious education contributes to the cultivation of intellectual activity.

Religious education is a visible and prominent feature of Rowshan life. Having returned home from classes in worldly education (*dunyavi sabaq*) in government or private schools in the morning, most Rowshan children attend classes of religious education (*dini sabaq*) in the mid-afternoon. Elderly men in the village often told me that when they were young, Sunni and Ismai'li children had studied the Qur'an together before the village's respected men of learning.[9] They told me that the era of their youth was one of calm (*sukoono zamana*) when villagers did not distinguish between Ismai'lis and Sunnis to the extent that they do today.

In present day Rowshan, however, Sunni children attend mosque schools (*dar-ul uloom*), whilst Ismai'li children attend religious education in the village's Jama'at Khanas (the Ismai'li place of worship). Both boys and girls attend such classes. However most Sunni girls stop receiving such

---

[9] Until about forty years ago, in addition to memorising the Qur'an and the Hadith, some Rowshan children were also taught Persian texts, especially the *Panj Ganj* ('Five Treasures') and the *Kulliyat-e Chahar Kitab* ('The Complete Four Books'). These works, often taught in Dari-speaking regions of Afghanistan, are written in rhythmic Persian prose, and 'contain the essential and fundamental facts and normative principles of Islamic belief and practice' (Shahrani 1991: 168). Compare Nichols 2001: 158–9 on older texts used in Pukhtun regions of the Frontier, and Khaleed 1998 on religious education in Central Asia.

religious education at the age of twelve, whilst Ismai'li girls continue to attend religious education courses until they are eighteen. I was often told that this is because Sunnis in the village practice stricter purdah than Ismai'lis and that it is improper (*najaiz*) for sexually mature girls (*chumut-keran*) either to enter the mosque (*masjid*) or to sit and study with boys. For many Sunnis in the village this shows that the ways they go about being Muslim are closely guided by the teachings of the *shari'a*, whilst for Ismai'lis in the village the commitment to educate even mature girls in religion is evidence of their 'open minds'.

There are also important differences in the courses that are taught in these centres of religious education, and the people who teach them. Mosque schools (*dar-ul uloom*) teach Sunni children the Qur'an as well as the Hadith (sayings attributed to the Prophet). The men who teach in these mosque are recognised as *dashmanan*: most of them have memorised the Qur'an and have certificates (*sana'at*) which show that they have undergone formal education in religious colleges (*madrasa*) in the Islamic sciences. Younger pupils (*talib-e ilm*), aged between five and twelve, are taught how to recite (*tilawat korik*) the Qur'an, and this is something that requires them to memorise (*yad korik*) the holy book. One little boy, aged about four, commented to me one day, when I was walking with him in the direction of the mosque school, that the 'little students' (*tstsekan*) memorise the Qur'an whilst the 'big students' (*zizaqe*) are taught the meanings (*maghnie*). Students first learn how to recite the Qur'an and how to read it, and only then are they taught to memorise a catechism of stock and standardised explanations of its meanings. Thus, mental activity is conceptualised as possible only after the cultivation of the ability to reproduce, in as perfect form as possible, the words of the holy book.[10]

The largest mosque school in Rowshan is located in a cluster of rooms attached to the Friday mosque (*jama' ma'jid*), which is located at the end of Rowshan's polo ground (*jinali*). In 1995, when I first visited Rowshan, the Friday mosque was simply a larger version of other Sunni mosques in the village: it comprised one large room covered with a tin roof where men gathered for congregational prayers on Fridays. Between 1995 and 2002, however, the mosque was rebuilt: it is now a three-storey structure with seven to eight rooms that make up the mosque school. The finances for this construction have come from a variety of sources. The *dashmanan* in the village sought contributions (*chandah*) from Sunni Muslims in the

[10] On mosque schools and Islamic learning in other settings, see Bledsoe and Robey 1993; Lubeck 1988; Messick 1993; Sanneh 1997; Yamba 1995: 79–83.

village: most Sunnis in the village contributed some money, and even the women of the village were asked to give what little they had to help in the completion of the mosque. When the present President of Pakistan, Pervez Musharaf, visited Rowshan in July 2000, he donated a considerable sum of money (about 120,000 Pakistan rupees, about £1,000) on behalf of the government of Pakistan for the construction of the new mosque.[11] Religious education and the need to construct a mosque school is at the forefront of the minds of many of Rowshan's Sunni Muslims.

I spent many afternoons siting with Rowshan's Sunni *dashmanan* in their houses, in shops in the bazaar and in minibuses. I was never invited to enter the village mosques, however. In this I was not alone. The majority of Rowshan's Ismai'lis had also never seen inside the Friday mosque, did not attend Friday prayers there, and never sent their children for religious education there. If they did visit other mosques in the village it was to deliver meals of rice and meat which they distributed to villagers after an especially happy occasion. Whilst there are many contexts in which Rowshan's Ismai'lis and Sunnis from a variety of personal backgrounds sit together and share views, the village's places of religious worship are not among these. Sunnis and Ismai'lis in the village do sit and study *islamiyat* (Islamic studies) together in classes at the government and private schools they attend in the village, but with regards to religious education outside the context of state education they build a rigid boundary. This boundary throws interesting light on the different conceptions that they have about learning and the cultivation of the mind, and it is on these differences that I now focus.

I walked past the Friday mosque on most afternoons when I went to visit friends who lived in a house nearby. On my way to my friend's house, I would almost certainly be accompanied by scores of young boys with small white prayer caps (*topi*) on their heads and girls with veils (*petek*) neatly fastened around their heads with safety pins. They made a special effort to look pious when they went to the mosque: little girls who usually went to school with their scarves loosely draped around their necks, would be sure to cover their heads for their afternoon in the mosque. Yet these children would also do what children in the village were most renowned for: *shaytani* (devilish behaviour). They would run to the mosque pretending to be horses by smacking their bottoms with their right hand, which they used as an

---

[11] I did not hear of there being any foreign funding for this mosque-school complex. In Markaz, one Jama'at-e Islami school was said to have received funding from the Government of Kuwait, and some people told me that a *madrasa* in the town was financed by the Government of Saudi Arabia. For details of the funding of mosque-schools and *madrasa*s elsewhere in Pakistan, see Nasr 2000: 144.

imaginary whip, and their little white prayer caps would fly off their heads into the dust underfoot. Bodies one minute pious and self-disciplined soon fluidly transformed into those of naughty and devilish children.

These young children – usually aged between four and twelve – would all be clutching slates, for one dimension of the religious education they undergo at the mosque school is learning how to write verses (*sura*) of the Qur'an in the Arabic script. When I walked past the *dar-ul uloom*, I would usually see Sunni children rocking back and forth (*aih af dik*) reciting from the Qur'an under the supervision of one of the village's *dashmanan* who often brandished a stick (*vetuk*).[12] As in other contexts in the Muslim world, the deeply embodied nature of the learning and memorisation of the Qur'an was always apparent when children recited the Qur'an for me on their way to the mosque. It was only after having hitched their trousers up to their ankles and folded their arms neatly across their stomach as in preparation for prayer, in the way they were taught to by their teachers (*ustazan*) at the mosque, that they would proudly recite from the Qur'an for my benefit. Sometimes they would even start the call to prayer (*adhan*), by first raising their cupped hands to their ears, and reciting the first line, *allahu akbar* (God is great).[13] For these Sunni children, then, religious knowledge required specific bodily postures, yet these postures themselves easily gave way to the devilish bodies (*sheytani jism*) said by many Rowshan people to be what childhood (*tseki*) is all about.

This is important for our understanding of the complexity of intellectual life in present day Rowshan because it points to the complex interaction between different styles of embodied knowledge. One style values knowledge as 'fixed and enduring' (Eickelman 1998: 289) and emphasises religious piety as a bodily state of self-discipline. The other entails a conception of the intellect that values individual intellectual creativity, and bodily freedom. Both of these are experienced as embodied states. And, as with the Nobles and the different styles of 'secular' education we encountered in chapter 4, we see how the boundary that separates them is fluid, and that, in the course of their daily lives, Rowshan's Sunni children move readily in and out of these two categories of being-in-the-world.[14]

---

[12] For a comparative study of the experience of Islamic education in West Africa see Sanneh 1997. On Islamic education in other contexts both within and beyond the Muslim world, see: Haddad (ed.) 2001; Kepel 1997; Lewis 1994, Starrett 1998.

[13] On Qur'anic recitation, see Nelson 1985; Rasmussen 2001.

[14] Compare Mahmood's study of prayer in a women's mosque movement in Cairo, Egypt (Mahmood 2001). Mahmood 2001 argues that it is important to 'recognise the disparate organizations of the body-self undergirding these different conceptions of ritual and to analyse the conditions under

Ismai'li children are taught from religious printed textbooks that are produced by the Ismai'li Tariqa Board, and designed for Ismai'li children across the world. The Ismai'li Tariqa Board is the international Ismai'li body that co-ordinates, amongst other things, the religious education of the world's Ismai'lis. Its central office is in France, close to the residence of the spiritual leader (*ruhani peshwa*) of the Ismai'lis, the Aga Khan. But it also has offices in all the countries where there are substantial populations of Ismai'lis, and in Pakistan the main office is in Karachi. The textbooks, called *Talim* (education) teach central Islamic and Ismai'li beliefs and doctrines. They teach children about the Islamic notion of the oneness of God (*tawhid*), the religious lessons learned from the life of the Prophet, and the role that the Aga Khan plays in Ismai'li belief. Children also learn about general Islamic history (*islami tarikh*). Yet they also discuss historical events pertaining more especially to Ismai'li history, such as the battle of Karbala (AD 680) – the historical moment at which the differences between Shi'a and Sunni traditions in Islam were created and sharpened – and the establishment of an Ismai'li state by Hassan Sabbah in Alamut Iran.[15] These textbooks also provide information on social aspects of life, especially the importance of education, the status of women and issues surrounding health and cleanliness. Far from seeing religious education as being confined only to the teaching of the Qur'an and the sayings of the Prophet Ismai'li religious education as it is taught in Rowshan involves a broader conception of what religious knowledge comprises.

Whilst Sunni children have no other educational tools than the teacher, his stick, the Qur'an and slates for writing on, Rowshan Ismai'lis' textbooks are full of colourful drawings and pictures. They show images of women in other parts of the Muslim world weaving mats, washing their children, and sending them to school, and there are line drawings of the holy lands in the early years of Islam. As I discuss below, for many Sunni students who have undergone advanced training in the Islamic sciences, any form of visual representation of the world is considered to be un-Islamic. For many Sunnis, then, the instruction of religious knowledge requires a blank mind upon which the powerful words of the Qur'an are permanently imprinted. In

which parallel and overlapping traditions of reasoning and moral formation exist, not also within different historical and cultural contexts, but also within a single cultural milieu' (Mahmood 2001: 837). I am suggesting that such variation is not only important within different groups in society, in Mahmood's case liberal-nationalists and those engaged in the construction of new forms of Islamic practice, but also within persons themselves.

[15] Hassan Sabbah established an Ismai'li state 'with its territories scattered from Syria to eastern Persia' for 166 years in the thirteenth century, and this era of Ismai'li history is often talked about as a golden era by Chitral's Ismai'lis. See Daftary 1998: 3–4.

striking contrast, Ismai'li textbooks integrate worldly and religious knowledge, and both are taught in the religious space of the Jama'at Khana.
Further, Ismai'li religious education has a strong modernist dimension with
an emphasis on women's agency as promoters of hygiene, education and
morality for their households and the Ismai'li community (*jama'at*).

Young Sunni children are taught how to read and write Arabic and recite
the Qur'an by Rowshan's *dashmanan*. Ismai'li children, on the other hand,
are taught religious knowledge by both young men and women who are
literate in Urdu and have undergone only brief courses of religious training
at the offices of the Ismai'li Tariqa Board in Rowshan. Indeed, the Ismai'li
religious authorities in the village (the *waizeen*) are trained in very different
courses and surroundings to the Sunni *dashmanan*. Unlike the Sunni
dashmanan, the Ismai'li *waizin* do not attend *madrasas* for religious training; instead they attend shorter courses (usually two to three years) in
Ismai'li doctrine and history in the offices of the Ismai'li Tariqa Board in
Karachi. Whilst the *waizeen* are mainly men, during my stay in Rowshan
women also attended *waizeen* training courses.

Whilst the *waizeen* give occasional sermons in the evening, the teachers
of religious knowledge in the Jama'at Khana in the hamlet in Rowshan in
which I lived were all young women aged between seventeen and twenty-
two. These women had passed their matriculation (class ten) examinations,
and occasionally attended seven-day courses in religious education training
at the offices of the Tariqa Board in Rowshan. Each afternoon at 2:30, after
having put on their smartest *shalwar kamiz* and washed and combed their
hair, these young women would grab the young children from their homes
and walk along the village paths to the Jama'at Khana. These female
teachers (*ustani*) were accused by some of the other Ismai'li girls in the
village of being not in the slightest bit interested in religion. These other
women often told me that the teachers only went to the Jama'at Khana so
that they could wear their white veils and fashionable green *shalwar kamiz*.
There are thus Ismai'lis in the village who subject their own community's
styles of religious education to critical analysis and debate, and women and
girls play a significant part in this debate. Rather than there being unreflecting and uncontested consensus about the need for modern religious
education, Ismai'lis hold and express a wide range of opinion about how
religion should be taught to the young ones.

The Ismai'li elders in the village also often expressed concern about the
fact that not all the Ismai'li children in the village were attending the
Jama'at Khana for religious education. They frequently called 'meetings'
(*meeting*) in the Jama'at Khana at which they told the Ismai'li parents of the

village to ensure that all their children attended religious classes each afternoon. The Ismai'li elders would often tell parents that children could only be successful in their 'worldly education' (*dunyavi sabaq*) if they learned the Qur'an and about religion. Having a mind capable of competing in the world requires the sustenance of religious knowledge.

Thus, there are important differences in the way that Ismai'lis and Sunnis seek to transmit religious knowledge in Rowshan, and these reveal a great deal about the way Rowshan people conceive of the complex interaction between learning and the training of cultivated minds. For many Sunnis in the village, religious education involves the transmission of a distinct category of knowledge that can only be taught in a proper way by men who have undergone long-term training in the Islamic sciences. Thus, the emphasis here is on the perfected writing, recitation and memorisation of the Qur'an in an environment cleansed of worldly images and concerns. This mnemonic perfection also requires bodily perfection: washed hands, folded arms, prayer caps, and veils are all a central feature of how Sunni children go about learning about Islam.

In contrast, Rowshan's Ismai'lis see religious knowledge (*dini ilm*) as integrated with other types of knowledge: instruction in religious know-ledge is seen as a necessary component of cultivating the mind so that it may be responsive to worldly knowledge and the challenges of modernity. For many Ismai'lis, then, religious learning is about more than mnemonic perfection, and, correspondingly, this different vision of religious educa-tion and knowledge is displayed in different forms of bodily comportment. Veils are loosely draped on heads, prayer caps are rarely worn, and hands not washed before instruction begins. Moreover, lay Ismai'lis – both men and women – are just as capable of transmitting this knowledge to the village young ones as are people with more formal training in the Islamic sciences.

Having explored the place of educating the small ones of the village, I now explore higher levels of religious education, and the impact that those educated in religious colleges are having on the intellectual and emotional climate of village life.

YOUNG DASHMANAN, AND 'DOWN COUNTRY' MADRASAS

How do Rowshan people think the experience of long-term religious training affects their fellow villager's thought processes, and how are returnee *madrasa* students conceived of as affecting the intellectual and emotional climate of the village?

Whilst there are many mosque schools where young Rowshan children learn the Qur'an, there is no *madrasa* in Rowshan that is qualified to issue students with certificates (*sanad*) enabling them to be recognised as fully trained *dashmanan*.[16] However, some Sunni children from the village travel to 'down Pakistan' (*aff pakistan*) to attend such religious teaching institutions. In the thirty-household hamlet in which I stayed, six boys were studying in *madrasas* in Peshawar. In the context of this region of Pakistan, this is a relatively small proportion of the village's children. In the predominantly Sunni valley which neighbours Rowshan – Mulkho – only a thirty-minute jeep journey away over a low and barren plateau, it is usual for at least one boy from each household to be enrolled in religious education in a 'down country' *madrasa*. Mulkho people (*mulkhowichi*), though, have an important influence on Rowshan as they often come to Rowshan to use its relatively well-stocked bazaar, hospital, courts and government offices.

The relatively few numbers of boys from Rowshan who study in *madrasas* must partly be seen in the context of the village's large Ismai'li population: Ismai'lis never seek education in Pakistan *madrasas*. Yet, at a deeper level, it is a further reflection of the ways in which Rowshan people value cultivated, open and free minds, and see 'narrow minds' as being threatening and dangerous for village life. For many Rowshan people, long spells of religious education in Pakistan's down-country *madrasas* are conceptualised as having an array of negative outcomes on the minds, bodies, and emotions of the *talib-e ilm*. Rowshan people themselves often use the English word 'brainwash' to describe the degree to which *madrasa* education has the potential to make individuals incapable of individual and critical intellectual activity.

There is no set age at which parents decide to send their children to a *madrasa*: some boys aged about six or seven start their religious training courses without having received any formal education in the village's government schools. Other boys leave the village after having attended school for four to five years. It is generally held by Sunni people to whom I spoke in the village, that it is better for a young boy to be 'left' (*petsik*) in a *madrasa* when his brain (*dimagh*) is still fast (*tez*) and receptive to new words and ideas. Most of the *madrasas* that Rowshan boys do attend are free, and they also provide free accommodation and food – something that makes them very attractive in the eyes of poorer Sunni families. They are often financed by foreign governments (especially Saudi Arabia and

---

[16] On religious colleges in Islamic history, see Makdisi 1981.

Kuwait), and they are frequently affiliated to religious parties that are active in present day Pakistani politics (especially the Jama'at-e Ulama-e Islam and the Jama'at-e Islami).[17] The children who study in these village schools are typical Rowshan boys, who play in the lanes, are naughty at home, and help their fathers in the fields.

During this long education process, Rowshan men and boys are separated from village life even though many of them return home annually, and are said by villagers to become 'like outsiders' (*berieo royoghon*). Having an in-depth knowledge of the Qur'an is something that is respected by many of the villagers, and the young *dashmanan* are listened to and often deferred to. There are also, however, surprising things about how these new *dashmanan* think and act, and about how other people in the village think they act.

Most of the young boys from Rowshan who are sent for advanced religious education attend *madrasa*s in the old city (*shahar*) of Peshawar, most especially the Deobandi Dar-ul Ulum Sarhad, and there are several *madrasa*s there that have been established by *dashmanan* from Chitral who are now settled in Peshawar.[18] Rowshan boys also train in *madrasa*s that have a high profile in state-level politics, for instance, young men from Chitral study at the Jama'at-e Ulama-e Islam (JUI) dar-ul haqqania *madrasa* run by the powerful JUI *'alim* Sami-ul Haq.[19]

When young boys leave the village it is usually the first time they have seen the city, or have found themselves amongst people speaking in unfamiliar languages, and have had to learn to speak these languages themselves.[20] Meeting people from other countries in the Muslim world is an important dimension of what it means to an experience *madrasa* education for many of the *talib-e ilm* I spoke to in Rowshan. Beyond learning the Qur'an and other

---

[17] On the affiliation of *madrasa*s to Islamist political parties and movements in present day Pakistan, see Kepel 2002; Nasr 2000; Malik 1998. Many of these parties and movements have played an important role in supporting and instigating 'holy war' in Kashmir.

[18] The Dar-ul Ulum Sarhad is of historical importance for Chitral Sunni Muslims: Chitral Muslim have studied there for at least the past fifty years, see also Malik 1998: 241, fn. 29. More generally, on the relationship in the Frontier between regional origin and choice of *madrasa*, see Malik 1998: 235–44.

[19] On the international dimension of *madrasa* education in Pakistan, see Nasr 2000: 179. On the historically multi-ethnic and linguistic experience of *madrasa* education in South Asia, see Metcalf 1982.

[20] This *madrasa* had close links with the Afghan Taliban government: many key figures in the Taliban government had studied there. See Kepel 2002 for the political significance of the Frontier's *madrasa*s. I heard only rumours about one Rowshan young man, a son of one of Rowshan's senior *dashmanan*, who was said by some in the village to have left Rowshan in order to fight *jihad* in Kashmir.

important religious texts, interacting with non-Chitrali people is a particularly memorable feature of the time they spend in the *madrasa*. I was often told by *madrasa* students from Rowshan that there were 'all colours of people' (*har qesma rango roi asuni*) in the religious colleges they attended. Whilst there were always other Khowar-speaking boys from Chitral, there were also Pukhtu-speaking, Urdu-speaking as well as Malaysian and Filipino students studying with them.[21] Rowshan boys, then, are placed in a very different cultural and linguistic setting when they go the *madrasas* of 'down Pakistan', and this is something that they conceive of as an especially important dimension of life in 'down Pakistan'.

Leaving the village to attend a *madrasa* is seen by Rowshan people to be a major event in a person's life, and it entails separation (*tanha 'iee*) from the daily patterns of village life and the affection and love of one's family (*doro royean khuloos*). Even studying in Peshawar, a sixteen-hour bus journey from Rowshan, means that a boy will not be able to return home more than once a year. Some men and boys in the village travel as far afield as Karachi for their religious education, and they often do not return to the village until they have completed their studies. Leaving the village and travelling to live in such a distant city is seen as being difficult for both the young child and his family, especially his sensitive and loving mother. Yet the 'pain of separation' (*juda 'ieeo chameik*) is conceptualised as an important feature of what it means to live a Muslim life. The sayings of Prophet 'for knowledge one should travel as far as China', and 'for knowledge a person must experience hunger and homesickness', are often recited by families who complain that they are missing their little boys living far away from home.

The decision to send a young child to one of Pakistan's major cities is a difficult one for a family to take, and it is not simply an unthinking response to calls for commitment made from influential *dashmanan* in the village and beyond. In the summer of 1998 *madrasa* students had been widely reported in the Pakistani television and radio news as involved in fighting against the Indian military forces in Kashmir. They had also participated in protests organised by the *ulama* to oppose Nawaz Sharif's (then the Prime Minister of Pakistan) decision (July 1999) to remove Pakistani troops from across the line of control that separates Indian from Pakistan's Northern Areas. The widowed and uneducated mother

---

[21] Compare Edwards' discussion of changes in identity, as exemplified through clothing and bodily appearance, of a powerful religious scholar in Afghanistan through his education career, Edwards 2002: 219–24.

of one of my Sunni friends who was in his late thirties had urged her son to visit his younger brother who was studying in a *madrasa* in the Jama'at-e Islami Markaz (Centre of the Jama'at-e Islami) in Lahore. She told him to tell his younger brother that he should not 'go for *jihad*' in Kashmir, and that he should not attend protests against the government, as she was frightened that he would be killed or wounded. My Sunni friend agreed with his mother, and he told me that whilst his younger brother was a sensible man (*sanjidah mosh*), *madrasa* students are often 'emotional' (*jezbati*) and that even his younger brother might be driven to do something dangerous. His younger brother, he told me, needed reminding that he had a mother, and that his first commitment was to her. He quoted from a saying of the Prophet, 'heaven lies at the feet of one's mother' (*jannat tan nano ponga mula sher*).

There are striking implications here about the ways in which Rowshan people conceptualise the processes of intellect and emotion. Above all for Rowshan *madrasa* education is important with regard to the role religious learning plays in the making of the adult Muslim whose thought and actions are a proper reflection of Islamic values. Rowshan people see the effects of *madrasa* education in very ambivalent ways, however. They send their sons to *madrasa*s for many reasons, but also fear some of its potential effects. In particular, they conceptualise its potential effects on their sons in ways that emphasise the complexities of the act of thought and the experience of emotion, and this is an especially sensitive dimension of Rowshan life. They understand particular kinds of education to elicit quite specific kinds of changes from thinking and emotionally active human beings. They often say that *madrasa* education can make young men 'emotional': it can upset in young minds the balance between reason and emotion. More particularly, they think that this can have the effect of arousing unhealthy forms of emotion that are very intense, and not a good thing. An interesting demonstration of this is in the thinking of the mother who sends an older son as an emissary to redirect her younger boy's mental processes by evoking memory and consciousness of her love and care. In particular, she does so to ensure that her son will not be so inclined to act on the basis of this pernicious religious emotion directing him to deny family affective ties, act thoughtlessly and unreasonably and go off to be a suicidal *shaeed* (martyr) for Islam. What we see here, then, are views that are much more complex than unreflecting deference to the authoritative calls of religious authorities, and that are deeply ambivalent about the virtues of 'purist' Islamic education. At the same time, however, Rowshan people do not reject Islamic education in any one-dimensional way.

The rhythms of the *madrasa* year have an important impact on life in Chitral: as the *madrasas* call their *chuhti* (holiday) during the hot summer months, young religious students from Chitral flood back to their villages to escape the heat (*garmi*) of Pakistan's sweltering planes. The minibuses which make their way over the 12,000 feet Lowari pass to Chitral from Peshawar are crammed full of the returnee *madrasa* students keen to assert their newly found religious authority over their Chitrali 'countrymen' (*watandaran*). Drivers are urged to turn off music tapes for the duration of the journey, and replace them with *qur'anic* recitations (*tilawat*). Men are encouraged to offer their prayers, and men travelling with women in the small bus are asked to ensure that their wives and sisters observe full purdah throughout the course of the journey. These attempts to Islamise the minibus are often the source of debate, and sometimes conflict, during the journey (*safar*). Young men eager to listen to Khowar, Urdu and Pashto music cassettes plead with the 'bearded ones' (*rigishweni*) to allow them to relieve the boredom of the journey by listening to some music. They call to the *dashmanan* sitting with them, Oh my sweet scholar (*ma shirin dashman*), our knees are in our faces, our backs are aching; please let us listen to a little music. What harm will it do (*kia nuqesan taroor*)?'

It is not only in the confined space of the minibus, however, that returnee *madrasa* students seek to make their mark on life in Chitral. Boys who left the village as loveable young children return to Rowshan as young men. Indeed, many returnee *madrasa* students seek to mark their newly found status by dressing in distinctive ways.[22] As opposed to donning the traditional white woollen Chitral cap of the village, they place brightly decorated 'down country' style prayer caps on their heads, and they sometimes even tie black turbans around their heads – a practice that symbolically identifies them with the strict dress code of the Afghan Taliban.

For many Ismai'lis in the village, for whom the Taliban is associated with the persecution and killing of non-Sunni Muslims, the sight of these turbans elicits complex emotional responses. Ismai'lis and some Sunnis in the village would often comment to me that 'seeing a *dashman* makes my heart tremble' (*hardi shenik*). Men who wanted to earn a reputation for bravery (*bahderi*) often told me, 'Only I don't feel frightened when I see a religious student (*talib*); other people see them and shut up (*aam roye tsrap bonie*), but they can't catch my penis (*mu puchi chokiko no bonie*). Why

---

[22] Yet, as Malik 2002 discusses, a significant proportion of students educated in Pakistan's *madrasas* remain unemployed, see also Malik 1998: 303.

should I fear?' These young religious men, then, are seen as having the capacity to silence villagers, prevent them from engaging in free (*azad*) discussion, but they also offer men a chance to display bravado. As the imitations of the religious scholar in chapter 5 demonstrated, there is a subtle culture of how to display and show off manliness. This in itself entails independent critical intellectual prowess: bravely parading critical attitudes to mullahs is one particularly important focus for this.

Young *dashmanan* also make significant attempts to change their bodily comportment, and, whilst they are feared by many villagers, it is striking that they are also the source of much amusement and joking for Rowshan people. In their hands the young *madrasa*-returnees carry rosary beads (*dazbeh*), which they finger whilst reciting under their breath the ninety-nine names of God they now know by heart. Rather than engaging in discussion, they repeat the names of God and the verses of the Qur'an, and this makes them very different from ordinarily more vocal Rowshan people. In the top pocket of their *kameez* (shirt) they place a piece of walnut wood, which they, as the Prophet had once done, use to brush their teeth. Their body-centred attempts to follow the *sunna* (customs associated with the Prophet) is the source of critical comment by many Rowshan people, especially Ismai'lis, who see this as proving that the young *dashman* are not only 'narrow minded' but are devoid of the power to think at all. One woman exclaimed to me, 'Look at the way they put bits of wood in their pocket! Don't they have any intellect? The reason the Prophet used wood to brush his teeth was because in his time there were no toothbrushes, but they can't even see this.' For this young woman, then, the embodied piety of the young *dashmanan* symbolised not so much heightened level of religiosity as an inability to think and, indeed, a total lack of rational mental activity.

Girls of the village say that the eyes of these men, unlike the infamous immoral (*badikhlaq*) 'girls watchers' (*kumoru lolak*) of the village, are *purdadar*: rather than looking in the direction of women, they divert their eyes by piously staring blankly at the floor. Keeping purdah, then, is not something that only requires women to wear veils and be prudent in their bodily comportment: it also calls upon men to 'control their eyes' (*ghechan khabara angik*) and discipline their bodies and their animal-like instincts and emotions. Yet the *purdahdar* eyes of the young *dashmanan*, I was often told, conceals a much deeper reality: 'They are just hiding, when it comes to looking at girls they are the most interested of us all.' Here, then, the young *dashman* are thought of by many Rowshan people – especially Ismai'lis – as being very crude in the way they go about concealing their real thoughts beneath the surface level accoutrements of Islamic piety. In doing so, they have the capacity to ruin the conceptions villagers have of Rowshan as a place of lively and open-minded intellectual exchange.

It is striking that there is so much overt disparagement and mocking of the *dashmanan*, and one thing that makes jokes about them so enjoyable is that there is a considerable amount of fear mixed with the humour. The pleasure of laughing at the *dashmanan* is not only, therefore, something that is given expression, as we saw in chapter 5, in one-off dramatic displays of manly bravado: the ability to make comical remarks about the *dashmanan* is a recurrent feature of everyday life in the village. Moreover, both men and women rejoice in this domain of humorous yet critical intellectual activity.

Many Rowshan people take the young *dashmanan* seriously and approve of them, however. Having a newly trained *dashman* in the house is also a source of considerable prestige and pride for many families. Sending a child to study in a 'down country' *madrasa*, like economic migration, is a further way of rescuing the 'little ones' from what so many people see as the immoral state of contemporary village life. Moreover, newly trained *dashmanan* also have the ability to bring much needed sources of income into the house as those with *madrasa* training now possess the necessary qualifications for employment in government jobs as teachers of Islamic studies and Arabic in the region's schools.[23]

Yet, having a *dashman* in the house also creates complex conflicts in many households in Rowshan. Young *dashmanan* often seek to mark their presence and new Islamic standards first of all in their homes. The returnee *madrasa* students are not like the scores of village boys who have studied in the mosque school: they return from their long spells of religious education as young *dashmanan* equipped with a certificate (*sanad*) of study. This certificate is an important source of their religious authority, although villagers also often distinguish between the number of certificates different *dashmanan* hold, and the quality (*jami*) of the *madrasas* in which they studied. The young *dashmanan* may try to change household practices that, after having 'learned Islam' in 'down Pakistan', they now finds un-Islamic (*ghair islami*). They tell their family members to stop making home-brew red wine (*drocho ogh*), demand that they remove photographs from the walls of their guest houses, and urge them to stop holding musical

---

[23] Compare Brenner 2000 for a discussion of religious colleges that teach both 'worldly' and 'religious' subjects in Mali.

programmes at times of family happiness such as marriages and the birth of a son.

When returnee *madrasa* students do return to their homes and seek to enforce their new Islamic standards, villagers react in complex ways. Ashraf, a Sunni villager in his late thirties, had sent his younger brother to a Jama'at-i Islami *madrasa* in Lahore, located at the Jama'at-e Islami *markaz* (The Jama'at-e Islami Centre). The boy had wanted to study biological science in one of Markaz's most prestigious and expensive private English-medium colleges. But his secondary results were too poor for him to gain admission. There was also a concern about the high cost of this college, and so his elder brother decided – with the boy's agreement – that he would secure admission for him at a religious college in Lahore. Yet the decision to send his brother to a *madrasa* was not simply a matter of economic considerations or the boy's poor matriculation results; it also entailed an important element of choice. The issue of choice is important here: it throws light on the complex ways Rowshan people conceptualise the degree to which *madrasa*s contribute to the cultivation of active minds.

Ashraf told me that the *madrasa* to which he was sending his brother was one that promoted the education of 'broad-minded' and intelligent Muslim scholars. He said he did not want to send his younger brother to a college where he would just return as a rough (*loq*) *dashman* who could do nothing but recite the Qur'an without understanding it. Thus, Ashraf regarded some *madrasa*s as being places of religious training rather than education, and it was such religious colleges that had the potential of narrowing or making inactive mindly activity. Ashraf had spent a considerable amount of money on a visit to the college in Lahore; when he returned, he told me that unlike other religious colleges in the country it taught sciences and English-medium secular subjects as well as the Islamic sciences. It was recognised by the government of Pakistan and issued its students with BA and MA degrees, and the teachers at the college were all well educated with degrees in 'worldly' (*dunyavi*) subjects, as well as holding certificates of religious education.[24] He was sending his brother to a religious college not just to give him religious training, but also in the hope that the experience of religious education could contribute to the cultivation of his mind.

This older brother was shocked, then, when on returning home for the first time for two years his now bearded 'little brother' (*tsek brar*) strode into the family guest house and removed the photographs of their deceased

---

[24] See, especially, Brenner 2000; Eickelman 1992a, 1992b; Metcalf 1978, 1982; Robinson 2000.

father that had occupied pride of place over the fireplace (*bukhario tek*). His young brother had told his distressed family members that houses in which photos were to be found would never be visited by the 'angels of kindness' (*rakhumo farashtiganan*) and the blessings these creatures of paradise brought with them. As a result, those in the house would all be doomed to go to hell (*duzakh*) on judgement day (*qiyamato anus*). The visual representation of the human form, according to this newly educated *dashmanan*, was prohibited (*najaiz*) in Islam, and, he told them in a commanding voice, he would no longer live in a house where he could see un-Islamic and corrupting images. Two months later when the young brother returned to his *madrasa* in Lahore, the photographs were once again displayed above the fireplace.

There was an important emotional dimension to the way in which Ashraf's young brother sought to impose his new Islamic standards on the household. For Ashraf, his young brother's fervent and newly found religiosity was partly a result of the effect that religious knowledge had on his emotional state. He told me that his young brother was emotional (*jezbati*), and that this emotion was made manifest in his horrified reaction to the presence of photographs in his house. Any thoughtful and affectionate young man would never have spoken to his elders in such a rude and impolite way. Like other young men in the village, Ashraf said that his young brother was emotional (*jezbati*), and he hoped that his brother would 'become even' (*bara bar boye*) as he grew older and matured. But for Ashraf there was something particularly potent about this man's emotion, and he called this emotion *mazhabi jezbat* (religious emotion). Ashraf told me his young brother had spent so much time reading religious books and thinking about them that he had become especially emotional about religion. His intellect, Ashraf said, had been 'tied' (*'aql boti sher*). A potent combination of youthful and religious emotion, is seen as having the potential of making reasoned mental activity impossible, and this absence of mindful activity is something that makes interacting with returnee *madrasa* students a difficult task for Rowshan people.

Yet not all of Rowshan's young *dashmanan* are said to be incapable of mental activity, and not all of them behave and think in predictable ways, and, when they do not they are the focus of complex reflection and thought by Rowshan people. On one occasion the educated Sunni Aftab, whom we first met in chapter 4, had travelled to one of his relative's houses in a nearby village in order to attend the marriage of one of the sons of the house. The groom had recently returned from four years of study in a *madrasa* in Karachi, and Aftab had told me that today's wedding would be 'no fun': the groom would not allow people to play music, and the event would be a very serious (*sanjidah*) affair. He advised me not to join him because he thought the whole event was going to be boring, and that attending it would be a waste of my time.

On returning from the wedding the next day, however, Aftab told me that he had been amazed by what had happened. As he was about to leave the home, the groom – wearing a beard and with a prayer cap on his head – had told him that he should not leave because there was no one in the house or, indeed, the village, who could sing Chitrali love songs. Aftab was well known for being an excellent vocalist; and the young *dashman* persuaded him to say. Aftab told me that his 'intellect was amazed' (*ma 'aql hairan hoye*). Here was a young *dashman* who had recently returned from a *madrasa* in Karachi, yet who wanted him to sing Chitrali love songs – an activity that many other *dashmanan* in Chitral decried as being impermissible within Islam (*islama najaiz*).

This young *dashman* had, against all expectations, shown that he had an 'open mind': he actually encouraged people to sing, dance and play music at his wedding. Aftab told me that he had said to the groom, 'but you are a *dashman*, I can't play before you', to which the young *dashman* had replied that it made no difference and hoped, one day, that he could shave off his beard. The shaving of a beard is a deeply meaningful and controversial statement in Chitral: even men who let their stubble grow for a few days before shaving are accused of failing to respect the traditions of the Prophet (*sunnato beizzat korik*). An uncut beard should be representative of a conscious and permanent decision to live a pure and pious Muslim life. In saying that he wanted to cut his beard this young *dashman* was suggesting that even his many years of *madrasa* education had not resulted in a permanent change in his attitudes to faith: he was still able to act and take decisions in an active and flexible way. This had deeply surprised Aftab, and led him to question his assumptions about what *madrasa* education does to the mind.

Yet this was not the only thing he did that surprised Aftab. The newly married returnee *madrasa* student took Aftab into the house that was now full of women from the village who had gathered to congratulate his family on their son's marriage. On seeing these women the sensitive Aftab had become shy, and, he told me, sat with his face staring at the floor, crippled with embarrassment and wanting to escape from this difficult situation as soon as possible. Aftab's embarrassment was further compounded by the fact that he said he had noticed one of the women in the house staring at him with her big wide eyes (*bilour ghechie*). Aftab told me that he and the groom left the house, and went to sit outside in the orchard. The young *dashman* now, once again, made a surprising comment to Aftab. He told him that he had seen the woman looking at him in the house, and that she was the wife of one of his cousins. This bearded one, was not only ready to broach this sensitive topic, but also now, rather than accusing the woman of being a person of 'bad morals' (*badikhlaq*), asked Aftab if he would like him to convey a message to her. Despite the fact he had spent many years in a *madrasa* in Karachi, despite his long beard, prayer cap and rosary beards, this man was still 'open-minded'. It was the fact that a young *dashman* was making these comments, and not an 'immoral' son of the village (*deho zhaou*), that made them all the more interesting and stimulating for Aftab, and, indeed, why he thought that I too would find them fascinating.

Religious education and returnee *madrasa* students are the focus of widely varying judgements on the part of Rowshan people. These judgements throw light on the way that Rowshan people conceive of the interaction between religious education and the cultivation of active minds. They also illuminate the ways in which thought and emotion are believed to work, and reveal much about conceptualisations of people's active role in the making and leading of a Muslim life. Living a Muslim life is not something that comes automatically, but requires reflection, intellectual action and emotional sensitivity on the part of the believer.

At one level, returnee *madrasa* students who have spent years memorising the Qur'an as well as studying religious books in 'down Pakistan' are like strangers conceptualised as having 'narrow minds', and as seeking to restrict the degree to which the village is a place of critical intellectual activity. An important dimension of this narrow-mindedness is the notion that powerful emotions are said to make these men incapable of rational thought. Having been separated from their families for so many years, affectionate kindness for parents is replaced by uncontrollable religious passion. On the other hand, however, religious education is a source of respect in the village; and is something that can refine young village minds, and improve both the moral standards by which they live their lives as well as the environment (*mahaul*) of the village as a whole.

Yet, at a deeper level, despite their uncut beards and the black marks on their foreheads, the thoughts of the young *dashmanan* have not been permanently transformed in the minds of many Rowshan people. What is more, if a person tries hard enough, he may provoke even these emotional, narrow-minded and pious young men to stimulating and creative thought. Indeed, it is the very fact that these young *dashmanan* are now public figures of piety that enables them to conceal their more authentic inner thoughts and feelings, and when they do say surprising things Rowshan people rejoice in the opportunity to see how the village's bearded ones really think.

Having explored how villagers conceptualise religious learning as affecting the thinking and emotions of the village's young men, I now ask in greater detail how far intellectual activity plays a role in the thought processes of the village's senior *dashmanan*.

LOVE AND ROWSHAN'S AMULET-MAKING ULAMA

The ways in which new types of religious knowledge and greater emphasis on older styles of religious learning have transformed the thought processes and subjectivity of Muslims both within and beyond the contemporary Muslim world has been the focus of considerable research.[25] Many of these accounts point to relatively recent shifts in the nature of religious knowledge as currently transmitted in the Muslim world. Muslim religious authorities – including the certified *ulama* and saintly men of spiritual power – were once the key figures in the transmission of esoteric Islamic knowledge, knowledge above all that is hierarchical and spiritual. As early as the eighteenth century, however, there was a shift towards the transmission of rationalistic Islamic knowledge – that which is available to all and is separated from acts of devotion and notions of spiritual power – in the contemporary Muslim world, and especially South Asia. This shift was certainly visible in the teaching, writing and thinking among the *ulama* throughout the late nineteenth and early twentieth centuries.[26] However, it is in the contemporary Muslim world that rationalistic religious knowledge has gained even greater importance. Powered by the expanding wealth of the Gulf countries after the 1970s – especially Saudi Arabia and Kuwait – movements of Islamic reform have sought to purify Muslim thought and practice of what they see as being 'innovative' and 'un-Islamic' local customs.[27] Movements of Islamic purification have employed both top down and bottom up tactics in their attempts to homogenise the thought and practices of Muslims across the world. Both have sought to educate Islam's religious authorities in the teachings of reform-oriented Islam. Historians of South Asian Islam have argued that Pakistan's *madrasas*

---

[25] On the place of 'the rational' and opposition to 'mystical' Islamic practice in nineteenth century Egyptian thought, see Hourani 1997 [1962]: 149–50. On this conflict in South Asia, see Robinson 2000: 216–17; C. Bayly 1998: 48.

[26] On attempts to purify Islamic practice and thought in West Africa, see Brenner (ed.) 1992.

[27] This is especially powerful in Pakistan's Frontier Province. See Nasr 2000: 117.

have played an especially critical role in processes of 'Islamisation' (Robinson 2000: 5).[28] At the same time, 'ordinary' Muslims across the Muslim world have organised themselves in order to preach to their fellow Muslims the importance of purifying themselves of 'un-Islamic' local practices.[29]

As I discuss below, both 'ordinary' Muslims and the *dashmanan* in Rowshan are concerned about rational thought and the danger of practices they see as being irrational and un-Islamic as well as rooted in the deployment of secret knowledge. Yet the practices and diverse makeup of Rowshan's senior *dashmanan,* as well as the ways in which Rowshan people talk about them, reveal surprising things about a region of the world supposedly dominated by reform-oriented *madrasas.* And it raises important questions about the relationship between the interaction between secret religious knowledge (*khoasht dini- ilm*) and the rational religious sciences in the Islamic tradition in Rowshan.

I now explore these issues by documenting the emotional and intellectual dimensions of the making of amulets by trained *dashmanan* in Rowshan. I do this in order to explore the place of amulet making in a village where *madrasa* education is a major dimension of life and where people are sophisticated about books, learning and education, and value those who think in critical and sophisticated ways. I focus particularly on the making of amulets to throw light on the ways in which Rowshan people conceive of the interaction between thought, rationality, the intellect and 'strong feelings'. In particular, the ways in which Rowshan people conceptualise the use of amulets for love illuminates both the ways in which they think about the village's *dashmanan,* and on the key issues of this book: faith, intellectual life and emotion.

Men who make amulets in Rowshan are numerous and from a diverse array of backgrounds. They are both Ismai'lis and Sunnis, and whilst some amulet-makers come from poor and uneducated backgrounds, others are relatively wealthy and have received education in either 'secular' schooling or the Islamic sciences in Pakistan's *madrasas.* My focus here is on trained and certificate-holding *dashmanan* who make amulets. The importance of earning a reputation for being an amulet-maker is most striking amongst this category of men because they are so often depicted both in the Frontier and elsewhere in the Muslim world as the founts of puritanical

---

[28] The worldwide preaching movement, Tabligh-e Jama'at, has been particularly influential in bottom-up 'Islamisation', see below.

[29] Even in the supposedly 'secular' and 'rational' West, magic remains an important dimension of spiritual experience. See Luhrmann 1989 for a discussion of magic and witchcraft in London in the present day.

and reform-minded Islam. When Rowshan's *dashmanan* do make amulets, however, they do so in a world where there are deep anxieties about what it means to display rational thought, and where many people hold reformist visions of Islam that decry 'popular Islam' practices as un-Islamic innovations.[30] Thus, it is not surprising that in this complex setting there is an important element of defensiveness in the explanations Rowshan's *dashmanan* give when asked why they make amulets.

There are eight senior (*zaq*) *dashmanan* in Rowshan, and these *dashmanan* are thought of, and distinguished between, by Rowshan people, as individuals and not as a general class of 'religious authorities'. Especially striking here is the ways in which both Rowshan's *dashmanan* and 'ordinary' Rowshan Muslims do not categorise individual *dashmanan* in any simply binary way as either Sufis or *shari'a*-oriented. Rather, they systematically distinguish the different classes of religious knowledge deployed by Rowshan's *dashmanan* in different domains of village life. Historians have explored the ways in which the complex interaction between different styles (*maslak*) of Islamic learning and knowledge contributes to the authority men of learning hold in the Muslim world.[31] However, there have been few attempts to explore both the forms that this interaction is taking place in the contemporary Muslim world, and the degree to which it entails independent intellectual activity. Nor have anthropologists explored the extent to which 'ordinary' Muslims understand these complex combinations of religious knowledge and subject them to critical thought and judgement.

The differences between Rowshan's individual *dashmanan* are the source of great discussion amongst Rowshan people. Arkhon Sahib, aged in his early seventies, is Rowshan's senior most *dashman*. Arkhon Sahib studied in a *madrasa* in Peshawar, the *Dar-ul Uloom Sarhad* (the Mosque School of the Frontier), established by the famous Deobandi *'alim* Yusuf Banuri in the early twentieth century. At that time, the Arkhon proudly told me, few Chitral people even left their villages let alone made the arduous nine day journey by foot to Peshawar, a journey that now takes little over sixteen hours in a minibus. The *madrasa* that Arkhon Sahib attended was a Deobandi foundation, and the courses he followed were in Islamic jurisprudence (*fiqh*), logic (*mantiq*) and theology (*kalam*). The

---

[30] See especially Robinson 1984 on the Indian Faranghi Mahal *ulama*. Metcalf 1982, 1996 emphasises the complex levels of interaction and opposition between Deobandi and Sufi-oriented styles of Islamic knowledge.

[31] On the Tabligh-e Jama'at, see Metcalf 1993, 1994, 1999.

Arkhon has a reputation amongst Rowshan people for following the principles of *shari'a* law in a very strict way, both as compared to 'ordinary' Muslims in the village and other Rowshan *dashman*. Arkhon Sahib himself seeks to Islamise village life in Rowshan by purifying the practices and thoughts of Rowshan people. He has been responsible, by collecting money and organising Rowshan's Sunni Muslims, for the building of mosques and the expansion of religious education for Sunnis in the village. Moreover, he has also been involved in attempts to make village women more knowledgeable about the teachings and doctrines of Islam. In particular, he has encouraged elderly and respected *dashmanan* in Rowshan to arrange preaching gatherings for the village women, and Arkhon Sahib himself spent many years teaching the Qur'an and the Hadith (the sayings of the Prophet) to Rowshan girls in the government high school for girls.

Like 'ordinary' Muslims in the village, Arkhon Sahib regularly complains about the way the lives of Rowshan's Muslims have become dominated by inauthentic affections. For Arkhon Sahib, though, it is not English-medium education, employment or migration, but, correct Islamic practice (*sahi islami 'amal*), that is the cure to the emotional failure that lies at the heart of village life.

We are only Muslims by tongue: in truth we do no work that is Islamic (*ispa liginio sura musulman, haqiqata no*). As a result we Muslims are anxious (*pereshan*) and the world is anxious. There is no love in the house (*dori muhabbat niki*), there is no love in our parents (*nan-taato muhabbat niki*), there is no love in our women and there is no love in our children. The reason is because we do not have correct and proper faith (*iman*) in God.

For Arkhon Sahib, then, the upside-down (*ulta pulta*) nature of the villager's emotions, is the product of Rowshan Muslims' weak faith and the insincere ways in which they go about living a Muslim life. Unlike the comedians of the Nobles, then, Arkhon Sahib takes very seriously the common assumption held by Chitral people, that they are Muslims who are weak in faith and lax in carrying out their duties as Muslims. So emotion and especially love, in addition to strictly conformist thought and behaviour, are central to Arkhon Sahib's ideas about what it means to be a proper Muslim. Arkhon Sahib believes in the need to Islamise village life and feels that the only way to improve the morality of the villagers is by teaching them a pure and perfect vision of Islam, and by improving their religious practices (*'amal*).

Arkhon Sahib is committed to reforming and purifying village life from the bottom up. Fifteen years ago he joined the Tabligh-e Jama'at,

worldwide movement of Islamic purification, and started to join them on
their preaching tours within and beyond Chitral. This is important for the
arguments of this chapter: movements such as the Tabligh-e Jama'at, of
which Arkhon Sahib is a member, label practices such as amulet-making as
being unlawful innovations. They say that they are un-Islamic and the
product of cultural accretion with non-Islamic traditions and religions.[32]
So it would be expected that a man like Arkhon Sahib would seek to oppose
those known for making amulets he is, rather, also a wellknown amulet-
maker (*tait korak*) himself. In the figure of Arkhon Sahib we see how *shari'a*
conformity can coincide with his knowledge of amulet-making, a practice
for which secret knowledge is of critical importance. Moreover, both
Ismai'li and Sunni villagers, rather than seeing this as an invalidating or
contradictory dimension of Arkhon Sahib's religious personhood, conceptualise it as enriching his status as both a man of learning (*'alim*) and a
saintly figure (*buzurg*).

Arkhon Sahib was always keen to point out that the amulets he made
and the reasons he made them were permissible (*jaiz*) and pure (*pak*). He
told me when I asked him about this sensitive issue, that he never received
payments for the making of amulets, and only made them for reasons that
were permissible from an Islamic perspective (*islami nazria*). As he once
told me, 'He who receives payments for the making of amulets, is selling
the verses of the Qur'an. This is a great sin (*lot gunah*) in Islam, and is
infidelity (*kufr*).' Other 'less reputable' amulet-makers in Chitral, however,
are famous for making amulets of love, that are used to ensnare women into
marriage with their amorous admirers. And what makes it even worse is
that these *dashmanan* receive payments and gifts for making successful
amulets, and do it as a profession (*kasb*).[33]

The amulet is a visible feature of life in Rowshan. Amulets usually
consist of paper on which special *sura* from the Qur'an, and auspicious
sequences of numbers, are written. The paper containing the holy words of
God is then sewn in cloth parcels. I often saw these parcels tied loosely
around the necks of small children, placed above the hearth in the household, strapped onto the legs of horses, and hung from the front mirror of

---

[32] For discussions of religious gifting in other contexts, see, especially, Parry 1994, 1989; Laidlaw 1995, 2000; Raheja 1988.

[33] In his study of amulet making in Buddhist Thailand, Tambiah (1984) explores the role played by amulets in the construction of the interconnected Thai Kingdom. Azeem lives in a small village in one of Pakistan's most remote regions. Yet some villagers told me that the former Prime Minster of Pakistan, Nawaz Sharif commissioned Azeem to make an amulet to ensure that he won an election campaign which he was contesting.

jeeps and minibuses. My friends in Rowshan often told me that they are used to ensnare people into love with one another, stop children from being frightened, curing those with speech impediments (*kakhachi*), bringing cows into milk, and to cure headaches.

The amulets Arkhon Sahib makes are mostly for everyday problems. I have seen him make amulets for a woman with a headache, a man suffering from 'tension', and a cow not coming into milk. The making of an amulet requires both a memorised knowledge of Islamic scriptural texts, and the ability to perform specific bodily gestures and comportment. Arkhon Sahib carefully writes Qur'anic verses and special combinations of numbers onto scraps of paper, 'blows' (*phu'ik*) certain verses of the Qur'an over them, and then puts them into a little envelope for the 'patient' to take home. Arkhon Sahib tells his 'patients' how to use the amulet. Some amulets must be rotated around something or somebody a certain number of times, others tied to a particular type of wood, whilst some must be put in a little cloth pocket and tied around the neck of the person for whom it has been prepared. Amulets have to be cared for. On them is blown the word of God, and they must never be allowed to touch the floor, and they must never be lost or dropped. Far from being in opposition to scriptural visions of the Islamic tradition, then, the making of amulets itself builds on a love of text and a precise knowledge of the Qur'an, and it is the bodily dimension of amulet use that plays a key role in mediating this complex interaction.

On one occasion, for instance, one of the young daughters in the Ismai'li household in which I was staying became ill, and was taken to the village hospital were she saw a doctor and received an expensive prescription of medicine that her father bought. When she was brought back home, however, her father immediately went in search of Arkhon Sahib to ask him to prepare an amulet that would help his daughter recover quickly and safely. The girl was placed in a bed outside my room, given a drip and also had amulets tied around her neck and arms. The girl's father told me that it was only with the help of the amulet that the medicine would be able to have its desired effects (*taito soom justa davaie asar koye*).

That this Ismai'li man was prepared to choose Arkhon Sahib to make an amulet for his daughter is significant. There are Ismai'lis who are also renowned for their ability to make amulets, and, as is discussed below and in greater detail in chapter 7, tensions between Rowshan's Ismai'lis and Sunnis are growing and have resulted in incidents of violence. Yet this Ismai'li man chose to see the Sunni Qazi, rather than an Ismai'li amulet maker. Despite his reputation as a strict Sunni, then, Arkhon Sahib was seen by this man as possessing a form of mystical power (*ruhani taqeat*) that transcended the sectarian division in the village. This mystical power was seen as having the potential of being accessed by both the village's Sunnis and Ismai'lis. This was especially important because Arkhon Sahib was known by both Ismai'lis and Sunnis in Rowshan for thinking that Ismai'lis are non-Muslims, and he often made comments saying this in his sermons in the village mosque. At one level, then, religious knowledge and education is a dimension of life where cognitive differences between Ismai'lis and Sunnis are held to be pronounced and unbridgeable. At another level, however, spiritual power and the practices to which this is put, have the potential of generating shared sources of faith and values for the village's Ismai'lis and Sunnis.

Arkhon Sahib manages, then, to combine the use of secret knowledge about amulet-making and a reputation for being a *shari'a*-oriented *dashman*. By making amulets Arkhon Sahib is behaving as 'a worshipper who assumes from the outstart that divinity is within him/her and whose task in prayer and devotion is to express and reinforce this ontological oneness with the Absolute that is God' (Parkin 2000: 12). Yet, at the same time, Arkhon Sahib has also committed himself to more strictly defined knowledge of Islamic law and learning. In doing so he is a Muslim 'who perceive[s] there to be an unbridgeable ontological gap between themselves as humans and God, who is therefore always likely to be in some way external to mankind' (12). By emphasising the extent to which the amulets he makes and the reasons he makes them conform to the *shari'a*, Arkhon Sahib manages to combine these two religious paradigms in a way that is acceptable to Rowshan's Muslims. Thus, what is important here is not that Arkhon Sahib is a 'Sufi' or an 'anti-Sufi' nor a monist or an ontological dualist, but, rather, that he draws on distinct classes of Islamic knowledge during his daily life. Rather than being in opposition to one another, *shari'a* conformity and the making of amulets are both important features of Arkhon Sahib's personhood, but this is not something that is effortless and unproblematic either for Arkhon Sahib himself or for Rowshan people. Rather, it requires mindful activity on Arkhon Sahib's part, and this entails him thinking carefully and aloud about what type of amulets he makes, for whom he makes them, and what type of amulet-maker he wishes to be seen as by the villagers. It is the product of this careful thought that makes him an *'alim*, whilst being known by Rowshan people as a committed and strict Sunni *dashman*, who is respected and seen as a man of authority for both Rowshan's Sunnis and Ismai'lis. In the context of the picture chapter 7 paints of the current shape of Sunni-Ismai'li relations in the village, Arkhon Sahib has accomplished a decidedly complex and fraught task.

There are several other amulet makers in Rowshan are particularly renowned for their ability to make amulets. These men, however, do not only make amulets for 'everyday' problems like Arkhon Sahib, they, rather, specialise in the making of 'love amulets' and amulets that help polo, football, cricket and volleyball teams win sporting tournaments. As we have seen, for Arkhon Sahib, and many 'ordinary' Muslims in Rowshan, such amulets are beyond the pale of Islam: those who make them are guilty of committing a great sin.

The Sunni amulet-maker upon whose work I now focus, however, has very different interpretations of the secret and hidden knowledge he is able to use for the benefit of his clients, and he has undergone a very different experience of Islamic education. This amulet-maker (*tait korak*) and trained *dashman*, Azeem, is said by many villagers to be a deviant (*apakar nisiru*) *dashman*. Azeem is widely rumoured not merely to accept gifts for his toils, but, rather, to actively request them, and this, for some villagers I spoke to, is something that invalidates his status as properly trained and sincere *dashman*. One Ismai'li man in his late thirties commented to me that when he walked past Azeem's house sometimes he saw a refrigerator and sometimes a television. He told me that he always knew when Azeem had made an amulet because the next day a fat ram was to be seen tethered outside his house awaiting slaughter. This man told me that he suspected Azeem of requesting gifts, and, therefore, committing the sin of selling the verses of the Qur'an. Amulet-making is, then, something that takes place in the vision of Rowshan people, and it is a domain of village life they find especially fascinating. Villagers distinguish carefully between different *dashmanan* who make amulets, and this is something that influences both the ways in which they reflect on amulet-making, and the extent to which it enriches or invalidates a *dashman*'s authority.

Azeem is a widely reputed and prestigious amulet-maker known and sought out beyond the immediate locality of Rowshan and even Chitral. Azeem is famous not only amongst Chitralis for his ability to persuade girls' 'hearts to catch' (*hardi chokiek*) with their male admirers, but also, according to my friends in Rowshan, across the whole of Pakistan.[34] Azeem

---

[34] Anthropologists and historians have documented the levels at which scholarly and legal proficiency are bestowed on Islam's legal experts, see Masud, Messick and Powers: 1996: 15–20; Powers 1996. Gilsenan 1990a: 134–138 documents the tools Lebanese villagers used to bestow and deny authenticity to Sheikhs.

lives in a small hamlet located about five miles down valley from Rowshan: he is the son of a *dashman*, and claims descent from a family of religious teachers who came to Chitral from the Central Asian city of Bukhara about three hundred years ago. Azeem's father also had a reputation of being a 'man of special prayers' (*duagoo*) who was able to make amulets, as well as see things hidden to the ordinary man's eye. Religious knowledge, then, is something that is a defining feature of Azeem's family history, but the way Azeem himself conceptualises his unique ability to make amulets does not rest on the transition of secret knowledge handed down from generation to generation (*nasil ba nasil*) alone. The transmission of secret knowledge, for Azeem, is also something that comes through effort and work. Azeem emphasis the work he has invested into learning the skill (*mahir*) of making amulets.

Azeem, now his mid-thirties, short, rotund and with a neatly trimmed beard, had in his youth studied in a *madrasa* in Karachi, and had later become a journalist for an Urdu paper in the city. Whilst Azeem is said to hold fewer certificates (*sana'at*) proving his religious training than other *dashmanan* in the region, he is still said to be a *dashman*. Although villagers also told me that Azeem was 'less of a scholar' than other *dashmanan* in the region who held more certificates and had attended higher-status *madrasas*. So villagers do interrogate the basis of a *dashman's* claim to religious authority, and reflective consideration of the qualifications that individual *dashmanan* hold is an important dimension of this.[35]

Azeem is nowadays most renowned for being able to make amulets that allow love-sick 'boys' (*daqan*) to elope with 'girls' (*kumoran*). For many in Rowshan, a girl who elopes brings not only disrespect on her family, but also destroys her own life: a woman who elopes is often not allowed to 'appear before the eyes' (*ghechi nisik*) of her father and her family for many years, and sometimes never.

For Azeem the use of secret knowledge (*khoasht ilm*) – something that involves the direct interaction between humans and the spirits (*jinaat*) – constitutes what he refers to as a science.

For spiritual power a person must do *practical* [he used the English] work and effort that is like a *science* [English]. After doing this effort (*mehnat*) it is possible to see the spirits and to take services from them (*hetan sar khidmat ganing boyen*). For example, you can write 'Allah' beautifully on a wall. You need to be in a state of purity – not having smoked a cigarette, not having been intoxicated and not

---

[35] Compare Gilsenan 2000 for a discussion of the sheikh's ability to 'see into the secrets of others and to penetrate the disciple and to demand his complete submission' (Gilsenan 2000: 610).

having told a lie. If you then remember Allah over and over again a fire will catch light and the room will become filled with a light just like the light that comes from an electric light bulb. Then you will start speaking to the spirits and they will give you a gift, like a ring or something else. Then you can start taking service from them. The spirits are just hidden creatures (*khoasht makhluk*), and it is possible to see them with one's own eyes and hear with one's own ears, just like they are speaking to you down a telephone, if you know how to and are prepared to work hard.

Azeem sees his special ability to perceive hidden dimensions of the world as a product of his hard work (*mehnat*), and deep understanding of the Qur'an. Strikingly, Azeem sought to help me to understand his complex craft by likening it to the electrical devices of modernity: telephones and light bulbs were the things that allowed Azeem to most easily relay what he did to the sceptical outsider.

For many in the village, Azeem's ability to know about things that are secret is a source of deep anxiety. One Ismai'li man in his thirties told me how he had taken two women from his village to see Azeem. One of the women had told Azeem that he was a liar (*changatu*) and a fraud (*doukhabaz*) and unable to perform the miracles (*mojiza*) he said he was able to. In response Azeem told the woman that she had a scar (*zakhmi*) on the left side of her back, something she admitted was true, and shocked her by his ability to see even the most hidden parts of her body (*jism*). The man who told me the story commented that Azeem is so skilled at what he does that 'he is able to see the bodies of others'. If the body is the source of hidden thoughts and emotions, then Azeem is conceptualised as able to penetrate even the most secret domains of people's lives, and this, in the eyes of Rowshan people makes him a dangerous and ambiguous feature of their lives.[36] Yet Azeem was also accused of receiving improper financial benefit for possessing the skills he did: it was widely rumoured that a constant stream of gifts – televisions, video players, washing machines – could be seen outside the door of Azeem's house.

The power of the amulets Azeem makes is talked about by many in the village. One man in his mid-thirties told me the following story.

A boy had fallen in love with a girl who lived in a village about twenty miles from the boy's home. The boy had little contact (*rabita*) with the girl – he had just seen her 'on the paths', fallen in love with her and conducted research (*tafsish*) to discover who she was. The boy was unemployed and realised that there was no way his father would allow him to marry, or persuade the girl's father to give him his

---

[36] Compare Overing and Passes 2000.

daughter. So he went to Azeem [the famous amulet-maker], told him his problem and asked for an amulet. Azeem made the amulet and asked the boy to pay him three thousand rupees [a great deal of money in Chitral]. The boy was able to do this by taking loans from some of his friends. The next day the girl, of her own accord, left her house and took a jeep to the boy's village, went to his house and asked him to marry her. The boy had arranged for an *'alim* to perform the *nikkah* between them, and they were married.

Azeem's amulets, then, have the power to make girls do irrational things that are driven by their passions and emotions.[37] Women who do not even usually consider leaving the confines of their homes are instrumentally directed to walk to the public road and ride in jeeps alongside unknown and unrelated male drivers.

The man who told me this story was married with three children, and worked as a gardener and driver for one of the district's most successful advocates and respected 'intellectuals'. The advocate who employed the driver prided himself for being 'rational' and 'scientific'; and his polite and self-effacing driver often told me that much of his employer's intellectual sophistication had rubbed off on him. The advocate's driver commented to me one day that he had little of a belief in the power of amulets. It was, he told me, only tales of girls making the risky and dangerous decision to 'flee' in order to marry with the boy they loved that really proved the power of the amulet.

Many other young and educated men told me that all the commotion about amulet-making was 'a load of rubbish' (*saf bagwaz*). When I asked them what they thought of amulet-making they would tell me that above all it is lies, and that I should not waste my time with Rowshan's amulet-makers. Yet, even these critical and rational-minded men often said they believed that the only amulets that did work were those that helped boys elope with the girls they loved. 'What else', I was often asked, 'would make a girl run away from her home and bring disrespect to her entire family?' For these men, there was simply no other way to explain why a girl would risk severing contact with her father and mother.

At one level, then, there is the sense in the minds of Rowshan people that, 'strong feelings can affect cognition by clouding or distorting it'. In doing so, strong feelings are seen as having the potential of limiting the extent to which thought is able to inform the decision-making that I have argued to be an important and stressful feature of what it means to live a

---

[37] On important divisions within the *ulama* in South Asia, see, especially, Metcalf 1982; Sanyal 1996; Werbner 2002.

Muslim life in Chitral. Yet, what is interesting here is where Rowshan people conceptualise these 'strong feelings' as having their origin. Rather than simply being the result of animalistic emotions or uncontrollable passions, they are, instead, the products of a mechanical device that can make an intense emotional state happen; and this mechanical device itself is something into which both intellectual work and religious knowledge has been invested. One dimension of living a Muslim life in Rowshan involves the self-fashioning of balanced levels of affection and emotion that allow cultured and mindful activity. Yet there are also deeply held anxieties about the ways in which selfhood, the body, and ideally moral and rational emotions can be directed and violated in a manipulative way by others. And this is a particularly pernicious dimension of life because it has the potential of poisoning the reputation of both individual people as well as their families.

Azeem is known by many Rowshan people as a 'great scoundrel' (*bo badmash*), and it is the way he uses the words of the Qur'an to manipulate and alter villagers' emotional states that makes him, for many people, a dangerous figure in village life. Some of the village's *dashmanan* claimed he was using his religious knowledge in ways that were 'not acceptable' in Islam. For these *dashmanan*, marriage without parental permission is impermissible (*najaiz*) and, thus, so is the work of this renowned maker of 'love amulets'. In making amulets of love he was stepping outside the boundaries of Islam and the *shar'ia*, and in doing so he had, I was often told, 'reached infidelity' (*kufra tortei*). These *dashmanan* often complain about what he and other amulet-makers do in their discussions with villagers and in their sermons in Rowshan's mosques. Here, then, Azeem in the minds of many of Rowshan's *dashmanan* is deviant and he has gone beyond the pale of correct and proper Islamic doctrine and practice.

The controversial *'alim* has a reply for his critics who are both trained *ulama* and 'ordinary' Muslims, however. When I asked him about these accusations he told me that in making such amulets he was in fact doing a great service for the young Muslims of Chitral. The region's 'narrow-minded' religious authorities were not able to appreciate this because of their very limited and confined understanding of Islam, and the 'complex-ities' (*pechidagi*) and 'compulsions' (*majboori*) of people's lives. Was the act of 'illegal fornication' (*zina*) between a boy and girl outside marriage (*wenikaho*) not a greater sin than the conducting of a recognised Islamic marriage rite between a man and a woman without the permission of their parents? In making these amulets Azeem argued that he was, in fact, directing the region's Muslims back to the 'straight path' (*sirat-al musta-qim*) of Islam. In arguing so he was also demonstrating that, unlike other *dashmanan* in the region, he could deploy his critical faculties flexibly in a way that is beneficial for the faith at a time when, as never before, it is threatened by social change and modern values.

Azeem has his own understanding of Islam and his own vision of Islamisation, then, even though he seems to be a very different kind of *dashman* from the young *dashmanan* and Arkhon Sahib whom I have discussed earlier in the chapter. Even more important is the fact that intellectual categories and reasoned thought come into play even in his account of what he is doing, and this is surprising since what he is doing is making love magic and dispensing amulets. The interaction between love, reason and thought, then, in the minds of Rowshan people is multidimensional, is grounded in in-depth understandings of contrasting Islamic intellectual traditions, and it is something that contributes to the intellectual vibrancy of village life. In chapter 4 the experience of the emotion of love was seen, in the case of Israr, as having the potential of inducing deep and inward thoughts that contributed to the cultivating of a sophisticated mind, and villagers made connections between this and classic Persian Sufi texts. Here, however, love is conceptualised by Rowshan people in quite different ways. In the context of the way in which Azeem conceptualises amulet making, love is an overpowering emotion that has the potential of leading people away from Islam's 'straight path': there is a fear that lovers may sin (*gunah korik*) by having sexual relations outside of marriage. It is for this reason that Azeem rationally and religiously justifies his making of amulets: he can use his special knowledge of Islam and embodied techniques that allow him to communicate with the spirits, to bring lovers together in marriage and save them from sin (*gunah*) and evil (*shumi*). In his own way, Azeem conceives what he does as 'preventing evil and promoting virtue', but in ways very different from that of the Taliban. For Azeem, then, the mechanical cultivation of emotional states that make rational thought impossible has a positive dimension, and as a last resort, is the only way of ensuring that lovers live a correct and proper Muslim life.

The continuing power of the amulet in Rowshan is not then a reflection of the inability of village Muslims to understand the 'formal requirements' of Islam (Robinson 2000: 5). Nor does the fact that religious scholars trained in Deobandi *madrasa*s make amulets suggest that even when village Muslims do come into contact with 'revivalist Islam' they are unable to understand the complexities of the courses which they follow. Rather, the *dashmanan* who make amulets bring their reform-oriented learning into their understandings of the sensitive and much-debated practice of amulet-making. And villagers who commission *dashmanan* to make amulets for them themselves distinguish in subtle ways between those amulet-makers whom they see as operating within the pale of Islam, and those they see as having 'reached infidelity'. Moreover, even *dashmanan* who are widely seen by Rowshan people to be making amulets in a way that goes 'beyond the pale of Islam' justify their practices by calling upon their villagers to recognise the challenges the Islamic tradition faces in the 'modern era of reform' (*tajdido zamana*).

Reformist and rationalising trends in Islamic scholarship and religiosity have had a powerful impact on the thinking of Rowshan Muslims, yet secret knowledge continues to be a powerful component of the Islamic tradition in Rowshan. Thus revivalist Islam has not simply homogenised Muslim thought in Rowshan, made more vivid the differences between the village's Sunnis and Ismai'lis, and eradicated 'magical' local traditions. Rather, the ideas and visions of reform-oriented Islam has contributed to the vibrant intellectual environment of debate that is a central feature of contemporary village life.

CONCLUSION

Rowshan people thus think in a multidimensional ways about the village's *dashmanan*, and the way they do so reveal much about the status and role of the *ulama* in this Muslim society. What I found in Rowshan is that villagers exercise a far greater degree of choice, thought, and reflection in these matters than might be expected from many accounts of *ulama, madrasas* and Taliban-style 'brainwashing' both within and beyond South Asia. But I also discovered a great deal about what Chitral people think about the nature of the interaction between thought and emotion.

This chapter suggests that conventional ways of classifying Muslims as being either traditionalist or Islamist, strict or liberal, Sufi or anti-Sufi are overly simple in the context of the Islamic tradition in Rowshan. It is not only the poets and musicians of Markaz or the social science educated young Rowshan men, then, who creatively combine different dimensions of the Islamic tradition through processes of intellectual creativity. Rather, thought, reasoned contemplation, and living a mindful Muslim life are things that also weigh heavily on the minds of Rowshan's *dashmanan* and ordinary villagers.

Intellectual work and religious learning are conceptualised in the minds of Rowshan people as having the power to transform emotional states, and these processes of transformation are seen to play an important role in the functioning of the critical faculties. There is a spectrum of ways in which emotional states and religious learning interact. Religious knowledge and piety have the capacity to make young *dashmanan* emotional about religion in ways that can limit their ability to think, and may sometimes make their minds altogether incapable of thought. At the same time, religious knowledge may also be used mechanically by *dashmanan* in order to alter the emotional states of others in the village, and may make people act in a way that prevents them from recognising the consequences of their actions. Even where strong feelings 'cloud rational thought' (Elster 2000), Rowshan people see intellectual work as having an important role to play in everyday village life.

An important dimension of this chapter, then, has been the ways in which the changing economy of religious knowledge in Rowshan is affecting the shape of Ismai'li-Sunni relations in the village. It has shown that Rowshan people hold deep anxieties about the danger of the bodies and minds of the village's young being violated both by excessive learning and by the improper deployment of religious knowledge. In the next chapter I explore in greater detail the nature of the Sunni-Ismai'li divide in Rowshan life and the potential that overpowering feelings have to violate what should ideally be the mindful bodies of Chitral people.

CHAPTER 7

To eat or not to eat? Ismai'lis and Sunnis in Rowshan

INTRODUCTION

As was seen in chapter 6, Rowshan people value the experience of emotion as a rational, educated, intellectual and articulated endowment of a person. Strong feelings are conceptualised by Rowshan people as dangerous: they have the potential to narrow minds and preclude rational thought and decision-making. And this is particularly significant for Chitral people, and for the broader arguments of this book, because decision-making in fraught and emotionally charged social contexts is such an important element of Muslim life in Chitral. This chapter too is concerned with emotions, but here I explore the ways in which strong feelings feature as a dimension of faith and spiritual experience for Rowshan people. I also ask where Rowshan people at times of heightened emotional experience conceptualise strong feelings as having their source. The ethnographic focus for this chapter are the multifaceted relations between Sunnis and Ismai'lis in the village.

As we have already seen, there are underlying tensions between Rowshan's Sunnis and Ismai'lis that manifest themselves especially in their conceptions of women and purdah, as well as in their thinking about religious education and the status and role of the Sunni *dashmanan.* Yet Ismai'lis and Sunnis also join together in the shared experience of the play of the mind and creative musical and intellectual performance, and the village is widely conceptualised by Rowshan people as a single moral unit. But what I document in this chapter is the other side of the experience of Sunni–Ismai'li relations in Rowshan: the experience of violent conflict showing how Rowshan people both experience and reflect upon the altered emotional states that come into being during moments of heightened sectarian tension and conflict.

There is a rich anthropological literature on Muslim life in religiously and culturally diverse social contexts, and there is also a large body of anthropological writing on religious syncretism.[1] Of particular significance to this chapter is the role of cognitive processes in the erecting of boundaries in settings where there are also powerful shared sources of faith and values.[2] There is also a major body of scholarly writing on communal and sectarian violence in South Asia, and of relevance to this chapter are the ways in which these works theorise the presence of 'discourses of difference' and religious hostility as well as frameworks of syncretism (C. Bayly 1998: 210).[3]

Both within and beyond South Asia, anthropologists have sought to account for and analyse forms of political violence. A key issue here is the extent to which violence in certain cultural settings is a routinised feature of daily life and an implicit dimension of sociality, or, rather, if moments of violence represent uncharacteristic and pathological breakdowns of the social order.[4] One important dimension of this debate is a concern with the place that emotional modes play in moments of political violence. For some commentators feelings of both aggression and fear facilitate the process by which underlying tensions rise to the surface (see, especially, Tambiah 1996: 266–96). Other works treat communalism as something very different: the product of instrumental actions by strategising politicians and the use of violence by the state, and not a result of passion, emotion and mass feeling (e.g. Brass 1997, 2003). Yet both of these paradigms have been challenged both for over exaggerating the power and instrumentality of 'the state' as a causal agent in moments of violence (Peabody 2000), and for underestimating the agency of local 'critics of violence or advocates of non-violent resolution' (Didier 2004: 66).

Yet one theme that is common to much of this body of literature is the critical emphasis that it assigns to the role that 'public arenas' have played in defining the nature of communal conflict in both colonial India and in the post-independence South Asian states (see, especially, Freitag 1989). From this perspective, the emergence of so-called communal riots is intimately linked to 'public arenas' and the 'popular collective activities' that are enacted within them (Freitag 1989: 25). Collective sacred ceremonial performance and popular protest were central components of public

---

[1] On Islamic 'syncretism' in India and elsewhere, see Barth 1983, 1993; S. Bayly 1989, 2000; Beatty 1999; Dale 1980; Eaton 1993; Hefner 1985; Lambek 2000b; Roy 1983; Topan 2000. On anthropological studies of religious pluralism in other world religions, see especially Laidlaw 1995 and Gombrich 1971.

[2] See especially, Barth 1983, 1993; C. Bayly 1983; Beatty 2002; Bringa 1996; Laidlaw 1995; van der Veer 1992.

[3] On communal violence in South Asia, see, especially, C. Bayly, 1983; Brass 1997; Das (ed.) 1990; Freitag 1989; Hansen 1999; O'Hanlon 1993; Pandey 1990.

[4] On the anthropology of political violence, see, especially, Daniel 1996; Kapferer 1988; Richards 1996; G. Robinson 1995; Spencer 1990a, 1990b; Tambiah 1992, 1996.

activity in South Asia. Under the conditions of colonialism, when personal forms of identity were invested with greater political power, public arena activity was critical in determining the form of so-called 'communal conflict' in South Asia: a thin line divided popular protest from the emotionally charged urban riot. More generally, the 'public sphere' in Muslim majority contexts is increasingly understood as the central domain in which Muslim identity is constructed and invested with political import-ance, and the 'site where contests take place over the definition of the common good' (Eickelman and Salvatore 2002: 94).

I document here how urban public spaces, public protests, and riots have also played a central role in the recent history of Sunni-Ismai'li relations in Chitral. Yet I also seek to illuminate a dimension of religious conflict in South Asia that has hitherto been largely overlooked: the role that anxieties concerning secret knowledge and concealed action play in moments of religious conflict. In the previous chapters of this book I have emphasised the powerful role that anxieties about the concealed and secret dimensions of Rowshan life play in villagers' experiences of the world in which they live – in this chapter I seek to bring this dimension of Rowshan life to our understanding of Ismai'li-Sunni relations in the village. By doing so, I seek to offer insights into forms of covert and hidden violence that, whilst having been explored by anthropologists in other regions, most especially the Middle East, have not been the focus of sustained analysis in the study of communal violence in South Asia where the urban riot is the focus of most major discussions.

Sectarian conflict and violence between Sunnis and Shi'a Muslims have intensified to such an extent in present day Pakistan that some scholarly commentators suggest that it is threatening the very viability of the country.[5] A combination of targeted killings of religious scholars and Shi'a profes-sionals and communal sectarian warfare has brought severe dislocation and upheaval to many regions of the country. Sectarian conflict in Pakistan is itself part of a broader spectrum of violence in the country, and, as Oskar Verkaaik has recently shown, the boundary between sectarian and other forms of conflict in the country is a fraught and partial one (Verkaaik 2004). This spectrum of 'political violence' includes the involvement of neofunda-mentalist para-military organisations in conflict in Kashmir as well as full-scale war with India. There have also been prolonged periods of ethnically, politically, and linguistically motivated urban violence, especially in

---

[5] On Shi'a–Sunni conflict elsewhere in Pakistan, see Aase 1999; Nasr 2000, Zaman 2002. On Pakistan's Shi'a, see Ahmad, M. D. 1987 and Schubel 1993: 1–34.

Pakistan's largest city, Karachi, and these have often served to blur the boundary between episodic conflict and full-scale civil war.[6]

Violence in Rowshan, and Chitral generally, is much rarer than what both many popular and academic commentators suggest is the norm elsewhere in Pakistan, but it is a matter of intense concern and debate in village life. The Frontier Province has long been portrayed in both colonial and more modern ethnography as home to a distinctive kind of violence, not so much 'communal' as 'tribal'. 'Revenge', the 'feud' and tests of prowess and masculinity are supposedly central to Pukhtun life (Ahmed 1980; Lindholm 1982, 1996). This is a dimension of Pukhtun life that is interestingly reflected on and questioned by Banerjee (2000) in her account of Abdul Ghaffar Khan and his non-violent and anticolonial independence movement especially influential in the 1930s and 1940s, the *Khudai Khidmatgars* (The Servants of God). The form of honour-oriented violence often associated with Pukhtuns is deeply problematic for Chitral people, however. Indeed, they distinguish themselves from Pukhtuns on precisely these grounds: they talk about themselves as 'peace lovers' (*aman pasand*) compared to the 'wild' (*jangali*) Pukhtuns, and there have between influential socioeconomic movements in the region which have sought to limit the growth of Pukhtun influence in Chitral. That the potential for Sunni–Ismai'li relations to become violent is a focus of concern, raises profound questions directly relevant to the concerns of my book, and is a very painful dimension of life for Rowshan people.

There is also a further layer of complexity concerning the nature of sectarian conflict in Chitral; this is a reflection of the specific configuration of Islamic doctrinal traditions in the region, and it is something of which Chitral people themselves are deeply aware. There are no Shi'a Muslims in Chitral, and Ismai'lis say, in particular, that the absence of Shi'a Muslims in Chitral has resulted in the relatively few incidents of violent conflict that have taken place in the region. Indeed, Ismai'lis often say that 'if only there had been Shi'a Muslims in Chitral, then we Ismai'lis would have lived totally peaceful lives as the aggressive Shi'a Muslims fought against the Sunnis, and ignored us'.[7] This, my Ismai'li friends often told me, was the situation in Gilgit where Sunni, Shi'a, and Ismai'li Muslims are all represented, but where most sectarian clashes have involved Sunni and Shi'a

---

[6] On ethnic and linguistic violence in Pakistan, see Harrison 1986; Hussain 1990; Tambiah 1996: 163–210. Though see Brass 1997 and Das 1995 on the problem of assigning causal labels to such events.
[7] The 1979 Islamic revolution played a major role in promoting Shi'a revolutionary activism in Pakistan, see Nasr 2002.

Muslims (see Aase 1999).[8] Indeed, Sunni Muslims from Gilgit I knew often commented to me that they were shocked by the degree of open animosity towards Ismai'lis that they encountered whilst speaking to Chitral's Sunni Muslims. I was often told by my Ismai'li friends, as well as some Sunnis, that Ismai'lis are especially soft (*narum*) and forgiving (*mu'af korak*) people. The reason for this, according to Ismai'lis and Sunnis is because the Aga Khan tells Ismai'lis, and especially Chitral Ismai'lis, to live in peace with what he calls their 'sister community' (the Sunnis). Thus, there is a difference between attitudes towards Sunnis and Ismai'lis who are of the village, and those held towards Sunni, Ismai'li and, especially, Shi'a Muslims both within and beyond Pakistan.

The ethnographic material presented in this chapter reflects this array of theoretical, regional and theological complexities. I begin by presenting a series of vignettes that illustrate the key complexities in the experience of Sunni–Ismai'li interaction in 'normal' times. I then document a number of terrifying 'critical events' (Das 1995) involving severe sectarian violence.[9] I conclude the chapter with a discussion of a 'spiritual journey' made by one Ismai'li family to see the Aga Khan – the spiritual leader of the Ismai'lis – on his October 2000 visit to Gilgit in northern Pakistan. By treating this journey as form of personal 'critical event', I show how not all 'critical events' are inevitably about public outbursts of rioting and – they also have the potential to generate surprising moments of intercommunal 'peace' (*aman, sukoon*).

TO EAT OR NOT TO EAT: SUNNIS AND ISMAI'LIS IN ROWSHAN

Beatty's recent article on a religiously plural village in Java raises important issues for the analysis of Ismai'li–Sunni relations in Rowshan (Beatty 2002). He argues that social harmony is such a powerful component of village values that it is not how villagers maintain village harmony in the context of religious plurality that needs to be explained, but rather how they learn to recognise the differences that divide them. Barth's account of the interaction between Sunni, Shi'a and Ibadi Muslims in the Omani town of Sohar also explores the interaction between religious plurality and notions of social harmony (Barth 1983). In contrast to Beatty's discussion of Java, Barth argues

---

[8] On the complexity of the exchange of theological doctrines between the Northern Area's Ismai'li and Shi'a communities, see Nasr 2002: 339–40.
[9] For Das, critical events result in 'new modes of action' and the redefining of 'traditional categories' (Das 1995: 4–5).

that, whilst Muslims of different doctrinal traditions interact in Sohar, they also go to great lengths to avoid discussing matters that have the potential to threaten the surface calm of town life. Difference in Sohar, then, needs to be denied in public to allow harmony to be maintained.[10]

As was seen in chapter 3, harmony (*aman*) and peace (*sukoon*) are important dimensions of the village as a moral unit in the minds of Rowshan people. They exist, however, alongside discourses that divide the village's Ismai'lis and Sunnis, and it is the complex interaction between these discourses and sets of values that I focus on here. How do Rowshan people distinguish between Ismai'lis and Sunnis in the village, and how do villagers go about maintaining village harmony at the same time as recognising the important doctrinal differences that divide them?

The doctrinal differences that divide Rowshan's Muslims are deeply rooted in the division between open and secret knowledge, a division that is also important in the ways in which Rowshan people make moral valuations, partake in spiritual experience and classify the village's *dashmanan*. The Ismai'li tradition of Islam has historically emphasised the spiritual and practical importance of keeping sacred knowledge secret. Ismai'li doctrines focus particularly on the need to understand the inner (*batin*) meanings of the Qur'an. Ismai'li Qur'anic interpretation (*tafsir*) emphasises the importance of esoteric hermeneutics (*ta'wil*) in which the surface words of the Qur'an are understood as having a deeper meaning than the doctrines they elicit.[11] Ismai'lis in Rowshan often discussed these issues with me, as well as amongst themselves, often saying that the best way of understanding the difference between *ta'wil* and surface-level interpretations of the Qur'an (*tanzil*) was by likening the holy book to a rose (*gulab*). Whilst the beauty of the rose's petals can be seen by a human's naked eyes, the original (*asil*) beauty of the rose – its perfume (*wourie*) – is hidden from sight.[12]

Ismai'lis are taught that they have special access to spiritual truth (*haqiqat*) because they have faith in the spiritual guidance (*ruhani hidayat*) of the 'Present Imam' (*hazir-e imam*) – the Aga Khan. The Present Imam is the direct descendent of the Prophet, and is imbued with a spiritual power that places him at the centre of the Ismai'li faith. He is the spiritual father

---

[10] Compare F. Bailey's (1997) discussion of 'ritualised politeness' and ethnic conflict in eastern India.

[11] For discussions and translations of one important Ismai'li thinkers whose works are read and recited by many Chitral Ismai'lis, see Hunsberger 2000. On the importance of the hidden in the identity and faith of Turkish Alevis, see Yalman 1969, and compare Mir-Hosseini 1994 the hidden in Iranian Kurdish religious doctrines.

[12] Compare Andreyev 1999 on the ways in which the sixteenth century Pukhtun Rawshaniyya movement transformed 'Pashtunistan into a truly Muslim society which was concerned not only with exoteric Islamic rituals but with deeper spiritual matters as well' (Andreyev 1999: 317).

(*ruhani tat*) of the world's Nizari Ismai'lis.[13] This spiritual power makes him the *qur'an-e natiq* (the talking Qur'an), in that he has the unique ability to understand the hidden meanings of the Book.[14] He transmits his special knowledge of the Qur'an through sermons (*farmans*) that are read out to Ismai'lis across the world in the Ismai'li place of worship, the Jama'at Khana.

Esoteric hermeneutics (*ta'wil*) pervades the Ismai'li understanding of religious practice and thought, and forms an important division between the Ismai'li and Sunni 'doctrinal clusters' (Eickelman 1992a). For Sunni Muslims, the month of Ramadan requires Muslims to abstain from food and drink during daylight hours as a way of strengthening their faith and trust in God. Yet for Ismai'lis, life itself is a fast during which Muslims must resist evil temptations and enjoin better morals and works in their daily lives. Likewise if Sunnis perceive undertaking pilgrimage to Mecca as a religious duty, for the Ismai'lis life's real pilgrimage is the attempt to destroy the carnal soul (*nafs*), and replace it with pure spiritual perfection.[15]

The central tenets of Islamic doctrine and thought, then, are a matter of very great differences in religious interpretation for Rowshan's Sunnis and Ismai'lis living side by side in this intimate village setting. This division is something of which Ismai'lis and Sunnis in Rowshan – educated and uneducated – are cognisant, and these differences in doctrinal interpretation also inform their different conceptions of how villagers set to the task of being Muslim.

An Ismai'li woman in her early twenties, educated to higher secondary level, told me, 'The difference between us and the Sunnis is that we believe in spiritual truth [*haqiqat*] and they believe in the *shari'a* [Islamic law].' This young woman went on to say that it was because Ismai'lis lived in an 'era of spiritual truth' (*haqiqato zamana*) made possible by their belief in the present Imam that they do not need to observe purdah. She said that Ismai'lis practice a deeper form of 'purdah of the heart' (*hardio purdah*), and that only those who believe in the *shari'a* and do not recognise the Aga Khan as being the spiritual leader (*ruhani peshwa*) need to physically 'hide their faces' (*mukhan khoashteik*). This woman told me that the only reason

---

[13] There have been a number of doctrinal splits during the course of Ismai'li history. The Nizari Ismai'lis are the largest Ismai'li doctrinal cluster and came into being as a result of a schism over the succession to the Imamate in 1094; see Daftary 1998: 2. The other Ismai'li group is the Tayyibi Ismai'lis, known in South Asia, as the Bohras, see Blank 2001. The Ismai'lis in Chitral and, indeed, northern Pakistan, are all Nizari Ismai'lis.

[14] There are strong parallels between the Ismai'li concept of the Present Imam and he importance of people of special mystical insight (*pirs*) in Sufism. See Daftary 1999 on Ismai'li Sufi relations in Safavid Persia.

[15] See, for instance, Hunsberger 2000: 193.

she veiled in public was because she had to respect the practices of her Sunni neighbours. Not all Ismaiʾlis in the village talk of purdah in terms of the heart and true emotions. As was seen in chapter 4, however, when they do not think of purdah in these terms, they are often accused by other Ismaiʾlis in the village of not being proper Ismaiʾlis, and of having only a partial understanding of Ismaiʾli teaching and the *farman*s of the Aga Khan. Being a proper (*sahi*) Ismaiʾli, then, involves having a deep understanding of Ismaiʾli doctrines and thought, and being able to distinguish the way Ismaiʾlis are required to go about leading a Muslim life from that of the village's Sunnis. Yet, critically, it also entails showing respect to the religious sensibilities of Rowshan's Sunnis. Differences between Ismaiʾlis and Sunnis about how the Qurʾan should be read and interpreted thus have a real impact on village life and the experience of lived Islam for Rowshan people.

Yet showing indifference towards the practices and beliefs of others is not something of which all Rowshan people are capable, and maintaining the division between secret and open knowledge is also a dimension of life that is fraught and complex. I have shown throughout the book thus far, especially in chapter 4, that many Rowshan Ismaiʾlis and Sunnis maintain long-lasting friendships that cross the sectarian divide, and that many if not all Rowshan people are prepared to engage in discussions and debates about issues of great sensitivity with their fellow villagers. Moreover, in chapter 5 I also documented how even in Sunni-dominated Markaz Ismaiʾlis and Sunnis perform together in musical groups, and gather to join in the shared experience of attending musical programmes. Thus, at one level, many forms of Ismaiʾli–Sunni relationships in the Chitral region entail a degree of openness and shared forms of both daily and special experiences. This challenges the assumption made by many scholars of Pakistan that emerging forms of sectarian identities have hardened in a one-dimensional way the boundary between Sunni and non-Sunni Muslims in Pakistan.

At the same time, however, Rowshan people also go to considerable lengths to avoid discussing things that have the potential to damage other people's religious sensibilities. In Rowshan this is especially important when villagers discuss the role and status of the Aga Khan in Ismaiʾli religious thought and practice. Whilst many Rowshan Sunnis do express misgivings about the degrees to which Ismaiʾlis respect the Aga Khan as their spiritual leader both to themselves and to their Ismaiʾli friends and neighbours, most if not all Sunni villagers are also careful to talk of the Aga Khan in a deeply respectful way, often referring to him as 'His Highness' or pre-fixing his name with the honorific 'Sahib'. So, living a harmonious (*sukoon*) and peaceful (*aman*) life is a notion that villagers have. This is an ideal they explicitly seek to preserve and promote, and it entails showing a certain level of indifference about the different ways in which villagers set to the task of being Muslim.

Yet showing indifference towards the practices and beliefs of others is not something of which all Rowshan people are capable, and maintaining the division between secret and open knowledge is also a dimension of life that is fraught and complex. I have documented in chapter 3 especially how some villagers are seen as having the capacity to disrupt the calm of everyday village life, and there is also a great fear that devilish children may transmit secret information about the village that they do not know how to conceal. Indeed, during my stay in Rowshan they were several occasions when both Sunni and Ismaiʾli children accused each other of not being 'proper Muslims'. Such tensions and anxieties about when to reveal and when to conceal are also a critical dimension of the way in which the boundary between Ismaiʾlis and Sunnis in the village is constructed and maintained.

Thus, beyond the show of polite indifference, maintaining calm relations between Sunnis and Ismaiʾlis also depends on the continuing efforts of people who are capable of rational and measured thought, and who are able to distinguish between the open and the concealed. A sophisticated and fully working mind must be complemented, however, by the ability to control emotions. People must neither lose control of their own emotions in ways that makes them incapable of rational thought, nor must they rejoice in the dangerous ability they have to make others in the village angry and emotional.

For Ismaiʾlis, hiding contentious features of their beliefs and practices is also about more than the place of secret knowledge in Ismaiʾli philosophy. There is also an important political dimension to the importance of the hidden in the thought processes of Rowshan's Ismaiʾlis. Many of them feel threatened and fearful about their status as Ismaiʾli Muslims not only in the village itself, but also within the broader context of present day Pakistan.[16] As I showed in chapter 6, many Ismaiʾlis in Rowshan say that they fear (*bukhtueik*) to see the Sunni *dashmanan* in their midst. At a time when Chitral Ismaiʾlis are regularly targeted by purist Sunni organisations as enemies of the Islamic 'brotherhood' (*umma*), they have to conceal important dimensions of their religion in the face of very real threats to their safety.

---

[16] Compare Ehmadi 1993, 1998 on the status of Ismaiʾlis in Afghanistan.

Many of Rowshan's Sunni *dashmanan* have publicly vilified the village's Ismai'lis, proclaiming that Sunnis should consign Ismai'lis to the category of *kafir* (enemy unbeliever), and they want their fellow Sunni villagers to change their thinking about their Ismai'li neighbours. Even the mild mannered Arkhon Sahib who is respected by many Sunnis and Ismai'lis in the village, says that Ismai'lis are beyond the pale of correct and proper Islam. For Ismai'lis, the danger of being categorised as unbelievers was greatly heightened in the 1970s when another of Pakistan's large non-Sunni 'heterodox' community, the Ahmediyas, were officially classed as *kafirs* by the government of Zulfikar Bhutto.[17] For Ismai'lis to be bracketed legally or even quasi-officially would have profoundly serious consequences: they would lose civic rights including being able to hold the highest government positions and marry 'mainstream' Muslims.[18] Moreover, for an array of orthodox Muslim movements and organisation, *kafirs* are an enemy for all true Muslims to abjure and extirpate. As ongoing attacks on the Ahmediyas and Shi'a Muslims and the recent bombings and shootings of Christians in Pakistan graphically illustrate, being legally classed as a *kafir* results in real danger for Pakistan's non-Sunni communities.

Rowshan's Ismai'lis are fully aware of this danger, and they often comment that Pakistan's Sunni *ulama* are 'ready to slaughter us' (*ispa kushikotan tayar*). Many *dashmanan* in Rowshan say that Muslims who do not offer prayers five times a day, observe the fast during Ramadan, or travel to Mecca for pilgrimage, and who display pictures of the Aga Khan in their place of worship are not real Muslims (*sahi musulman no*). Significant numbers of *dashmanan* in Rowshan accuse Ismai'lis of commit- ting one of the greatest of all sins (*gunahan*) – the association of a human with God (*shirk*). They say that Ismai'lis worship the Aga Khan as if he is God, and that this is what makes them non-Muslims.

In present day Rowshan even the most basic of day-to-day activities are saturated by concerns of a sectarian nature, and these concerns have the potential of raising the temperature of villagers' emotions and feelings. In particular, some of Rowshan's *dashmanan* have focused on food and *halal* slaughter practices as the key test of correct Sunni–Ismai'li relations. Rowshan's Muslims are very aware of this and it provokes much anxiety and comment. For instance, I was often told that many of Rowshan's Sunni

---

[17] On the successful campaign led by Pakistan's *ulama* and religious parties to label the Ahmediyas as a non-Muslim minority, see Jalal 1990: 153; Nasr 1992: 132–41; 2000, 2002: 94–6; Tambiah 1996: 195–97.

[18] Throughout the 1990s Sunni Islamist parties sought to pressurise the Pakistan government into declaring Shi'as a non-Muslim minority, see Nasr 2002: 343.

dashmanan claim that to eat meat from an animal slaughtered by an Ismai'li is prohibited in Islam: meat is only lawful (*halal*) if killed in the correct Islamic way by a Muslim. Sunnis are told 'not to eat from the hands' (*hostar no zhibik*) of Ismai'lis.[19] Even if Ismai'lis do slaughter animals in the correct Islamic way, the fact that Ismai'lis are 'outside the fold of Islam' makes the meat slaughtered by them, according to many *dashmanan*, prohibited for Sunnis.

For many of Rowshan's ordinary Sunnis following the verdicts of the village's *dashmanan* presents complex problems and is a cause of deep anxieties. It often results in moments of heightened emotional intensity that inflect on the day-to-day shape of Ismai'li-Sunni relations in the village. At one level, the village is a moral unit, and consuming village products, as I showed in chapter 4, is an important way in which social relations are enriched through moral nourishment. The refusal by many Sunni *dashmanan* to eat Ismai'li killed meat and their efforts to make ordinary Sunnis do likewise throws into doubt the very existence of the village as a moral unit for Rowshan people. At another level, however, Rowshan's Sunni Muslims are also under pressure from the village's religious authorities to display religious commitment, and this means erecting boundaries between themselves and their Ismai'li neighbours.

At public ceremonial events such as weddings, for instance, Sunnis must make the decision of either refusing or agreeing to eat meat that is placed before them by Ismai'lis. Not to eat will inevitably make Ismai'li neighbours or even relatives upset (*khafa*) and angry (*qahri*). A Sunni who refuses to eat meat will earn a reputation in Ismai'li eyes as 'extremist' (*intiha pasand*) and 'narrow-minded' (*trang dimagho*). Eating the meat, however, may result in *dashmanan* criticising Sunnis either publicly in Rowshan's mosques or secretly in the village's houses, for their lack of faith and commitment towards pure Sunni Islam. So, Sunnis in the village must continually decide how to situate themselves regarding the place that the Ismai'li–Sunni boundary occupies in their lives, and choices are made and actions taken both within the household and in the wider public gaze. If some Sunnis flout the dictates of the region's anti-Ismai'li *dashmanan* by publicly eating Ismai'li-killed meat, others refuse to eat the meat and some do not even drink water from glasses that have touched Ismai'li lips. So Rowshan people do not simply inhabit fixed sectarian categories. In all kinds of painful and problematic ways, being either Sunni or Ismai'li

---

[19] For a comparative discussion of the important role played by pronouncements over what is and is not *halal* in the form taken by Sunni–Shi'a conflict in Gilgit, Northern Pakistan, see Sokefeld 1999.

entails continual choice-making and continual demands on people to take public initiatives.

More broadly, where we find striking manifestations of 'tolerance' in Rowshan life, where we see Rowshan people not behaving in ways consistent with Muslims as 'unthinking fundamentalists', this is not a matter of indifference to religion. Nor is it that Rowshan people happen to have 'tolerant' attitudes that are just a pre-existing feature of 'Chitral society'. On the contrary, they have to work and choose all the time, and they do so in very problematic and sometimes dangerous circumstances. So, the appearance of relatively harmonious relations between Sunnis and Ismai'lis, of a village of exceptionally tolerant people, is a matter of work and striving and anxiety; and not just an unproblematic fact of life in Chitral in general and Rowshan in particular.

LOVE, ANGER, GREED AND THE ROTTING OF FAITH

The village's Ismai'lis also distinguish between thoughtfully explaining difference in a way that makes living a plural life possible, and building a sectarian boundary that displays their commitment to Ismai'li doctrines. Maintaining faith, religious commitment, and doctrinal differences are things that both Sunnis and Ismai'lis in the village are deeply concerned about. In short, the sectarian divide in the village is connected by Rowshan people to deeper and underlying concerns about the role that emotions and the intellect play in the lived experience of Islam.

Rowshan people also continually grapple with the issue of whether an individual's or a family's sectarian allegiance is fixed, or subject to willed transformation: can or should people convert from one 'doctrinal cluster' to another? This is a very fraught question for Rowshan Muslims, who are well aware of the sensitivities of the issues of religious conversion in Pakistan and elsewhere in the Muslim world.[20] Islam is of course a religion of conversion, yet 'changing religion' (*mazhabo petsik*) is often said by Rowshan people to be something that 'should never happen' (*kiawat di no belik*). Ismai'lis who are even seen to be coveting the doctrines and practices of Sunni Islam, are accused by others Ismai'lis in the village of going astray (*abatha bik*), and of having let their faith (*iman*) go 'rotten' (*pulie*). It is not

---

[20] On the anthropology of conversion, see, especially, Bayly 1989; Hefner 1993; van der Veer 1996; Viswanathan 1998; Levtzion (ed.) 1979. These works focus on the cognitive 'reorientation to the world' (Beatty 2002: 472) and conversion's political importance. My interest here, however, is on the emotional dimension of religious conversion.

only Rowshan's Sunni *dashmanan*, then, who convey a message to villagers that they should set about building much firmer lived boundaries between the village's Ismai'lis and Sunnis, Ismai'lis are also deeply aware of, and involved, in these processes. Beyond the form the sectarian boundary takes in village life, the fact that faith is seen as having the potential of going 'rotten' illuminates the ways in which Rowshan people consider matters of faith to be deeply implicated in questions of emotion. It is to these concerns that I now turn.

Sunni *dashmanan* in the village not only call for the building of lived boundaries between Rowshan's Ismai'lis and Sunnis, they also call for an equally problematic form of action: conversion across the sectarian boundary. Both Ismai'lis and Sunnis have to grapple with this further element of the *dashmanan*'s emotionally charged teachings: they enjoin Sunnis in the village to persuade Ismai'lis to 'convert', and to become 'proper' (*sahi*) Muslims by embracing Sunni Islam. In present day Rowshan, religious conversion is rare, and when it does occur it is conversion from Ismai'li to Sunni Islam. In the thirty-household hamlet in which I lived there had only been one incident of religious conversion over the past ten years when an Ismai'li man converted to Sunni Islam, and then persuaded all his family to join him. This man was uneducated and worked as a driver, and other Ismai'lis in the village often told me that it was because he spent so much time with Sunni drivers that they had *brainwashed* (in English) him. Thus, this Ismai'li driver's conversion to Sunni Islam was not seen as a product of a thoughtful changed vision of Islam. Rather, this man's uneducated and uncultivated mind had made him susceptible to Sunni attempts to encourage him to 'change' (*badel korik*) his religion.

Yet conversion is also about more than unsophisticated minds and poorly developed critical faculties. When Rowshan's Ismai'lis talk about religious conversion they also emphasise the important role played by overpowering emotions in the process. I was told that Ismai'li women converted to Sunni Islam because their 'senses had been tied' by love amulets made by the Sunni *dashmanan* I discussed in the previous chapter. Ismai'li men, I was often told, left the Ismai'li faith because they had become angry when their families had refused to allow them to marry the (Ismai'li) girl they loved, and in 'changing religion' (*mazhabo badel korik*), they were venting their anger on their parents. I was also told that some Ismai'lis converted for the 'greed of money' (*paisao lalichi*): Sunnis in the village were said to promise them financial reward if they converted to Sunni Islam. Their greed meant that their intellect was tied, and that they could not see through the lies of their cunning so-called (*bara-enam*) Sunni friends. Love, anger and greed, then, are seen as powerful emotions that result in the destruction of Ismai'li faith, and the weakening of the Ismai'li community.

Yet, at the same time, such powerful emotions are also conceptualised as a necessary component of what it means to live a good Ismai'li life. At one level, Rowshan people see faith as having the potential to go rotten (*pulie*), and heightened levels of worldly emotion weaken the intellect and the activity of the critical faculties. At another level, however, the implication in referring to faith as 'rotting' is that it is something that needs nurture, continual furbishment and upkeep, or it is possible that it will weaken and decay. This nurturing must at once be based in thought, for Ismai'lis must learn to understand the full depths of Ismai'li teachings, but at the same time faith must also be nurtured through powerful emotions that maintain heightened levels of religious commitment.

Great pressure is placed upon Muslims in Rowshan to be either Sunni or Ismai'lis properly, and proving this to other villagers involves drawing distinct boundaries between the two 'communities' in the village. At the same time, however, many Rowshan people do not simple defer to these calls for them to construct boundaries between Ismai'lis and Sunnis in the village. Rather, they make decisions and take initiatives in specific social settings about how they want to be viewed by others in the village. There are moments of fraught interaction during which the emotional temperature of village life rises, and when decisions made over seemingly minor issues have the potential of hurting sensitive religious feelings. There are moments when Sunnis and Ismai'lis are able to joke and discuss in a relaxed way the most contentious of issues in village life, and when they value the living of a contemplative and plural Muslim life.

Despite the increasing rigidity of the sectarian boundary in the village, Sunnis and Ismai'lis in still have a great many shared values, and one key value that they do share is a view of faith as something that they have to nurture. Yet this shared notion of faith as needing to be nurtured is also something that can cause severe conflict between Rowshan's Ismai'lis and Sunnis, and I now focus in detail on moments of violent conflict between Chitral's Ismai'lis and Sunnis.

SUNNI–ISMAI'LI 'CRITICAL EVENTS' IN CHITRAL: 1982–2001

Stanley Tambiah has argued that violent conflict 'has become an everyday and seemingly permanent state of affairs' that actually 'structures and directs political action' in South Asia (Tambiah 1996: 223). For Tambiah, an important dimension of the 'routinisation' of violence has been its 'ritualisation': 'festivals, rallies, demonstrations, and riots may spill over into one another as collective enactments, involving the participation of crowds experiencing heightened sensibilities' (242). Sectarian violence is a relatively recent feature of Chitral's history, and so I now ask how far such violence is a routinised feature of life in the village, and what role is played by heightened emotional sensibilities during moments of violent sectarian conflict.

I describe two 'critical events' that have occurred in Chitral over the past twenty-three years. These events took place in the context of a serious incident of sectarian violence that occurred in the summer of 1982. The violence is said by Rowshan people to have started in Rowshan and then spread to Markaz. Other violent incidents between Sunnis and Ismai'lis in Chitral in August 1999 and April 2001 have their immediate roots in the 1982 conflict, and are widely recognised by Chitral people as a continuation of it. Many people also fear the possibility that the conflict will continue, and say that the enmity (*dushmani*) that has developed between Ismai'lis and Sunnis in the region will not easily break (*shau no chhiyoor*). I first give a brief description of what I was told happened in 1982 with the aim of explaining the place sectarian violence occupies in the thoughts of Rowshan people. Then, in more depth, I describe and analyse the moments of sectarian conflict and tension that I witnessed whilst in Chitral in 1999 and 2001.

Rowshan Ismai'lis think in multidimensional ways about the history of sectarian relations in the region. At one level, many of the village's Ismai'lis, especially those belonging to the older generation, claim that before the creation of Pakistan and during the 'era of the Chitral state' (*riyasato zamana*), Chitral Ismai'lis suffered 'cruelty' (*zulm*) at the hands of the region's Sunni ruling family. Narratives of forced Ismai'li conversion to Sunni Islam, the appropriation of Ismai'li land and property, and the expulsion (*jela watan korik*) of influential Ismai'li families to other regions in what is now northern Pakistan and to Afghan Badakshan are common themes of conversation for elders in many Ismai'li homes in the village. Within this historical narrative, the creation of Pakistan in 1947 culminated in an 'era of freedom' (*azadio daur*) in which it became possible for Chitral Ismai'lis, generally, to practice their religion openly, and, more particularly, to build separate Ismai'li places of worship.

At another level, however, Rowshan Ismai'lis also claim that the nature of interpersonal relations between 'ordinary' (*aam*) Ismai'lis and Sunnis in the region underwent a radical change only after the events of 1982. 'Before 1982' (*1982ar prooshti*), I was often told, 'nobody really differentiated between Ismai'lis and Sunnis in the village, but after 1982 (*1982ar achi*) religious fighting (*mazhabi janjal*) has been a part of life in the village.' In particular, people in the village would repeatedly tell me that before 1982 marriage between Sunnis and Ismai'lis had been common, and that it was only after 1982 that marriage between Sunnis and Ismai'lis became rare. This is especially important because ideally any Muslim should have the right to marry another Muslim, so when marriage became largely impossible between Ismai'lis and Sunnis a discourse of difference came to define sectarian relations in the region. The incident in 1982 was a critical event, for, following Das, it resulted in 'new modes of action' and the redefining of 'traditional categories' (Das 1995: 4–5) in ways clearly recognised by Rowshan people themselves.

The events of 1982, I was told, arose from the activities (*korum*) and words (*lu*) of a Sunni religious scholar (*'alim, dashman*) from a village about fifteen miles down valley from Rowshan. This *'alim* had studied in a religious college (*madrasa*) in Peshawar, and was said to have close contacts with the then President of Pakistan, General Zia ul Haq. General Zia himself was at the time Islamising the legal system of Pakistan in an attempt to get the support of the country's Sunni *ulama* for his military government.[21] In 1982 the religious scholar returned to his village in Chitral, where he gave a series of inflammatory speeches from the pulpit of his mosque calling upon Chitral's Sunni Muslims to recognise Ismai'lis as *kafir*s, enemy unbelievers. He was also said to have made insulting and offensive remarks about the spiritual leader of the Ismai'lis, the Aga Khan. 'They are committing sins', Rowshan Ismai'lis I spoke to reported the Sunni scholar said. 'Why else should they not allow us to enter their Jama'at Khanas?'[22] These allusions to hidden knowledge and secrecy were well calculated to arouse Chitral Sunni Muslims to anger, as they touched on matters that Chitral Sunni Muslims find emotionally arousing and inflammatory.[23]

Days after giving these addresses in his own village, the *'alim* came to Rowshan where he addressed the village's Sunni Muslims at the Friday mosque near the village polo ground. There he claimed that he had suffered an outrage in the hands of the village's Ismai'lis: he said that two young

---

[21] See, especially, Nasr 2002; Kepel 2002. See also Weiss (ed.) 1986.

[22] Similar remarks were made to me by 'bearded ones' I knew in Markaz.

[23] On the power of *ulama* sermonising, see Gaffney 1994; Hirschkind 2001.

Ismai'li men had removed his sacred prayer hat and thrown it on the ground. Worshippers were summoned to the mosque where the *'alim* told them that he had suffered a gross and intolerable outrage incident at the hands of non-Muslim Ismai'lis, and so he called upon Sunnis in the village to take revenge. On giving this call, large numbers of Sunnis were said to have come to Rowshan from surrounding Sunni villages, and they gathered at the mosque and polo ground adjacent to it. Many of these men were armed.

Rumours that Sunnis were under attack in Rowshan soon reached Markaz – at that time a four-hour jeep journey along a *kacha* (dirt) road down valley; today a two-and-a half hour drive along a metalled road. Religious scholars addressed Sunnis in the mosques of Markaz. They were reported to have said that the 'house of god' was under attack by the non-Muslims in Rowshan, and that it was a duty (*farz*) on Muslims in the region to fight the *kafir*s. A large crowd of Sunni men gathered in the bazaar of Markaz, where they burned down an Ismai'li-owned hotel. Some of these men were said to be Pukhtun-speaking Afghan refugees who had settled in Chitral after the Soviet invasion of Afghanistan in 1979; others were Khowar-speaking Chitral people. United in their defence of the faith, this mixed crowd hunted out prominent Ismai'li people and places. They now moved to a hostel built by the Aga Khan for Ismai'li students studying at colleges in Markaz. They were burning this hostel when an Ismai'li preacher (*waiz*) stood in defence and dispersed the mob by firing a Kalshnikov assault rifle at the Sunni assailants.[24] The Sunni *'alim* whose speeches had incited the initial acts of violence was banned from returning to Chitral for anything other than short visits to his village, where he was no longer allowed to address congregations in his mosque. In addition, several prominent Ismai'lis were also arrested and jailed in an attempt to prevent further violence.

Dry Land, Revenge and the Taliban: Critical Event No. 1

I now present a first-hand account of five days of heightened emotion and fear, after a further incident of sectarian violence occurred in August 1999 whilst I was in Markaz and Rowshan.

---

[24] I heard deeply contrasting figures concerning the number of people killed in this attack, I was told by some Rowshan people that at least four Sunnis had been killed, other people told that no deaths occurred as a result of the firing. This was not, however, an issue that I felt I could broach with the region's official administration or police.

In August of 1999 the same *'alim* who had been involved in the 1982 clashes returned to his village from his Peshawar religious college (*madrasa*). Sixteen years after the 1982 clashes, he was now one of the provincial leaders of the Jama'at-e Ulama-e Islam (JUI) party in the Frontier Province.[25] This *'alim* was also said by people in the village to be an influential figure in the Sipah-e Sahaba-e Pakistan (SSP, the Organisation of the Companions of the Prophet).[26] This organisation has been responsible for inciting anti-Shi'a riots and involvement in the killings of prominent members of Pakistan's Shi'a population, and there are SSP members in Markaz although I heard only rumours that one Sunni man was sympathetic to this organisation in Rowshan.

On returning to his village, the *'alim* gave a number of speeches in his local mosque denouncing the activities of the Aga Khan Development Network (AKDN) in the region. He pointed in particular to the work of the Water and Sanitation Programme of the AKDN. The organisers of this programme were attempting to provide his village with drinking water for both Sunni and Ismai'li households. According to an Ismai'li man from the *'alim*'s village, he accused the Aga Khan Foundation of plotting to create a giant Ismai'li state encompassing the Ismai'li-populated regions of northern Pakistan, northern Afghanistan, central Asia and China.[27] It was the goal of the organisation, he told gatherings in his village mosque, to convert the region's Sunnis to the Ismai'li faith. Moreover, he said that the money the Aga Khan Foundation was using to construct the water system was *haram* (unlawful), because it was from the personal finances of the Aga Khan. The *'alim*, as in 1982 was, then, seeking to heighten the emotional sensibilities of his listeners by making them feel fear, and by portraying both them and the Sunni faith as under threat. What is striking here is that he sought to do this in the context of Sunni-dominated Pakistan and Chitral, where the influence of Sunni religious authorities and legal codes had been steadily intensifying over the past thirty years. For the *'alim*, it was this strategy that had the greatest potential of encouraging Sunnis in the region to build a lived boundary between themselves and Ismai'lis. This entailed more than just not eating Ismai'li-killed meat or

---

[25] This party is associated with Deobandi teachings. It has a support-base that is connected to a network of religious schools largely attended by poor students from rural backgrounds (Kepel 2002: 58). See also Nasr 2000.

[26] The SSP is a paramilitary organisation whose main goal is to persuade the Government of Pakistan to declare the country's Shi'a a non-Muslim (*kafir*) minority (*akhliat*), see Kepel 2002: 224; Nasr: 2000: 163. In January 2002 it was officially banned by the Government of Pervez Musharaf.

[27] On the Aga Khan Development Network activities in Tajikistan, see Rashid 2002: 92.

ignoring Ismai'li neighbours. It meant systematically rejecting the financial support of the Aga Khan Foundation, and he was calling upon Sunnis to sacrifice worldly comforts – here a clean and reliable supply of drinking water – in order to maintain the strength of their faith in the face of corrupting and 'non-Muslim' forces.

But there was more to this than matters of faith, however, and Chitral people I spoke to interpreted these events in very different ways. The *'alim* was involved in a long-running land dispute with an extended Ismai'li family, whose four houses are located on a small hillock (*dok*) that over-looks his house. This case had been proceeding in the Chitral district court in Markaz over the past twenty years. It was over a small piece of dry land (*chuchu zamin*) on the slope that separated the *'alim*'s house from the Ismai'li household. This piece of land was historically and religiously important for the Ismai'li family. The shrine (*ziyarat*) and grave (*qabur*) of one of their ancestors who died as a martyr (*shaheed*) fighting the British in the famous 'siege of Chitral' in 1895, was located at the edge of the piece of land. That their ancestor had died in martyrdom fighting the British had a double significance in the context of present day Chitral: Sunni *dashma-nan* frequently labelled Ismai'lis as non-Muslims, and as such that meant they could never achieve martyrdom.[28]

The *'alim* had now been in his village for three weeks, despite a government ban placed on him staying there for more than ten days after the 1982 incident. During this period he had given a number inflammatory speeches in his mosque, and throughout all of these events I had been in Rowshan and had even once visited the *'alim*'s village. Now the tensions between this Sunni *'alim* and his Ismai'li neighbours reached a climax. One day the *'alim* began the construction of a thorn fence (*polough*) around the piece of disputed land. On seeing the *'alim* doing this, a young and educated Ismai'li man employed as a teacher and about twenty-six years old, told him that if he laid one more stick on the fence he would be compelled to kill him. The *'alim* continued to build his fence. On seeing this, the Ismai'li man walked into his house, picked up a Kalashnikov, returned to the hill, and killed the *'alim* and the *'alim*'s nephew who was working with him. The Ismai'li man then turned the gun upon himself and committed suicide.

---

[28] In August 1999 I attended the funeral of a Rowshan Ismai'li man who had been killed fighting with the Chitral Scouts in India. Whilst he was buried as a martyr by the Pakistan Army, many of Rowshan's Sunni *dashmanan* did not attend the burial, and it was widely rumoured that this was because they did not believe Ismai'lis could attain martyrdom because they were 'non-Muslim'.

Within three hours this news reached Rowshan. Immediately there were fears that there would be reprisal killings by Sunnis against Ismai'lis in the village. Several Rowshan Ismai'li families were closely related to the Ismai'li family in the *'alim*'s village. During the course of that day, an armed contingent of the Chitral police surrounded the Ismai'li households overlooking the *'alim*'s land, for 'their own protection' (*hetan hifazato bachen*). The four adult male members of the households were arrested, and taken for interrogation in secret locations across Chitral. In addition, a wellknown Ismai'li politician who had stood for one of Pakistan's most important political parties in the 1997 elections from Rowshan was also arrested and accused of inciting the killings. This individual was one of the two boys who had thrown dust on the *'alim*'s prayer cap in the 1982 conflict. The next day several hundred members of the Frontier Corps – a unit of a special security force deployed especially to control sectarian and ethnic violence in the country – were sent to Rowshan in order to prevent any further incidents of Ismai'li–Sunni violence. These Frontier Corps troops were Pukhtun-speakers, and none of them were from Chitral. They stayed in the police station (*thana*) in Rowshan, and patrolled Rowshan's small bazaar during the day and night. All of them were armed with automatic weapons.

Moreover, a night curfew was imposed by Chitral's District Commissioner, and any person outside his home after dark subject to arrest. One night when I was returning from a musical evening in Rowshan with some Sunni and Ismai'li friends, we were stopped by a Pukhtun-speaking policeman who was armed with a Kalashnikov. It was only because one of my friends was carrying a *sitar* that we were able us to persuade the policemen to let us go to our homes. The men I was with were incensed that they could no longer walk freely even in the streets of their own 'country' (*mulk*) without being stopped by strangers (*nagoni*).

The District Commissioner also banned gatherings of more than five people in public places, imposed an order that banned the use of loud speakers in mosques for anything other than the call to prayer and the Friday sermon, so in effect martial law was declared in Rowshan and nearby localities.[29] These orders were displayed in the form of a small typed poster that was pinned to a notice board at the crossroads (*chowk*) of Rowshan's small bazaar.

Two days later the *'alim* was buried. Thousands of Sunnis from Chitral attended the funeral and travelled there in processions (*juloos*). On that day

---

[29] Compare Ahmed 1983 on comparable moves made by District Commissioners elsewhere in the Frontier.

I was travelling to Markaz and saw about 200 men carrying sticks and marching in an ordered military-style procession to the place of the funeral.[30] The burial ceremony was also attended by thousands of his religious students (*talib-e ilm*), as well as JUI party members from across Pakistan who came to his village by road from Peshawar. At that time Afghanistan was under Taliban rule, and many Taliban officials and fighters crossed the border from Afghanistan to attend the funeral. In order to reduce the number of people entering Chitral for the funeral, the Chitral police closed the roads to Afghanistan and made checks on people entering Chitral from other regions of Pakistan. I was told by Ismai'lis in Rowshan that these checks were so tight that anyone with a beard or wearing a turban was barred from entering Chitral. All this was reported in Pakistan's English-language national newspapers. Moreover, those associated with sectarian organisations in Chitral and elsewhere in Pakistan were placed under close surveillance by the Chitral police. I learned this from an Ismai'li Havildar in the Chitral police force, who told me that his duty was to follow men suspected of involvement with such organisations, and enquire about their activities.

Thus far in this chapter and in the book more generally, I have sought to argue that Rowshan Muslims are not tamely and unthinkingly deferential to local Islamic purists in such matters as the status of Ismai'lis as *kafir*s, or the acceptability of girls' education. I now connect these issues with the notion pervading much social science writing about communal riots that such moments of violence are merely constructions placed on local conflicts by the state, or strategising outsiders and self-seeking politicians (Brass 1997).

Besides the Taliban officials, and the Chitral police and Frontier Corps, powerful public figures also became implicated in the 1999 killing. One of Pakistan's most prominent political leaders, Fazlur Rahman of the Jama'at-e Ulama-e Islam party, attended the funeral of the *'alim*.[31] At the side of the *'alim*'s grave he made a speech saying that the *'alim* had died the 'death of a martyr' (*shahadat*).[32] This comment had important implications

---

[30] The killing of the *'alim* gave rise to protests elsewhere in Pakistan, most notably in Peshawar where Chitrali migrant labourers and *madrasa* students staged large scale processions at which they burned effigies of the Aga Khan.

[31] On the Jama'at-e Ulama-e Islam, see Pirzada 2000.

[32] See Trench 1985 for a history of the Frontier Scouts. Martyrdom was very much on the minds of Chitral people at the time. In May and June of the summer of 1999, before the killing of the *'alim*, about fifteen Ismai'li and Sunni men were killed fighting for the Chitral Scouts – the local unit of the Pakistan Army – in the infamous Kargil conflict, where Pakistani military forces fought Indian military forces. On the Kargil conflict, see Cloughley 2000.

for people in the region. It signalled that this powerful and well-known 'alim and political leader wanted the death of the Chitrali 'alim to be seen as an incident of religious motivation. On the day of the killing, however, Rowshan people to whom I spoke were relieved to hear that both the BBC and the Iranian international radio news programmes had stated that the 'alim was killed as the result of a long-running land dispute. The leader of the JUI party was now seeking, my Ismai'li friends in Rowshan told me, to give the killing a 'religious colour' (*mazhabi rang*). Following Brass (1997), complex local conflicts may be reduced to categories such as 'land disputes' or 'religious-conflict' by powerful external actors. However, far from allowing others to define the incident for them as an outbreak of 'religious' or 'sectarian' violence, Rowshan people were themselves consciously aware of the complex array of forces involved, and had strikingly different interpretations of the event. Moreover, they also sought to exert their own agency and bring critical thought to the ways in which the violent events were interpreted by the wider world.

During these days of heightened emotion there was great anxiety in Rowshan about the possibility of further incidents of sectarian violence. Ismai'li families conducted night patrols around their houses, and some of these men armed themselves with pistols and guns. Even the four-year-old son in this household handed me a plastic toy pistol that he told me to place under my pillow to protect myself as well as his family. Ismai'li men also sat in the Jama'at Khanas all night in the fear that Sunnis would come to torch them.

The tensions impacted in a serious way on the interpersonal relations between Ismai'lis and Sunnis in Rowshan. Some Ismai'li men I knew claimed that their Sunni neighbours and friends had stopped visiting their houses, and no longer even conveyed their salaams when they met in the village bazaar. One Ismai'li man in the village accused one of his Sunni neighbours of using a government-owned motorcycle in order to travel to other nearby villages, and spread rumours about the role of Ismai'lis in the killing of the 'alim. In a conversation with another Sunni man in the village, this Ismai'li man said that his Sunni neighbour was a *sheytan* (devil), and that he was working behind the backs of his Ismai'li neighbours despite the fact they were from one village and had been his friends since school. He told this Sunni man that his family had done much to help people in the village, yet, he said, 'all these people can do now is try and make matters worse for us'. For this Ismai'li man, his Sunni neighbour was guilty of seeking to destroy the moral unit of the village as a place of shared happiness (*khoshani*), service (*khidmat*) and sadness (*gham*).

The accused Sunni man was told of the allegations made against him, and, in the bazaar, he confronted his Ismai'li neighbour asking him to give proof (*suboot*) to support the claims he had made against him. The Sunni man – at the time unmarried and aged about twenty-eight – responded to the accusations made about him in an aggressive tone of voice, and he already had a reputation amongst villagers for being angry (*qahri*) and emotional (*jezbati*).

You've been saying very bad things about me. Find proof for what you are saying. If you do then I'll let you take me to the bazaar crossroads (*chowk*) and wipe shit on my neck (*goro rich dik*). I consider you to be nothing less than my brother but even then you don't trust me (*ma soora ihtibar no kosan*).

Public defamation of the pure Muslim body, and not a physical beating, then, was seen by this Sunni man as the most extreme form of punishment for someone who stepped outside the boundaries of acceptable village morality. Violence again lay in the public desecration of personal purity.[33] The Ismai'li and Sunni men were speaking in loud voices clearly heard by other men in the bazaar at the time. Emotions had risen, and the bazaar had been transformed from a place of ideally polite (*sharif*) and controlled behaviour to a space of animosity. So these two men had failed to handle heightened levels of emotion at a time of great anxiety, and they become driven by unhealthily high levels of emotion, here anger and suspicion, in a way that restricted their capacity to think and act properly. And their failure was all the more denigrating for them because it took place in the bright light of Rowshan's bazaar.

The heightened sensibilities experienced during these days not only transformed the inter-personal relations between Ismai'li and Sunni men, and altered the structure of public bazaar life – they also impacted on life in the village itself. The Sunni women in one household, for instance, were said, by women in an Ismai'li household I often visited, to have cried so loudly that their wailing could be heard throughout the village.[34] Their displays of emotion and upset at the death of the religious scholar were said by Ismai'lis to be false (*faltu*) and a display (*pasheiko bachen*): what had the *'alim* ever done for these Sunnis? Why did they feel so saddened by his

---

[33] Compare Gilsenan 1996: 227–8.

[34] Mahmood 2001: 839–44 offers an interpretation strikingly different from Rowshan Ismai'lis of displays of weeping in the context of a women's mosque movement in Cairo. For Mahmood such displays of weeping are not simply 'conventionalised' behaviour but, rather, 'a tool or developable means through which certain kinds of ethical and moral capabilities are attained' (Mahmood 2001: 844). Rather than dismissing such a position I am here seeking to bring attention to the ways in which Rowshan people subject even the most intense forms of emotional modes to critical scrutiny.

death? For many Ismai'lis in the village I spoke to, these Sunni women were not displaying authentic and genuine emotions. They were, rather, they told me and exclaimed to one another, *acting* (an English word often used in Khowar). The reason they were crying, they commented amongst themselves and with me, was to create *tensien* (tension), and to make Ismai'lis in the village angry (*qahri*). The tears they were shedding were not real 'tears of sadness' (*ghamo ashru*), these women were, instead, 'forcing themselves to cry' (*zor korie kelinian*), and the tears flowing from their eyes were those of 'liars' (*changie kelik*). On the one hand, damaged religious sensibilities provoked legitimate displays of unbridled emotion, yet, on the other hand, such displays of powerful emotions were also conceptualised as being the result of rational and tactical mental activity.

In 1999, then, the killing of the *'alim* resulted in heightened emotional sensibilities and damaged religious feelings, and the place occupied by the sectarian divide in village life came to dominate the thoughts and feelings of Rowshan people. Yet, despite the heightened tensions, there was no further incident of sectarian violence, and no communal conflict.

Courts, terrorists and communal harmony: the April 2001 shootings

In April 2001 a third major incident of sectarian violence occurred, this time in Markaz. This event also involved the dispute between the family of the dead *'alim*, and the Ismai'li family that had purportedly been involved in his killing. The Ismai'li men accused of the killing of the *'alim* had remained in jail since the event some months sixteen months earlier. The Ismai'li politician from Rowshan had, however, been released six months after the killing. He, along with the other men, was facing charges of conspiracy to murder, however. The court case was taking place in the district court in Markaz. In the middle of April 2001 the son of the *'alim*, a young man aged about twenty-six years who had studied in a *madrasa* in Peshawar, whilst sitting in the court, took a pistol out of his short pocket and fired it at the Ismai'li men accused of killing his father. He injured three of the men present, although none were killed. Two of the men were admitted in hospital, whilst the Ismai'li politician received surface wounds to his shoulder and returned, under police escort, to his home in Rowshan.

The shape taken by this critical event was substantially different from that of 1999. After the April 2001, there was little talk of the potential escalation of the violence into sectarian conflict between Chitral's Ismai'lis and Sunnis. Rather, a discourse that emphasised Chitral as a place of social harmony and peace characterised many of the conversations that Rowshan people had about the event. The existence of this discourse of social harmony alongside a discourse of difference raises important questions about the intellectual dimension of notions of tolerance in Rowshan, and specifically about the ways in which Rowshan people reflect upon moments of emotional intensity.

I was returning from a walk along the village paths when I passed the Ismaiʾli politician's house, and stopped to speak to his sister who was standing outside the inner compound. She asked me if I had heard about the day's events. I said no and she then told me that there were rumours going around the village that her brother had been shot in the back in Markaz by the son of the dead *ʿalim*, and was now on his way back to Rowshan. I went into the house to speak to his mother, whom I found weeping inside the house. She told me, still crying, that she feared that people were trying to conceal from her what had happened to her son. She said she would only believe he was alive when he returned home, and asked me to go the bazaar, and telephone Markaz, to find out what had really happened.

When the injured Ismaiʾli man returned to his home in Rowshan, all the men and boys from the village gathered in his house to congratulate him on his survival. Many of these men and boys were Sunni. The atmosphere in the house was tense, and all the injured man's family – men and women – wept. After the killing of the *ʿalim* sixteen months previously, many Sunnis in the village had had stopped visiting Ismaiʾli homes in the village. Now they sought to show that they had feelings of affection and compassion for a household in the village that found itself in trouble, and a 'son of the village' wounded in an unprovoked attack. In the orchard outside the house village elders had gathered. Among them were Ismaiʾli prayer leaders and the Sunni *imam* of the hamlet's mosque; they all commented how what had happened was deeply sorrowful and they praised the Ismaiʾli man for his strength and bravery.

Yet even these shows of committed affection for the wounded man and his family at a 'time of need' (*zarurato wakhta*) were said by many Ismaiʾlis in the village to be lacking in authenticity (*asil*) but, rather, full of latent animosity and insincerity. The elder brother of the politician told me that the Sunni men and boys had really come to laugh at the plight of his brother, and that they were pleased to see the injuries caused by the young *dashman*'s gun.

My father keeps on sitting with these Sunni boys, but he doesn't realise that they are happy to see us in trouble, and that they take delight from the bad situation we are in. On the surface they are helping us, but underneath they are both happy that we are in trouble, and sad that our brother has survived the attack.

The elder brother of the wounded politician, then, judged the displays of affection of his fellow villagers critically and sceptically. Even when villagers claimed a sense of shared and neighbourly affection, this discourse was infused with latent tensions and divisions. This man's suspicions were added to when women from his household came back from their Sunni neighbour's home, and told the family that Sunni women in the household had said how brave (*bahder*) the young *dashman* was. These Sunni women had reportedly said that he was honourable (*ghairati*) because he had sought to avenge (*badela ganik*) the death of his father. If Rowshan people did perceive there to be a type of warm affection that infused relations between the villagers, they also told me that this affection had become rotten (*pulie*), and that few in the village were really sincere and compassionate.

Later that afternoon the Ismai'li man went to the Aga Khan hospital in the village where thousands of Sunni and Ismai'li Chitral people visited him. For the next three weeks Sunnis and Ismai'lis from throughout Chitral visited the injured man's house to share in his family's 'happiness', and to congratulate the man on surviving the attack on his life. As they drank tea and ate biscuits in the family's orchard, they repeatedly remarked that Chitral's Ismai'lis and Sunnis were 'all brothers' (*saf brargini*), and that events such as these were shameful for Chitrali people who are *sharif* (polite) and *aman pasand* (peaceful) folk. What had happened, they said, was not an instance of sectarian violence but, rather, a form of enmity (*dushmani*) killing that was new to Chitral and that threatened the peace for which the region was famed across Pakistan. They often commented that whilst enmity killing was a common feature of life in other regions of the country, it was not part of the Chitral way of life. Some said that what had happened in the court was an act of 'terrorism' (*dehshadgardi*) perpetrated by an 'extremist' (*intiha pasand*), and as such it 'looked bad' (*shum noyuko*) for Chitral's peaceful and polite folk.[35]

A notion of tolerance does, then, play an important role in the lives of the villagers, and it does have the power to harmonise Ismai'li–Sunni relations in the village. Importantly, this notion of tolerance is rooted in an ideal vision of balanced affection and emotions that call upon villagers to care for one another. Yet, where this notion of tolerance is important, it also tends to be the source of deeper debate and discussion, and may be

---

[35] In July 2002 the Ismai'li family had pardoned (*mu'af areni*) the young Sunni *dashman* and agreed that he should be released from jail. Chitral's *ulama* also in August 2002 planned to visit the Ismai'li family in order to come to a compromise (*sulah*) over the events. The Ismai'li men injured in the attack in the court were all also acquitted and allowed to return to their homes, four months after the attack in September 2001.

seen by many villagers as something that is far from sincere and authentic. So, Rowshan people seek to live a lives that meet an ideal vision of emotion as characterised by warmth, neighbourliness, humanity and self-sacrifice. Yet, at the same time, they value the display of critical and thoughtful reflection, and very often this reflection reveals the inconsistencies of village life. These inconsistencies are not easily resolved, they result in considerable levels of anxiety for Rowshan people, and this dimension of Chitral life is something that is recognised all too starkly by Chitral people at times of heightened emotion.

Analysis

These three critical events over the course of the past twenty-three years clearly indicate that relations between Ismai'lis and Sunnis have the potential to become hardened and hostile, and that this can and does result in incidents of violence that can be legitimately classed as 'sectarian'. However, such 'sectarian' violence takes multiple forms, and, in some cases at least, local people do not see violent episodes as straightforwardly sectarian: new and alien forms of 'enmity relations' (*dushamani*), 'terrorism', and 'land disputes' are seen by Rowshan people to further complicate the nature of Sunni-Ismai'li conflict in Chitral.[36] Since the events of 1982 Rowshan people expect a general level of anxiety about Ismai'li–Sunni relations, and this anxiety is now a feature of everyday village life.

Moreover, the anxiety expressed by many Chitral people concerning the deteriorating nature of Ismai'li–Sunni relations in Chitral also reflected another source of fear for many Chitral people. The long and ongoing nature of the conflict between the Ismai'li and Sunni families in the village also suggested to many Chitral people that the potential for Pashtun-style 'revenge' feuds becoming a dimension of Chitral life was a very real possibility. This was so concerning because, as I was often told, it was Chitral peoples' ability to resolve disputes in a 'sophisticated', 'peaceful' and 'polite' way that made them different from their 'wild' Pukhtun neighbours who dominated other regions of the Frontier. Thus, the form taken by the Ismai'li–Sunni dispute over the past twenty years was threatening to Chitral people not only because of its clearly negative impact on the nature of Ismai'li–Sunni relations in the region, but also because of the implications it had for a viable concept of shared a Chitrali selfhood. In this context of their status as non-Pashtuns in a Pashtun-dominated region of

---

[36] For contrasting accounts of the term 'communalism' see, especially, C. Bayly 1998 and Pandey 1990.

Pakistan, then, the dispute made Chitral people reflect in a critical way on the nature of life in the region, and the ethnic stereotypes Chitral people deployed in their everyday lives. Rather than in any simple way reinforcing crude ethnic distinctions between Chitralis and Pukhtuns, the conflict between Ismai'lis and Sunnis in the region had, rather, provoked many Chitral people to be critical of themselves and their society: many claimed that it proved how Chitralis were 'one thing on the surface, something different beneath'. For some Chitral people, at least, the killings had shown that Chitral people were more susceptible to the traditions of their Pahstun-neighbours in Pakistan and Afghanistan than many of them cared to believe, and, perhaps more pertinently, that there was a greater place for revenge conflict in the thought and actions of Chitral people than the ideal conception of Chitralis as people of 'peace and harmony' at first sight suggested.

Yet to interpret the conflict as a form of 'revenge feud' would also be to ignore the very real steps that many people took in the region to confront the complex issues that they did negotiate in a thoughtful and reasonable manner. The events of April 2001 shows how many Rowshan people were critically aware of the complex form of so-called 'sectarian conflict' in their region. Most if not all Rowshan people did not talk about the conflict between the Sunni Peshawar-based *alim* and the Ismai'li family in terms of the inevitably unfolding narrative of a 'revenge feud', and those that did were said to have misunderstood the dispute's more complex and sensitive dimensions. Rather, for many Rowshan people it was finer details of the dispute that were important factors in shaping the direction in which it evolved. Thus, many people I talked to did not simply debate the extent to which the dispute was either about land or about doctrinal differences between Sunni and Ismai'li Muslims, but, rather, it was the role played by education, and the desires and emotions that the acquisition of different forms of knowledge generate that was central to their understanding of the conflict.

Moments of Ismai'li–Sunni tension do involve the heightening of religious emotions and sensibilities in ways that prove this may constitute breaks from everyday life for Rowshan people. The processes by which religious sensibilities become heightened are multidimensional, and are often perceived so by Rowshan people. Heightened religious emotions are seen by many villagers as being instigated by addresses (*taqerir*) made by *dashmanan* from the pulpits of mosques in the region. These addresses especially emphasise feelings of being under threat and thus have the effect of instilling emotions of fear in the minds and bodies of their listeners. The division between the attacker and the group under threat is blurred in these addresses, and the heightened emotional states that they engender can play a powerful role in enhancing the sectarian boundary between Chitral's Ismai'lis and Sunnis.

Many Chitral people also claim that they are able to subject these addresses to critical intellectual activity, however, and that they are able to see the 'real' motivations behind the making of these speeches. The intellect is a something that is ideally critical and active for Chitral Muslims, and thus the cultivated mind is widely seen as playing a powerful role in controlling religious emotion, and preventing unbridled displays of religious passion. Moreover, emotion should be authentic, and many Chitral people are critical of displays of emotion that they conceptualise as fake and employed in tactical and 'rational' ways in order to heighten the emotional temperature of daily village life.

Yet they are often further complexities in the relation between the intellect and religious passion in the minds of many Rowshan people. Fast minds and fast intellects also have the potential of making folk emotional in potentially destructive ways: the Ismai'li man who eventually killed the *'alim* and then himself, was said to be educated and intelligent, but also frustrated and upset because all his hard work and study had rewarded him with was a poorly paid teaching post in a distant school. So once out of control and overly refined, the intellect has the potential to bring forth emotions of fear and anger, and unbridled passions themselves have an ultimate source in the intellect and the mind.[37]

Out of the three critical events explored above – all of which involved violence and took place at moments of heightened tension – only one, the riots of 1982, resulted in an instance of communal crowd violence, and this was in the bazaar of Markaz and not in Rowshan. Despite the processions, the addresses made by powerful Pakistan *ulama*, the influx of Taliban fighters from Afghanistan and *madrasa* students from other regions of Pakistan, the deployment of the armed police, and the employment of a language of self-sacrificial martyrdom, there were no incidents of communal violence after the critical events of 1999 and 2001. Violence may have become routinised in Pakistan: there are constant episodes of great violence including church and mosque massacres and the murders of politicians and religious leaders. Yet this does not mean that Ismai'li–Sunni conflict in Chitral inevitably involves physical violence.

---

[37] The connection between thinking and heightened emotions is one made in other regions of Pakistan, see Verkaaik 2004: 107.

How is it possible to explain this? In a recent book, Bailey asks why a caste-based temple dispute that he observed in a small Orissa village in India in the 1950s failed to result in communal violence (Bailey 1996). For Bailey, it was the villagers' 'quiet pragmatism', their dislike of excess, and their underlying vision of reality 'that had to do with calculation and rationality', in short, their 'civilised indifference', that meant the villagers he lived with avoided what could have been self-destructive communal violence (Bailey 1996: 159–74). Much has changed in South Asia since the 1950s: public displays of religious emotion and commitment are now an everyday feature of life, even in the most remote localities, of religious experience in the subcontinent (see, notably, Didier 2001). Rowshan people, like the villagers with whom Bailey lived, remain concerned about rational thought and the danger of excessive displays of inauthentic emotion. Yet, when they do show indifference to the religious beliefs and practices of others, they do so in a way that reflects complex processes of conscious thinking and reflection on their part. At the same time, however, they also conceptualise strong feelings and heightened states of emotion as a critical dimension of what it means to live a Muslim life: religious sensibilities are wounded, and when they are, an emotional response is required. What I have shown above, then, are some of the complex ways in which these discourses – one which emphasises balanced emotion and a thoughtful life of plurality, and the other heightened religious emotion and commitment – interact in the lives of Rowshan people. They both inform our understandings of why sectarian tensions grow in the village, and under what circumstance they may be controlled and confined, and this interaction is something that informs both the living of a daily life, and the experience of 'critical events'.

If bodies are not necessarily wounded, selves often are. What Gilsenan, in his study of violence and narrative in rural Lebanon, calls a 'carefully unspoken narrative of injury' (Gilsenan 1996: 63–4), is a pervasive feature of life in Chitral. Dirty looks by *dashmanan*, words spoken in anger by village women, and emotionally heated interchanges in the bazaar are the cause of great anxiety for Rowshan people. Indeed, according to the Khowar proverb I was often told, the word wounds in a way that the sword cannot. And, for Rowshan people, the poison of gossip and rumour is all the more painful because discussion, ideally, should be about the exchange of abstract ideas and the experience of the play of the mind. It is, then, in the wider context of a perceived state of emotional and intellectual failure that it is possible to discern the lived experience of the sectarian divide in Rowshan.

The experience of heightened levels of emotion interacts in a complex and multidimensional way with the cultivated mind and the critical faculties, and inflects deeply on the shape of Ismai'li–Sunni relations in Rowshan. How, then, do heightened levels of religious emotion contribute to religious experience in Rowshan?

DEEDAR MUBARAK! CATCHING A GLIMPSE OF THE AGA KHAN

To answer this question I now document the spiritual journey (*ruhani safar*) that one Ismai'li family made to 'catch a glimpse' of the Aga Khan when he visited his 'spiritual children' (*ruhani azhelie*) in the town of Gilgit, the headquarters of Pakistan's Northern Areas.[38] 'Catching a glimpse' (*deedar korik*) of the Aga Khan is a moment when Ismai'lis feel themselves to be in the presence of 'spiritual truth' (*haqiqat*); and it is a religious event that is without comparison for Ismai'lis. Gilgit lies no less than eighteen hours' drive over rough and difficult mountain roads from Rowshan, and for many of the family who went to see the Aga Khan it was the first time they had left Rowshan, let alone visited another region of Pakistan.

My aim is to ask what role heightened emotional states play in special moments of religious experience for Rowshan's Ismai'lis. One powerful force behind this family's decision to make the long and potentially dangerous journey to Gilgit was the women of the household. As a further dimension to my discussion, then, I explore how Ismai'li women's participation in moments of intense religious experience affects the shape of the sectarian divide in the village.

There is a significant body of anthropological writing on the role played by women in communal conflict and emergent religious identities in South Asia.[39] Particularly instructive for the account I present here, is the interaction between the ways in which visions of a world made perfect by religion are inscribed and imagined on women's bodies and the place that women's own agency occupies in these visions. In contexts where women find it difficult to engage in 'direct, confrontational verbal activity',

---

[38] See, especially, Gold 1988 for an ethnography of a religious journey with Hindus in India. For studies of the hajj and other forms of religious journeys in Muslim societies, see Delaney 1990; Eickelman 1976; Eickelman and Piscatori (eds.) 1990; Yamba 1995.

[39] For a general discussion of the ways women have 'engaged in activism within and against "communal politics"' (Basu 1997: 1) in South Asia, see Basu 1997 and Jatyawardena and de Alwis (eds.) 1996.

women's bodies are held to have a 'discursive agency' in and of themselves (Hegeland 1998a, 1998b).[40]

In September 2000 Rowshan's Ismai'li religious authorities (the *waizin*) announced that the Aga Khan was planning a visit to Pakistan and Chitral in the middle of October. As well as these *waizin*, prominent Ismai'li men in Rowshan even announced that the Imam was planning to make a visit to Rowshan, and that preparations for his arrival (*tashrif angik*) must begin. The Imam is an ever-present feature of life for Ismai'lis in the village: framed photographs and portraits of him are hung on the walls of all Ismai'li households, and many people, especially young women, hang small lockets with an embedded photograph of the Imam around their necks. The last time the Imam had visited Chitral was in 1987, and so for many of Rowshan's Ismai'lis this was to be the first time they saw the Aga Khan. On hearing the good news (*mushqari*), Ismai'lis in the village started to prepare a piece of land in Rowshan where the Aga Khan would land his helicopter, perform *deedar* and read out his *farman* to the region's Ismai'lis.

The *deedar* would be performed within an enclosed space shielded by cloth and blankets from public view. Only Ismai'lis would be able to enter this secluded area (*pindal*) and obtain a glimpse of the Aga Khan. Young Ismai'li men especially selected for their commitment to the Ismai'li faith (the *volunteeran*), would ensure that Sunnis would not be allowed to enter, and any that tried to do so would be politely asked to leave. The only reason Sunnis would want to enter, I was told, was so that they could ruin the event for the village's Ismai'lis, and learn things that were secret about Ismai'li doctrines and practices, which they would then use to spread as *propaganda* as proof (*suboot*) that Ismai'lis were un-Islamic. Only those who believed in the spiritual powers and leadership of the Aga Khan would be able to glimpse the spiritual truth (*haqiqat*), and non-Ismai'lis would ruin the special nature of the occasion, misinterpret what they saw and even cause commotion (*halagula*) inside, thus ruining the proceedings. In particular, my friends told me, Sunnis would misinterpret the displays of crying and emotion that would take place in the *pindal*, and would accuse Ismai'lis of worshipping the Aga Khan as if he were god. Some Ismai'lis told me that many of the Ismai'lis present would not be able to see the Imam because of the special spiritual light (*nur*) that radiated from his face inside the *pindal*. I was often told that the Aga Khan whom we saw when

---

[40] On purdah practices in India, see Jeffery 1979, and, in the Muslim world more generally, see Barron and Keddie (eds) 1991. For ethnographic material on women and purdah in other Muslim socities, see Beck 1986; Grima 1992; N. Tapper 1990a; Tapper and Tapper 1987.

we watched the television or looked at his pictures in books, was not the same Aga Khan who met his followers (*muridan*) in the confines of the *pindal*. When in the *pindal* he would take on a different (*khur*) and even more beautiful (*sheli*) shape (*shikil*). This was something that those who did not believe in the Imamate (spiritual leadership) of the Aga Khan could never experience or understand, and it was only those moved by the religious emotion (*mazhabi jezbat*) of the event who would see the bright light (*roshi*) emanating from the Imam.

Here, then, it is Ismai'lis who are delineating and firming up the sectarian divide in the village, and the reasons they are doing so are complex. At one level they are seeking to maintain the purity of Ismai'li faith and worship – something that non-believers have the potential to dirty and erode. At another level, however, they feel that the boundary between Sunnis and Ismai'lis in the village needs to be hardened in order to protect threatened Ismai'li selves from Sunni attack – attack that has both a religious and a physical dimension. Some Ismai'lis in the village even felt that some Sunnis in the region were so extremist that they may even try to assault and attack the Imam himself. Many remembered how Sunnis in Chitral, after the killing of the *'alim* in Peshawar in August 1999, had burned effigies of the Aga Khan. Thus, whilst the sectarian boundary is an ever-present feature of Rowshan life, its importance is heightened during both violent 'critical events' and important religious occasions.

In mid-October 2000 the Aga Khan arrived at Islamabad airport, where he was met by Pakistan's Foreign Minister and then went on to have meetings the next day with the Chief Executive of Pakistan, General Pervez Musharaf. Pakistan Television broadcast in the evening news film of the Aga Khan arriving in Pakistan. On seeing these pictures, the Ismai'lis in the house I was living in had to wipe tears from their moist eyes. 'Oh how beautiful he is', they said. 'He becomes more beautiful each time we see him; rather than becoming older he becomes younger (*zaru biko zhagha bar bar sheli boyen*).' 'Look at his smile', I was told. 'look at the deep respect (*sifat*) in that smile.'

In the days leading up to the expected arrival of the Aga Khan in Rowshan, Ismai'li women were particularly visible in the preparations.[41]

---

[41] See Torab 1997 for a comparative discussion of Shi'a women's involvement in rituals in Iran; Hegeland 1998a, 1998b for a discussion of the role of women in Shi'a rituals in Peshawar, Pakistan; and Mahmood 2001 for a discussion of a women's mosque movement in Cairo, Egypt. These works emphasise the embodied and emotional dimension of women's experience of the Islamic. I am here emphasising that if emergent forms of Ismai'li identity are embodied then they also have a powerful verbal and mindful dimension.

As was noted in chapter 6, whilst Sunni women never visit the village's mosques, Ismai'li women and girls worship, study and teach in Rowshan's Jama'at Khanas, and this has important implications for their lived religious experience.

Many girls and young women in the village are Ismai'li 'volunteers', and they, along with the young men, were to be responsible for preparing for the Aga Khan's visit to Rowshan. They wrote invitation cards to Ismai'li people in the village asking them to attend especially arranged meetings to discuss preparations for the *deedar*. They were also told that on the day of *deedar* they would have to help Ismai'li women enter the *pindal* and find places to sit. Ismai'lis also gathered each evening to recite special prayers (*tazbeh*) which would make the Aga Khan's visit to Rowshan certain. All the women in the Ismai'li household in which I lived attended these prayer sessions without fail, and many started to get up exceptionally early in the mornings so that they could offer special prayers in the Jama'at Khana. Days before these young women had been regularly scolded by their grandmother for their laziness and their love for sleep; never would anyone marry them, she had often told them. Yet now when I strolled into the house at 7:30 am these young women had been awake and busy for hours. Thus, the days leading up to the visit of the Aga Khan were characterised by an intensification of the religious activities and sensibilities of Rowshan Ismai'lis, and this was something particularly noticeable in the lives of Ismai'li women.

All this occasioned much comment from Rowshan's Sunnis. Sunni men kept telling me how 'strange' (*namunar, ajeeb*) they found it when they saw Ismai'li girls and women making their way to the Jama'at Khana each day for prayers and religious instruction. One of my Ismai'li friends, Hassan, often told me that seeing Ismai'li women live an active life outside the home made Sunnis angry and irritated (*hetan qahar goyen*). Hassan told me that even if Sunni people in Rowshan saw him walk with his wife along the paths of the village they became angry. 'Why', they would ask him, he told me, 'does this man need to take his wife wherever he goes?' Even by appearing with his veiled wife in public, Sunnis in the village would accuse him of being immoral and of stepping outside the fold of correct and proper in Islam. The sight of Ismai'li girls and women walking in groups to the Jama'at Khana each evening, then, would inevitably make some of Rowshan's Sunnis angry. Thus, the concealment of women and purdah practices are conceptualised by Rowshan people as being a further visible manifestation of the sectarian boundary in the village, an important dimension of this is the view that it raises the emotions and tempers of the village's Sunnis.

So it was with great sadness and distress that Rowshan's Ismai'lis received the news that the Aga Khan would not be visiting Rowshan or Chitral. Most Ismai'lis gave two reasons for the Aga Khan's decision to cancel his visit. First, a rumour had circulated that the Chitral District Commissioner had informed the Aga Khan's advisors that he could not ensure his security if he were to visit Chitral. As a result of the killing of the religious scholar in 1999, officials were allegedly insisting that the region was still experiencing dangerous levels of sectarian tension. There was the prospect that Sunnis in the region would try to disrupt the Aga Khan's visit to Chitral, and Taliban fighters in Afghanistan, still angry at the killing of the *'alim* by an Ismai'li, could also once again flood into the region if the Imam were to visit.

Secondly, Ismai'lis blamed their own 'bad intentions' (*bad niyat*) for the cancellation. The Ismai'li community (*jama'at*) was said to be divided, and this was a cause of great anxiety for Rowshan's Ismai'lis. Prominent Ismai'li leaders in Chitral had purportedly argued about where the Aga Khan should perform *deedar*. The Ismai'li leadership in one valley was even said to have threatened Ismai'lis in other regions that if the Aga Khan were to visit Rowshan then they would refuse to join the gathering, and would boycott the *deedar*. So, ordinary Ismai'lis in Rowshan blamed their own defective morality and thoughts to explain the Aga Khan's decision to cancel his visit. The Aga Khan could understand them and see into their minds and, many Ismai'lis said to me; he had decided that they did not deserve to see him. Only those truly faithful to the Aga Khan deserved to see him and this, they told me, they obviously were not.

The Aga Khan's visit to Ismai'lis in Gilgit, however, was to go ahead, and now that catching a glimpse of the Aga Khan in Rowshan was not possible, many talked of making the long journey to Gilgit. For most Ismai'lis in the village making such a journey would be impossible: to hire a vehicle to Gilgit would cost, at least, 12,000 rupees, and the journey would take about three days. Yet for many in the village this was their first chance even to obtain a holy sighting of the Present Imam, and it was not one to be missed. On glimpsing the Aga Khan, I was told, sins (*gunah*) would be forgiven, and those present would be returned to a state of purity (*pak*) and spiritual cleanliness (*ruhani safa'iee*). For Rowshan's Ismai'lis sin is not something than can be easily purified,[42] and for many Rowshan Ismai'lis it is only the white light of the 'present Imam' that has the potential to burn

---

[42] On Ismai'li moral thought, see Cook 2000: 301–4.

(*puleeran*) away worldly sins that have become grafted onto the carnal human soul (*zhan*).[43]

Shabnam is an unmarried Ismai'li woman aged about twenty-seven years. She has a BA degree in Urdu, and at the time of this planned visit by the Aga Khan, she had worked for five years in a government office in Rowshan. She walks to her office each day, sometimes on her own and sometimes with other employed women from her hamlet. Whilst many women in the village rarely leave their homes without being accompanied by a close male relative or their husband, Shabnam enjoys 'walking' (*kosik*) and says that she has a 'free mood' (*azad tabyat*).

Shabnam is a devout Ismai'li: she rarely misses the evening prayers in the Jama'at Khana, and often also attends prayers early in the morning. She had high expectations that the Aga Khan was to visit Rowshan, and had been going to the Jama'at Khana early every morning to pray that this would be the case. On hearing of the cancellation, Shabnam announced to her family that come what may she would travel to Gilgit to glimpse the Present Imam. She told them that it was particularly important for her to do so. Sitting in the house one day, she told her sisters that seeing the Imam meant that all sins were cleansed and that one's inner intention (*niat*) would come true (*sahi boye*). Shabnam's sisters did not take her seriously, and few of them believed she would really undertake the eighteen-hour long journey to Gilgit on her own. Laughing, they teased her about exactly what 'inner intention' it was that she wanted to become true. I gathered by the tones of their voices and the faces they pulled, and having had many 'secret' conversations with Shabnam, that they assumed that this was something to do with marriage. Shabnam told her sisters, 'I'll show you (*pisa pasheim*), then you won't be able to laugh at me; I'm a dangerous (*khatarnark*) and brave (*bahder*) woman (*kimerie*), not ordinary village girls like you.'

Two days before the Imam was to arrive in Gilgit, Shabnam told me that she was ready to leave early the next morning. Shabnam planned to travel with only one companion, her young teenage nephew, Mahsood, who had never travelled beyond Markaz before. Shabnam told me that she would make the journey without the knowledge or approval of her elder brothers, and insisted that under no circumstances should I tell either of them. Her brothers were both in their mid-thirties, educated, employed, well travelled and whilst one of them was married the other was not. In particular, her

---

[43] Compare Laidlaw 1995: 28–9 on the relationship between sin, the soul and heat in Jain religious thought and practice.

unmarried brother, who was widely said by Rowshan people to have one of the 'fastest brains' in Chitral, had been angry with Shabnam before when she had travelled with her then thirteen-year-old nephew to Markaz in order to obtain treatment for an eye infection. On this occasion her brother had told her that she had gone mad, and that no woman in Chitral dared to travel around on her own in the way that she did.

The journey Shabnam was now preparing to make was quite different from the previous trip to Markaz. Other young women in Rowshan, elsewhere in Chitral and Pakistan in general would be very unlikely to make such a daring and, indeed, physically dangerous journey, and doing so would certainly result in serious domestic arguments and maybe even physical reprisals. This journey would involve travelling outside of Chitral, and staying overnight in the houses of people with whom she had no recognised relations, Shabnam had decided that she would arrange these overnight stays by trying to find a place in a jeep carrying other Chitral Ismai'lis to Gilgit. Her brothers would most certainly not allow her to travel alone on such a long and potentially dangerous journey.

Shabnam left the home early in the morning, and her departure created a stir in the house. Fortunately the brother with whom she had fought in the past had already left for Gilgit with some wealthy Ismai'li friends, one of whom was a bank manager in Markaz. Her mother was worried about her daughter, but told me that there was nothing she could do about her: she lived, according to her mother, a life 'according to her own choice' (*tan chita baig*). Not only was this woman independent and determined, but she was now driven by religious emotion and desire (*arman*), and this made stopping her from going to Gilgit impossible. Thus, the spiritual reason for Shabnam's journey, was seen by her elderly mother both as making her daughter more determined, and the journey itself greatly more acceptable. The context and repercussions of Shabnam's decision to make the long journey to see the Aga Khan are important. Far from an unthinking moment of intense religious faith and emotion, Shabnam's decision to take this risky initiative involved considerable work on her part. Moreover, in doing so, as I now explore, she also generated discussions amongst other members of her family.

The newly married youngest brother in the house now announced that he and his wife, along with his mother and his wife's parents, would be booking a vehicle to go to Gilgit. This would leave in the house the eldest brother, the father, the eldest brother's children and four of his sisters. None of these people – from the three-year-old twin daughters to a twenty-two-year-old sister – were prepared to miss out on the possibility of catching a glimpse of the present Imam. If Shabnam could make the journey by herself, and if the youngest brother of the household could take his wife, together with his in-laws (*ishpashur bolu*) and mother, then the others were not prepared to sit at home and watch proceedings on the television. The elder brother was left no option but to agree to take the remaining ten family members to Gilgit, despite the fact that doing so would almost inevitably involve him taking a large loan from one of the shops in the village or from his relatives and friends.

Yet the journey made to see the Aga Khan was not attended exclusively by Ismai'lis. Besides my own presence on the journey, the family also decided to invite a male Sunni neighbour aged about thirty-three, and an elderly Ismai'li man who was their close relative and neighbour. The fact that a Sunni man was accompanying the Ismai'li on their 'spiritual journey' was highly unusual. The decision to invite this man had been a difficult one for the eldest brother, Mehboob, of the Ismai'li household. He realised that many of his Ismai'li relatives in the village would want to accompany his family on their trip to Gilgit, yet he was worried about upsetting his close Sunni friend and neighbour.

If we don't take Aftab then he will be sad with us (*ispa sar khafa boye*). He will say they were friends with me but then they went to Gilgit and left me behind. He will say that they are Ismai'li and don't like me because I am Sunni. There are many other people we should take in the village, but I think that it is most important that we take Aftab. Aftab is not a normal Sunni, he won't say anything about us when he gets back. Indeed, taking him on the trip to Gilgit will improve his relations with us and make us better friends.

It is striking that Mehboob did not want to be seen to exclude Aftab from the trip to Gilgit. He was making conscious decisions about the way in which he wanted to be seen as an Ismai'li, and the ways in which he felt his Ismai'li identity should shape the relations he had with Rowshan's Sunnis. Aftab had never seen Gilgit, loved to travel, he recognised what an important moment the visit of the Aga Khan was to be for the region's Ismai'lis, and he wanted to join me so he could discuss and analyse the journey as we went along. Aftab had recently failed his Pakistan civil service exam, had become increasingly interested in my anthropological research, and often told me that even if he had no money he wanted to live a life of study and research and would no longer try and become a 'boring' civil servant.

Yet when Aftab was invited to join us on our trip to Gilgit he too had a difficult decision to make. On the one hand he was keen to see Gilgit and the Northern Areas – a region of Pakistan that he had never visited. Yet at the same time he was worried about how he might be received by this Ismaʾli family on their trip to Gilgit. Whilst he was close to them and the women did not observe purdah in front of him, he was also concerned that his being Sunni may diminish some of the special enjoyment (*khaz mazah*) of their religious journey.

I don't think I will come, Magnus. If I come, then the daughters and sisters may feel that they cannot say things about the Aga Khan that they want to because I am there. When they see me they will think that they have to hide things, and that they cannot enjoy themselves in the way they want to.

Yet, despite Aftab's worries about joining the family on their journey to Gilgit, he eventually decided to come after Mehboob had repeatedly urged him to do so.

Aftab had other worries beside the possibility that he might impair the Ismaʾli family's enjoyment of the trip. He also worried about what his own family and what other Sunnis in the village would say about him joining this Ismaʾli family on this trip to see the Aga Khan. He told me that whilst his mother and brothers had approved of his going, he was worried that it would anger his wife. Indeed, the day after we returned from Gilgit, I met Aftab on a village path and he told me that he was facing a very angry wife. 'Do you not know', she had shouted at him, 'that all the Sunnis in the village are saying that you have become an Ismaʾli because you went to Gilgit.'

Thus a particularly important dimension of this journey was the negotiation of religious differences between this Sunni man and the Ismaʾli family. Both the Ismaʾlis and Aftab were deeply aware of the religious differences dividing them, and this special religious event brought these differences into even greater relief. Yet, on the behalf of the Ismaʾli family, there was also an intense emphasis on the need not to 'make him upset', and Aftab was deeply worried that he might 'take away from the enjoyment' of his Ismaʾli friends. This sensitive man and his polite Ismaʾli neighbours emphasised their acceptance of each other's beliefs. The politeness and etiquette that characterised the interactions between them throughout the journey involved more than the 'tea party politeness' that I explored in the context of the musical gatherings attended by the Nobles in Chapter 5. The decision to take the Sunni man to Gilgit and his decision to accept the invitation, came only fourteen months after the killing of the Sunni *ʿalim*. It also represented a direct attempt to ensure that the relations between Mehboob and Aftab were to become even deeper, and more deeply resonant with even greater levels of trust. Aftab was being encouraged to travel with Ismaʾlis on a journey to the most secret and spiritual

Ismai'li occasions, in preference to inviting other Ismai'li friends and relatives from the village.

Yet, once on the road, the situation was not so simple. The driver of the minibus – a Sunni from 'down Chitral' with an uncut beard and a prayer cap perched on his head – was intent on emphasising his Sunni identity throughout the journey. He showed none of the sensitivity to Ismai'li sensibilities exhibited by our friend Aftab, and this driver's impolite behaviour was a source of anxiety throughout the course of the journey.

After a six-hour drive on the first day, and still within the boundaries of Chitral district, we stopped at an Ismai'li house for the night. This family were closely related to the family of Rowshan Ismai'lis with whom I was travelling. They welcomed the male members of the party into the guest house, and the women and children were taken into the inner confines of the home. As a mark of respect to us, the eldest man in the house slaughtered a young lamb (*verku*), which took several hours to cook. The village we were staying in was remote – it had no bazaar and only a few shops, and was connected to other regions of Chitral and Gilgit by only a rough dirt road. So there was no meat available for purchase in the village. Butchers in Chitral are all Sunni, and they are mostly Afghan refugees from the Panjshir valley. The fact that they are Sunni means that Ismai'lis can invite their Sunni guests to eat bazaar-killed meat without having to worry that they might refuse to eat Ismai'li-slaughtered animals. No such possibility presented itself in this village. The Sunni driver was irritated by the wait: the time was already twelve o'clock, he told us, and the next day we would have to leave at five in the morning if we were to have any chance of reaching Gilgit before nightfall. The driver decided that he would sleep without taking food, and he went and rested in his minibus.

Eventually our host brought the boiled lamb, plates of rice and freshly cooked bread, and all of the men present, including the Sunni Aftab, tucked in. We were all worried about why the driver had gone off 'in a sulk' (*krui bik*), and told one of the men to try to persuade him to eat with us. The driver again refused, and so the host kept the driver's share (*zhira*) of rice and meat, and said that he would give it to him early in the morning for his breakfast. Aftab left the room. Now the Ismai'li men in the room started speculating about whether it was the fact that the meat was killed by an Ismai'li that was making the driver so moody and difficult. They compared the 'pearl-like' (*durdana*), educated (*talimi yafta*), and open minded (*khulao dimagho*) Aftab (the family's Sunni friend) to the wild and rude driver. The next morning the driver ate the rice, but pointedly refused to eat the meat, saying that he had stomach problems and did not want to get an upset stomach. This excuse (*bahana*) was not a plausible one and the Ismai'li men present agreed that the family should never have agreed to take a Sunni driver on *deedar* in the first place. They decided that the best way of dealing with him was to ignore him: this would make sure that he did not become proud (*tsarak*) and out of his place. He was, after all, *their* driver and they were paying him to take them to Gilgit.

It was not only this driver's refusal to eat Ismai'li-killed meat that caused tension on the journey to see the Aga Khan. Once again we also see how music and travel are a rich source of insight into the ways in which Chitral people handle the pressures of 'Islamisation'. The girls and young women in the mini-bus were particularly fond of listening to the tapes of Ismai'li devotional hymns (*ginan*) recited in Urdu and Persian by a wellknown Ismai'li woman from Gilgit, Mehrangiz.[44] These hymns, recited by both men and women, extol the greatness and spiritual light of the present Imam, the Aga Khan, and also extol the first Imam, Ali, the son-in-law and cousin of the Prophet. Some of these *ginans* are based on the spiritual poems of the eleventh century Ismai'li philosopher from Balkh in present day Afghanistan, Nasir Khusraw.[45] But when these hymns were played in the cassette deck of the minibus our Sunni driver objected, claiming that the hymns were 'boring' and were putting him to sleep. He kept removing the tapes and replacing them with cassettes of loud Indian film music. This music was interspersed with comedy dialogues about an uneducated Pukhtun man who had fallen in love with a sophisticated Karachi woman. Hymns praising the Imam were replaced by the voices of two lovers arguing about where they would have their next secret meeting. These Indian music cassettes and comedy dialogues were a particular favourite of these young women when they were at home, and the whole family enjoyed watching on their television video cassettes of the ribald commentaries on the *ulama* by the Nobles.

Yet there was a feeling that as they were going on *deedar* in a minibus that they were paying for, it was only proper for them to have their way about the appropriate music to play, and particularly to be allowed to play their own devotional music. Thus, it is striking that people who communicate through

---

[44] The largely Persian and Urdu *ginans* recited by Ismai'lis in Rowshan are different from those recited by Gujerati-speaking Khoja Ismai'lis living in Karachi and Bombay. On Ismai'li devotional music in South Asia, see Asani 2002; Esmail 2002. For English translations of the type of *ginans* of the kind listened to by Ismai'lis in Rowshan, see Hunzai 1996, and on the musical traditions of Afghan Badakhshani Ismai'lis, see van Belle 2002.

[45] See Hunsberger 2000. Nasir-e Khusraw is said by many Ismai'lis to be their original *pir* (spiritual master).

and appreciate daring music in other settings see this trip as a time when Hindi film music is improper, impious and insulting. Normally Ismai'lis are not able to play such music in public minibuses as they travel around Chitral, even if the driver is Chitrali, in the fear of exciting Sunni anger and comments about the improper nature of Ismai'lis veneration for the Aga Khan. Once again this 'dirty' (*gandah*) and 'rough' (*jalash*) driver was trying to establish the power of Sunni Islam on what was meant to be an Ismai'li spiritual journey.

After two long days of travel across mountain terrain, we arrived at seven o'clock in Gahkuch, the town in the Gilgit region in which the Aga Khan was to perform *deedar*. Our arrival in Gahkuch was the cause of much public discussion. This was the first time, we were told by admiring and amazed local people in Gahkuch, that a minibus had made the journey from Chitral, a journey that involved scaling the 3,500 metre Shandur pass, and travelling through steep and windy mountain tracks. The driver we had hired, it turned out, may have been moody, but he was also one of the most skilled (*mahir*) and experienced (*tajrubah kar*) men of his profession in northern Pakistan. Beyond the skill of the driver, I was told, it was the spiritual nature of the journey that had allowed us to travel to Gilgit so safely. 'It is astounding', the elder brother told me, 'that none of the children have cried and even the weakest and sickest of my sisters has not even suffered from travel sickness. They have not even felt dizzy. This really has been a spiritual journey.'

As we drove into the town, the girls and women in the minibus commented on the enthusiastic and committed way in which the town's young male Ismai'li volunteers were guiding the long queues of traffic along the dangerous and narrow road. Watching these boys, dressed in khaki *shalwar kamiz* and vigorously blowing at their whistles, the girls said what good and devoted Ismai'lis these young men were. The travellers looked out of the windows of the minibus, onto the steep and barren mountain slopes to the side of the road, to see messages such as '*deedar mubarak*' (congratulations on *deedar*) and 'Welcome to the Hazir Imam' written in huge letters in white stones. The large and bustling crowd of both men and women walking around the town, they said, seemed 'like a dream' (*ispaten khoshpo ghon tsereiran*). Both the young women and the men in the vehicle commented how the people of Gilgit 'turned out' to be 'more modern' and considerably 'more advanced' than themselves (*ispa sar modern, ispa sar kafi prooshti bi asooni*). It was seeing women walking around the bazaar with their head-scarves loosely covering their heads or even draped around their necks (*petek goli petsi*), that especially made them comment on how 'behind' (*achi*)

Rowshan's Ismai'lis were in when compared to their co-religionists in Gilgit. The driver, however, was less concerned with thinking about modernity, and had his mind and eyes on other things on the road ahead. Nudging me in my ribs, he dared me to film the 'pretty, pretty girls' (*sheli, sheli kumoran*) with 'white as white' (*phuk ishperu*) faces he saw walking along the road ahead.

Deedar was to be performed early next morning, and all had an early night. The girls, women and elderly father were invited to stay in an Ismai'li house in the town, whilst the rest of us slept in a school building that had been set aside for people who had travelled to the town to see the Aga Khan. We woke early in the morning and the Ismai'li men prepared themselves for *deedar*. They washed their hair, scented themselves with perfume (*spray*), shaved, and polished their boots. The elder brother had even bought a new white woollen Chitral hat and a Chitrali woollen jacket for this special event, and other men donned blue blazers and attached pre-fastened cravats around their necks.

The Ismai'li family all succeeded in 'catching a glimpse' of the Aga Khan, and were able listened to the message (*farman*) the Imam delivered in which the Aga Khan implored his 'spiritual children' (*ruhani azhelie*) to promote unity in the Ismai'li community and to live in peace with non-Ismai'li Muslims. Despite attempts made by Mehboob to persuade us to enter the *pindal* with him, Aftab and I did not participate in *deedar*. Both Aftab and I were pleased and moved that Mehboob had asked us to join him for this special moment. It was with great regret, however, that we decided we had to refuse Mehboob's gracious invitation. We were both concerned that some people in attendance would know that we were not Ismai'lis and ask us to leave the sacred area, and we were also worried about what Sunnis back at home in Rowshan would say about us when they discovered that we had performed *deedar*.

When the Ismai'li family came out of the *pindal* they all talked of how beautiful (*sheili*) the Aga Khan had appeared to them, and how all in attendance had wept to see him. The eyes of the women and the men were wet and red with tears, and the girls used colourful handkerchiefs they had sewn at home to dry their eyes. They had also emerged from the crowds with Shabnam, whom they had spotted sitting with her little brother in the *pindal*. Her elder brother, Mehboob, looked at me and said, laughing, 'Oh Magnus, you don't have a Chitrali sister – you have a Chitrali brother; no other woman in Chitral could have done such a thing.' Even for her elder brother, the lengths his sister had gone to attend *deedar* were commendable, and proved to him that 'pure religious emotion' (*pak mazhabi jezbat*) could move a person to do great things.

Heightened levels of religious emotion and sensibility are an important dimension of Muslim life in Chitral beyond the context of sectarian violence. Besides working to strengthen faith and display religious commitment, religious emotion is also an important feature of meaningful spiritual experience. Moreover, even heightened religious emotion and the spiritual experience it cultivates is also held as being a rational and articulated component of the person, and all this is evident both in this incident and in Rowshan life more generally. Shabnam, in her quest to see the present Imam during his 2000 trip to Pakistan did the unthinkable: she travelled alone to the distant city of Gilgit without the permission of her elder brothers. Yet there was planning involved in her journey, and Shabnam was determined to prove to her sceptical sisters that she was not a woman of words alone (*khali lu*), but also a woman of action (*korum, ʿamal*). Moreover, even her elder brother recognised that Shabnam, powered by special religious emotion, had proven herself capable of accomplishing difficult tasks that involved not only bravery (*bahderi*) but also intellectual ability (*qabiliyat*). So, unlike the overly emotional returnee *madrasa* students, Shabnam had been successful in handling, generating and cultivating a special type of emotion whilst not being taken over or dominated by it in a way that restricted her capacity to think.

Shabnam's decision to make the daring and challenging trip to Gilgit also resulted in the women and girls remaining behind in the house to press their case to their elder brother as to why he should take them on the long and expensive trip to Gilgit. They did this through speech and not just embodied gestures. The agency of these Ismaiʾli women, far from being confined to the 'discursive body', was, rather, 'direct, confrontational verbal activity' (Hegeland 1998a: 255). This is important for the general argument of this book: an important dimension of living a Muslim life is creativity, and this creative activity is not a matter of male action only, nor is it to be found solely in the writing of poetry or the singing of love songs. As Lambek notes, if 'religion is inevitably bound up with the naturalisation of power and the legitimation of or sanctification of the world it constructs, it also enables (and directs) meaningful agency' (Lambek 2000a: 309). In Shabnam's visit to see the Aga Khan, we see how heightened states of religious sensibility and independent decision-making contributed to the meaningful agency of one Ismaiʾli woman and her family. This was not this was not a unique situation, as I have noted in other chapters of this book, such initiatives were a pervasive element of Rowshan life during my stay.

The trip made by this Ismaiʾli family to see the Aga Khan in Gilgit has thus provided unexpected insights into the sectarian divide in Rowshan, demonstrating the importance of the role played by emotions, affections and the intellect in the construction and experience of that divide. At one level, the elder brother's decision to invite his Sunni friend to accompany them, and Aftab's decision to accept, reveals much about the importance of showing sensitivity to the sensibilities of others in the living of a Muslim life in Chitral. Living a thoughtful life that has plural dimensions requires cultivated and sensitive minds and feelings. Aftab was taken on *deedar* because he was educated and therefore, he thought, able to be properly 'broad-minded' and 'human'. The dangers of the uncultivated mind capable only of low thoughts (*pust sooch*) was confirmed by the sulky and sometimes even aggressive behaviour of the Sunni driver. At another level, however, the complex composition of the travellers was a cause of intense anxiety and conflict. When Rowshan people do try and live a thoughtful and plural religious life they do so in the face of intense opposition from some of their fellow villagers who think that the boundary between Ismaiʾlis and Sunnis should be hardened.

CONCLUSION

Recognising and actively erecting the boundary between Sunnis and Ismaiʾlis in the village is an important dimension of what it means to live a proper Muslim life in Rowshan, and an important dimension of this is the display of heightened religious emotions. Yet, at the same time, villagers also value people who are 'social' and 'broad-minded', and critical thought and decision-making are important dimensions of the most contentious and heated issue in present day Rowshan. For Chitral people, it is cultivated and critical minds that have meant that their region has not been beset by the incidents of communal sectarian violence which have so bedevilled other regions of Pakistan. Rowshan people can and do live a calmly thoughtful life, and this entails actively explaining and thinking about difference in ways that make it reasonable to be plural. But in some cases the emotional temperature rises, and when it does it affords significant insights into the ways in which Rowshan people conceptualise the interaction between emotions and the intellect, and how this in turn affects the cultivation of rational thought.

Heightened states of religious emotion are, however, about more than the erecting of a sectarian boundary in the village. They are also about concerns that transcend the division between Ismaiʾlis and Sunnis in the village. These concerns are about the transitory nature of religious faith in the village, and the need for Muslims to nurture and renew their faith through displays of emotional commitment and the acquisition of religious knowledge. Moreover, I have also shown how these often public displays of 'religious emotion' are themselves linked in complex ways to the importance that secret knowledge plays in village life, for if much emotional energy goes into the public display of faith, then so too do Rowshan people devote a great deal of effort to conceal their religious practices and beliefs, as well as the opinions they hold about the religious dispositions of their neighbours. Conceptually, then, the sectarian division that is such an important feature of Muslim life in Rowshan, is about doctrinal difference, but it is also about deeper and underlying concerns about what it means to have faith and display faith in a world of faith. And whilst there are occasions in their daily lives when Rowshan people must display faith in public arenas before their fellow villagers, it is also often the case that having true faith also entails the ability to hide and conceal.

Beyond the study of sectarian violence, this chapter has also explored the ways in which the experience of religious emotion interacts in complex ways with the cultivated critical faculties in the lives of Rowshan people. At one level, heightened states of religious emotion have the potential, in Rowshan people's minds, of blinding people of reasoned and critical thought. Yet, it is not only emotions that can become out of control and unbridled – so can the intellect. It is young and educated men with quick minds and fast tongues who are liable to become emotional and act irrationally. Finally, religious emotion, besides making possible intense religious experience, is also conceptualised as having the potential to facilitate reasoned thought and calculated action.

CHAPTER 8

Conclusion

Thinking has made the intellect astonished, but the heart is compelled (*dunie ʿaql hairan, magam hardi majboor*)
(Modern Khowar love song)

THE LIFE OF THE MIND IN NORTHERN PAKISTAN

I have argued throughout this book that Rowshan people are willing and indeed eager to reflect upon and not just to attack or disparage alternative views, and that my experience of Chitral people was very consistently one involving the exchange of and reflection upon ideas. These processes of exchange and reflection entailed valuing intellectual engagement with ideas and points of view often very much at odds with what one believed, and with fellow Chitral Muslims whose response to Islamising messages were markedly different from ones own. Indeed, the relationship between Chitral people who respond in diverse ways to radical Islamising messages is the source of much discussion in the region's villages and small towns. Yet what is striking is that whilst in some cases such relations result in open and even aggressive moments of conflict, other relations involve debate that is heated but is, nevertheless, considered intellectually stimulating and of inherent value to those involved. Moreover, many of the subjects under discussion were often about matters of deep importance and great sensitivity in the highly charged political and religious context of present day Pakistan. So value judgement and intellectual analysis were addressed to matters of faith and emotion, and it is through the examination of this process that this study has sought to generate new perspectives on the nature of Muslim life, and also to illuminate the richness and complexity of the interaction between emotional and intellectual activity.

Above all else, the lives of Chitral Muslims challenge the notion that northern Pakistan is a place brimming with unthinking village conformists and, thus, inevitably in the grip of Islamising fanatics. I have documented, rather, how being Muslim in Chitral involves dynamic and creative processes that reflect a complex interaction of decision-making, intellectual energy, debate and critical discussion, and ideally balanced levels of affect and emotion. Yet there is also a darker side to the intellectually and emotionally vibrant lives that so many Chitral people strive to live: anxiety and the fear of the unseating consequences of the experience of powerful emotions is also a recurring dimension of Chitral people's experience. Finally, the experience of anxiety pervades many Chitral people's ideas about their moral universe, and Chitralis exert a great deal of their energies in deciding which dimensions of their lives should be concealed and which revealed.

WHERE RUMI AND ROUSSEAU MEET: ISLAM IN SOUTH ASIA

This book has had two key concerns. First, I have sought to contribute to the anthropology of Islam and of sociality in Pakistan, south Asia and the broader Muslim world. In order to understand Islam in the context of Chitral I have employed distinctly anthropological approaches and methods: I found that my analysis of the ways in which Chitral Muslims handle the pressure to 'Islamise' required a consideration of Chitral people's conceptions and experiences of the life of the mind, intellectual activity and emotional sensitivity. So, secondly, by exploring Islam from this perspective I have also sought to contribute more broadly to the anthropology of emotion, thought, the intellect, personality and morality.

My discussion has been about the capacity of 'village Muslims' to be critical and reflective in the face of global Islam. By arguing in these terms, I have explored the ways in which reform-oriented Islam has impacted on the Islamic tradition in present day Chitral. I have sought to show that the intellectual traditions of classic Persian Sufi texts are still important in a part of the world where reform-oriented Muslim movements and organisations deeply hostile towards Sufi thought and practice are also influential and pervasive. More broadly, my exploration of the input of Sufic texts and ideas on the thought processes of Chitral Muslims has allowed me to demonstrate the complexities of the experience of thought in Chitral: Sufi values and teachings are an omnipresent feature of Chitral Muslims' emotional and spiritual repertoire. Thus, this ethnographic dimension of the study has also generated complex questions concerning the ways in which Chitral people think about the mind, the body and the emotions, and the complex nature of the interactions between these domains of their everyday experience. In relation to the anthropology of Islam and religion more specifically, all this is striking because it remains widely assumed in both scholarly and more popular accounts that so-called 'Islamic reformism' is the dominant trend in the Muslim world today, and that this form of Muslim spirituality is above all else a rationalising force that leaves little or no space for emotion and experience.

In order to understand the full complexities of Muslim thought and identity, it is not possible to simply ask how Muslims think about the claim of faith: what is needed, rather, is an appreciation of the ways in which Muslims engage – intellectually and emotionally – with different classes of religious knowledge, and, importantly, to recognise that they often do so in deeply critical ways. In Chitral there is no simple correlation between types of Muslims and the classes of religious knowledge they employ in their everyday lives: revivalist Deobandi scholars make love amulets, and reformist Jama'at-e Islami supporters cultivate reputations for being Sufis and love poets. Influential reform-oriented religious scholars have sought to impart a 'new meaning of Sufism' in which it becomes not 'an esoteric dimension of Islam, but merely a gauge to measure concentration and morals' (Nasr 1996: 123), yet secret knowledge is a powerful feature of religious experience for many Chitral people, and the language of emotion continues to be central to being Muslim for most if not all Chitral Muslims. The diverse classes of knowledge that are part of the Islamic repertoire of Chitral people, and the connections they make between these and emotional experience, informs the ways in which Chitral Muslims structure their conceptions of morality, deploy their critical faculties, think about the relation between rationality and strong feelings, and experience the spiritual dimensions of the world. In formulating these arguments, I have questioned many recent studies of the Islamic tradition which treat processes of 'rationalisation' as the dominant force in the structure and making of Islamic knowledge and Muslim identity in the world today (Starrett 1998).

Other Muslims in Pakistan and beyond also have visions of Islam that are deeply influenced by Sufi values and concepts, as Ansari's work on Sufi saints in Sind and Werbner's research on Pakistanis in Britain and in the country itself have shown (Ansari 1992; Werbner 2002, 2003). What is important and distinctive about the power and creative vitality of the Sufi tradition in Chitral is that its focus is on intellectual and emotional engagement with Sufi texts and ideas, rather than ecstatic worship at shrines and affiliation to formalised Sufi lodges and brotherhoods. In my account of village debate in chapter 4 I showed how this engagement, for many Chitral people, entails the cultivation of inner insight as well as heightened forms of bodily sensitivity and understanding. Chitral Muslims themselves make connections between everyday life and Sufic values and teachings: reaching spiritual truth (*ruhani haqiqat*), understanding the sounds of the heart (*hardio hawaz*), and experiencing the pains and delights of ecstatic love (*ishqo dardochen gham*) are all forms of experience that are both a vibrant focus of conversation in the village and a source of the region's rich tradition of musical and poetic performance. There is a living presence of classic Sufi texts in the minds of Chitral Muslims – both Sunni and Ismai'li – at the same time as the absence of the accoutrements of ecstatic Sufi Islam in the region. So I have argued that where the teachings of Sufi texts have provided a source of values for Chitral Muslims, these values remain primarily about thought and emotion, and that this is something that is itself reflected in the great value Chitral people place on the experience and act of thought.

At the same time, however, the processes of intellectual creativity and exchange that I have documented in Chitral are made even more complex by changes in religious education that have affected the Muslim world more generally. Drawing on the anthropology of religious knowledge, learning and education in Muslim societies, I have argued that the impact of mass education in the Muslim world, and newly emergent styles of religious education, can be fully understood only if religious knowledge is itself placed in a broader economy of knowledge than simply that which is taught in the region's schools, mosques and *jama'at khanas*. At one level, the dominance of religious colleges and mosque schools teaching reform-oriented Deobandi styles of religious knowledge has given rise to import-ant changes in Muslim subjectivity in Chitral. Mystical Persian Sufi texts, such as Rumi's *Mathnawi*, are no longer formally taught to Rowshan children in mosques or schools; it is, rather, the Urdu works of Deobandi scholars like Ashraf Ali Thanawi that form the central focus of Islamic education in the region. This change, in particular, has important implications for Rowshan people's experience of the sectarian divide as a lived feature of village life. While at least some Sunni and Ismai'li children in the village thirty years ago sat together and were taught mystical Persian texts like Rumi's *Mathnawi* and Sa'di' s *Bustan*, which imparted religious concepts valued by both doctrinal traditions, this shared experience of religious learning is impossible in Rowshan today. In present day Rowshan, Ismai'lis and Sunnis learn about religion in different places and have very different conceptions of what constitutes religious knowledge: it has, as in other contexts in the Muslim world, become increasingly 'systematised' and 'objectified' (Eickelman 1992a, 1997, 1999).

At another level, however, I found that it is not only in mosques, *madrasas*, and Jama'at Khanas that religious knowledge is transmitted, and that there are people other than Ismai'li volunteers and Sunni *dashmanan* who play an active role in Chitral's economy of religious knowledge. 'New Muslims' (Eickelman and Anderson 1999) in musical groups such as the Nobles are now also an active force in the transmission of Sufi-centred knowledge and thought, and they employ the instruments of modernity – tapes and compact discs – in order to popularise their styles of music, performance and writing. The music they perform, their styles of dancing and the words they sing, are all deeply rooted in Sufi texts and traditions, so much so that they themselves even accuse poets in the region of plagiarising Rumi. The vision of Islam that they promote is an aesthetic – it calls upon Muslims to be creative in intellectual and bodily ways, conscious of form and beauty, and also to partake in embodied enjoyment. Their work is also deeply, yet subtly, political: they use both poetry and their skills as impersonators to poke fun at those of Chitral's *ulama* whom they see as being hypocritical and 'narrow-minded'. This Islamic aesthetic is not, however, something that is separated off from more sober ways of going about being Muslim: prayers are performed and God's name is frequently uttered, and many in the audience are supporters of the Jama'at-e Islami party.

So the spirituality of Chitral's Muslims is both deeply intellectual and experienced in embodied ways, and this is something experienced widely by Chitral people: having ideas and tolerating the pain of inward thoughts and reflections are what make a local philosopher for many Chitral people. Yet Chitral Muslims do not simply know or defer to old Persian Sufi literary materials, they also creatively build upon them, especially so in their making of poetry which they recite in both musical and spoken forms. Music and poetry is thus a mindful domain of Chitral life where Chitral people creatively make their rich literary heritage relevant to their contemporary concerns.

New forms of knowledge and sources of educational experience have contributed to the complexity of these interactions. Muslims in Rowshan and Chitral more generally, study a wide variety of social science subjects – especially sociology, political sciences and international relations – both in their homes, in the region's degree colleges and in Peshawar University. The modernist courses that Chitral people follow have not simply resulted in growing scepticism of the values of the Persianate Sufi canon. Rather,

I have argued, especially in my account of education and debate in Rowshan in chapter 3, that there is a complex interaction between the themes of modernist degree courses and classic Sufi texts. This interaction is one that is actively participated in by many Chitral Muslims whose daily discussions draw both on modernist ideas about healthy minds, bodies, sexuality and sociality, as well as ideas about the heart, the mind and truth, that emanate from their own interpretations of classic Persian Sufi texts. It is in Chitral's villages where Rumi, Hobbes and Rousseau meet: this interaction contributes to the distinct texture of the Islamic tradition in the region, and it does so in a way that heightens the intellectual vibrancy of village life.

Long-running debates in the anthropology of religion about the relationship between religious texts and lived religion, and more recent discussion of religious morality and ethics, have shaped my approach to the nature of the role that Persianate Sufi texts play in the living of a Muslim life in Chitral. I have argued that important themes in the Persian Sufi canon – especially the division between the concealed and the revealed – are a source of debate and internal moral conflict for Chitral Muslims. And this conflict is one that is partially resolved through stressful intellectual work, decision-making, and the taking of risks in fraught social contexts.

'SECTARIAN CONFLICT' OR 'ISLAMIC PLURALITY'?

Life in Chitral is also stressful because of the division between the region's Sunnis and Ismai'lis. My findings thus also contribute to anthropological debate about so-called religious conflict within and beyond south Asia. Whilst Chitral's Ismai'lis and Sunnis subscribe to very different Islamic doctrinal traditions, recognise the differences that divide them, and actively seek to construct hardened boundaries between themselves in certain contexts and at certain moments, there remains the potential for the sharing of religious doctrines and values. The emphasis on the secret (*batin*) is an important dimension of Ismai'li doctrines – it lies at the very core of Ismai'li identity and philosophy. What I found, however, was that villagers talk about the world as being divided between what is said and done on the surface; and what takes place in the hidden: these villagers are both Ismai'li and Sunni. Shared sources of faith and values is not only a feature of life in contexts of plural harmony: transmission of religious doctrines and the sharing of ethical and moral frameworks takes place even in contexts where religious boundaries are hardened.

In the context of present day Pakistan where there is much violent conflict between Sunni and Shi'a Muslims, the fact that Ismai'lis and

Sunnis continue to live relatively peacefully in the intimate village setting of Rowshan is important. Along with growing levels of women's education and employment, and relatively relaxed purdah practices it points to the distinctive nature of village life in Chitral as compared other regions of Pakistan, and, indeed, other regions of the Muslim world. Yet some parts of Chitral are considerably less open to the types of discussions and activities that are possible in Rowshan. Most importantly, I have sought to show throughout the book that even Rowshan people have a broad spectrum of views about a contentious array of issues that are important in the region today. Indeed, Rowshan people may hold deeply contrasting views about emotive issues, and yet they can engage in discussion with other villagers, have friendships that traverse the sectarian divide, and bring critical thought and a complex variety of intellectual traditions to their discussions. Moreover, as recent ethnographies suggest (Werbner 2003; Verkaaik 2004) it would certainly be overly simplistic to claim that what Chitral people refer to as 'down Pakistan' is homogeneously more influenced by 'radical Islam' and more prone to violent sectarian conflict than Chitral. So my ethnographically dense exploration of Isma'li-Sunni relations in Rowshan challenges approaches to the study of sectarian conflict in Pakistan that, I suggest, over emphasise both the instrumentality of 'the state' and so-called 'extremist' and armed 'Islamist' groups in determining the nature of the relationships between Muslims in Pakistan who claim affiliation to a diverse array of Islamic doctrinal traditions.

There is an expanding body of anthropological literature that emphasises the importance of compromise, principled reflection and vigorous debate in the negotiation of diversity and plurality in South East Asian Islamic traditions (Beatty 1999; Bowen 2003; Peletz 2002), and there is an older anthropological tradition which explores the strategies employed by Muslims holding diverse opinions about 'Islam' in order to live together if not always socially. In the study of Pakistan in particular and South Asia more generally the scholarly understanding of conflicts linked to internal doctrinal differences between Muslims focus largely on their manifestation in *fatwas*, accusations of heresy, and acts of violence (Tambiah 1996; Nasr 2000; Zaman 2002).[1] My account of Ismai'li-Sunni relations throughout this book has sought to recognise the importance of both approaches to the study of Muslim diversity but also to extend the discussion. Not simply documenting that Muslims living in a world of no consensus are capable of

---

[1] Although Didier 2004 argues that violence in South Asian societies may be less 'rountinised' than many anthropologists suggest.

recognising that their fellow Muslims hold opinions about Islam and Muslim life that are different from their own, I have sought to show that they also take their different perspectives to open discussions, and engage in arguments that seek to test one another's opinions. In so doing, I have challenged the assumption that violence is now a homogenously routinised feature of Sunni and non-Sunni relations in Pakistan. I have argued that there is a need to pay greater attention to Muslims in Pakistan who are critical both of the deployment of sectarian discourses and the increasingly violent nature of relations between the country's diverse Muslim communities.

Yet, as was seen in chapter 7, *fatwas*, killings and riots have played a significant role in structuring the relationship both between Chitral's Ismai'lis and Sunnis, as well as the nature of the conflict between the members of each of these doctrinal clusters. At the same time, many Chitral Muslims negotiate religious difference through skilled mindful work on a daily basis, and one result of this is the generally peaceful nature of Ismai'li-Sunni relations in Chitral. Critical thought on the part of both Sunni and Ismai'li people is an important dimension of even the most contentious domains of life in the region. When plural and tolerant views do play an important role in life in the region they are not simply a pre-existing feature of Chitral society, but are rather the result of intellectual work on the part of Chitral Muslims.

There is a distinctive and ongoing interaction of Ismai'li and Sunni values taking place in Chitral. More particularly, the type of knowledge that constitutes the Ismai'li and Sunni Islamic traditions in the region, is some-thing which has both facilitated an exchange of ideas between the two communities and prevented major incidents of communal sectarian vio-lence. Unlike the wealthy Khoja Ismai'lis whose rich and complex literary heritage draws powerfully on syncretistic devotional works of the great Hindu and Muslim saint cults of South Asia (Asani 2002), it is the works of the Ismai'li philosopher Nasir Khusraw that are known and recited by Chitral Ismai'lis. The different kind of spiritual heritage of Chitral's Ismai'lis means that they pose fewer theological problems for Chitral Sunnis than Khoja Ismai'lis. Whilst Ismai'lis remain a considerable problem for many of the region's Sunnis, they do have shared sources of faith and values and this has facilitated close relations between followers of these two 'doctrinal clusters' into the present day in Chitral. Though tense at times, the generally peaceful nature of Sunni–Ismai'li relations in Rowshan is even more remark-able because hardened religious forces powerful in Pakistan and beyond have sough to generate violent conflict in the region. Moreover, Chitral Ismai'lis' intellectual history has also powered the valuing of critical and intellectual activity in the region. The Ismai'li faith, for Nasir Khusraw, entailed a rich combination of belief in the Present Imam, as well as reflection, contemplation, and the exercise of the reasoning intellect; (Hunsberger 2001) these are dimensions of life that are clearly visible in the lives of Chitral Muslims – both Ismai'li and Sunni – today.

Yet it would be wrong to explain the generally peaceful nature of 'sectarian relations' in Chitral as exclusively relating to the Ismai'li tradition. At the same time, both Sunni and Ismai'li Muslims in Chitral are deeply knowledgeable about the Persian writings of other great Persian Sufi masters including Rumi, Hafiz, and Sa'di. Their knowledge of this intellectual tradition means that Chitral Muslims are mindfully aware of the emphasis on perspective (*nazar*), contemplation, (*fikr*), and the intense experience of thought-provoking love (*ishq*) extolled by these great writers. These are values important both in Ismai'li philosophy and a great deal of Sufi writing. So, besides mediating a creative encounter between Deobandi and Sufi Islamic traditions, the specific impact of Sufi values and teachings on the form of Islam in Chitral has also facilitated multidimensional interactions between the Ismai'li and Sunni doctrinal traditions. This is especially significant because these are Islamic 'doctrinal clusters' (Eickelman 1992a) that are often held to be inherently irreconcilable by Pakistan's Sunni religious authorities.

Whilst Ismai'lis and Sunnis do live together in intimate village settings in Chitral, there have been moments of violent conflict, however, and Chitral people's experience of this conflict sheds light on the complex interaction between the place of thought and the experience of emotion in the living of a Muslim life in Chitral. Chitral Muslims actively and vocally think and engage in discussions about this deeply sensitive dimension of their lives, yet they are also painfully aware of the dangerous nature of the heightened emotions that competing forms of religious sectarian identity have the power of inculcating. As I have argued, many Chitral people conceptualise such heightened emotions as precluding the possibility of mindful activity. Recognising the importance of experiencing heightened emotional states for Chitral people has allowed me to explore in detail the processes whereby 'principled reflections' (Bowen 2003) give way to violent dispute.

At the same time, the findings of the present book highlight the important role that non-public spaces, forms of action and classes of knowledge play in determining the nature of Sunni-Ismai'li conflict in this generally rural region of Pakistan. This is important because a great deal of scholarship on communal violence in South Asia has focused on its relationship to 'public arenas', and much of this body of literature analyses violence that takes place in urban settings. Sectarian conflict in Chitral does have a complex history in public spaces and the forms of collective action and participation that such space engenders. The 1982 riot was a critical event because during it tension between Sunnis and Ismai'lis in Chitral arose to the surface in violent public acts, and something that had long-term consequences: Ismai'li–Sunni marriages largely became a thing of the past.

Yet in chapter 7 I sought to demonstrate that Ismai'li–Sunni conflict in Chitral is about underlying anxieties about inner dimensions of life and self shared by both Ismai'lis and Sunnis. I therefore challenge the idea that sectarian violence arises largely from the emergence of more open and public awareness about doctrinal difference as a result of mass education and growing levels of literacy in the contemporary Muslim world (Eickelman 1992a). The shared anxieties that lie at the heart of Ismai'li–Sunni conflict in Chitral are primarily concerned with what it means to live an emotionally legitimate and intellectually significant Muslim life. There is a tension between showing correct displays of emotional commitment to religious doctrine, and the impulse to show balanced emotion and critical intellectual activity – dimensions of life considered essential to living well and in tune with divine will. This tension is all the more important because what is at stake is faith in a world where faith counts: faith perishes, it rots; and it is only through vigorous emotional renewal that faith can be nurtured to become an inherent part of the Muslim person. Sectarian divisions and conflicts are, then, themselves rooted in deep and internal anxieties shared by Ismai'lis and Sunnis in Rowshan.

Finally, the arguments I make in relation to sectarian conflict in Chitral are also of broader anthropological concern, for the experience of fear and pain are not only important in relation to sectarian violence in Chitral. Chapter two documented the extent to which the anxieties resulting from 'gossip' and 'talk' are considered painful dimensions of village life by Rowshan people. Moreover, Chapter five showed how Rowshan's *madrasa*-educated *dashmanan* connect this domain of village experience with their understandings of Islamic philosophical approaches to human speech. A key dimension of violence as experienced by Rowshan people, then, is the violence of the word, and this is seen as being even more damaging than physical violations of the body. While there have been no major incidents of sectarian violence in Rowshan itself, the violence of the word, whose wounds, unlike those of the sword, never heal, is a source of deep anxiety for Rowshan people. And it is precisely because discussion and debate for Rowshan people should be about the handling of abstract concepts in a way that facilitates the play of the mind that wounds caused by words are especially painfully for Chitral people. What is more, complicity in this morally problematic underside of Rowshan life – making 'useless gossip', harbouring of 'dirty thoughts', displaying blind anger – means that participation in violence directed at others is only one side of the coin. More painful is the experience of self-inflicted violations of the ideally emotionally legitimate and intellectually adept person – something that, in the context of an emotionally 'upside-down' Rowshan, many Rowshan people conceptualise as being impossible to avoid.

THE ISLAMIC REVIVAL

In my account of Muslim life in Chitral I have revealed the vitality of local ways of being Muslim in the face of an array of homogenising 'Islamist' movements. Anthropologists of Islam theorised the nature of tensions between local and global Islam long before the current focus on globalisation became central to much ethnographic writing. Islam is a world religion that connects Muslims in diverse cultural settings. Trading routes, Muslim travellers, men of learning and piety, networks of religious knowledge and learning, and complex political entities, have for many centuries connected the world's Muslims (see, for instance, Bennison 2002). In the contemporary world the tensions between the local and the global are an especially powerful dimension of Muslim experience. Many reform-minded Islamic movements have sought to homogenise the world's Muslims, and any diversity within the Muslim 'community' (*umma*) is conceptualised as promoting division, weakness, syncretism and impurity. In my account of musical creativity in the small town setting of Markaz I have sought to show that local responses to this process have also been inherently global. The Nobles use the technologies of modernity to promote their work, but, moreover, they draw too on styles of thought and creative expression that embody the global set of meanings, texts, experiences and intellectual connections which make up Islam. And even religious authorities who are widely known and praised as makers of love amulets use the global language of modern science to reply to their reform-minded detractors. Thus, by addressing issues raised in the anthropological literature on the intellect and the emotions, I have sought to challenge social science assumptions about the so-called 'Islamic revival' and 'political Islam'.

For Olivier Roy, Islamism is above all the quest to create a universal Islamic state based on individual virtue, and it is has failed for two reasons (Roy 1994). First, nowhere has the attempt to create an Islamic state succeeded: where *shari'a* law has been implemented it has only been partial (Saudi Arabia, Pakistan, Sudan), and Islamic revolutions have always met the forces of segmentary Muslim society (Iran, Afghanistan, Algeria). Second, it has failed at a deeper intellectual level: the ideas of the Islamists themselves are the product of modern and Western thought. Yet, according to Roy, this very failure has itself fanned neofundamentalism: the attempt to re-Islamise society bottom-up, as opposed to Islamise the state from the top-down (see also Kepel 2002). Yet like Hirschkind I am not convinced that 'political Islam' 'involves an extension of the Islamic tradition outside of the properly religious domain it has historically adopted' (Hirschkind 1997).[2] This construction of 'political Islam' fails to appreciate the extent to which religion and politics have fused even in Western political entities, and, at a deeper level, it reduces forms of religious experience and morality to a 'posited distortion or corruption of properly religious practice' (Hirschkind 1997).

In contrast to these accounts, I have argued throughout this book is that the anthropological attempt to understand so-called 'revivalist Islam' must also incorporate the voices of Muslims who are themselves critical of emergent styles of Muslim thought and identity. Chitral people themselves refer to some of their fellow Muslims as being 'hardened' (*sakht*), 'extremist' (*intiha pasand*), and 'narrow-minded' (*trang dimagho*), and in doing so they are not simply replicating the modernist and antifundamentalist values of Pakistan's ruling elite, or those of the more narrowly Islamaphobic Western media. Rather, they are reflecting in a sophisticated and historically informed way about what dimensions of movements of Islamic reform they find threatening or troubling, and how their visions of Islam are located in contrasting intellectual traditions, values, moral states and modes of religious experience.

Not all Chitral Muslims are critical of the teachings of reform-minded Islam: there are many Chitral people who vocally claim to support the values of movements of Islamic purification and reform, including the Afghan Taliban. And so this book is also a contribution to the anthropological understanding of the form taken by the so-called 'Islamic revival' in the contemporary Muslim world. First, I have sought to show that if there is a plurality of ways of living a Muslim life in Chitral then, at the

---

[2] See also Dresch and Haykel 1995.

same time, there is also no one way of being a 'pro-Taliban' or 'hardened' Muslim in the region. This was the key theme both in my discussion of Rowshan's *dashmanan* but also in relation to Chitral Muslims who voice support for Pakistan's influential Islamist parties: Majid – a supporter of the Jama'at-e Islami party – emphasises the importance of a strict *shari'a* code for Pakistan, despite the fact that he continues to be friends and share his secrets with Ismai'il yet nevertheless fellow Rowshan people. So to conceptualise 'the Islamic revival' as a trend sweeping the Muslim world that engenders irreversible changes in Muslim consciousness at either a collective or individual level, conceals the ways in which individual Muslims thoughtfully adopt reform-oriented teachings to suit both their personal preferences and understanding of the Muslim life, as well as the particularities social settings in which they live. The diversity of ways in which so-called reform-minded Muslims in Chitral set to the task of living a Muslim life shows that even those folk Chitral people themselves call 'hardened Muslims' think and reflect about the religious life in complex and multidimensional ways, and, indeed, are sometimes ready to change their perspectives as a result of such thought processes.

Secondly, I have argued that there is more to reform-minded forms of Muslim spirituality than piety alone, and that to suggest that such forms of Muslim spirituality are above all else about embodied dispositions of self-discipline replaces one form of essentialism of the 'Islamic revival' with another. For as I have documented, most notably in relation to my account of amulet making mullahs in chapter 6, whilst piety for religious-minded men like Azeem may be one important dimension of what it means to live a Muslim life, it is not the only one. Indeed, many Chitral Muslims say that those who depict themselves as living a life of piety alone, besides not 'knowing the secrets of the enjoyable life', are fraudulent at best. It is certainly not the case that those who criticise new standards of Muslim piety in the region are old and uneducated Chitral folk, who are ignorant of the normative requirements of doctrinal Islam, and either wistfully remember a golden era of bygone Chitral life or passively transform themselves as part of an inevitable generational process by which young 'village scoundrels' become respected 'bearded ones'. Indeed, my account of village life in chapter 3 showed that young and educated men and women, the very category of Muslims so often assumed to be most vulnerable to the messages of 'reformist Islam', are regularly outspoken in their criticisms of the values of Pakistan's Islamist parties.

This is all notable because the dominant trend in much recent anthropology is to call the 'Islamic revival' a 'piety movement' (Hirschkind 2001;

Mahmood 2001, 2003; Abu-Lughod 2000: xiii–xiv): embodying pious dispositions and seeking to conform society to Muslim values are often held to be central to emergent forms of identity and thought in the Muslim contemporary world. I have shown, however, how piety, far from being a widely valued religious disposition for Chitral Muslims, a clear and shared standard by which they mark out a transformation towards living a proper Muslim life, is, rather, subject to complex judgement, discussion and criticism, and seen as being needed to be carefully matched with balanced levels of love, affection and humour.

It is in this context, then, that I have argued that the Islamic revival in Chitral is taking very different directions from interpretations of political Islam advanced both by political scientists (especially Roy 1994; Kepel 2002) and anthropologists (especially Hirschkind 2001; Mahmood 2001; Starrett 1998). Islamists' attempts to create Islamic states have not only run up against 'ethnic and tribal segmentation, political manoeuvring, personal rivalries' (Roy 1994: 26). More critically, so-called reform-oriented or neofundamentalist movements have also failed to bring about the homogenisation of thought and practice on which their ideologies and experience of Islam are implicitly founded. One factor of great importance for the explanation of this diversity, I suggest, is the diverse political cultures in which so-called Islamic revivalism is emerging and evolving. The Muslim men and women in Cairo studied by Hirschkind (2001) and Mahmood (2001) attempt to live piously in a country that is, according to these authors, 'increasingly ruled by a secular rationality' (Mahmood 2001: 830). Yet in Pakistan the *ulama* have grown in stature and power over the past two decades (Zaman 2002): the *ulama*, and Islamist parties with whom they are associated, have exerted their power in ways that significantly constrain the ability of ordinary Muslims to make decisions about how they want to live a Muslim life. Marriage, women's movement and comportment, education, and the relations between Sunnis and Ismai'lis, have all been areas of life where the forces of hardened Islam have sought to exert their power and influence. More broadly, Chitral Muslims inhabit a region of the world deeply influenced by war in Afghanistan and the profoundly purifying and proselytising visions of Islam that have emerged as a result of the past twenty years of conflict there. This vision of a *jihad*-centred and largely Sunni-dominated world made perfect by Islam is one that threatened the very future ability of Chitral's Ismai'li Muslims to continue to live in the region. Thus, any study of so-called revivalist Islam must take into account the visions of power and authority it entails, the constraints on individuality it imposes, the forms of exclusion it develops, and the multiple types of resistance it generates.

CHITRAL AND THE WIDER WORLD

My account of Muslim life in Chitral differs, then, in striking and sub-stantial ways from other recent treatments of the nature of the Islamic tradition in contemporary Muslim-majority settings. Thus, this book's findings pose significant questions concerning both how it is possible to account for diversity in the contemporary Muslim world, and the extent to which the findings presented here are of relevance for understanding the nature of Muslim life in other contemporary settings.

Chitral is different in many ways not only from other regions of the Muslim world but also from other regions of Pakistan, and this difference is recognised, indeed rejoiced in, by many Chitral people. A full explan-ation of this would require a more historically informed work, and one that addressed issues of regional identity in addition to those of everyday religious life that I have focused upon here.[3] One issue, however, is central here. The setting for my study of Muslim life is one of great cultural, religious and ethnic diversity: Chitral is a frontier region where the nego-tiation of boundaries between nation-states, administrative regions, ethnolinguistic groups and religious communities is a feature of everyday life. As a number of recent anthropological studies have shown, 'borders are contradictory zones of culture and power, where the twin processes of state centralisation and national homogenisation are disrupted' (Wilson and Donnan 1998: 26), and this is something that Mukulika Banerjee has recently argued is central to understanding Pukhtun culture and society (Banerjee 2000: 28). Chitral life is perhaps even more multidimensional than that of Pukhtun society: Chitral people are not a part of a national majority, nor do they share ethnic or linguistic ties with neighbouring Muslim populations either in Pakistan or in Afghanistan, and their region is also home to a substantial population of Shi'a Ismai'li Muslims – a comparatively small Islamic doctrinal cluster that occupies a threatened position in the Sunni-dominated Pakistan state.

Thus, in my account of village life in chapter 3, I showed how Chitral people feel threatened by an encroachment of Pukthun cultural values and religious modes into their villages, and, as the comic routines of the Nobles illustrated, there is a strong sense amongst many Chitral people that their 'homeland' is a culturally isolated region within a Pukhtun-dominated Frontier and a Punjab-dominated Pakistan nation state. Moreover, Chitral

---

[3] For a comparative historical treatment of regional and Muslim identity in Kashmir, see Zutshi 2004 and Rai 2004.

people must not only negotiate the complex ethno-linguistic world in which they live, their lives are also deeply affected by the volatile political setting of the region. In particular, they are called upon to register change within Pakistan and also in neighbouring countries, especially Afghanistan. Thus, in my account of Sunni–Ismaiʼli conflict in Rowshan I showed how many Rowshan Ismaiʼlis were deeply concerned about the potential of a Taliban attack on Chitral Ismaiʼlis.

The boundaries that Chitral people negotiate in their daily lives are not only ethnic and political, however, they are also religious. This further layer of complexity in Chitral peopleʼs lives means that being Muslim in Chitral entails engaging with fellow Chitral people who also have very different ideas about Islamic life and practice, and handling these differences is yet another source of thought and debate in the region. The presence of Ismaiʼlis in a region of Pakistan where Deobandi-educated Sunnis Muslims occupy most of the key positions of religious authority, means that many if not all Chitral people are painfully aware of the great danger that affiliating themselves to either Sunni Islamist or exclusively Ismaiʼli values holds for the future coexistence of the regionʼs people.

Existing on the periphery of a largely Pukhtun-dominated Frontier, experiencing moments when sectarian divisions become fraught and vio- lent, yet investing great significance on the distinctive and shared Chitrali nature of their society, Chitral peopleʼs lives involve the ongoing negotia- tion of multiply layered claims on their personal commitment to a variety of forms of regional and Muslim identity, as well as Islamic faith. My account of life in Chitral has sought to show how the complexity of life in frontier regions affects not only the formation of national, regional, ethnic and gender identities, but also the nature of religious life. Chitral people live in a region of the world where they are required to constantly engage with competing conceptions of national, regional and religious identity, thus, they have also negotiated with emerging forms of Muslim identity in thoughtful, critical and multidimensional ways.

Yet whilst it is important that we do not disregard the distinctiveness of life in Chitral, Chitral people are aware and informed about the wider world in which they live. Sectarian conflict, support for movements of Islamic revival and reform, and the impact of mass education policies on Muslim conceptions of selfhood are all dimensions of Muslim life that are the focus of everyday discussion by Chitral people. Moreover, even if the striking features of Muslim life that I have documented here are a reflection of Chitralʼs culturally and politically complex frontier setting, then such zones, far from being peripheral to the formation of more encompassing forms of national and religious entities are, rather, arenas in which states exert great efforts to establish their influence and control, and, thus, spaces where the tensions of the centre are clearly illuminated in everyday life. I contend, therefore, that the need to recognise Muslim voices that are critical of forms of Muslim thought and action associated with the 'Islamic revival' has important ramifications for the anthropological study of Islam beyond Chitral, south Asia and geographically remote regions of the Muslim world.

First, the emphasis I have placed on the importance of recognising the capacity of Muslims to be critical and reflective of reform-oriented forms of global Islam is perhaps so striking because it is the outcome of ethnographic research in a poor and relatively isolated rural setting. Indeed, choosing to conduct a study of the responses of 'village Muslims' to the teachings and organisations of the Islamic revival itself diverged from recent work on this dimension of Muslim thought and identity: in much of this work there is an almost exclusive focus on urban movements of Islamic reform and revival. Moreover, when anthropologists have focused in recent years on rural regions of the Muslim world what they have found has tended to be predictable: local Islamic traditions are weakened by the levelling forces of Islam's 'piety movement' as village Muslims embark on more self-conscious and religious-minded approaches to living the Muslim life (Abu-Lughod 2000). In the context of this teleological framework, urban forms of Muslim religiosity and identity continue to be conceptualised as central for understanding the current state of religiosity in the Muslim world: 'village Muslims' are treated as peripheral to wider trends in Islamic disputation, thought and identity. Of course, other anthropologists have challenged older forms of analytical divisions made between 'urban' and 'rural' Islam, and they have shown that village Muslims are not a peripheral feature of the Muslim world because they are economic producers within broader Islam networks and contexts (Asad 1986; Mundy 1995). What I have argued though is that village Muslims are important for understanding Muslim thought and identity more widely because they are capable of critical intellectual exchange, and it is through such complex processes that their opinions and, importantly, attitudes have an impact on the societies and networks of which they form an integral part.

Second, the arguments advanced in this book are a product of more than just the rural nature of the setting in which I undertook fieldwork, they are also a reflection of the broader ethnographic concerns and approach of my work. I embarked on the anthropology of conversation and intellectual activity in Rowshan because I recognised that the 'village Muslims' with whom I lived were as serious about thought as they were about talk. Many anthropologists of the Middle East have employed linguistic and narrative analysis techniques to understand the 'unending talk' they encountered during fieldwork. These types of approach failed to encompass both the value that many Chitral people placed on experiencing the play of the mind and their conceptions concerning the degree to which thought and intellectual work were processes that had negative as well as positive dimensions and outcomes. Indeed, it was through my recognition that the talk I encountered in Chitral was about more than narrative or performance that I saw the different perspectives and intellectual traditions that Chitral people brought to their discussions, and also found evidence of intellectual creativity interacting with known and valued literary heritage in 'village' society.

Yet the debates that I have argued are a central feature of Chitral village life were also often contentious and emotional, and my friends in Rowshan themselves were deeply concerned about how to handle powerful and potentially unseating emotions. In order to explore these dimensions of Chitral life, I took part both in debates and conversations with groups of villagers, as well as engaged in ongoing discussions with individual Chitral people. Critical here was my previous engagement with Chitral society: I had been visiting the region since 1995, when I was eighteen years old and treated as a brother of the family with whom I stayed. This meant, perhaps most importantly, that I was able to speak to women of a variety of ages from the village, and it is my account of their perspectives on life and religion in Chitral throughout the book that enriched my understanding of the degree to which Rowshan people think and talk in sensitive and complex ways about an array of issues for Muslims that are often assumed to be beyond the remit of daily conversation, or even thought.

At the same time, by conceptualising emotional processes in Chitral as connected to the act of thought I was also able to make broad arguments about religious life and morality. In this regard, my treatment of illicit cross-gender relations, children's lives, anxiety, music and 'secular' education, all furnished me with insights into Muslim life in Chitral. These are dimensions of Muslim life that anthropologists have often been unable to explore in great depth because of constraints of gender and the duration of fieldwork. Moreover, where such ethnographic insights are the focus of anthropological analysis they are often compartmentalised into distinct studies of education, the domestic sphere, gender, or Muslim 'personal life'. My approach, rather, sought to explore the connections between these domains of Chitral life and their relationship to Chitral people's understandings of Islam. Affect and emotions were conceptualised by many Chitral people as central to the living of a Muslim life, this was an issue of much thoughtful discussion in village life, and whilst some villagers claimed that Muslims should first of all fear God, there were many others who argued that emotions were moral only if they were an expression of a person's own desires (*arman*) and feelings.

The Muslims we have heard voicing their anxieties about purifying Islam live, then, in a remote and poor region of Pakistan where high literacy levels are very much a new development. Thus, I have argued that greater emphasis needs to be placed on the extent to which village as well as small-town Muslims constitute an active force in current processes of change in the Muslim world. Within Pakistan, it is not only educated, urban, wealthy or middle class Muslims who have increasingly rejected the formulations of political Islam (Kepel 2002). In Chitral at least, village Muslims have also subjected the aims and goals of Islamist movements to searching critiques. Recent historical writing has shown how regions of the world that were once thought to be peripheral and inconsequential from the perspective of world history have played actually powerful roles in the forming of the contemporary world (e.g. C. Bayly 1989, 2002). An anthro-pology of Islam that seeks to reflect on current trends in the Muslim world must also seek to establish the myriad of connections that link supposedly 'out-of-the-way-places' (Tsing 1993) with global processes of change and transformation.

I have contested anthropological and social scientific accounts of the Muslim world which tend to locate change and intellectual sophistication in urban settings. For Rowshan Muslims, the village is at once a place of constraint and boredom, yet, at the same time, it is ideally a space of authentic emotions and critical discussion and intellectual exploration. Many Rowshan people expend considerable social and economic energy on the attempt to create an atmosphere of intense intellectual activity. It is 'donkey-like' army men, young *dashmanan* with 'closed intellects', and returnee migrants who speak Pashto and have 'narrow minds' returning from Pakistan's cities who are seen to constrain the intellectual dimension of village life. Ideally, it is Rowshan that is seen as a potentially stimulating intellectual environment.

We have seen in both Rowshan and Markaz, deeply critical and surpris-ing views about the verdicts and pronouncements of trained religious scholars, the Taliban and other powerful Islamist movements, and the intellectual capacities of women. And, whilst there are villagers who hold much more 'narrow-minded' views on these issues, on the whole being 'narrow-minded' is an uncommon dimension of Rowshan life. It is also notable that Rowshan people laugh at many of these contentious issues which we might expect to arouse fear, shame and anxiety. Yet there should be no temptation to replace the old stereotype of unthinking and deferential villagers with a new homogeneous vision of the collective Muslim village mind as good humoured and unwaveringly critical of emerging forms of religiosity and religious authority. Indeed, in my account of village debate in chapter 4 I argued that an important feature of experiencing the play of the mind in Rowshan is the ability to handle and think about a wide array of views and abstract concepts in debate; and if Rowshan people live together socially, they do so in an independent minded way. Moreover, whilst we have also met people in fraught situations who seem to live a more good humoured life than we would expect, the jokes they tell and the things they laugh at have both a barbed dimension, and a more relaxed and genuinely cheerful side. Thus, the intense experience of the joy of the joke and the pleasure of laughter are themselves testament to the deeply stressful lives that Chitral Muslims lead. So, whilst highly concerned about living an intellectually significant life, then, flesh and the body are also on the minds of Rowshan people.

THE ANTHROPOLOGY OF THE INTELLECT AND THE EMOTIONS

Thought and the intellect are central features of a Muslim life in Chitral, but I have also shown how emotion and flesh need too to be recognised as central to Chitral people's ideas about the proper Muslim life. Chitral people conceptualise the intellect and the emotions as interacting in a complex way. Moreover, whilst Chitral Muslims see thought has having both positive and negative outcomes, so too do they talk about the significant and problematic dimensions of the experience of emotion and affection.

Brains boil in anger, love cooks hearts, fathers' sticks burn, and faith rots: 'strong feelings' (Elster 2000: 198) are an important dimension of living a Muslim life in Rowshan and Markaz. Ideally, emotion should be experienced as an authentic, rational, educated, intellectual, thoughtful, and articulated component of the person, and, when it is not, emotional failure weighs heavily on the minds of Rowshan people. Muslims should have 'souls that burn for others', but they often do not, and, when they do, they do so for the wrong reasons, in the wrong places and for the wrong people. Women cry when they should not, and do not when they should. Instead of showing affection to their parents, girls fall in love with boys, and even this they do insincerely. Men lose their tempers and become angry in full public view in the bazaar. Emotions are the subject of 'normative assessments' (Elster 2000: 202), and the making of such assessments itself entails the deployment of the cultivated critical faculties.

The emphasis that Chitral Muslims place on living an emotionally balanced and legitimate life is something that is rendered even more strenuous by the poor and unstable region of the world in which they live. Sectarian violence, international conflict, and the Taliban are just some of the factors that have and continue to heighten the emotional temperature of life in Chitral. So, Chitral Muslims seek to successfully handle, cultivate and generate the emotions, but they are also deeply concerned about the consequences of their being taken over or dominated by 'strong feelings' in a way that precludes thought. Many Chitral Muslims embark on this delicate and complex task with considerable ease and success. Yet there are times when they are less successful, and it is when the ideally mindful body becomes directed by irrepressible emotions and makes carefully calculated and morally informed decision-making impossible, that emotional and intellectual failure emerges to the surface of Chitral people's understandings of themselves.

Yet the connections that Rowshan people make between the domains of the intellect and the emotions are deeper, and if they experience the world through emotions, these emotions themselves have an important seat in the mind. As I was often told, 'intelligent people are always angry' (*laiq roye qahri tan boynie*). At one level, cultivated faculties of feeling and perception are conceptualised by Rowshan people as contributing to intelligent and informed mindly activity. 'Sensitive humans' are able to understand the inner thoughts and feelings of their cunning neighbours, poets are skilled in extemporising the 'sounds of the heart', and heightened levels of religious emotion provide a focus for personal decision-making. At another level, as was seen in chapter 6, the overly active intellect has the potential of eliciting uncalculated and uncontrolled emotions: young and intelligent men with 'fast minds', 'quick tongues' and 'hot heads' lose their tempers, insult powerful religious scholars, and even kill. And religious knowledge can also be deployed in a mechanical way by amulet makers so that it 'ties the intellect', and makes people act without contemplating the consequences of their actions. Reasoning intellect (*'aql*) must discipline the carnal soul, but so too must balanced affections exert a controlling influence on the overly excitable and critical intellect.

Yet the critical and creative use of the intellectual faculties that I have identified as a critical dimension of Chitral life exists in a world of faith and

religious prescription. While Rowshan people value the creative and flexible deployment of the intellect, these ideas also exist alongside visions of
knowledge that are 'fixed and enduring', and with styles of learning that
emphasise the importance of 'acute memorisation', together with a notion
of debate that values a 'certain style of argument and questioning'
(Eickelman 1998: 289). These seemingly discordant visions of the intellect,
of knowledge, of learning – in short, of being Muslim – themselves exist
within persons and within bodies, and it is recent anthropological developments in the study of embodiment that are particularly instructive in
helping to explain how this is possible.

The shaking shoulders of 'local intellectuals', the crossed arms of young
talib-e ilm, the clapping hands of men sitting in musical programmes,
soiled prayer caps, uncut beards, veiled and unveiled heads, and the
purdah-keeping eyes of young *dashmanan* – the body has been an important dimension of the ethnographic material analysed presented here. In a
recent article on the practice of listening to cassette recordings of sermons
in contemporary Egypt, Hirschkind has argued that these practices cultivate listeners' 'knowledge, emotions, and sensibilities in accord with
models of Islamic moral personhood' (Hirschkind 2001: 640; see also
Mahmood 2001, 2003). Despite this common concern for the embodied
character of emotion, perception and morality, in short, 'embodiment as
the existential ground of culture and self' (Csordas 1994: 6) my analysis
departs from other anthropological accounts of embodiment.

I have argued that attempts to live a moral and thoughtful Muslim life
in Rowshan and Markaz do not result in feelings of calm and harmony,
but rather are stressful, and a source of deep anxiety. For Hirschkind and
Mahmood, Islamic morality is about self-discipline, self-scrutiny, and
being reminded about the need to 'monitor their behaviour for vices
and virtue'; and these are things that are achieved through the practice of
listening to cassette sermons which evoke embodied ethical responses. For
Chitral, this conception of Islamic morality and personhood fails to fully
appreciate the extent to which living a moral Muslim life and making
ethical decisions is always a fraught process that entails thought and active
processes of reflection and moral verification. With regard to the study of
Islam beyond the context of Chitral, approaches to Islam that emphasise
self-discipline as central to the living of a Muslim life remain reliant on a
vision of Islamic morality that is above all exceptionally coherent. In turn,
these studies obscure the degree to which spiritual and moral authority in
present day Muslim societies is the source of complex judgements and
debates. This emphasis on coherence means that such approaches to

Islamic morality are unable to confront the ways in which Muslims are called upon to face, explain and contend with inconsistencies and complexities in their attempts to live virtuous lives.

Fundamentally what all this amounts to is an understanding of Muslim personhood and Islam as a world religion that questions the long held scholarly assertion that Muslims first of all submit and, therefore, expect a moment of surrender in their strivings to meet God's expectations. In the context of this assertion it was a surprise for me, and, indeed, for many of the people with whom I lived in Chitral, to encounter not only so much intellectual enterprise in Chitral, but also such a great degree of independent thought and action. I have argued throughout the book that many Chitral Muslims invest a great amount of energy in the creative and provocative play of the mind, and they regard such activity as important, valuable and pleasurable. Moreover, in their daily lives, many Chitral people also embark on courses of action that are risky and threatening, and that are the focus of great public criticism: sometimes they emerge from such contests successful, other times less so. Such strivings do certainly not come without a cost, and many villagers in Chitral are also concerned by the sources of stress and pressures that they see as affecting the quality of their lives: there is an ever present concern with the dangers that *tensien* and anxiety hold for the mental and bodily states of well being of Chitral people. So, the constant struggle to demonstrate the possibility of generating independent intellectual and emotional ideas and standards, and taking individual stands on matters of great personal significance, is one that is recognised as having the potential of unleashing unseating anxieties, yet, despite these dangers, it is considered good, valuable and worthy of personal sacrifice.

Beyond understanding the nature of Muslim selfhood and the relationship between faith and personhood in the contemporary world, what is at stake here is the place that the independent self should occupy in anthropological analysis. I have argued that – far from being externally imposed categories of Western thinking – notions of thought, freedom, individuality and the ways they are creatively expressed are values that matter for Chitral Muslims. Many Chitral people believe in and cherish the ability to display their individuality (*khusoosiyat*), and they work hard to maintain the place that critical, free and independent thought plays in their lives. Not all Chitral people feel able to express their individuality, but those who do not often rejoice in seeing other people doing so. Moreover, far from being a lost hope, even people in the region who are said to be 'narrow-minded' are 'worked upon' and the focus of directed mental energies by others, in the hope that they too will change the way they think. Sometimes, indeed, even those who are expected to be incapable of thought at all, such as the young *dashman* we encountered in chapter 6, surprise Chitral people, dissolve their stereotypes and ask them to rethink their assumptions. What is striking is that all this takes place in a world of strict Deobandi-influenced scriptural Islam. The ways in which many Chitral people work hard to maintain a sense of individuality in the context of prescribed faith and the powerful constraints imposed by this suggests that the independent self as a category for anthropological analysis should be the subject of further exploration.

What I perceive as the need for anthropologists to explore in greater depth the claims of the independent self, the constraints imposed on individual intellectual activity and the forms of anxieties these result in, connects to a further theoretical dimension of this book. I have argued that the anthropology of embodiment needs to be complemented by the exploration of thought and thought processes as a marked feature of human experience. Chitral people call themselves 'intellectuals', 'thinkers' and 'open-minded' and they combine their prize of the intellect with an emphasis on the role that sensory perception plays in their experience of the world. For Hirschkind, 'the mind' and 'the heart' are 'two contrasting modes of sensory organisation, one purely intellectual, the other ethical and grounded in Islamic disciplinary practices' (Hirschkind 2001: 639). This division only partially explains how Chitral Muslims conceptualise the interaction between the faculties of the intellect and the emotions. The body in Chitral stimulates discussion, debate and emotional responses: men's eyes, girls' veils, the beards of *dashmanan*, and the dancing bodies of children are all things that generate conversation, and the ideas and emotions they stimulate are complex and multi-dimensional. But the body is also something that bears the imprint of thought: the thin bodies of those locked in inward and self-destructive thought that eats the flesh, and the fat bodies of those with thoughts that fly higher and freer than even the sky.

Thus, it is the shadowy interface between the intellect and the emotions, thought and perception that, I suggest, transcends the mind–body duality. Yet this interface also allows anthropologists to theorise the ways in which active thought processes play a powerful role in the making of moral valuations and ethical decisions. And it offers a distinct window into the ways in which people reflect on and experience authority, engage in resistance, and live in, as well as engage with, the changing world in which they live. By exploring the experience of thought and emotion in Chitral, in an era of globalisation and disorienting social change, I have shown that Chitral people's visions of Islam are about more than self-discipline, self-control and the 'prevention of evil' and the 'promotion of good'. Rather, the Chitral people I know all felt that the life of a good Muslim is a mindful life, in which the play of refined and emotionally sensitive thought processes is and should be a critical element of everyday human interaction. It is because of this that Taliban-inspired and other Islamist or purist visions of a word made perfect by Islam – far from gripping the attentions of Chitral people – have, rather, provoked continual debate in the houses, bazaars, orchards, polo grounds and jeeps of Chitral.

Bibliography

Aase, T. 1999. The Theological Construction of Conflict, Gilgit, Northern Pakistan. In L. Manger (ed.), *Muslim Diversity: Local Islam in Global Contexts.* Richmond: Curzon, pp. 58–79.

Abu-Lughod, L. 2005. *Dramas of Nationhood: The Politics of Television in Egypt.* Chicago and London: University of Chicago Press.

2000. *Veiled Sentiments: Honour and Poetry in a Bedouin Society.* Updated with a new preface. Berkeley and Los Angeles: University of California Press.

1993. *Writing Women's Worlds: Bedouin Stories.* Berkeley and Los Angeles: University of California Press.

1990. The Romance of Resistance: Tracing Transformations of Power Through Bedouin Women. *American Ethnologist* 17 (1): 41–55.

1989. Zones of Theory in The Anthropology of the Arab World. *Annual Review of Anthropology* 18: 276–306.

1986. *Veiled Sentiments: Honour and Poetry in a Bedouin Society.* Berkeley and Los Angeles: University of California Press.

Abu-Lughod, L. and Lutz, C. (eds) 1990. *Language and the Politics of Emotion.* Cambridge: Cambridge University Press.

Ahmad, M. 1994. The Jamaat-i-Islami and the Tablighi Jamaat of South Asia. In M. Marty and S. Appleby (eds), *Fundamentalism Observed.* Chicago: Chicago University Press, pp. 457–30.

Ahmad, M. D. 1987. The Shi'is of Pakistan. In M. Kramer (ed.), *Shi'ism: Resistance and Revolution.* Boulder: Westview Press, pp. 275–87.

Ahmed, A. S. 1986. *Pakistan Society: Islam, Ethnicity and Leadership in South Asia.* Karachi: Oxford University Press.

1983. *Religion and Politics in Muslim Society: Order and Conflict in Pakistan.* London: Routledge and Kegan Paul.

1980. *Pukhtun Economy and Society.* London: Routledge and Kegan Paul.

1977. *Social and Economic Change in the Tribal Areas.* Karachi: Oxford University Press.

1976. *Millenium and Charisma among Pathans.* London: Routledge and Kegan Paul.

1994. Ahmed, A. and Donnan, H. (eds). *Islam, Globalization, and Postmodernity.* London: Routledge.

Akiner, S. 2001. *Tajikistan: Disintegration or Reconciliation?* London: Royal Institute of International Affairs.

Alam, M. 1998. The Pursuit of Persian: Language in Mughal Politics. *Modern Asian Studies*, 1998, **32** (2): 317–49.

Ali, D. 2004. *Courtly Culture and Political Life in Early Mediaeval India.* Cambridge: Cambridge University Press.

Ali, T. 1981. Ceremonial and social structure among the Burusho of Hunza. In C. von Fürer-Haimendorf (ed.), *Asian Highland Societies in Anthropological Perspective.* Delhi: Sterling Publishers, pp. 231–44.

Anderson, J. 2000. Producers and Middle East Internet Technology: Getting Beyond Impacts. *Middle East Journal* **54** (3): 419–31.

1985. Sentimental Ambivalence and the Exegesis of 'Self' in Afghanistan. *Anthropological Quarterly* **58** (4): 203–11.

Andreyev, S. 1999. The Rawshaniyya: A Sufi Movement on the Mughal Periphery. In L. Lewisohn and D. Morgan (eds), *The Heritage of Sufism, volume III. Late Classical Persianate Sufism (1501–1750): The Safavid and Mughal Period.* Oneworld: Oxford, pp. 290–318.

Ansari, S. 1992. *Sufi Saints and State Power: The Pirs of Sind, 1843–1947.* Cambridge: Cambridge University Press.

Antoun, R. 1989. *Muslim Preacher in the Modern World: A Jordanian Case Study in Comparative Perspective.* Princeton, NJ: Princeton University Press.

Appadurai, A. 1993. Global Ethnoscapes: Notes and Queries for a Transnational Anthropology. In R. Fox (ed.), *Recapturing Anthropology: Working in the Present.* Santa Fe: School of American Research, pp. 191–210.

1986. Commodities and the Politics of Value. In A. Appadurai (ed.), *The Social Life of Things: Commodities in Cultural Perspective.* Cambridge: Cambridge University Press, pp. 3–63.

1981. Gastro-Politics in Hindu South Asia. *American Ethnologist* **8** (3): 494–511.

Arkoun, M. 2001. Present-Day Islam Between Its Tradition and Globalization. In F. Daftary (ed.), *Intellectual Traditions in Islam.* London and New York: I.B. Tauris in association with The Institute for Ismaili Studies, pp. 179–221.

1994. *Rethinking Islam: Common Questions, Uncommon Answers.* Boulder: Westview Press.

Asad, T. 2003. *Formations of the Secular: Christianity, Islam, Modernity.* Stanford: Stanford University Press.

1993. *Genealogies of Religion: Discipline and Reasons of Power in Christianity and Islam.* Baltimore: John Hopkins University Press.

1986. *The Idea of an Anthropology of Islam.* Washington: Smithsonian Institute Press.

1972. Market Model, Class Structure, and Consent: A Reconsideration of Swat Political Organisation. *Man* (NS) **7** (1): 74–94.

Asani, A. 2002. *Ecstasy and Enlightenment: The Ismaʾili Devotional Literature of South Asia.* London: I.B. Tauris in association with the Institute of Ismaili Studies.

Ask, K. 1993. Ishq aur Muhabbat: Ideas about Love and Friendship in a Northern Pakistani Community. In V. Broch-Due, I. Rudie and T. Bleie (eds). *Carved Flesh: Gendered Symbols and Social Practices.* Oxford: Berg, pp. 207–23.

Azoy, W. 1982. *Buzkashi: Game and Power in Afghanistan.* Philadelphia: University of Pennsylvania Press.

Baig, R. K. 1997. *Hindu Kush Study Series: Volume 2.* Peshawar: Rehmat Printing Press.

1994. *Hindu Kush Study Series: Volume 1.* Peshawar: Rehmat Printing Press.

Bailey, F. 1996. *The Civility of Indifference: On Domesticating Ethnicity.* Ithaca: Cornell University Press.

1971. The Management of Reputations and the Process of Change. In F. G. Bailey (ed.), *Gifts and Poison*, Oxford: Basil Blackwell, pp. 281–301.

Bailey, J. 1994. The Role of Music in the Creation of an Afghan Identity, 1923–1973. In M. Stokes (ed.), *Ethnicity, Identity and Music: The Musical Construction of Space.* Oxford: Berg, pp. 45–60.

1987. *Music in Afghanistan: Professional Musicians in the City of Heart.* Cambridge: Cambridge University Press.

Bakar, O. 1999. *The History and Philosophy of Islamic Science.* Cambridge: Islamic Texts Society.

Baldick, J. 2000. *Mystical Islam: An Introduction to Sufism.* London: Tauris Parke.

Banerjee, M. 2000. *The Pathan Unarmed: Opposition and Memory in the North West Frontier.* James Currey: Oxford.

Barron and Keddie, N. (eds) 1991. *Women in Middle Eastern History: Shifting Boundaries in Sex and Gender.* New Haven and London: Yale University Press.

Barth, F. 1993. *Balinese Worlds.* University of Chicago Press: Chicago and London.

1992. Towards Greater Naturalism in Conceptualising Societies. In A. Kuper (ed.), *Conceptualising Society.* London and New York: Routledge, pp. 17–33.

1990. The Guru and The Conjurer: Transactions in Knowledge and the Shaping of Culture in Southeast Asia and Melanesia. *Man* (NS) 25: 640–53.

1987. *Cosmologies in the Making: a Generative Approach to Cultural Variation in Inner New Guinea.* Cambridge: Cambridge University Press.

1983. *Sohar: Culture and Society in an Omani Town.* London: Johns Hopkins University Press.

1981. *Features of Person and Society in Swat: Collected Essays on Pathans.* London: Routledge and Kegan Paul.

1969. Pathan Identity and its Maintenance. In F. Barth (ed.), *Ethnic Groups and Boundaries.* Oslo: Universitetsforlaget, pp. 117–34.

1959. *Political Leadership Among Swat Pathans.* Athlone: London.

1956. *Indus and Swat Kohistan: an Ethnographic Survey.* Oslo: Forenede Trykkerier.

Bashir, E. 1996. The Areal Position of Khowar: South Asian and Other Affinities. In E. Bashir and Israr-ud-Din, (eds), *Proceedings of the Second International Hindukush Cultural Conference.* Karachi: Oxford University Press, pp. 165–79.

Basu, A. 1997. Appropriating Gender. In A. Basu and P. Jeffrey (eds), *Appropriating Gender: Women's Activism and Politicized Religion in South Asia.* London and New York: Routledge, pp. 3–14.

Bayly, C. 2002. 'Archaic' and 'Modern' Globalization in the Eurasian and African Arena, *c.* 1750–1850. In A. Hopkins (ed.), *Globalization in World History.* London: Pimlico, pp. 47–73.

  1998. *Origins of Nationality in South Asia: Patriotism and Ethical Government in Making of Modern India.* Delhi: Oxford University Press.

  1992. *Rulers, Townsmen and Bazaars: North Indian Society in the Age of British Expansion 1770–1870.* Delhi: Oxford University Press.

  1989. *Imperial Meridian: The British Empire and the World.* London and New York: Longman.

  1983. The Pre-History of 'Communalism'? Religious Conflict in India 1700–1860. *Modern Asian Studies,* **19** (2): 177–203.

Bayly, S. 2004. Vietnamese Intellectuals in Revolutionary and Postcolonial Times. *Critique of Anthropology* **24** (3) :320–44.

  2000. Cult Saints, Heroes and Warrior Kings: South Asian Islam in the Making. In K. Yandel and P. John (eds) *Religion and Public Culture: Encounters and Identities in Modern South Asia.* Richmond: Curzon, pp. 211–32.

  1999. *Caste, Society and Politics in India from the Eighteenth Century to the Mordern Age (New Cambridge History of India).* Cambridge: Cambridge University Press.

  1989. *Saints, Goddesses and Kings: Muslims and Christians in South Indian Society: 1700–1900.* Cambridge University Press: Cambridge.

Beatty, A. 2002. Changing Places: Relatives and Relativism in Java. *Journal of the Royal Anthropological Institute.* **8** (NS): 469–91.

  2000. Islamic and Non-Islamic Prayer in Java. In D. Parkin and C. Healey (eds), *Islamic Prayer across the Indian Ocean: Inside and Outside the Mosque,* pp. Curzon Press: Richmond, pp. 39–61.

  1999. *Varieties of Javanese Religion: An Anthropological Account.* Cambridge: Cambridge University Press.

Beck, L. 1986. *The Qashqai of Iran.* New Haven and London: Yale University Press.

Beeman, W. 1986. *Language, Status and Power in Iran.* Bloomington and London: Indiana University Press.

Bennett, A. 1990. In Nanda Baba's House: The Devotional Experience in Pushti Marg Temples. In O. Lynch (ed.), *The Social Construction of Emotion in India.* Delhi: Oxford University Press, pp. 182–211.

Bennison, A. 2002. Muslim Universalism and Western Globalization. In A. Hopkins (ed.), *Globalization in World History.* London: Pimlico, pp. 74–97.

J. Biddulph, 1972 [1880]. *Tribes of the Hindu Kush.* Lahore: Ali Kamran.

Blank, J. 2001. *Mullahs and the Mainframe: Islam and Modernity Among the Daudi Bohras.* Chicago and London: University of Chicago Press.

Bledsoe, C. and Robey, K. 1993. Arabic Literacy and Secrecy Among the Mende of Sierra Leone. In B. Street (ed.), *Cross Cultural Approaches to Literacy.* Cambridge: Cambridge University Press, pp. 110–34.

1986. Arabic Literacy and Secrecy Among the Mende of Sierra Leone. *Man* 21: 202–66.

Bloch, M. 1992. What Goes Without Saying: The Conceptualisation of Zafimaniry Society. In A. Kuper (ed.), *Conceptualizing Society*. London: Routledge.

Boddy, J. 1988. Spirits and Selves in Northern Sudan: The Cultural Therapeutics of Possession and Trance. *American Ethnologist* 15 (1): 4–27.

Boesen, I. 1980. Women, Honour, and Love: Some Aspects of the Pashtun Woman's Life in Eastern Afghanistan. *Afghanistan Journal* 7 (2): 50–9.

Bose, S. 1997. *The Challenge in Kashmir: Democracy, Self-Determination and a Just Peace*. New Delhi: Sage.

Bose, S. and Jalal, A. 1998. *Modern South Asia: History, Culture, Political Economy*. Cambridge: Cambridge University Press.

Bose, S. and Jalal, A. (eds) 1997. *Nationalism, Democracy and Development: state and politics in India*. Delhi: Oxford: Oxford University Press.

Bourdieu, P. 1990. *The Logic of Practice. Richard Nice*, Stanford: Stanford University Press.

Bowen, J. 2003. *Islam, Law and Equality in Indonesia: An Anthropology of Public Reasoning*. Cambridge: Cambridge University Press.

2000. Imputations of Faith and Allegiance: Islamic Prayer and Indonesian Politics Outside the Mosque. In D. Parkin and C. Healey (eds), *Islamic Prayer across the Indian Ocean: Inside and Outside the Mosque*. Curzon Press: Richmond, pp. 23–83.

1998. What is Universal and Local in Islam. *Ethos* 26 (2):258–61.

1993. *Muslims Through Discourse. Religion and Ritual in Gayo Society*. Princeton University Press: Princeton.

1992a. Elaborating Scriptures: Cain and Abel In Gayo Society. *Man* (NS) 27 (3): 495–516.

1992b. On Scriptural Essentialism and Ritual Variation: Muslim Sacrifice in Sumatra and Morocco. *American Ethnologist* 19 (4): 656–71.

1989. Salat in Indonesia: The Social Meaning of an Islamic Ritual. *Man* 24 (4): 600–19.

Boyer, P. (ed.) 1993. *Cognitive Aspects of Religious Symbolism*. Cambridge: Cambridge University Press.

Brass, P. 2003. *The Production of Hindu-Muslim violence in contemporary India*. Washington: Washington University Press.

1997. *Theft of an Idol: Text and Context in the Representation of Collevtive Values*. Princeton University Press: Princeton.

Brenner, L. 2000. *Controlling Knowledge: Religion, Power and Schooling in a West African Muslim Society*. London: Hurst and Company.

Brenner, L. (ed.) 1992. *Muslims and identity and social change in Sub-Saharan Africa*. London: Hurst and Company.

Bringa, T. 1996. *Being Muslim the Bosnian Way: Identity and Community in a Central Bosnian Village*. Princeton: Princeton University Press.

Brison, K. 1992. *Gossip, Meetings and Power in a Papua New Guinea Village*. Berkeley and Los Angeles: University of California Press.

Buchta, W. 2002. The Failed Pan-Islamic Program of the Islamic Republic: Views of the Liberal Reformers of the Religious 'Semi-Opposition'. In N. Keddie, and R. Matthee (eds), *Iran and the Surrounding World: Interactions in Culture and Cultural Politics*. Seattle and London: University of Washington Press, pp. 281–304.

Caroe, O. 1965. *The Pathans*. London: Macmillan.

Carruthers, M. 1990. *The Book of Memory: A study of Memory in Medieval Culture*. Cambridge: Cambridge University Press.

Carsten, J. 2000. Introduction: Cultures of Relatedness. In J. Carsten (ed.), *Cultures of Relatedness: New Approaches to the Study of Kinship*. Cambridge University Press: Cambridge, pp. 1–36.

——— 1991. Children in Between: Fostering and the Process of Kinship on Pulau Langkawi, Malaysia. *Man* 26 425–43.

Caton, S. 1990. *Peaks of Yemen I Summon: Poetry as a Cultural Practice in a North Yemeni Tribe*. Berkeley: University of California Press.

Chughtai, A. (ed.) 1997. *Bazm-e Khowar*. Chitral: Anjuman Taraqqi-e-Khowar.

Cloughley, B. 2000. *A History of the Pakistan Army: Wars and Insurrections*. Second edn, with a new chapter on the Kargil Issue. Oxford: Oxford University Press.

Cohn, B. 1987. *An Anthropologist Among The Historians*. Delhi: Oxford University Press.

Cole, J. 2002. Iranian Culture and South Asia, 1500–1900. In N. Keddie and R. Matthee (eds), *Iran and the Surrounding World: Interactions in Culture and Cultural Politics*. Seattle and London: University of Washington Press, pp. 15–35.

Comaroff, J. and J. Comaroff (1993) 'Introduction' in J. Comaroff and J. Comaroff (eds), *Modernity and its Malcontents: Ritual and Power in Postcolonial Africa*, Chicago: University of Chicago Press, xi–xxxviii.

Cook. M. 2000. *Commanding Right and Forbidding Wrong in Islamic Thought*. Cambridge: Cambridge University Press.

Corbin, H. 1997. *Alone with the Alone: Creative Imagination in the Sufism of Ibn 'Arabi*. Princeton: Princeton University Press.

——— 1983. *Cyclical Time and Ismai'li Gnosis*, tr. R. Manheim and J. Morris. London: Kegan Paul International in association with Islamic Publications.

Csordas, T. 1994. Introduction: The Body as Representation and Being-in-the-World. In T. Csordas (ed.), *Embodiment and Experience: The Existential Ground of Culture and Self*. Cambridge: Cambridge University Press, pp. 1–24.

Curzon, Marquess of Keddlestone. 1984. *A Viceroy's India: Leaves from Lord Curzon's Note-book*. Edited by Peter King with an introduction by Elizabeth Longford. London: Sidgwick and Jackson.

Daftary, F. 2001. Intellectual Life Among the Ismailis: An Overview. In F. Daftary (ed.), *Intellectual Traditions in Islam*. London and New York: I.B. Tauris in association with The Institute for Ismaili Studies, pp. 87–111.

——— 1999. Ismai'li–Sufi Relations in Early Post Alamut and Safavid Persia. In L. Lewisohn and D. Morgan (eds), *The Heritage of Sufism, volume III. Late*

Classical Persianate Sufism (1501–1750): The Safavid and Mughal Period. Oxford: Oneworld, pp. 275–85.

1998. *A Short History of the Ismailis.* Edinburgh: Edinburgh University Press.

1990. *The Ismailis: Their History and Doctrines.* Cambridge: Cambridge University Press.

Dale, S. F. 1980. *Islamic Society on the South Asian Frontier: The Māppilas of Malibar, 1498–1922.* Oxford: Clarendon Press.

Dani, H. 1989. *History of the Northern Areas of Pakistan.* Islamabad: Lok Virsa.

Daniel, V. 1996. *Charred Lullabies: Chapters in an Anthropology of Violence.* Princeton: Princeton University Press.

1984. *Fluid Signs: Being a Person the Tamil Way.* Berkeley: University of California Press.

Das, V. (ed.) 1990. *Mirrors of Violence: Communities, Riots, and Survivors in South Asia,* Delhi: Oxford University Press.

Das, V. 1995. *Critical Events: An Anthropological Perspective on Contemporary India.* Delhi: Oxford University Press.

1984. For a Folk Theology and Theological Interpretation of Islam. *Contributions to Indian Sociology* 18 (2): 293–300.

Day, H. J. 2001. Sufism and the Indonesian Islamic Revival. *The Journal of Asian Studies* 3 (August): 701–29.

Delaney, C. 1990. *The Seed and the Soil: Gender and Cosmology in Turkish Village Society.* Berkeley and Los Angeles: University of California Press.

Didier, B. 2004. Conflict Self-Inflicted: Dispute, Incivility and the Threat of Violence in an Indian Muslim Community. *Journal of Asian Studies* 63 (1): 61–80.

2001. The Scars of Piety: Islam and the Dynamics of Religious Dispute on Androth Island, South India. Unpublished PhD dissertation, University of Cambridge.

Donnan, H. (ed.) 2002. *Interpreting Islam.* London: Sage.

Donnan, H. and Stokes, M. 2002. Interpreting Interpretations of Islam. In H. Donnan (ed.), *Interpreting Islam,* pp. 1–19. London: Sage.

Donnan, H. and Werbner, P. (eds) 1991. *Economy and Culture in Pakistan: Migrants and Cities in Muslim Society.* Basingstoke: Macmillan.

Dresch, P. and Haykel, B. 1995. Stereotypes and Political Styles: Islamists and Tribesfolk in Yemen. *International Journal of Middle East Studies.* 27 (4): 405–31.

Dumont, L. 1980. *Homo Hierarchicus: The Caste System and Its Implications.* Revised edition. Chicago: University of Chicago Press.

Durand, A. 1899. *The Making of a Frontier: Five Years Experiences in Gilgit, Hunza, Nagar, Chitral and the Eastern Hindu Kush.* London: John Murray.

Eaton, R. 1993. *The Rise of Islam and the Bengal Frontier, 1204–1760.* Berkeley and Los Angeles: University of California Press.

1996 [1978]. *Sufis of Bijapur, 1300–1700: Social Roles of Sufis in Medieval India.* New Delhi: Munshiram Manoharlal Publishers.

Edwards, D. 2002. *Before Taliban: Genealogies of the Afghan Jihad.* Berkeley: University of California Press.

1998. Learning from the Swat Pathans: Political Leadership in Afghanistan, 1978–97. *American Ethnologist* **25** (4): 712–28.

1996. *Heroes of the Age: Moral Faultlines on the Afghan Frontier.* Berkeley: University of California Press.

1995. Print Islam: Media and Religious Revolution in Afghanistan. *Anthropological Quarterly* **68** (3): 133–9.

Ehmadi, H. 1998. The end of Taqiya: Reaffirming the Religious Identities of Ismailis in Shughnan, Badakshan – Political Implications for Afghanistan. *Middle Eastern Studies* **32** (3): 687–716.

1993. Minority Group Politics: The Role of Ismailis in Afghanistan's Politics. *Central Asian Survey* **12** (3): 689–716.

Eickelman, D. 1999. Communicating and Control in The Middle East: Publication and Its Discontents. In D. Eickelman and J. Anderson (eds), *New Muslim Media in the Muslim World: The Emerging Public Sphere.* Bloomington: Indian University Press, pp. 29–40.

1998. *The Middle East and Central Asia: An Anthropological Approach.* Third edition. New Jersey: Prentice Hall.

1997. Muslim Politics: The Prospects for Democracy in the Muslim Middle East. In J. Entelis (ed.), *Islam, Democracy and the State in North Africa.* Bloomington and Indianapolis: Indiana University Press, pp. 17–42.

1992a. Mass Education and the Religious Imagination in Contemporary Arab Societies. *American Ethnologist* **19** (4): 643–55.

1992b. The Art of Memory: Islamic Knowledge and its Social Reproduction. In J. Cole, (ed.), *Comparing Muslim Societies: Knowledge and the State in a World Civilization.* Ann Arbor: University of Michigen Press, 97–132.

1985a. *Knowledge and Power in Morocco: The Education of a Twentieth Century Noble.* Princeton NJ: Princeton Univ. Press.

1985b. Introduction: Self and Community in Middle Eastern Societies. *Anthropological Quarterly* **58** (4): 135–40.

1982. *The Study of Islam in Local Contexts.* Contributions to Asian Studies **17**: 1–16.

1976. *Moroccan Islam: Tradition and Society in a Pilgrimage Centre.* Austin: University of Texas Press.

Eickelman, D. and Anderson, J. (eds) 1999. *New Muslim Media in the Muslim World: The Emerging Public Sphere.* Bloomington: Indian University Press.

Eickelman, D. and Anderson, J. 1999. Redefining Muslim Publics. In D. Eickelman and J. Anderson (eds), *New Muslim Media in the Muslim World: The Emerging Public Sphere.* Bloomington: Indian University Press.

1997. Print, Islam, and the Prospects for Civic Pluralism: New Religious Writings and Their Audiences. *Journal of Islamic Studies* **8** (1): 4–62.

Eickelman, D. and Piscatori, J. 1996. *Muslim Politics.* Princeton NJ: Princeton University Press.

Eickelman, D. and Piscatori, J. (eds) 1990. *Muslim Travellers: Pilgrimage, Migration, and the Religious Imagination.* Berkeley and Los Angeles: University of California Press.

Eickelman, D. and Salvatore, S. 2002. The Public Sphere and Muslim Identities. *European Journal of Sociology* 33 (1): 92–115.

Elster, J. 2000. *Strong Feelings: Emotion, Addiction and Human Behaviour.* Cambridge, Massachusetts: MIT Press.

1998. *Alchemies of the Mind: Rationality and the Emotions.* Cambridge: Cambridge University Press.

El Zein, A. 1977. Beyond Ideology and Theology: The Search for an Anthropology of Islam. *Annual Review of Anthropology* 6: 227–54.

Esmail, A. 2002. *A Scent of Sandlewood: Indo-Ismaili Religious Lyrics.* London: I.B. Tauris in association with the Institute of Ismaili Studies.

Ewing, K. P. 1998. Crossing Borders and Transgressing Boundaries: Metaphors for Negotiating Multiple Identities. *Ethos* 26 (2): 262–7.

1997. *Arguing Sainthood: Modernity, Psychoanalysis, and Islam.* Duke Univ. Press: Durham and London.

1984. Malangs of the Punjab: Intoxication or *Adab* as the Path to God? In B. Metcalf, (ed.), *Moral Conduct and Authority: The Place of Adab in South Asian Islam.* Berkeley: University of California Press, pp. 357–71.

1983. The Politics of Sufism: Redefining the Saints of Pakistan. *Journal of Asian Studies* 18: 106–14.

Faizi, I. UPMS. The Development of Khowar as a Literacy Language, Results of Interaction Between Linguists and Language Community: Case Study in Chitral, Northern Pakistan.

1996. *Wakhan: A Window into Central Asia.* Islamabad: Al Qalam.

Feierman, S. 1990. *Peasant Intellectuals: Anthropology and History in Tanzania.* Madison: University of Wisconsin Press.

Ferguson, J. and Gupta, A. 1992. Beyond Culture: Space, Identity and the Politics of Difference. *Cultural Anthropology* 7 (1): 6–23.

Ferme, M. 2001. *The Underneath of Things: Violence, History and the Everyday in Sierra Leone.* Berkeley: University of California Press.

Fischer, M. 1980. *Iran, from Religious Dispute to Revolution.* Cambridge, Mass.: Harvard University Press.

Friedl, E. 1989. *Women of Deh Koh: Lives in an Iranian Village.* Washington DC: Smithsonian Institution Press.

Freitag, S. 1989. *Collective Action and Community. Public Arenas and the Emergence of Communalism in North India.* Berkeley: University of California Press.

Fuller, C. 2001. Orality, Literacy and Memorization: Priestly Education in Contemporary South India. *Modern Asian Studies* 35 (1): 1–31.

1989. Misconceiving the Grain Heap: A Critique of the Concept of the Indian Jajmani System. In J. Parry and M. Bloch (eds), *Money and the Morality of Exchange.* Cambridge: Cambridge University Press, pp. 33–63.

Gaffney, P. 1994. *The Prophets Pulpit: Islamic Preaching in Contemporary Egypt.* Berkeley and Los Angeles: California University Press.

Gardener, K. 1999. Global Migrants and Local Shrines: The Shifting Geography of Islam in Sylhet, Bangladesh. In Manger, L. (ed), *Muslim Diversity: Local Islam in Global Contexts.* Richmond: Curzon.

1995. *Global Migrants, Local Lives: Travel and Transformation in Rural Bangla Desh.* Oxford: Clarendon Press.

1993. Mullahs, Migrants, Miracles: Travel and Transformation in Sylhet. *Contributions to Indian Sociology* **27** (2): 213–35.

Geertz, C. 1968. *Islam Observed: Religious Development in Morocco and Indonesia.* New Haven: Yale University Press.

1960. *The Religion of Java.* Chicago: University of Chicago Press.

Gellner, E. 1981. *Muslim Society.* Cambridge: Cambridge University Press.

Ghomi, H. 1999. The Image of Annihilation (Fana') in the Poetry of Sai'b Tabrizi. In L. Lewisohn and D. Morgan (eds), *The Heritage of Sufism, volume III. Late Classical Persianate Sufism (1501–1750): The Safavid and Mughal Period.* Oxford: Oneworld, pp. 493–517.

Gilmartin, D. 1988. *Empire and Islam: Punjab and the Making of Pakistan.* Berkeley: California University Press.

Gilsenan, M. 2000. Signs of Truth: Enchantment, Modernity and the Dreams of Peasant Women. *Journal of the Royal Anthropological Institute* (NS) **6**: 597–615.

1996. *Lords of the Lebanese Marches: Violence and Narrative in an Arab Society.* London: I.B. Tauris.

1990a. *Recognizing Islam: Religion and Society in the Modern East.* London: I.B. Tauris.

1990b. Very Like a Camel: The Appearance of an Anthropologists Middle East. In R. Fardon (ed.), *Localizing Strategies: Regional Traditions of Ethnographic Writing.* Washington, DC: Smithsonian Institution Press, pp. 222–39.

1989. Words of Honour. In R. Grillo (ed.), *Social Anthropology and the Politics of Language.* London: Routledge, pp. 193–221.

1982. *Recognizing Islam An Anthropologist's Introduction.* London: Croom Helm.

1973. *Saint and Sufi in Modern Egypt: an Essay on the Sociology of Religion.* Oxford: Clarendon Press.

Gladney, D. C. 1999. Central Asia and China: Transnationalization, Islamization and Ethnicization. In J. Esposito (ed.), *The Oxford History of Islam.* Oxford and New York: Oxford University Press, pp. 433–73.

Gold, A. 1988. *Fruitful Journeys: The Ways of Rajasthani Pilgrims.* Berkeley: University of California Press.

Gombrich, R. 1971. *Precept and Practice: Traditional Buddhism in the Rural Highlands of Ceylon.* Oxford: Clarendon Press.

Goodman, J. 1998. Singers, Saints and the Construction of Postcolonial Subjectivities in Algeria. *Ethos* **26** (2): 204–88.

Goody, J. (ed.) 1968. *Literacy in Traditional Societies.* Cambridge: Cambridge University Press.

Goody, J. 1987. *The Interface between the Written and the Oral.* Cambridge: Cambridge University Press.

1986. *The Logic of Writing and the Organisation of Writing.* Cambridge: Cambridge University Press.

Grima, B. 1992. *The Performance of Emotion among Paxtun Women.* Austin: The University of Texas Press.

Gupta, A. 1995. Blurred Boundaries: The Discourse of Corruption, the Culture of Politics, and the Imagined State. *American Ethnologist.* **22** (2): 375–402.

Gurdon, B. E. M. 1934. Chitral Memories: The Siege of Chitral. *Himalayan Journal* **6**: 1–30.

⸻ 1933. Chitral Memories: Events Leading up to the Siege. *Himalayan Journal* **5**: 1–27.

Haakonssen, K. 2002. Introduction. In A. Smith 2002 (1870) *The Theory of Moral Sentiments.* Edited by K. Haakonssen. Cambridge: Cambridge University Press, pp. vii–xxi.

Haddad, Y. (ed.) 2001. *Muslims in the West: From Sojourners to Citizens.* New York: Oxford University Press.

Hammoudi, A. 1997. *Master and Disciple: Cultural Foundations of Moroccan Imperialism.* Chicago: University of Chicago Press.

Hansen, T. 2001. *Wages of Violence: Naming and Identity in Postcolonial Bombay.* Princeton and Oxford: Princeton University Press.

⸻ 2000a. Predicaments of Secularism: Muslim Identities and Politics in Mumbai. *Journal of the Royal Anthropological Institute* **6** (2): 255–72.

⸻ 2000b. Bridging the Gulf: Migration, Modernity and Identity among Muslims in Bombay. In C. Bates (ed.). *Empire, Migration and Community.* London: Macmillan.

⸻ 1999. *The Saffron Wave: Democracy and Hindu Nationalism in Modern India.* Princeton: Princeton University Press.

Hansen, T. and Stepputat, F. 2001. Introduction: State of Imagination. In T. Hansen and F. Stepputat (eds) *States of Imagination: Ethnographic Explorations of the Postcolonial State.* Durham and London: Duke University Press, pp. 1–38.

Harrison, S. 1986. Ethnicity and Political Stalemate in Pakistan. In A. Banuazizi and M. Weiner (eds), *The State, Religion and Ethnic Politics: Afghanistan, Iran and Pakistan.* Syracuse: Syracuse University Press.

Hart, D. 1985. *Guardians of the Khaibar Pass: The Social Organisation and History of the Afridis of Pakistan.* Lahore: Vanguard Books.

Hassan, N. and Mufid, A. S. 2002. When Executives Chant *Dhikr. International Institute for Asian Studies Newsletters,* August 2002.

Hefner, R. 1993. Introduction. In R. Hefner (ed.), *Conversion to Christianity; Historical and Anthropological Perspectives on a Great Transformation.* Berkeley: University of California Press.

⸻ 1985. *Hindu Javanese: Tengger Tradition and Islam.* Princeton: Princeton University Press.

Hefner, R. and Horvatich, P. (eds) 1994. *Islam in an Era of Nation-States: Politics and Religious Renewal in Southeast Asia.* Honolulu: University of Hawai'i Press.

Hegeland, M. 1998a. Flagellation and Fundamentalism: (Trans)forming Meaning, Identity, and Gender Through Pakistani's Women's Rituals of Mourning. *American Ethnologist* **25**: 240–66.

1998b. The Power Paradox in Muslim Women's *Majales*: North-West Pakistani Mourning Rituals as Sites of Contestation over Religious Politics, Ethnicity and Gender. *Signs: Journal of Women in Culture and Society* 23 (2): 392–428.

Herzfeld, M. 1997. *Cultural Intimacy: Social Poetics in the Nation-State*. New York and London: Routledge.

Hirschkind, C. 2001. The Ethics of Listening: Cassette Sermon Audition in Contemporary Cairo. *American Ethnologist* 28 (3): 623–49.

1997. What is Political Islam? *Middle East Report* 27: 4.

1996. Heresy or Hermeneutics: The Case of Nasr Hamid Abu Zayd. *Stanford Humanities Review* 5 (1): 35–49.

Hollis, M. and Lukes, S. (eds) 1982. *Rationality and Relativism*. Oxford: Basil Blackwell.

Hopkins, A. (ed.) 2002. *Globalization in World History*. London: Pimlico.

Hopkins, A. 2002a. Introduction: Globalization – An Agenda for Historians. In A. Hopkins (ed.), *Globalization in World History*. London: Pimlico, pp. 1–10.

2002b. The History of Globalization – and the Globalization of History? In A. Hopkins (ed.), *Globalization in World History*. London: Pimlico, pp. 11–46.

Holzwarth, W. 1998. Chitral History, 1540–1660: Comments on Sources and Historiography. In E. Bashir and Israr-ud-Din (eds), *Proceedings of the Second International Hindukush Cultural Conference*. Karachi: Oxford University Press, pp. 117–34.

1994. *Die Isma'iliten in Nordpakistan. Zur Entwicklung einer Religiösen Minderheit im Kontext Neuer Außenbeziehungen*. Berlin: Verlag Das Arabische Buch.

Horvatavich, P. 1994. Ways of Knowing Islam. *American Ethnologist* 21 (4): 811–26.

Howell, E. 1979. *Mizh: A Monograph on Government's Relations with the Mahsud Tribe*. Karachi: Oxford University Press.

Hourani, A. 1997. *Arabic Thought in The Liberal Age: 1798–1939*. Cambridge: Cambridge University Press.

Howe, L. 2000. Risk, Ritual and Performance. *Journal of the Royal Anthropological Institute* (N.S.) 6: 63–79.

Hunsberger, A. 2001. Nasir Khusraw: Fatimid Intellectual. In F. Daftry (ed.), *Intellectual Traditions in Islam*. London and New York: I.B. Tauris in association with The Institute of Ismaili Studies, pp. 112–29.

2000. *Nasir Khusraw, The Ruby of Badakshan: A Portrait of the Persian Poet, Traveller and Philosopher*. London and New York: I.B. Tauris in association with The Institute of Ismaili Studies.

Huntington, S. 1993. The Clash of Civilisations? *Foreign Affairs* 72 (3) (summer): 22–49.

Hussain, A. 1990. The Karachi Riots of December 1986: Crisis of State and Civil Society in Pakistan. In V. Das (ed.), *Mirrors of Violence: Communities, Riots and Survivors in south Asia*. Delhi: Oxford University Press, pp. 185–93.

Hunzai, F. 1996. *Shimmering Light: An Anthology of Ismaili Poetry*. London: I.B. Tauris in association with the Institute of Ismaili Studies.

Huq, M. 1999. From Piety to Romance: Islam-Oriented Texts in Bangladesh. In D. Eickelman and J. Anderson (eds) *New Muslim Media in the Muslim World: The Emerging Public Sphere*. Bloomington: Indian University Press, pp. 133–162.

Jackson, M. 1983. Knowledge of the Body. *Man* 18: (2) 326–45.

1989. *Paths Towards a Clearing*. Bloomington: Indiana University Press.

Jaffrelot, C. (ed.) 2002. *Pakistan: Nationalism Without a Nation*. London: Zed Books.

Jahanzeb, M. 1985. *The Last Wali of Swat: An Autobiography as Told to Frederick Barth*. New York: Columbia University Press.

Jalal, A. 2000. *Self and Sovereignty: Individual and Community in South Asian Islam Since 1850*. London and New York: Routledge.

1995a. *Democracy and Authoritarianism in South Asia: A Comparative and Historical Perspective*. Cambridge: Cambridge University Press.

1995b. Conjuring Pakistan: History as Official Imagining. *International Journal of Middle East Studies* 27: 73–89.

1991. The Convenience of Subservience: Women and the State of Pakistan. In D. Kandiyoti, (ed.) *Women, Islam and the State*. Macmillan: Basingstoke and London, pp. 77–114.

1990. *The State of Martial Rule: the Origins of Pakistan's Political Economy of Defence* Cambridge: Cambridge University Press.

James, S. 1997. *Passion and Action: The Emotions in Seventeenth-Century Philosophy*. Oxford: Clarendon.

Jatyawardena, K and de Alwis, M. (eds). 1996. *Embodied Violence: Communalising Women's Sexuality in South Asia*. London: Zed Books.

Jeffery, P., Jeffery, R. and Jeffrey, C. 2004. Islamisation, Gentrification and Domestication: An 'Islamic Course for Girls' and rural Muslims in Western Uttar Pradesh. *Modern Asian Studies* 38 (1): 1–52.

Jeffery, P. 1979. *Frogs in a Well: Indian Women in Purdah*. London: Zed Books.

Kandiyoti, D. (ed.) 1996. *Gendering the Middle East: Emerging Perspectives*. London: I.B. Tauris.

1992. Women, Islam, and the State: A Comparative Approach. In: J. Cole (ed.), *Comparing Muslim Societies: Knowledge and the State in a World Civilization*. Ann Arbor: University of Michigan Press.

1991a. Introduction. In D. Kandiyoti (ed.) *Women, Islam and the State*. Basingstoke and London: Macmillan, pp. 1–21.

(ed.) 1991b. *Women, Islam and the State*. Basingstoke and London: Macmillan.

Kapferer, B. 1988. *Legends of People, Myths of State: Violence, Intolerance and Political Culture in Sri Lanka and Australia*. Washington and London: Smithsonian Institution Press.

Keay, J. 1996. *Explorers of the Western Himalayas 1820–1895*. Cambridge: Cambridge University Press.

Keiser, L. 1991. *Friend By Day, Enemy by Night*. Fort Worth: Holt, Rienhart and Winston.

Kennion R. L. 1910. *Sport and Life in the Further Himalaya*. London and Edinburgh: William Blackwood and Sons.

Kepel, G. 2002. *Jihad: The Trail of Political Islam*. I.B Tauris: London and New York.

——— 1997. *Allah in the West: Islamic Movements in America and Europe*. Cambridge: Polity Press.

——— 1994 [1991]. *The Revenge of God: The Resurgence of Islam, Christianity, and Judaism in the Modern World*. Translated by Alan Braley. Cambridge: Polity Press.

Khaleed, A. 1998. *The politics of Muslim Cultural Reform: Jadidism in Central Asia*. Berkeley and Los Angeles: University of California Press.

Knysh, A. 2001. The Tariqa on a Landcruiser: The Resurgence of Sufism in Yemen. *Middle East Journal* **55** (3): 399–414.

Kreutzmann, K. 1991. The Karakorum Highway: the Impact of Road Construction on Mountain Societies. *Modern Asian Studies* **25** (4): 711–36.

Kurin, R. 1993. Islamization in Pakistan: The Sayyid and the Dancer. In D. Eickelman, (ed.), *Russia's Muslim Frontiers: New Directions in Cross Cultural Analysis*. Bloomington and Indiana: Indiana University Press, pp. 175–89.

Laidlaw, J. 2002. For an Anthropology of Ethics and Freedom. *Journal of the Royal Anthropological Institute* (NS) **8**: 311–32.

——— 2000. A Free Gift Makes No Friends. *Journal of the Royal Anthropological Institute* (NS) **6**: 617–34.

——— 1995. *Riches and Renunciation: Religion, Economy and Society Among the Jains*. Oxford: Oxford University Press.

Lambek, M. 2000a. The Anthropology of Religion and the Quarrel between Poetry and Philosophy. *Current Anthropology* **41** (3): 309–20.

——— 2000b. Localising Islamic Performances in Mayotte. In D. Parkin and C. Headley (eds), *Islamic Prayer Across the Indian Ocean: Inside and Outside the Mosque*. Richmond: Curzon, pp. 63–97.

Lambert, H. 2000. Sentiment and substance in North Indian forms of relatedness. In J. Carsten (ed.), *Cultures of Relatedness: New Approaches to the Study of Kinship*. Cambridge: Cambridge University Press, pp. 73–89.

Lawrence, B. 1999. The Eastward Journey of Muslim Kingship: Islam in South and Southeast Asia. In J. Esposito (ed.), *The Oxford History of Islam*, pp. 395–431. Oxford: Oxford University Press.

Leach, J. 2003. *Creative Land: Place and Procreation on the Rai Coast of Papua New Guinea*. Oxford: Berghahn.

Lelyveld, D., 1979. *Aligarh's First Generation: Muslim Solidarity in British India*.

Levtzion, N. (ed.) 1979. *Conversion to Islam*. New York: Holmes & Meier.

Lewis, P. 1994. *Islamic Britain: Religion, Politics and Identity among British Muslims: Bradford in the 1990s*. London and New York: I. B. Tauris.

Lievre, V. and Loude, J. 1990. *Le Chamanisme des Kalash du Pakistan: Des Montagnards Polytheistes Face l'Islam*. Lyon: Centre Regional de Publication de Lyon.

Lindholm, C. 2001. Kissing Cousins: Anthropologists on Islam. In H. Donnan (ed.), *Interpreting Islam*. London: Sage, pp. 110–29.

1998. Prophets and *Pirs*: Charismatic Islam in the Middle East and South Asia. In P. Werbner and H. Basu (eds), *Embodying Charisma: Modernity, Locality and the Performance of Emotion in Sufi Cults*. London: Routledge, pp. 209–33.

1999. Justice and Tyranny: Law and State in the Middle East. *Journal of the Royal Asiatic Society* 3, 9, 3: 375–88.

1996. *Frontier Perspectives: Studies in Comparative Anthropology*. Karachi: Oxford University Press.

1995. The New Middle-East Ethnography. *Journal of the Royal Anthropological Institute* (NS) 1 (4): 805–20.

1982. *Generosity and Jealousy Amongst the Swat Pukhtun*. Columbia: Columbia University Press.

Loeffler, R. 1988. *Religion in Practice: Religious Beliefs in a Persian Village*. Albany: State University of New York Press.

Lubeck, P. 1988. Islamic Political Movements in Northern Nigeria: The Problem of Class Analysis. In E. Burke III and I. Lapidus (eds), *Islam, Politics and Social Movements*. London: I.B. Tauris, pp. 244–60.

Luhrmann, T. 1989. *Persuasions of the Witch's Craft: Ritual, Magic and Witchcraft in Present-Day England*, Oxford: Basil Blackwell .

Lynch, O. (ed.) 1990. *Divine Passions: The Social Construction of Emotion in India*. Berkeley: University of California Press.

Lynch, O. 1990. The Social Construction of Emotion in India. In O. Lynch (ed.), *Divine Passions: The Social Construction of Emotion in India*. Berkeley: University of California Press.

McChesney, R. D. 1991. *Waqf in Central Asia: Four Hundred Years in the History of a Muslim Shrine, 1480–1889*. Princeton New Jersey: Princeton University Press.

McKenna, T. M. 1998. *Muslim Rulers and Rebels: Everyday Politics and Armed Separatism in the Southern Philippines*. Berkeley: University of California Press.

Madan, V. (ed.) 2002. *The Village in India*. New Delhi: Oxford University Press.

Maggi, W. 2001. *Our Women are Free: Gender and Ethnicity in the Hindu Kush*. Ann Arbor: University of Michigan Press.

Mahdi, M. 2001. The Rational Traditions in Islam. In F. Daftary (ed.), *Intellectual Traditions in Islam*. London and New York: I.B. Tauris in association with The Institute of Ismaili Studies, pp. 43–65.

Mahmood, S. 2003. Ethical Formation and the Politics of Individual Autonomy in Contemporary Egypt. *Social Research* 70 (3): 1501–30.

2001. Rehearsed Spontaneity and the Conventionality of Ritual: Disciplines of *Salat. American Ethnologist* 28 (4):827–53.

Makdisi, G. 1981. *The Rise of Colleges: Institutions of Learning in Islam and the West*. Edinburgh: Edinburgh University Press.

Maley, P. (ed.) 1998. *Fundamentalism Reborn?: Afghanistan and the Taliban*. London: Hurst and Company.

Malik, J. 2002. Dynamics of Islamic Religious Scholars and their Institutions in Contemporary Pakistan. In J. Meuleman (ed.), *Islam in the Era of Globalization: Muslim Attitudes Towards Modernity and Identity*. New York: Routledge Curzon.

1998. *Colonialization of Islam: Dissolution of Traditional Institutions in Pakistan.* New Delhi: Manohar.

Mandel, R. 1990. Shifting Centres and Emergent Identities: Turkey and Germany in the Lives of Turkish *Gastarbeiter.* In D. Eickelman and J. Piscatori (eds), *Muslim Travellers: Pilgrimage, Migration, and the Religious Imagination.* London: Routledge, pp. 153–71.

Masud, K. 2002. Religious Identity and Education. In J. Meuleman (ed.), *Islam in the Era of Globalization: Muslim Attitudes Towards Modernity and Identity.* New York: Routledge Curzon.

Manger, L. 1999. Muslim Diversity: Local Islam in Global Contexts. In L. Manger (ed.), *Muslim Diversity: Local Islam in Global Contexts.* Richmond: Curzon, pp. 1–36.

Manuel, P. 1993. *Cassette Culture: Popular Music and Technology in North India.* Chicago and London: University of Chicago Press.

Marr, D. G. 2000. Concepts of 'Individual' and 'Self' in Twentieth-Century Vietnam. *Modern Asian Studies* 34 (4): 769–96.

Marsden, P. 1998. *The Taliban: War, Religion and the New Order in Afghanistan.* London: Zed Books.

Masquelier, A. 2001. *Prayer Has Spoiled Everything: Possession, Power and Identity in an Islamic Town of Niger.* Durham and London: Duke University Press.

Masud, K., Messick, B. and Powers, D. 1996. Muftis, Fatwas and Islamic Legal Interpretation. In Masud, K., Messick, B., Powers, D. (eds), *Islamic Legal Interpretation: Muftis and Their Fatwas.* Cambridge, MA and London: Harvard University Press.

Meeker, M. 2003. *A Nation of Empire: The Legacy of Turkish Modernity.* Berkeley: University of California Press.

1991. The New Muslim Intellectuals in the Republic of Turkey. In R. Tapper (ed.), *Islam in Modern Turkey: Religion, Politics and Literature in a Secular State.* London: I. B. Tauris, pp 189–219.

1980. The Twilight of a South Asian Heroic Age: A Rereading of Barth's Study of Swat. *Man* (NS) 15: 682–701.

1979. *Literature and Violence in North Arabia.* Cambridge: Cambridge University Press.

Mehran, G. 2002. The Presentation of the 'Self' and the 'Other' in Postrevolutionary Iranian School Textbooks. In N. Keddie and R. Matthee (eds), *Iran and the Surrounding World: Interactions in Culture and Cultural Politics.* Seattle and London: University of Washington Press, pp. 232–53.

Messick, B. 1996. Media Muftis: Radio Fatwas in Yemen. In K. Masud, B. Messick and D. Powers (eds), *Islamic Legal Interpretation: Muftis and Their Fatwas.* Cambridge MA and London: University of Harvard Press, pp. 310–20.

1993. *The Calligraphic State: Textual Domination and History in a Muslim Society.* Berkeley: University of California Press.

Metcalf, B. 2004. *Islamic Contestations: Essays on Muslims in India and Pakistan.* Oxford: Oxford University Press.

1999. Nationalism, Modernity, and Muslim Identity in India Before 1947. In P. van der Veer and Lehmann (eds), *Nation and Religion: Perspectives on Europe and Asia.* Princeton NJ: Princeton University Press, pp. 129–43.

1996. Two Fatwas on Hajj in British India. In Masud, K., Messick, B., Powers, D. (eds), *Islamic Legal Interpretation: Muftis and Their Fatwas.* Cambridge, MA and London: Harvard University Press.

1994. 'Remaking Ourselves': Islamic Self-Fashioning in a Global Movement of Spiritual Renewal. In M. Marty and R. S. Appleby (eds) *Accounting for Fundamentalism: The Dynamic Character of Movements.* Chicago and London: Chicago University Press, pp. 706–25.

1993. Living Hadith in the Tabligh-i Jamaat. *Journal of Asian Studies* 52: 584–608.

1990. *Perfecting Women: Maulana Ashraf 'Ali Thanawi's Bihishti Zewar. A Partial Translation with Commentary.* Berkeley: University of California Press.

1987. Islamic Arguments in Contemporary Pakistan. In W. Roff (ed.), *Islam and the Political Economy of Meaning: Comparative Studies of Muslim Discourse.* London and Sydney: Croom and Helm, pp. 131–59.

1983. The Case of Pakistan. In P. Merkl and N. Smart (eds), *Religion and Politics in the Modern World.* New York and London: New York University Press.

1982. *Islamic Revival in British India: Deoband, 1860–1900.* Berkeley: University of California Press.

1978. The Madrasa at Deoband: A Model for Religious Education in Modern India. *Modern Asian Studies* 12 (1): 111–34.

Mills, M. 1991. *Rhetoric and Politics in Afghan Traditional Storytelling.* Philadelphia: University of Pennsylvania Press.

Mir, A. K. 1994. *Firdausi Firdausi.* Chitral: Anjuman Taraqqi Khowar.

Mir-Hosseini, Z. 2000. *Islam and Gender: The Religious Debate in Contemporary Iran.* London: I.B. Tauris.

1994. Inner Truth and Outer History: The Two Worlds of the Ahl-I Haqq of Kurdistan. *International Journal of Middle East Studies* 26 (2): 267–85.

Mody, P. 2002. Love and the Law: Love-Marriage in Delhi. *Modern Asian Studies* 36 (1): 223–56.

Mottahedeh, R., 1985. *The Mantle of the Prophet: Religion and Politics in Iran.* New York: Pantheon Books.

Mousavi, S. 1998. *The Hazaras of Afghanistan: An Historical, Cultural, Economic and Political Study.* Richmond: Curzon.

Mundy, M. 1995. *Domestic Government: Kinship. Community and Polity in North Yemen.* London: I.B. Tauris.

Murphy, R. 2000. The Hairbrush and the Dagger: Mediating Modernity in Lahore. In W. Armbrust (ed.), *Mass Mediations: New Approaches to Popular Culture in the Middle East and Beyond.* University of California Press: Berkeley, pp. 203–23.

Naipaul, V. 1981. *Among the Believers: A Journey.* London: Deutsch.

Naji, N. 2001. *Troq Zualoo.* Peshawar.

Najmabadi, A. 1998. Crafting an Educated Housewife in Iran. In L. Abu-Lughod (ed.), *Remaking Women: Feminism and Modernity in the Middle East.* Princeton: Princeton University Press, pp. 91–125.

Nandy, A. 1990. *At the Edge of Psychology: Essays in Politics and Culture.* New Delhi: Oxford University Press.

Nanji, A. 1995. Aga Khan. In J. Esposito (ed.), *Encyclopaedia of the Modern Islamic World.* New York: Oxford University Press.

   1978. The Nizari Ismaili Tradition in the Indo-Pakistan Sub-Continent. Delmar: Caravan.

Nasr, S. V. R. 2002. The Iranian Revolution and Changes in Islamism in Pakistan, India and Afghanistan. In N. Keddie and R. Matthee (eds), *Iran and the Surrounding World: Interactions in Culture and Cultural Politics.* Seattle and London: University of Washington Press, pp. 327–52.

   2001. *Islamic Leviathan: Islam and the Making of State Power.* Oxford: Oxford University Press.

   2000. The Rise of Sunni Militancy in Pakistan: The Changing Role of Islamism and the Ulama in Society and Politics. *Modern Asian Studies* 34 (1): 139–80.

   1999. European Colonialism and the Emergence of Modern Muslim States. In J. Esposito (ed.), *The Oxford History of Islam.* Oxford and New York: Oxford University Press, pp. 549–99.

   1996. *Mawdudi and the Making of Islamic Revivalism.* New York and Oxford: Oxford University Press.

   1994. *The Vanguard of the Islamic Revolution: The Jama'at-i Islam of Pakistan.* Berkeley: Berkeley University Press.

   1992. Students, Islam and Politics: Islami Jami'at-I Tulaba in Pakistan. *The Middle East Journal* 46 (1): 59–76.

Navaro-Yashin, Y. 2002. *The Faces of the State: Secularism and Public Life in Turkey.* Princeton University Press: Princeton and Oxford.

Nelson, K. 1985. *The Art of Reciting the Qur'an.* Austin: Texas University Press.

Newman, A. 1999. Clerical Perceptions of Sufi Practices in Late Seventeenth Century Persia: Arguments over the Permissibility of Singing (*ghina*). In L. Lewisohn and D. Morgan (eds), *The Heritage of Sufism, volume III. Late Classical Persianate Sufism (1501–1750): The Safavid and Mughal Period.* Oxford: Oneworld, pp. 135–64.

Nichols, R. 2001. *Settling the Frontier: Land, Law, and Society in the Peshawar Valley, 1500–1900.* Karachi: Oxford University Press.

O'Brien, D. B. Cruise. 1971. *The Mourides of Senegal: The Political and Economic Organization of an Islamic Brotherhood.* Oxford: Oxford University Press.

O'Brien, D. J. T. 1895. *Grammar and Vocabulary of the Khowar Dialect (Chitrali), with introductory sketch of country and people.* Lahore: Civil and Military Gazette Press.

O'Hanlon, R. 1993. Historical Approaches to Communalism: Perspectives from Western India. In P. Robb, (ed.), *Society and Ideology. Essays Presented to*

Professor Kenneth Ballhatchet. New Delhi: Oxford University Press, pp. 247–66.

Ortner, S. B. 1978. *Sherpas Through their Rituals.* Cambridge: Cambridge University Press.

Osella, C. and Osella, P. 1998. Friendships and Flirting: Micro-Politics in Kerala, South India. *Journal of the Royal Anthropological Institute* (NS) 4: 189–206.

2000. Migration, Money and Masculinity in Kerala. *Journal of the Royal Anthropological Society* (NS) 6: 117–33.

Overing, J. (ed.) 1985. *Reason and Morality.* London and New York: Tavistock Publications.

Overing, J. and Passes, A. 2000. Introduction: Conviviality and the Opening Up of Amazonian Anthropology. In J. Overing and A. Passes (ed.), *The Anthropology of Love and Anger: The Aesthetics of Conviviality in Native Amazonia.* London and New York: Routledge.

Pandey, G. 1990. *The Construction of Communalism in North India.* New Delhi: Oxford University Press.

Parkes, P. 2001a. Alternative Social Structures and Foster Relations in the Hindu Kush: Milk Kinship and Tributary Allegiance in Former Mountain Kingdoms of Northern Pakistan. *Comparative Study of Society and History* 43 (1):4–36.

2001b. Unwrapping Rudeness: Inverted Etiquette in an Egalitarian Enclave. In J. Hendry and C. W. Watson (eds), *An Anthropology of Indirect Communication.* London and New York: Routledge, pp. 232–51.

1999. Enclaved Knowledge: Indigent and Indignant Representation of Environmental Management and Development among the Kalasha of Northern Pakistan. In R. Ellen, P. Parkes, and A. Bicker (eds), *Indigenous Environmental Knowledge and its Transformations: Critical Anthropological Perspectives.* Amsterdam: Harwood Academic Publishers.

1996a. Kalsha Oral Literature and Praise Songs. In E. Bashir and Israr-ud-Din (eds), *Proceedings of the Second International Hindukush Cultural Conference.* Karachi: Oxford University Press, pp. 315–28.

1996b. Indigenous Polo and the Politics of Regional Identity. In J. MacClancy (ed.), *Sport, Identity and Ethnicity.* Oxford: Berg, pp. 43–67.

1994. Personal and Collective Identity in Kalasha Song Performance: The Significance of Music-making in a minority enclave. In M. Stokes (ed.), *Ethnicity, Identity, and Music.* Oxford: Berg, pp. 157–88.

1991. Temple of Imra, Temple of Mahandeu: a Kafir Sanctuary in Kalasha Cosmology. *Bulletin of School of Oriental and African Studies* 54 (1): 145–58.

1987. Livestock Symbolism and Pastoral Ideology Among the Kafirs of the Hindu Kush. *Man* 22: 637–60.

Forthcoming. A Minority Perspective on the History of Chitral: Katore Rule in Kalasha Tradition. Paper presented at the 1995 Hindu Kush Cultural Conference.

Parkin, D. 2000a. Inside and Outside the Mosque: a Master Trope. In D. Parkin and C. Healey (eds), *Islamic Prayer across the Indian Ocean: Inside and Outside the Mosque.* Curzon Press: Richmond, pp. 1–21.

2000b. Invocation: Salaa, Dua, Sadaka and the Question of Sef-Determination. In D. Parkin and C. Healey (eds.), *Islamic Prayer Across the Indian Ocean: Inside and Outside the Mosque.* Curzon Press: Richmond, pp. 137–68.

Parry, J. 1994. *Death in Banaras.* Cambridge: Cambridge University Press.

1989. On the Moral Perils of Exchange. In J. Parry and M. Bloch (eds), *Money and the Morality of Exchange.* Cambridge: Cambridge University Press, pp. 64–93.

1985. The Brahmanical Tradition and the Technology of the Intellect. In J. Overing (ed.), *Reason and Morality.* London and New York: Tavistock.

Peabody, N. 2000. Collective Violence in Our Time. *American Ethnologist* 27 (1): 169–78.

Peletz, M. 1996. *Reason and Passion: Representations of Gender in a Malay Society.* Berkeley: University of California Press.

2002. *Islamic Modern: Religious Courts and Cultural Politics in Malaysia.* Princeton: Princeton University Press.

Pilot, C. 1999. *Remotely Global: Village Modernity in West Africa.* Chicago and London: University of Chicago Press.

Pirzada, S. A. S. 2000. *The Politics of the Jamiat Ulema-I-Islam in Pakistan, 1971–1977.* Karachi: Oxford University Press.

Pocock, D. 1973. *Mind, Body and Weath: A Study of Belief and Practice in an Indian Village.* Basil Blackwell: Oxford.

Powell, A. 1993. *Muslims and Missionaries in Pre-Mutiny India.* Richmond: Curzon Press.

Powers, D. 1996. The Art of the Legal Opinion: al-Wansharisi on *Tawlij.* In Masud, K., Messick, B. and Powers, D. (eds), *Islamic Legal Interpretation: Muftis and Their Fatwas.* Cambridge, MA and London: Harvard University Press.

Quigley, D. 1993. *The Interpretation of Caste.* Oxford: Clarendon.

Qureishi, R. 2000. How Does Music Mean: Embodied Memories and the Politics of Affect in Indian Sarangi. *American Ethnologist* 27 (4): 805–38.

1995. *Sufi Music in India and Pakistan: Sound, Context and Meaning in Qawwali.* Chicago: University of Chicago Press.

Racy, A. J. 2003. *Making Music in the Arab World: The Culture and Artistry of Tarab.* Cambridge: Cambridge University Press.

Radcliffe-Brown, A. 1964. *The Andaman Islanders.* New York: Free Press.

Raheja, G. 1988. *The Poison in the Gift: Ritual, Prestation and the Dominant Caste in a North Indian village.* University of Chicago Press: Chicago.

Rahman, T. 1996. *Language and Politics in Pakistan.* Karachi and New Delhi: Oxford University Press.

Rai, M. 2004. *Hindu Rulers, Muslim Subjects: Islam, Community and the History of Kashmir.* Hurst and Co.: London.

Al-Rasheed, M. 2002. *A History of Saudi Arabia.* Cambridge: Cambridge University Press.

Rashid, A. 2002. *Jihad: The Rise of Militant Islam in Central Asia.* New Haven and London: Yale University Press.

2000. *Taliban: Islam, Oil and the New Great Game in Central Asia.* London and New York: I.B. Tauris.

Rasmussen, A. 2001. The Qur'an in Indonesian Daily Life: The Public Project of Musical Oratory. *Ethnomusicology* 45 (1): 30–57.

Richards, P. 1996. *Fighting for the Rain Forest: War, Youth and Resources in Sierra Leone.* London: International African Institute.

Robertson, G. S. 1976 [1896]. *The Kafirs of the Hindu Kush.* Lahore: Sang-e Meel.

1899 *Chitral: The Story of a Minor Siege.* Methuen: London.

Robinson, A. 2002. I Had No Idea That Madness in the Islamic World Had Gone So Far. *The Times* 7 August 2002: 16–17.

Robinson, F. 2000. *Islam and Muslim History in South Asia.* New Delhi: Oxford University Press.

1998. The British Empire and Muslim Identity in South Asia. *Transactions of the Royal Historical Society*: 271–89.

1997. Ottomans-Safavids-Mughals: Shared Knowledge and Collective Systems. *Journal of Islamic Studies* 8 (2): 151–84.

1991. Persio-Islamic Culture in India from the Seventeenth to the Early Twentieth Century. In Canfield, R. L. *Turko-Persia in Historical Perspective.* Cambridge: Cambridge University Press.

1984. The 'Ulama of Farangi Mahal and Their *Adab.* In B. Metcalf (ed.), *Moral Conduct and Authority: The Place of Adab in South Asian Islam.* Berkeley: University of California Press, pp. 153–83.

1983. Islam and Muslim Society in South Asia. *Contributions to Indian Sociology* 17: 185–203.

Robinson, G. 1995. *The Dark Side of Paradise: Political Violence in Bali.* Ithaca: Cornell University Press.

Roff, W. 1996. An Argument about how to Argue. In K. Masud, B. Messick and D. Powers (eds), *Islamic Legal Interpretation: Muftis and Their Fatwas.* Cambridge MA and London: Harvard University Press.

Rosaldo, R. 1980. *Knowledge and Passion: Ilongot Notions of Self and Social Life.* Cambridge: Cambridge University Press.

Rostam-Kolayi, Y. 2002. Foreign Education, the Women's Press, and the Discourse of Scientific Domesticity in Early-Twentieth-Century Iran. In N. Keddie and R. Matthee (eds), *Iran and the Surrounding World: Interactions in Culture and Cultural Politics.* Seattle and London: University of Washington Press, pp. 182–202.

Roy, A. 1983. *The Islamic Syncretistic Tradition in Bengal.* Princeton, NJ: Princeton University Press.

Roy, O. 1998. Has Islamism a Future in Afghanistan? In W. Maley (ed.), *Fundamentalism Reborn? Afghanistan and the Taliban.* London: Hurst and Company, pp. 199–211.

1994. *The Failure of Political Islam.* London: I. B. Tauris.

1990. *Islam and Resistance in Afghanistan.* Cambridge: Cambridge University Press.

Sachedina, A. 2001. Woman, Half-the-Man? The Crisis of Male Epistemology in Islamic Jurisprudence. In F. Daftary (ed.), *Intellectual Traditions in Islam.*

London and New York: I.B. Tauris in association with The Institute of Ismaili Studies, pp. 160–78.

Sanneh, L. O. 1997. *The Crown and the Turban: Muslims and West African Pluralism.* Oxford: Westview Press.

Sanyal, U. 1996. *Devotional Islam and Politics in British India: Ahmed Riza Khan Barelwi and His Movement, 1870–1920.* Delhi: Oxford University Press.

Scheper-Hughes, N. 1992. *Death Without Weeping: The Violence of Everyday Life in Brazil.* Berkeley and Los Angeles: University of California Press.

Schimmel, A. 2001. Reason and Mystical Experience in Sufism. In F. Daftary (ed.), *Intellectual Traditions in Islam.* London: Tauris in association with Institute for Ismaili Studies, pp. 130–45.

1999. The Vernacular Tradition in Persianate Sufi Poetry in Mughal India. In L. Lewisohn and D. Morgan (eds), *The Heritage of Sufism, volume III. Late Classical Persianate Sufism (1501–1750): The Safavid and Mughal Period.* Oxford: Oneworld, pp. 416–34.

1975. *Mystical Dimensions of Islam.* Chapel Hill: University of North Carolina Press.

Schomberg, R. C. F. 1938. *Kafirs and Glaciers: Travels in Chitral.* London: Hopkins.

1935. *Between the Oxus and the Indus.* London: Hopkins.

Schubel, V. J. 1993. *Religious Performance in Contemporary Islam: Shi'I Devotional Rituals in South Asia.* Columbia: University of South Carolina Press.

Shakry, O. 1998. Schooled Mothers and Structured Play: Child Rearing in Turn-of-the-Century Egypt. In L. Abu-Lughod (ed.), *Remaking Women: Feminism and Modernity in the Middle East.* Princeton University Press: Princeton, pp. 126–70.

Shah, S. W. A. 1999. *Ethnicity, Islam, and Nationalism: Muslim Politics in the North-West Frontier Province 1937–47.* Karachi: OUP.

Shahrani, N. 1991. Local Knowledge of Islam and Social Discourse in Afghanistan and Turkistan in the Modern Period. In R. Canfield (ed.), *Turko-Persia in Historical Perspective.* Cambridge: Cambridge University Press.

1979. *The Kirghiz and Wakhi of Afghanistan: Adaptation to Closed Frontiers.* Seattle and London: University of Washington Press.

Shyrock, A. 1997 *Nationalism and the Genealogical Imagination: Oral history and Textual Authority in Jordan.* Berkeley: University of California Press.

Sikand, Y. 2002. The Emergence and Development of the Jama'at-I Islami of Jammu and Kashmir (1940s–1990). *Modern Asian Studies* 36 (3): 705–51.

Sirreyeh, E. 1999. *Sufis and Anti-Sufis: The Defence, Rethinking and Rejection of Sufism in the Modern World.* Richmond: Curzon.

Sokefeld, M. 1999. Debating self, identity, and culture in anthropology. *Current Anthropology* 40 (4): 417–47.

Southwold, M. 1983. *Buddhism in Life: The Anthropological Study of Religion and the Sinhalese Practice of Buddhism.* Manchester: Manchester University Press.

Spencer, J. 1990a. *A Sinhala Village in a Time of Trouble: Politics and Change in Rural Sri Lanka.* Delhi: Oxford University Press.

1990b. Collective Violence and Everyday Practice in Sri Lanka. *Modern Asian Studies* 24 (3): 609–23.

Sperber, D. 1985. Anthropology and Psychology: Towards an Epidemiology of Representations. *Man* 20: 73–89.

Stafford, C. 1995. *The Roads of Chinese Childhood: Learning and Identification in Angang.* Cambridge: Cambridge University Press.

Staley, J. 1982. *Words for my Brother: Travels between the Hindu Kush and the Himalayas.* Karachi: Oxford University Press.

1969. Economy and Society in the High Mountains of Northern Pakistan. *Modern Asian Studies* 3 (3): 225–43.

Starrett, G. 1998. *Putting Islam to Work: Education, Politics, and Religious Transformation in Egypt.* Berkeley: University of California Press.

1995. The Margins of Print: Children's Religious Literature in Egypt. *Journal of the Royal Anthropological Institute.* (NS) 2: 117–39.

Stewart, M. 2002. Erotic Dreams and Nightmares from Antiquity to the Present. *Journal of the Royal Anthropological Institute* 8: 279–322.

Stokes, M. 2002. Silver Sounds in the Inner Citadel? Reflections on Musicology in Islam. In H. Donnan (ed.), *Interpreting Islam.* London: Sage, 167–89.

1994. Turkish Arabesk and the City: Urban Popular Culture as Spatial Practice. In A. Ahmed and H. Donnan (eds), *Islam, Globalization and Postmodernity.* London and New York: Routledge, pp. 21–37.

1992. *The Arabesk Debate: Music and Musicians in Modern Turkey.* Oxford: Oxford University Press.

Street, B. (ed.) 1993. *Cross-Cultural Approaches to Literacy.* Cambridge: Cambridge University Press.

Street, B. 1990. Orientalist Discourse in the Anthropology of Iran, Afghanistan and Pakistan. In R. Fardon (ed.), *Localizing Strategies: Regional Traditions of Ethnographic Writing.* Washington, DC: Smithsonian Institution Press.

1984. *Literacy in Theory and Practice.* Cambridge: Cambridge University Press.

Talbot, I. 1998. *Pakistan: A Modern History.* London: Hurst and Company.

1996. *Freedom's Cry: The Popular Dimension in the Pakistan Movement and Partition Experience in North West India.* Karachi: Oxford University Press.

Tambiah, S. J. 1996. *Levelling Crowds: Ethnonationalist Conflicts and Collective Violence in South Asia.* Berkeley: University of California Press.

1992. *Buddhism Betrayed? Religion, Politics and Violence in Sri Lanka.* Chicago: University of Chicago Press.

1990. *Magic, Science, Religion and the Scope of Rationality.* Cambridge: Cambridge University Press.

1985. *Culture, Thought and Social Action.* Cambridge, MA: Harvard University Press.

1984. *The Buddhist Saints of the Forest and the Cult of Amulets: A Study in Charisma, Hagiography, Sectarianism, and Millenial Buddhism.* Cambridge: Cambridge University Press, 1984.

Tapper, N. and Tapper, R. 1987. The Birth of the Prophet: Ritual and Gender in Turkish Islam. *Man* 22: 69–92.

1986. Eat This, It'll Do You the Power of Good; Food and Commensality Among the Durrani Pashtuns. *American Ethnologist* **13** (1): 62–79.

Tapper, N. 1990a. *Bartered Brides*. Cambridge: Cambridge University Press.

1990b. *Ziyaret*: Gender, Movement, and Exchange in a Turkish Community. In D. Eickelman and J. Piscatori (eds), *Muslim Travellers: Pilgrimage, Migration, and the Religious Imagination*. London: Routledge, pp. 236–55.

Tapper, R. 2001. Anthropology and (the) Crisis: Responding to Crisis in Afghanistan. *Anthropology Today* 17 (6): 13–16.

2001. Blood, Wine and Water: Social and Symbolic Aspects of Drink and Drinking in the Islamic Middle East. In S. Zubaida and R. Tapper (eds), *A Taste of Thyme: Culinary Cultures of the Middle East*. London: Tauris, pp. 215–31.

1984. Holier Than Thou: Islam in Three Tribal Societies. In A. Ahmed and D. Hart (eds), *Islam in Tribal Societies: From the Atlas to the Indus*. London: Routledge and Kegan Paul, pp. 244–65.

(ed.) 1983. *The Conflict of Tribe and State in Iran and Afghanistan*. London: Croom Helm.

Taussig, M. 1980. *The Devil and Commodity Fetishism in South America*. Chapel Hill: University of North California Press.

Thomson, H. C. 1895. *The Chitral Campaign: A Narrative of Events in Chitral, Swat, and Bajaour*. London: W. Heinemann.

Titus, P. (ed.) 1997. *Marginality and Modernity: Ethnicity and Change in Post-Colonial Balochistan*. Karachi: Oxford University Press.

Titus, P. 1998. Honour the Baluch, Buy the Pashtun: Stereotypes, Social Organisation and History in West Pakistan. *Modern Asian Studies* **32** (3): 689–716.

Topan, F. 2000. Swahili and Ismai'li Perceptions of *Salat*. In D. Parkin and C. Healey (eds), *Islamic Prayer across the Indian Ocean: Inside and Outside the Mosque*. Curzon Press: Richmond, pp. 99–115.

Torab, A. 1997. Piety as Gendered Agency: A Study of Jalaseh Ritual Discourse in an Urban Neighbourhood in Iran. *Journal of the Royal Anthropological Institute* **2**: 235–52.

Toren, C. 1993. Making History: The Significance of Childhood Cognition for a Comparative Anthropology of the Mind. In *Man* **28**: 461–78.

Trench, C. 1985. *The Frontier Scouts*. London: Cape.

Trimingham, S. 1998 [1971]. *The Sufi Orders of Islam*. With a new forward by John Voll. New York and Oxford: Oxford University Press.

Trol, C. 1978. *Sayyid Ahmad Khan: A Reinterpretation of Muslim Theology*. New Delhi: Vikas Publishing House.

Tsing, A. 1993. *In the Realm of the Diamond Queen: Marginality in an Out-of-the-Way Place*. Princeton: Princeton University Press.

Van Belle, J. 2002. Living Musical Traditions of the Ismailis in Afghan Badakshan. *International Institute for Asian Studies Newsletter* March 2002: 9–10.

Van der Veer, P. 1996. Introduction. In P. van der Veer (ed.), *Conversion to Modernities: The Globalization of Christianity*. London: Routledge, pp. 1–23.

1992. Playing or Praying: A Saint's Day in Surat. *Journal of Asian Studies.* 51 (3): 545–65.

Verkaaik, O. 2004. *Migrants and Militants: Fun and Urban Violence in Pakistan.* Princeton: Princeton University Press.

2001. The Captive State: Corruption, Intelligence Agencies and Ethnicity in Pakistan. In T. Hansen and F. Stepputat (eds), *States of Imagination: Ethnographic Explorations of the Postcolonial State.* Durham and London: Duke University Press, pp. 345–64.

Viegas, S de. 2002. Eating with your Favourite Mother: Time and Sociality in a Brazilian Amerindian Community. *Journal of the Royal Anthropological Institute* (N.S.) **8**: 691–708.

Viswanathan, G. 1998. *Outside the Fold: Conversion, Modernity, and Belief.* Princeton: Princeton University Press.

Watkins, F. 2003. 'Save There, Eat Here': Migrants, Households and Community Identity Among Pukhtuns in Northern Pakistan. *Contributions to Indian Sociology,* 37 1&2: 59–81.

Weiss, A. (ed.) 1986. *Islamic Reassertion in Pakistan: Application of Islamic Laws in a Modern State.* Syracuse: Syracuse University Press.

Weiss, A. 1999. Pakistan: Some Progress, Sobering Challenges. In S. Harrison, P. Kreisberg and D. Kux (eds), *India and Pakistan: The First Fifty Years.* Cambridge: Cambridge University Press, pp. 132–52.

1998. The Slow Yet Steady Path to Women's Empowerment in Pakistan. In Y. Haddad, and J. Esposito, (eds), *Islam, Gender, and Social Change.* Oxford: Oxford University Press.

1994. Challenges for Muslim Women in a Postmodern World. In A. Ahmed and H. Donnan (eds), *Islam, Globalization and Postmodernity.* London: Routledge.

1992. *Walls Within Walls: Life Histories of Working Women in the Old City of Lahore.* Boulder CO: Westview Press.

Werbner, P. 2003. *Pilgrims of Love: The Anthropology of a Global Sufi Cult.* London: Hurst and Company.

2002. *Imagined Diasporas among Manchester Muslims: The Public Performance of Pakistani Transnational Performance.* Oxford and New York: James Currey and School of American Research Press.

Werbner, P. and Basu, H. (eds) 1998. *Embodying Charisma: Modernity, Locality and the Performance of Emotion in Sufi Cults.* London: Routledge.

White, J. 1999. Amplifying Trust: Community and Communication in Turkey. In D. Eickelman and J. Anderson (eds), *New Muslim Media in the Muslim World: The Emerging Public Sphere.* Bloomington: Indian University Press, pp. 162–79

Whitehouse, H. 1998. From Mission to Movement: The Impact of Christianity on Patterns of Political Association in Papua New Guinea. *Journal of the Royal Anthropological Institute.* (NS) 4: 43–63.

1996. Jungles and Computers: Neuronal Group Selection and the Epidemiology of Representations. *Journal of the Royal Anthropological Institute.* (NS) 2: 99–116.

1992. Memorable Religions: Transmission, Codification and Change in Divergent Melanesian Contexts. *Man* (NS) **27**: 777–97.

Wikan, U. 1990. *Managing Turbulent Hearts: A Balinese Formula for Living.* Chicago: Chicago University Press.

1982. *Behind the Veil in Arabia: Women in Oman.* Baltimore and London: Johns Hopkins University Press.

Wilce, JR. 1998. Communicating Multiple Identities in Muslim Communities: An Introduction. *Ethos* **26** (2):115–19.

Wilson, B. 1970. *Rationality.* Oxford: Basil Blackwell.

Wilson, T. and Donnan. H. 1998. Nation, State and Identity at international borders. In T. Wilson and H. Donnan (eds), *Border Identities: Nation and State at International Frontiers.* Cambridge, Cambridge University Press, pp. 1–30.

Yalman, N. 1969. Islamic Reform and the Mystic Tradition in Eastern Turkey. *European Journal of Sociology* **10** (1): 41–60.

Yamba, C. 1995. *Permanent Pilgrims: The Role of Pilgrimage in the Lives of West African Muslims in Sudan.* Edinburgh: Edinburgh University Press.

Younghusband, G. J. and Younghusband, F. E. 1895. *The Relief of Chitral.* London: MacMillan and Co.

Younghusband, F. E. 1895. Chitral. *Journal of the Society of Arts* **43**: 487–97.

Zaman, B. Q. 2002. *The Ulama in Contemporary Islam: Custodians of Change.* New Jersey: Princeton University Press.

1999. Religious Education and the Rhetoric of Reform: The Madrasa in British India and Pakistan. *Comparative Studies in Society and History.* 294–323.

1998. Sectarianism in Pakistan: The Radicalisation of Shi'a and Sunni Identities. *Modern Asian Studies.* **32** (3): 689–701.

Zakhmi, Z. Not dated. *Ma Ishq Ma Junoon.* Chitral and Booni: Khowar Chap.

Zirbel, K. 2000. Playing it Both Ways: Local Egyptian Performers Between Regional Identity and International Markets. In W. Ambrust (ed.), *Mass Mediations: New Approaches to Popular Culture in the Middle East and Beyond.* Berkeley: University of California Press, pp. 120–45.

Ziring, L. 1997. *Pakistan in the Twentieth Century: A Political History.* Karachi and Oxford: Oxford University Press.

Zubaida, S. 2001. Rice in the Culinary Cultures of the Middle East. In S. Zubaida and R. Tapper (eds), *A Taste of Thyme: Culinary Cultures of the Middle East.* London and New York: Tauris Parke, pp. 93–104.

Zutshi, C. 2004. *Languages of Belonging: Islam, Regional Identity and the Making of Kashmir.* London: Hurst and Co.

Index

adultery 60, 189
affection 53, 55, 60, 61, 73, 75, 77, 94, 98, 169, 181, 189, 218, 258, 259
Afghan refugees
　Dari speaking 39
　in Markaz 21, 125, 209
　in Rowshan 34, 39
　Pashto-speaking 39
　perceptions of 39
Afghanistan 1, 14, 24, 57, 115, 128, 209, 213
　Rowshan people's connections with 41
Aga Khan 164, 197, 223, 224
　attacks upon 119, 208, 225
　catching a glimpse of (see also *deedar*) 224–225, 227
　role in Ismai'li thought 16, 112, 198–199, 200
Aga Khan Development Network 210, 211
　activities in Rowshan 43–44, 59, 114
agriculture 63
Ahl-e Hadith 112
Ahmadiya 202
Alamut 164
alcohol 7, 69, 72, 76, 78, 96, 104, 106, 118, 132, 152, 173, 219
alleys 59
amulets 158, 179
　and body 183
　and love 182, 185, 188, 189, 205, 241
　gifts for 182, 185, 187
　illegality of 182
　makers of 179–180
Anderson, Jon 29, 110
angels 148, 175
anger 77, 259
Ansari, Sara 241
Anxiety 52, 55, 60, 70, 89, 98, 128, 142, 147, 181, 187, 192, 195, 215, 222, 240, 260, 261
Appadurai, Arjun 150
'Aql (see also intellect) 88
Arabic 13, 91, 163, 165, 173
Arabisation, of speech 146

Arkoun, Mohammed 129
Assabiyya 114
audiocassettes 3, 4, 122, 128, 139, 143, 156, 171, 243

back-stabbing 147
Badakshan 41, 125, 207
Badmash 68, 76, 127, 189
Bailey, F. G. 222
Bajaur 21, 40, 125
Banerjee, Mukulika 24, 196, 253
Banuri, Yusuf 180
Barth, Frederick 91, 111, 133, 197
bazaar 124, 222
　in Markaz 21, 42, 59, 62, 77, 209, 221
　in Peshawar 115
　in Rowshan 3, 38, 47, 89, 105, 212, 214
　women in 21, 127
Bazaaris 126
BBC 214
Beatty, Andrew 197
bearded ones (see also *dashmanan*) 2, 126, 127, 145, 154, 171, 176, 177
beards 117, 176
Bhutto, Zulfikar Ali 144
Bin Laden, Osama 25
blasphemy laws 123, 148
body, the 107, 111, 149, 166, 172, 183, 187, 192, 215, 260, 262
Bongi 131
border zones 24, 253
boredom 92, 94, 99
Bourdieu, Pierre 104
Boycott, Geoffrey 140
brain, the 88, 94, 167
brainwashing 159, 167, 191, 205
bravado 173
Bukhara 186
Burqa 38

Cairo 122
Cambridge 97

cassette players 124
childhood 163
children 70–72, 160, 162, 165, 171, 201
Chistiyya brotherhood 129
Chitral
    colonial accounts of 44
    distinctiveness of 245, 253
    history of 13–14, 207
    population of 14
    poverty in 25, 61
    sectarian conflict in 207
Chitral cap (*pakol*) 171
Chitral fort 125
Chitral Ismai'lis
    and creation of Pakistan 207
    conflict with Chitral Sunnis 17, 43
    fear of Afghan Taliban 17
    migration to Rowshan 43
    Pakistan 16
    perception of how different from Sunnis 102
    responses towards fall of Afghanistan's Taliban
        government 18
Chitral river 37, 125
Chitral Scouts 47
Chitrali, self-conceptions of 54
Christians 202
cigarettes 70
city life, village conceptions of 4, 82
Civil Service examinations 230
civility 117
clothing in Rowshan 37–38
communalism 194, 247
Communist, accusations of being 118
computer training centres 103
concealment (see also hidden)
    and violent conflict 195
    of emotions 22
    of faith and belief 238
    of immorality 57
    of thought 22, 118
    tactics of 7, 22, 54, 61, 77, 177
conversion 204–206, 207
conversation, anthropology of 255
creativity 93, 99, 107, 109, 123, 132, 147, 150, 156,
    158, 163, 191, 193, 236, 240, 243, 249, 256, 261,
    262
criminality 75
critical events 197, 207
cultural homogenisation 155

Damama 137
dance 96, 107, 123, 130, 140
Dar-ul Haqqania 168
Dar-ul Uloom 160 (see also mosque schools)
Dar-ul Uloom Sarhad 168, 180

Dari 13
Das, Veena 208
Dashmanan (see also *ulama* and bearded ones) 7,
    106, 145, 157, 171
    bodily comportment of 172
    employment of 173
    fear of 201
    mocking of 173
    Rowshan 179
    source of family pride 173
debate
    and religious education 165
    approaches towards within the study of
        Muslim societies 86, 159
    importance in Chitral 28, 85, 86, 92, 110, 240,
        256, 258
    involvement of Sunni and Ismai'lis together
        in 111
debt and public humiliation 62
decision-making 62, 188, 193, 259
Deedar 16, 223–237 (see also Aga Khan)
Deoband 22, 74, 129–130, 168, 180, 241, 242, 254,
    255–256, 262
    criticisms of Sufi practices 129
    hostility towards music 130
    madrasas 129
desire, sexual 117
devilish bodies 163
Dhikr 33
Dir 40
discipline 107, 108, 109, 172
    Islamic self 123, 156, 163, 260, 261
discussion 85, 93, 94, 97, 133, 242
District Commissioner 212, 227
diversity, of Islamic viewpoints 144
Dol 131
Down Pakistan 93, 102, 159, 167, 169
drinking circle 132
driving 48, 171
drunkards 126, 131

education
    and moral failings of village life 70–71
    and the anthropology of in Muslim societies 86
    as a dimension of fieldwork 5–6
    commitment towards 109
    contributing factor to the vitality of village
        intellectual life 115
    in Pakistan's major cities 41
    relationship to Islamic reformism 110, 113
    rising levels in Chitral villages 10, 11, 68, 94
    schools in Rowshan 42
Egypt 260
Eickelman Dale 19, 29, 101, 110
elders 65, 160, 165

elopement 76, 186, 188
Elster, Jon 53, 192
embodied piety 172
embodiment 163, 190, 260, 262
emotion 170, 191, 216
    and conversion 205
    and faith 193
    and human behaviour 118, 189
    and morality 79
    and religious knowledge 175
    and violent conflict 193, 194, 214
    anthropology of 27, 87
    masked by polite behaviour 118
    unhealthy forms of 170, 189, 190, 215
emotional failure 258, 259
enmity, relations of 60, 218, 219
esoteric hermeneutics 198, 199
ethnic stereotypes 220
etiquette (see politeness)

faith 176, 177, 181, 190, 204, 206, 211, 227
    display of 238
    and emotion 193, 205
    jokes about 141
    nurturing of 206
    rotting of 204
Farman 200, 224, 235
fashion 20, 37, 108, 127, 165
fatherhood 70, 77
feeling, sense of 88
fields 38
fighting 66, 72, 100, 102, 131, 169
food
    and sectarian conflict 202
    Ismai'li ritual 82
    sharing between Sunnis and Ismai'lis 162, 203
    sharing of within household 63, 104, 108, 134,
        135
freedom 163, 261
frontier corps 212
frontier regions 253–254
funerals 213

Gahkuch 234
gardens 61, 95, 122
Gellner, Ernest 34, 114
Generation gap 67
Ghalib, Mirza Assadullah Khan 69
Ghazals 131, 137, 140
Gilgit 196, 223, 227, 228
Gilsenan, Michael 91, 222
Ginan 233
globalization 30, 57, 263
gossip 94, 105, 126, 222, 248, 249–252
governance, Islamic 117

guesthouses 61, 95, 105, 130, 173
Gujars 15
Gurzen 41, 43

Hadith 161, 181
Hafiz 34, 124, 137
happiness, occasions of 115
Haqaiqat 117, 198, 199
Hashish 7, 72, 75, 76, 90, 96
Hazir-e Imam 198
heart 41, 60, 63, 77, 88, 97, 98, 108, 109, 118, 242,
        259, 262
    and thought 118, 121
hell 175
heroin 75
hidden knowledge 55 (see also concealment)
    and Islam 158, 179, 182, 186
    and Ismai'li tradition 198
    and morality 55
    and science 186
    and the making of amulets 158
    and the *ulama* 158
high society, in Chitral 151
Hindu Kush 37
Hindu Raj 37
Hirschkind, Charles 123, 250, 260, 262
homesickness 81
households
    and *dashmanan* 173
    description of in Rowshan 45
    economics and expenditure of 47–49, 108
    in Markaz 152
hospitality 60, 61–63, 94, 128, 135–136
    and women 135
Howe, Leo 142
Hudood Ordinance 75
human–animal relations 63–64
humanity 114, 219
humour 173, 258

illness (mental and bodily) 56, 60, 90, 104
imagery 164, 166, 173, 174–175, 202, 224
impersonation 140, 146–148, 155
    as a sin 146
independent self 261, 262
India 58, 129, 169, 194, 195
Indian films 58
indifference, display of 200, 201
individuality 147, 163, 261
inner insight 242
intellect, the (see also 'aql) 88, 99, 107, 163, 170,
        172, 205, 221, 238, 259, 262
intellectual failure 259
intellectual work 256
intelligence 88, 98

intoxication,
  and love 138
  and music 129
  curse of 132
Iqbal, Allama Muhammad 95, 106
Iran, radio station of 214
irrigation 65
Islamic festivals
  Eid-ul Fitr 37, 127
  Eid-ul Azhar 37
Islamic Law (*shari'a*) 56, 115, 117, 118, 144, 149, 161,
    189, 199, 250
  and Sufism 129, 182
Islamic practice 181, 189
Islamic revival and reform 9, 122, 156, 190, 191,
    240, 248
  and Sufism 158, 240
  critical attitudes towards 250
Islam
  and piety 251–252
  anthropology of 8, 193, 257
  as a source of moral criteria 53, 54, 55, 57
  attitudes towards 122
  debates over in northern Pakistan 110
  intellectual and emotional dimensions 23
  local and Global 9, 123, 151, 155, 156, 249
  revivalist movements within 58
Islamabad 41, 49, 225
Islamisation 2, 7, 9, 10, 12, 18, 51, 52, 127, 130, 150,
    155, 171, 233, 239, 250
  alternative forms of 190
  and *madrasas* 179
  attempts made by Jama'at-e Islami 117
  responses of village Muslims towards 11
  state-led 17, 25–26, 123
Islamisers 1, 159, 181
Islamism 250
Islamist political parties and movements 2, 123
Ismai'li Tariqa Board 164, 165

Jalalabad 39
Jama'at Khana 98, 160, 165, 214, 226, 228
Jama'at-e Islami Markaz 170, 174
Jama'at-e Islami party 6, 56, 87, 116, 117, 118, 144,
    145, 147, 149, 151, 241
Jama'at-e Ulama-e Islam 168, 210, 213
Jaqmara
Java 197
jealousy 59
jeeps, honoured seating within 132
Jeer can
Jihad,
  debates concerning 111
  in Pakistan 159, 170
Jinaat 185, 190

joking 133, 140–142, 172, 258
Judgement day 175

Kabul 128
Kalasha people
Kalashnikov 209, 211, 212
Karachi 41, 49, 99, 106, 126, 130, 164, 169, 176, 186
  and violence 196
Kashmir 24, 169, 170, 195
Kepel, Giles 159
Khaldun, Ibn 6, 114
Khan, Abdul Ghaffar (Frontier Gandhi) 196
Khayyam, Omar 34
Khoja Ismai'lis 246
Khowar 12–13, 40, 94
  Chitral people's perceptions of 2–3
  and music 130
Khudai Khidmatgar 196
Khusraw, Nasir 233, 246
Kinship and Afghanistan 41
knowledge (see also religious knowledge)
  and emotion 175, 189
  divisions between secret and open 157
  embodied 163
Kuwait 167, 178

Lahore 125, 170, 174
Laidlaw, James 53, 67
Lambek, Michael 66
landscape
  Rowshan people's perceptions of 4
language
  diversity of in *madrasas* 168
  multi-linguality in Chitral 40–41
laughter 96, 106, 140, 147, 258
lies 65, 87, 118
line of control 169
lineage group 114
literary knowledgeability 124
loans 48, 82, 188
London 117
lordly families 45, 57, 59, 62
  houses of 45
  parody of 130
  Rowshan people's perceptions of 46
love 117, 122, 242
  amulets for 179
  and thought 190
  between Sunnis and Ismai'lis 75
  illicit relationships of 58, 73–74, 98, 100,
    187–189

Madrasa 158, 159, 160, 167
  certificates of 161, 167, 173, 186
magic 60

Mahfil 122, 128
  and humour 140
  and women 132
  as arena of contestation 144
  commercial recordings of 122, 130, 139
  proper pace and tempo 152
  religious dimensions of 142–143
  risks associated with 142
marriage 67, 100, 115, 131, 174, 175, 189, 190, 205, 228
  Sunni and Ismai'li 208
  threats of forces ??
martial law, in Rowshan 212
martyrdom 170, 211, 221
masculinity 147, 172, 173, 196
Masoud, Ahmad Shah 39
Mawdudi, Mawlana 6, 56
Mecca 199, 202
Mehtar 13, 125
memorisation 101, 161, 163, 177, 183, 260
migration
  and Chitral 43
  rural–urban 25, 41, 47, 52, 79–82, 173
mind, the 262
  constraints placed upon activity of 109
  cultivation of 174, 192
  impact of education upon 109, 119
  play of 89, 94, 98, 193, 256, 258, 261
mindful body, the 192, 259
mindfulness 85, 86, 98, 99, 104, 111, 189, 246, 263
  constraints upon 175
miracles 112, 187
modernity 57, 58, 109, 117, 118, 166, 187, 190, 191, 234, 243
money 81, 108, 205
morality 23, 51, 53, 111, 117, 123, 227, 260
  and emotion 79
  and religious education 177
  and village relationships 67
  economic dimensions of 60, 61–63
  embodied states of 123
  Islamic 149, 156, 260–261
  two sources of moral standards in village life 54
Moscow 40
Mosque schools 160, 161, 163, 167 (see also *dar-ul uloom*)
Mosques 111, 126, 127, 142, 161, 211
  Friday Mosque, Rowshan 161, 162, 208
  Royal mosque, Markaz 125
motherhood 64–65, 80, 170
Mulkho 167
Mullah 127, 172
multiple identities 150
Musharaf, President Pervez 162, 225
music 123, 242

and travel 4
  disputes over 5, 171, 233–234
  during marriage 46, 176
  hostility of religious authorities towards 123
  in Markaz 123
  Indian and Bollywood 3, 58, 106, 109, 131, 233
  Ismai'li devotional 233
  power of in Chitral 122
musical gatherings
  and anxiety 128
  and religion 129
  opposition towards 145, 173
musicians
  amateur 130, 136, 150
  and patronage 154
  professional 131
Muttahida Majlis-e Amal 19

Nafs 88
Naqshbandiyya brotherhood 33
Narrow-minded 91, 150, 167, 177, 189, 193, 262
Nasr, Seyyid Vali Reza 25, 151
new elite, in Chitral 151
New Muslims 149
newspapers 42
nobles, the (Chitral musical group) 5, 163, 243
  audiences of 131, 137
  cassettes of 131
  composition of 130, 136, 143
  diversity within 144
  focus of investment 142
Northern Areas 169, 223, 230
North-West Frontier Province 10, 12
Nuristan 125
nursing 41, 99, 103

open, the
  and moral standards 55
  conversation in 105
  music in 132
Open university 102
open-minded 91, 97, 103, 108, 113, 125, 167, 176, 177
orchards 38, 46, 61, 115, 217
outdoor musical programmes 128, 131
outside world 58
outsiders 3, 39–41, 42, 75, 128, 168, 187

pain of separation 169
Pakistan, study of 159
Pakistan Army 24, 39, 47, 77
Pakistan People's Party 144
Pamir mountains 15, 42
paradise 175
paramilitary organisations 122

parenthood and parenting 68, 75
Pashto (see also language)
  Chitral people's conceptions of 14, 40
  Chitral people's fluency in 13
paths, of the village 38
Persian (see also language)
  influence on Khowar poetry 124
  Rowshan people's conceptions of 41, 138
Persian Sufi texts 117, 124, 143, 155, 190, 240
personal belief 113
Peshawar 14, 41, 64, 99, 169, 208, 259
  madrasas in 167, 168, 180, 210
  University 4, 68, 69, 111, 114, 115, 145, 149
philosophers, local 94, 103, 104, 260
picnic-tours 3
pilgrimage 199, 202
poetry
  and daily life 96, 242
  language of 73, 121
  love poetry 32, 37, 98, 131, 137–138, 148
  mystical/Sufi 69, 106
  novelty within 139
  reception of 137
  recitation of 136
police 47, 76, 77, 212, 213
politeness 117, 128, 133, 135, 136, 142, 215, 231
political Islam 250
polo 14, 46, 58, 131, 185
prayer 55, 118, 134, 152, 161, 163, 171, 226
prayer, call to 163
prayer cap 171, 209, 232
present Imam 198
princes 125
Prophet, the 110, 112, 161, 164, 169, 170, 172, 198
prostitution 115
psyche, experts in 89
public events 87
  ceremonial 203
  school 'programmes' 6, 93, 106–109
public sphere
  and anthropology of Islam 22, 195
  and communal conflict 194
  and faith 238
Pukhtuns
  and Frontier corps 234
  and violence 196, 219
  impact on Chitral life 253
  musical traditions of 124
  resident in Chitral 14
  society 253
  traders 75, 125
Punjabi 141
Punjabification 141
Purdah 21–22, 43, 45, 58, 89, 103–104, 111, 119, 127,
  132, 161, 171, 172, 231

Purdah of the heart 199

Qawwali 141
Qur'an 85, 96, 112, 116, 146, 147, 149, 160, 161, 163,
  167, 168, 181, 182, 189, 200
  interpretation of 198
  memorisation of 161, 163, 166
  recitation of 161, 166, 171, 174
  repetition of 172
Qur'an-e natiq 199

Rahman, Fazl-ur 213
Ramadan 141, 199, 202
rationality and irrationality 179, 180, 188, 193, 201
  and emotion 177
  anthropology of 27
reasoned argument 86, 175, 190
reasoned contemplation 191, 238
reform-minded Muslims 88, 112, 114, 150, 178
  and Pakistan's middle classes 151
  criticism of Persianate literary culture 138
religious authority, fractured nature of 149
  and ulama 159, 170, 180, 186, 189
  madrasa students 171, 173
religious education 30, 60, 159, 169, 242–243
  and intellectual activity 160–166, 174, 191
  differences between Sunni and Ismai'li
    traditions of 160–161, 162, 166
  girls 160
  in Rowshan 160
  impact on thought and emotions 166, 167, 170,
    177–178, 192
  Ismai'lis 160, 164, 165
  shared Sunni–Ismai'li experience of 160
religious emotion, dangers of 120, 170, 175, 177,
  220, 259
  and thought 238
  spiritual dimension 236–237, 238
religious knowledge (*ilm-e din*) 159, 178, 180, 190,
  192, 241, 259
  and Ismai'li–Sunni relations 192
religious sensibilities 200
religious syncretism, anthropology of 194
resistance 124, 142, 149
respect and reputation 55, 76, 90, 103, 105, 131
  acquisition and bestowal of 118
  threats to 135
revenge 196, 219, 220
revolution, Islamic 250
rice 134, 136
ritual 27, 38
rioting 195, 207, 210
  and South Asia 213
rosary beads 78, 114, 134, 172
Rousseau, Emile 114

Roy, Olivier 250
rubbish talk (see also gossip) 105
Rumi, Mawlana 34, 106, 124, 137, 139
rumour 209, 210
Russian Olive Tree 4

Sabbah, Hassan 164
Sa'di 34, 124, 137
Saintly figures 182
Sami ul-Haq, Mawlana 168
September (11 September 2001) 12
    ramifications for life in Chitral 25
Saudi Arabia 130, 151, 167, 178
secret, the
    experience of 147
    immorality of 117
sectarian conflict 219–223, 244–249
    and emotion 193
    and new forms of religious knowledge 192
    and secret knowledge 195
    anthropological perspectives of 19–20
    in Pakistan and South Asia 20, 194, 195, 196
    relationship to mass education 20
sectarian division 184, 193, 238
sectarian identities 200
self-control 133, 142, 263
self-sacrifice 55, 95, 98, 261
sensitivity 242, 259
sensory perception 262
serfs 46
sermons, Islamic 123, 125, 126, 127
    and the Aga Khan (see also *farman*)
        199, 200
    inflammatory 208, 211
    reception of 221
sex and sexuality 58, 68–70, 72, 75, 103, 190
shame 55, 63, 76, 92, 128
Sharif, Nawaz 169
Shi'a Ismai'lism (see also Chitral Ismai'lis)
    and secret knowledge 198
    cultural diversity amongst Ismai'li Muslims 16
    doctrines of 198, 200
    role played during the creation of Pakistan 16
    status of followers in contemporary Pakistan 17
Shi'a Muslims 195, 196, 197, 202
    killings of 210
shops
    in Rowshan 38, 48, 62
    music 139
shrines 211
Shughnan 125
siege of Chitral 211
sin 189, 190, 202
    Ismai'li conception of 227
singing 137

Sipah-e Sahaba-e Pakistan 210
sitar 137, 212
small-town Muslims 257
Smith, Adam 27
Sohar 133, 197
soul 87, 88, 111, 199, 228, 259
spare time 68
speech 105
spiritual light 224, 233
spiritual journeys 229, 230, 234
spiritual power 111, 117, 158, 178, 184, 186
    and the Aga Khan 198
    representation in Urdu and Persian poetry 138
spiritual truth 198, 223, 242
state
    Chitral 207
    Chitral people's criticism of 79
    Chitral people's engagement with 25, 41
    courses concerning the study of 101
    invasion into village life 78
    Islamic 57, 250
    rumours surrounding creation of an Ismai'li
        state 210
status and hierarchy
    in Rowshan 44
    moral complexities of 57–58
strangers 128
strong feelings 179, 188, 192, 193, 259
submission 260, 261
sufism 32–33, 240
    and hidden/esoteric knowledge 158
    and Islamic reformism 158
    Hinduised 129
    in Chitral 33–34, 97–98, 143
    role of brotherhoods in 33, 124, 241
    role of Shrine worship within 33, 124, 129, 241
    South Asian 124
    textual dimension 34, 118
    vibrancy of in the face of opposition towards 129
suicide 170, 211
sulking 104, 135, 142
Sunna, the 172, 176, 177
surface-level features of life 116
Surnai 131
Swat 21, 40, 125

Tabligh-e Jama'at 144, 181
    culture of 155
    relationship to Sufi thought and practice 33
Tajikistan 40, 95
Takbir 115, 119
Taliban 1, 2, 11, 12, 18, 31, 57, 115, 130, 171, 190, 254
    activities and presence within Chitral 123, 213
    debate concerning extent to which truly
        Islamic 116–117

fall of 42
  hostility towards music 128
  hostility towards visit of the Aga Khan 227
Talibanisation 10
Talib-e ilm 168
Talim 164
Tambiah, Stanley 206
tambourine 137
Tanzil 198
Tawhid 164
Tawil 198, 199 (see also esoteric hermeneutics)
technologies of modernity 156
television 42, 52, 58, 86, 169, 225
terrorism 218
textbooks 164–165
Thanawi, Ashraf Ali 242
thought 90, 246, 256, 261, 262
  and religious education 192
  as positive elements of daily Muslim life 85
  authentic and inauthentic 118
  feeling as an important dimension of 87, 93, 191, 215
  negative dimensions of 89, 190
thoughtful reflection 109
tolerance, notion of 218–219
transmission of refinement 154
transport 38
travel 171, 180
  Chitral people's enjoyment of 4
  experiences of Afghanistan 116
  spiritual 197
turban, Taliban-style 171

Ulama (see also *dashmanan*) 126, 127, 146, 169, 178
  and esoteric knowledge 179
  anti-alcohol strictures of 132
  anti-poetry 148
  commitment towards creativity 158
unemployment 39, 67, 68, 187
Urdu (see also language)
  and South Asian Muslim thought 30
  Chitral people's fluency in 13, 40, 95, 165, 186
  degrees in Literature of 69, 114, 145

veiling 162, 200
  diversity of forms in Rowshan 37
Verkaaik, Oskar 195
violence 60, 122, 127, 193, 194, 207, 212, 244, 247

and emotion 194
  and personal purity 215
  covert 195, 248
  ethnic and linguistic 195, 213
  political 194–195
  tribal 196
village intellectuals 92, 94
village life 51–54
  and politics 58
  and thought 85, 91, 163, 190, 191
  emotional attachment towards 52
  moral valuations of 23
  morally degraded state of 55, 68, 74
  role of the police in 77
village Muslims 254, 255–256, 257
  importance of Intellectual life for 10, 11
  negative stereotypes of 9, 10
volunteers, Ismai'li 226, 234

Waizeen 165, 209, 224
Wakhan corridor 40
Wakhiks 15, 40
weddings 115, 154, 203
Werbner, Pnina 134, 241
women
  access to during fieldwork 3, 256
  and agency 236
  and animal husbandry 64
  and Ismai'li religious education
  and Ismai'li religious experience 223
  and *madrasa* students 172
  and sectarian conflict 215, 223
  and the intellectual life of the village 99–109
  care for children 64
  clothing 37
  education of 22, 99
  in Markaz 127
  moral propriety of 58, 72, 106, 172
  training and vocational learning of 41, 99–100, 103
  transformation of village attitudes regarding 120
  unmarried 68
World Wide Web 3, 49
worldly education 160, 165, 166, 174

youth 67–70, 77

Zia, General ul-Haq 75, 123, 208